HUMAN RIGHTS LAW-MAKING IN THE UNITED NATIONS

Human Rights Law-Making in the United Nations

A Critique of Instruments and Process

THEODOR MERON

CLARENDON PRESS · OXFORD
1986

Oxford University Press, Walton Street, Oxford OX2 6DP
Oxford New York Toronto
Delhi Bombay Calcutta Madras Karachi
Kuala Lumpur Singapore Hong Kong Tokyo
Nairobi Dar es Salaam Cape Town
Melbourne Auckland
and associated companies in
Beirut Berlin Boston Nicosia

Oxford is a trade mark of Oxford University Press

Published in the United States
by Oxford University Press, New York

British Library Cataloguing in Publication Data
Meron, Theodor
Human rights law-making in the United
Nations : a critique of instruments and
process.
1. Civil rights (International law)
I. Title
341. 4'81   K3240.4
ISBN 0-19-825549-7

Library of Congress Cataloging in Publication Data
Meron, Theodor, 1930-
Human rights law-making in the United Nations.
Includes index.
1. Civil rights (International law)   2. United
Nations.   I. Title.
K3240.4.M485   1986   341.4'81   86-9654
ISBN 0-19-825549-7

Set by Grestun Graphics, Abingdon, Oxon
Printed in Great Britain
at the University Printing House, Oxford
by David Stanford
Printer to the University

To Monique

Preface

I WISH to express my gratitude to the New York University Law Center Foundation for supporting my research on this book and to the Max Planck Institute for Comparative Public Law and International Law in Heidelberg for making it possible for me to work on it at the Institute during sabbatical leave from New York University School of Law. Special thanks are addressed to the Directors of the Institute, Professors Rudolf Bernhardt, Karl Doehring, and Jochen-Abr. Frowein. I am most grateful to my research assistants Gwen Robosson, Manuel Vargas, John Gill, and Scott Coleman, and especially Donna J. Sullivan, without whose able help this study would not have been possible, and to my friends and colleagues who have been kind enough to read various parts of the draft manuscript and to comment upon them.

I also express appreciation to the American Journal of International Law, in which parts of the material contained in this book have previously appeared.

T.M.

Max Planck Institute for Comparative Public Law and International Law,
Heidelberg,
July 1985

Contents

Abbreviations

ACC	Administrative Committee on Co-ordination
ASIL	American Society of International Law
AJIL	American Journal of International Law
CDDH	Committee of Experts on Human Rights
CERD	Committee on the Elimination of Racial Discrimination
CFR	Code of Federal Regulations
ECOSOC	Economic and Social Council
ECR	European Court Reports (European Communities law reports)
EEOC	Equal Employment Opportunities Commission
ESC	Economic and Social Council
ESCOR	Economic and Social Council Official Records
FSC	Federal Supreme Court (Nigeria)
GAOR	General Assembly Official Records
IACHR	Inter-American Commission on Human Rights
ICJ	International Court of Justice
ICRC	International Committee of the Red Cross
ILC	International Law Commission
ILM	International Legal Materials
ILO	International Labour Organisation
NGO	Non-governmental organization
OAS	Organisation of American States
OEA	Organizacion de Los Estados Americanos
TIAS	Treaties and Other International Acts Series
TS	Treaty Series
UNCITRAL	United Nations Commission on International Trade Law
UNESCO	United Nations Educational, Scientific and Cultural Organization
UNTS	United Nations Treaty Series
USC	United States Code
USCA	United States Code Annotated
UST	United States Treaties and Other International Agreements ·
WHO	World Health Organization

Introduction

THE United Nations has made a tremendous contribution to the promotion and protection of human rights. It has adopted conventions and declarations regulating most aspects of the relationship between the governments and the governed and has established important procedures for the implementation and supervision of norms stated in these instruments. It has thus fostered the principle of international accountability of governments for the manner in which they treat individuals and groups. Without detracting from any of these great achievements, this book attempts to demonstrate some of the weaknesses inherent in the present methods of adopting human rights instruments employed by the United Nations and the resulting inadequacies of the instruments themselves. Since it would be impractical to attempt to analyse within the confines of this book all the human rights instruments which have been adopted by the United Nations, three of the major instruments have been selected as examples. The book also subjects to a critical analysis another aspect of law-making: the normative and the jurisdictional relations between the instruments and organs. Although a great many of the weaknesses result from the political realities prevailing in the United Nations, others could have been prevented by better law-making techniques, including higher levels of competence, more careful drafting and editing, more research, and so on. Some suggestions therefore have been made for the necessary reforms, both of the institutions and of the process itself.

The continued inadequacies of the present system of law-making cause considerable difficulties in the interpretation and application of the various instruments and in the relations between human rights instruments and organs. These problems encourage cynicism and endanger the credibility of this most important function of the organized international community, ensuring the respect of human rights. There are many examples of conflicting provisions within a single instrument, of provisions which are over broad and couched in vague terms, and there are problems of overlap and conflict between different instruments.

In many cases abstraction helps, of course, to obtain the necessary support of States. While it is true that rights stated in the Constitution of the United States and in constitutions and laws of other countries are also couched in general terms, these rights have been interpreted in the rich practice and jurisprudence of the national courts. In international human rights, however, the process of creating interpretative jurisprudence is slow in time and non-comprehensive in scope. The United Nations human rights system is thus characterized by weak and sporadic implementation. The weaker the implementation system, the greater the importance of a more precise formulation of human rights instruments. The quality of the instrument and the instrument's relationship to international practice and to the needs of the international community will affect, no doubt, the acceptability of the instrument as a treaty and of the norms stated in it as customary law by the international community.

Part I of this book comprises critical essays on three instruments, in a sequence progressing from the more specific — the International Convention on the Elimination of All Forms of Racial Discrimination (Chapter I) and the Convention on the Elimination of All Forms of Discrimination Against Women (Chapter II) — to the more general, the International Covenant on Civil and Political Rights (Chapter III). The first two instruments have been selected because of their special importance and because the international community has given the notion of equality a special priority level. The discussion focuses on selected aspects of each of the instruments considered.

To prevent conflicts and to avoid gaps and undesirable overlap, the lawmaker must take into account the ensemble of international human rights instruments, indeed, the entire system of international human rights law. Part II of the book is concerned with this broad perspective. Since substantive problems of law-making are closely related to problems of supervision or implementation, Chapter IV focuses on the former and Chapter V on the latter.

Chapter IV concerns the relations between norms stated in different instruments. Instruments may be inconsistent or incompatible with each other, may overlap (which may not always be undesirable for the effective protection of international human rights), or may fail to address subjects which require normative regulation. The risk of conflict between norms and values stated in various international instruments reflects difficulties in establishing a sound legislative policy for the Member States of the United Nations in view of the diversity of their stages of development, cultures, traditions, and conditions of social peace and security. The risk of conflict is enhanced by the fact that the general practice in the United Nations has been for each normative system to create its own system of supervision. The scope of competence of a particular 'control' organ is, therefore, of relevance to the avoidance and resolution of conflicts and the development of a rational and consistent jurisprudence.

Several questions which merit consideration will be addressed. For example, what is the actual scope for conflicts between instruments in general or between specific norms such as women's equality and freedom of religion? Are conflicts between human rights instruments inevitable in the present decentralized and poorly co-ordinated process of law-making? Are provisions of the Vienna Convention on the Law of Treaties helpful for resolving conflicts between various instruments? Has the international community developed a hierarchy of human rights norms, such as *jus cogens*? What principles or techniques are useful for the avoidance, reduction, or resolution of conflicts?

Jurisdictional relations between instruments and organs are the subject of Chapter V. What are the purposes and the means of rationalizing and co-ordinating the systems of supervision and implementation of international human rights? Is the resolution of jurisdictional conflicts the duty of the supervisory organs only, to be fulfilled by means such as due deference to other control organs and the exercise of 'judicial restraint', or is it also, and perhaps primarily, the task of the lawmaker, who, by careful, thoughtful, and imaginative drafting, can, in some cases, avoid conflicts altogether?

The quality and the effectiveness of each instrument and of the ensemble of instruments depends on the system of law-making in international organizations, that is on the international community's legislative organs and on their methods of work. The structure and the operation of these bodies is affected by a wide range of political, budgetary, administrative, and legal considerations. The law-making process is the subject of Part III of this book. Chapter VI focuses on the experience of the specialized agencies of the United Nations. Chapter VII concerns the United Nations itself. Since all worthwhile critique and analysis should be constructive, here, too, the object is to consider what reforms could be envisaged. It is my hope that this book will serve as the catalyst for reflection and, eventually, action.

This book focuses on human rights law-making in the United Nations, not in regional and other organizations. Reference to specialized instruments, for instance those of the International Labour Organisation, or to regional human rights instruments has been made when necessary, mostly for comparative purposes. Because the African Charter on Human and Peoples' Rights has not yet entered into force, only a small number of allusions have been made to its provisions.

PART I

A Critique of Selected Human Rights Instruments

I

The International Convention on the Elimination of All Forms of Racial Discrimination

I. INTRODUCTION

THE International Convention on the Elimination of All Forms of Racial Discrimination[1] (the Convention) is the most important of the general instruments (as distinguished from specialized instruments such as those pertaining to labour or education) which develop the fundamental norm of the United Nations Charter — by now accepted into the corpus of customary international law — requiring respect for and observance of human rights and fundamental freedoms for all, without distinction as to race.[2] It has been eloquently described as 'the international community's only tool for combating racial discrimination which is at one and the same time universal in reach, comprehensive in scope, legally binding in character, and equipped with built-in measures of implementation . . .'.[3]

The chain of events that ultimately led to the preparation and adoption of the Convention originated with swastika painting and additional 'manifestations of anti-semitism and other forms of racial and national hatred and religious and racial prejudices of a similar nature' in 1959-60.[4] But an explicit

---

[1] 660 UNTS 195, reprinted in 5 ILM 352 (1966).

[2] Concerning the status of this norm as customary law, see Restatement of the Foreign Relations Law of the United States (Revised) §702 (Tent. Draft No. 6, vol. i, 1985). Regarding human rights instruments on discrimination, see generally Marie, *International Instruments Relating to Human Rights: Classification and Chart Showing Ratifications as of 1 January 1984*, 4 Human Rights L. J. 503, 522-4 (1984).

[3] 33 UN GAOR, Supp. (No. 18) at 108, 109, UN Doc. A/33/18 (1978) (a statement by the Committee on the Elimination of Racial Discrimination at the World Conference to Combat Racism and Racial Discrimination).

[4] Schwelb, *The International Convention on the Elimination of All Forms of Racial Discrimination*, 15 Int'l & Comp. L. Q. 996, 997 (1966); N. Lerner, The UN Convention on the Elimination of All Forms of Racial Discrimination 1 (1980).

reference to anti-Semitism was not included in the Convention as adopted.[5] Nor does it mention other specific forms of racism, except for apartheid, which is addressed in Art. 3, as well as in the Preamble. Nevertheless, anti-Semitism may be regarded as encompassed by the general prohibitions of racial discrimination stated in the Convention.[6] Although expressions of discrimination on ethnic grounds and on religious grounds are sometimes closely related,[7] the Convention does not prohibit religious discrimination. The intention, of course, was to make it the subject of separate instruments.[8]

The Convention drew its primary impetus from the desire of the United Nations to put an immediate end to discrimination against black and other non-white persons. Because of the strong political support of the African, Asian, and other developing States, top priority was given to the Convention by the organs involved in its preparation, that is the Sub-Commission on Prevention of Discrimination and Protection of Minorities, the Commission on Human Rights, the Economic and Social Council (ECOSOC), and the Third (Social, Humanitarian and Cultural Questions) Committee of the General Assembly. Although the Sub-Commission began working on it only in January 1964, the Convention was adopted with record speed on 21 December 1965 and entered into force on 4 January 1969.[9] It has been ratified by more States[10] than any other human rights treaty except for the Geneva Conventions of 12 August 1949 for the Protection of Victims of War.[11]

On the preparatory work of the Convention, see generally Schwelb, above, at 997–1000; N. Lerner, above, at 1–6; 2 Review of the Multilateral Treaty-Making Process, UN Doc. ST/LEG/SER.B/21 at 70-2 (Prov. edn. 1982).

[5] For the background, see N. Lerner, above n. 4, at 2, 68–73; Schwelb, above n. 4, at 1011–15.

[6] Schwelb, above n. 4, at 1014–15; N. Lerner, above n. 4, at 72.

[7] See below text accompanying nn. 104–6.

[8] The Declaration on the Elimination of All Forms of Intolerance and of Discrimination Based on Religion or Belief was adopted by the UN General Assembly on 25 Nov. 1981, by Res. 36/55, 36 UN GAOR, Supp. (No. 51) at 171, UN Doc. A/36/51 (1981). A convention on the subject is still far from completion.

[9] Multilateral Treaties Deposited with the Secretary-General: Status as at 31 December 1984, at 99. UN Doc. ST/LEG/SER. E/3 (1985).

[10] A total of 124 States. 40 UN GAOR Supp. (No. 18) at 1, UN Doc. A/40/18 (1985).

[11] A total of 160 States. Int'l Rev. Red Cross, No. 242, Sept.-Oct. 1984, at 274.
Convention for the Amelioration of the Condition of the Wounded and Sick in Armed Forces in the Field (Geneva Convention No. I), Aug. 12, 1949, 6 UST 3114,

The Convention was signed on behalf of the United States on 28 September 1966. On 23 February 1978 it was transmitted by President Carter to the US Senate for advice and consent to ratification, with far-reaching reservations, declarations, and understandings.[12] These reservations, declarations, and understandings have been the subject of considerable discussion[13] and will not be addressed in detail in this study. The Senate Committee on Foreign Relations has not yet reported the Convention out and is not now actively considering it. None the less, the principle of law stated in Article 18 of the Vienna Convention on the Law of Treaties[14] obligates the United States not to defeat the object and purpose of the Convention prior to its entry into force for the United States.

The annual reports of the control organ established under Article 8 of the Convention — the Committee on the Elimination of Racial Discrimination (the Committee) — other documents of the Committee, the individual comments made by members of the Committee, and its practice and jurisprudence provide ample material for critical studies of the Convention and for assessing how well its object and purpose are being served.

The Committee's functions may be divided into three different categories. First, and most important for this study, the examination of reports from States Parties and the submission of annual reports to the General Assembly under Art. 9. Such reports may include 'suggestions and general recommendations based on the examination of the reports and information

TIAS No. 3362, 75 UNTS 31. Convention for the Amelioration of the Condition of the Wounded, Sick and Shipwrecked Members of Armed Forces at Sea (Geneva Convention No. II), Aug. 12, 1949, 6 UST 3217, TIAS No. 3363, 75 UNTS 85. Geneva Convention Relative to the Treatment of Prisoners of War (Geneva Convention No. III), Aug. 12, 1949, 6 UST 3316, TIAS No. 3364, 75 UNTS 135. Convention Relative to the Protection of Civilian Persons in Time of War (Geneva Convention No. IV), Aug. 12, 1949, 6 UST 3516, TIAS No. 3365, 75 UNTS 287.

[12] 1978 Digest of United States Practice in International Law 440-6 (M. Nash ed. 1980) (hereinafter cited as US Digest); 'Contemporary Practice', 72 AJIL 620, 621-2.

[13] See e.g., *International Human Rights Treaties: Hearings Before the Senate Comm. on Foreign Relations*, 96th Cong., 1st Sess. (1980).

[14] Opened for Signature 23 May 1969, UN Doc. A/CONF.39/27 (1969), reprinted in 63 AJIL 875 (1969), 8 ILM 679 (1969). See generally I. Sinclair, The Vienna Convention on the Law of Treaties 42-4 (1984); Restatement of the Foreign Relations Law of the United States (Revised) § 312(3) (Tent. Draft No. 6, vol. ii 1985).

received from States Parties'. Second, the consideration of complaints submitted by one State Party against another and alleging violation of the Convention, under Arts. 11-13. This function of the Committee will not be discussed in this study. Third, the consideration of individual communications under Art. 14, which will be mentioned in Section VII below.

Under Article 22 of the Convention any disputes between States Parties over the interpretation or application of the Convention that are not settled by negotiation or by Convention procedures or referred to another mode of settlement may be submitted to the International Court of Justice for decision at the request of any party to the dispute. So far, no such dispute has been referred to the Court. While the Committee has not been given general competence to interpret the Convention, as a treaty organ, the Committee may be competent to interpret the Convention insofar as required for the performance of the Committee's functions.[15] Such an interpretation *per se* is not binding on States Parties, but it affects their reporting obligations and their internal and external behaviour. It shapes the practice of States in applying the Convention and may establish and reflect the agreement of the parties regarding its interpretation.[16] Whether a particular interpretation or decision by the Committee serves such a function can, of course, be determined only *in concreto*.

The object of this chapter is to analyse and interpret some key provisions of the Convention — considerations of space compel selectivity — with attention to problems of their reach that have not been discussed in depth in the literature.[17]

[15] For a discussion of this question, see 28 UN GAOR Supp. (No. 18), paras. 46-8, UN Doc. A/9018 (1973).

[16] See Vienna Convention on the Law of Treaties, above n. 14, Art. 31.

[17] There is an extensive literature on the Convention. See generally Vincent-Daviss, *Human Rights Law: A Research Guide to the Literature — Part I: International Law and the United Nations*, 14 N.Y.U. J. Int'l L. & Pol. 209, 278-80 (1981); W. McKean, Equality and Discrimination under International Law (1983). N. Lerner, above n. 4, Schwelb, above n. 4; Greenberg, *Race, Sex and Religious Discrimination in International Law*, in 2 Human Rights in International Law: Legal and Policy Issues 307 (T. Meron ed., 1984); Buergenthal, *Implementing the UN Racial Convention*, 12 Tex. Int'l L. J. 187 (1977); Partsch, *Elimination of Racial Discrimination in the Enjoyment of Civil and Political Rights*, 14 Tex. Int'l L. J. 191 (1979). J. Inglés, Study on the Implementation of Article 4 of the International Convention on the Elimination of all Forms of Racial Discrimination, UN Doc. A/CONF.119/10 (1983). Regarding the conformity of US law with the Convention, see particularly

Beyond the Convention itself, the study may throw some light on the quality of human rights law-making in the United Nations.

II. DEFINING DISCRIMINATION: PURPOSE AND EFFECT

Article 1(1) defines racial discrimination as 'any distinction, exclusion, restriction or preference based on race, colour, descent, or national or ethnic origin which has the purpose or effect of nullifying or impairing the recognition, enjoyment or exercise, on an equal footing, of human rights and fundamental freedoms in the political, economic, social, cultural or any other field of public life'. Unlike Art. 2(1) of the International Covenant on Civil and Political Rights (Political Covenant), which only addresses distinctions in the enjoyment of the rights recognized by the Covenant, Art. 1(1) extends to all human rights and fundamental freedoms, whatever their source.

This definition of racial discrimination is different from the statement of the right to equality before the law, which appears in Art. 5 of the Convention, but the notion of equality before the law must be taken into account in interpreting the definition. It has been suggested that equality and non-discrimination can be seen as affirmative and negative statements of the same principle.[18] But what does 'equality' mean? In the US fair employment laws there is tension between equality in the sense of equal treatment (obligation of means) and equality in the sense of equal achievement (obligation of result).[19] The goal of equal achievement has, of course, a redistributive quality.[20]

N. Nathanson & E. Schwelb, The United States and the United Nations Treaty on Racial Discrimination: A Report for the Panel on International Human Rights Law and its Implementation (The American Society of International Law, 1975). See generally H. Santa Cruz, Racial Discrimination, UN Doc. E/CN.4/Sub.2/370/Rev.1 (1977); Ténékidès, *L'Action des Nations Unies contre la discrimination raciale*, 168 Recueil des cours 269 (1980–III).

[18] Ramcharan, *Equality and Nondiscrimination*, in The International Bill of Rights: The Covenant on Civil and Political Rights 246, 252 (L. Henkin ed., 1981).

The notions of non-discrimination and equality before the law were addressed by the Human Rights Committee in a case of discrimination on grounds of sex submitted under the Optional Protocol to the International Covenant on Civil and Political Rights. Communication No. R. 9/35, *Shirin Aumeeruddy-Cziffra* v. *Mauritius*, 36 UN GAOR Supp. (No. 40) at 134, UN Doc. A/36/40 (1981).

[19] Fiss, *A Theory of Fair Employment Laws*, 38 CHI. L. Rev. 235, 237–8 (1971).
[20] Ibid. at 244.

In a major policy statement, the Committee itself has explained that '[b]oth of these obligations [the obligation regulating the behaviour of the State and public authorities, institutions, and officials, whether national or local, *and* the prohibition of discriminatory conduct by any person or group against another] aim at guaranteeing the right of everyone to equality before the law in the enjoyment of fundamental human rights, without distinction as to race, colour, descent or national or ethnic origin, and at ensuring that that equality is actually enjoyed in practice.'[21] The Committee thus appears to regard equality of result as the principal object of the Convention. That goal is reflected in several provisions of the Convention (for instance Arts. 1(4) and 2(1) (c)), but is not explicitly stated in the Convention's definition of racial discrimination. The definition poses special problems because of the proviso limiting the prohibited distinctions to those leading to the denial or the impairment of human rights on an equal footing.[22]

Purposeful discrimination and discrimination that is the effect or consequence of actions undertaken for a non-discriminatory reason are evinced by facts of a different nature. When distinctions are made on the explicit basis of race, a violation of the Convention can often be established without great difficulty, since the discriminatory purpose may be apparent on the face of the instrument, policy, or programme in question. Establishing the existence of discriminatory effect,[23] however, may require information of appreciable specificity and breadth, especially where effect is observable only over time.[24] An authoritative commentator has described purpose as the subjective test and effect as the objective test of discrimination, implying perhaps that the latter is more easily applied.[25]

[21]   33 UN GAOR Supp. (No. 18) at 108, 110, UN Doc. A/33/18 (1978).

[22]   Schwelb, above n. 4, at 1001.

[23]   Section 1607.3 of the Uniform Guidelines on Employee Selection Procedures of the US Equal Employment Opportunities Commission (EEOC) states that the use of any selection procedure which has an adverse impact on the hiring, promotion, or other employment opportunities of members of any race, sex, or ethnic group will be considered to be discriminatory, unless certain conditions have been met. 29 CFR 153 (Rev. July 1, 1983).

[24]   Section 1607.4 of the EEOC Uniform Guidelines, above n. 23, provides that where the user has not maintained data on adverse impact of a selection process, the Federal enforcement agencies may draw an inference of adverse impact from that failure. Ibid. at 154–5.

[25]   N. Lerner, above n. 4, at 30–1.

Yet, depending upon the quantity and the quality of the data required, discriminatory effect may be very difficult to establish, for instance when it is attributed to the impact of economic policies and practices on ethnic groups that are already economically disadvantaged, or when the discriminatory aspects of social and cultural practices may be explained by other factors (such as religion). Information sufficiently detailed to support findings of violations in such cases will not always be available.

When egregiously racist practices are involved, these questions concerning proof are primarily of academic interest. However, the distinction between purpose and effect presents a basic question: is the Convention addressed to unintentional, as well as to intentional, acts of discrimination? It has been suggested that the drafters of the Convention wished to prohibit only racially motivated discrimination.[26] The word 'effect' may thus bring actions for which discriminatory purpose could not be established within the scope of the Convention by allowing the inference of purpose from effect;[27] consequences may be probative of an actor's intent.[28] This is of particular

[26] Ibid. at 28.

[27] Greenberg observes: 'The use of the standards of "purpose" and "effect" anticipated the full-blown controversy in the US law of racial discrimination which became important after the US Supreme Court decision in *Washington* v. *Davis* [426 U.S. 229 (1978)], that mere discriminatory effect without the *purpose* of discriminating does not violate the Constitution. Some *statutes*, however, have been held to forbid discriminatory *effect* [e.g., *Board of Education of the City of New York* v. *Harris*, 444 U.S. 130 (1979)]. One may speculate whether the Racial Discrimination Convention, had it been in force in the United States at the time *Washington* v. *Davis* was decided, would have brought about a different result.' Greenberg, above n. 17, at 322.

See also *Village of Arlington Heights* v. *Metropolitan Housing Development Corporation*, 429 U.S. 252 (1977).

For a major US example of legislation based on the purpose or effect of racial discrimination, see Title VII of the Civil Rights Act of 1964, 42 USC sections 2000e-2(a). In *Griggs* v. *Duke Power Co.*, 401 U.S. 424, 432 (1971), the Supreme Court stated: 'Congress directed the thrust of the Act to the *consequences* of employment practices, not simply the motivation.'

[28] See Bonfield, *The Substance of American Fair Employment Practices Legislation I: Employers*, 61 Nw. U. L. Rev. 907, 956–7 (1967). Regarding the relevance of effect to the determination of purpose, see *Village of Arlington Heights* v. *Metropolitan Housing Development Corporation*, 429 U.S. 252 (1977). The Supreme Court stated that determining whether invidious discriminatory purpose was a motivating factor demanded a sensitive inquiry. 'Sometimes a clear pattern, unexplainable on grounds other than race, emerges from the effect of the state action even when the governing legislation appears neutral on its face.' Ibid. at 266.

importance where subtle discriminatory purpose is not apparent on the face of statutes, policies, or programmes.

That the goal of *de facto* equality is central to the interpretation of the Convention is supported by references in the Preamble to enjoyment of certain rights 'without distinction of any kind',[29] and to 'discrimination between human beings on the grounds of race . . .',[30] as well as by the reference in Art. 5 to the right to equality before the law. Moreover, the phrase 'on an equal footing', in Art. 1(1), considered in conjunction with the exception created in Art. 1(4) allowing distinctions for the purpose of affirmative action 'to ensure . . . groups or individuals equal enjoyment or exercise of human rights', and the obligation imposed by Art. 2(2) to take certain affirmative action, indicate that the Convention promotes racial equality, not merely colour neutral values, 'not only *de jure* . . . but also *de facto* equality . . . designed to allow the various ethnic, racial and national groups the same social development'.[31] Of particular importance in this context is Art. 2(1) (c) which requires States to take policy measures and to amend, rescind, or nullify any laws or regulations which have the effect of creating or perpetuating racial discrimination.

Past acts of discrimination[32] have created systemic patterns of discrimination in many societies. The present effects of past discrimination may be continued or even exacerbated by facially neutral policies or practices which, although not purposely discriminatory, perpetuate the consequences of prior, often intentional discrimination. For example, when unnecessarily rigorous educational qualifications are prescribed for jobs, members of racial groups who were denied access to education in the past may be denied employment. Because the objective of the Convention is the attainment of equality, facially neutral policies or practices which have a disparate impact on some racial groups should be prohibited, despite the absence of

---

[29] Preamble, para. 2. Regarding reference to a preamble to interpret a treaty, see Vienna Convention on the Law of Treaties, above, n. 14, Art. 31 (1)-(2).

[30] Preamble, para. 7.

[31] 37 UN GAOR Supp. (No. 18) para. 468, UN Doc. A/37/18 (1982).

[32] Greenberg, above n. 17, at 313, notes the view permitting affirmative action to compensate disadvantaged groups for past discrimination. Regarding the difficulties involved in changing discriminatory habits and attitudes, see Shipp, *Across the Rural South, Segregation as Usual*, NY Times, Apr. 27, 1985, § 1 at 1, col. 3.

discriminatory motive.[33] The prohibition of practices which have a discriminatory effect or impact imposes an obligation upon States which may be more difficult to respect than the obligation to prohibit purposeful discrimination. States may fulfil the latter obligation, but still violate the Convention by failing to comply with the requirements of the former. While in US law effect is often taken into account in establishing purposeful discrimination, and the redistributive equal achievement goal 'is not to be pursued without restraint',[34] the Convention appears to prohibit discriminatory effect independently of the notion of intent. We shall return to the notion of intent in Section IV, below.

It is primarily with regard to measures to ensure the development and protection of certain racial groups that the Convention, in Art. 2(2), permits this obligation to be carried out 'when the circumstances so warrant', leaving a certain degree of discretion to the State. These measures will be further considered in Section V below. Discretion is also recognized in Art. 1(4), which excludes from the definition of racial discrimination such affirmative action measures 'as may be necessary . . .'. Other provisions of the Convention, such as Art. 2(1) (c), obligate the State to 'take effective measures to review governmental, national and local policies, and to amend, rescind or nullify any laws and regulations which have the effect of creating or perpetuating racial discrimination wherever it exists', without leaving it a wide margin of discretion.

Thus, the Convention states far-reaching and burdensome obligations. Could it be argued, for example, that general fiscal or social policies which have the effect, though not the intent, of perpetuating the disadvantaged position of certain racial groups, must be changed without delay, whatever the cost and without regard to competing priorities? The Convention does not indicate that States can invoke a range of considerations to

---

[33] In discussing Title VII of the Civil Rights Act of 1964, above n. 27, the Supreme Court stated that the Act was 'to achieve equality of employment opportunities and remove barriers that have operated in the past to favor an identifiable group of white employees over other employees. Under the Act, practices, procedures, or tests neutral on their face, and even neutral in terms of intent, cannot be maintained if they operate to "freeze" the status quo of prior discriminatory employment practices.' *Griggs* v. *Duke Power Co.*, 401 U.S. at 429–30.

[34] Fiss, above n. 19, at 297.

justify the failure to take immediate steps towards implementing the equal achievement goal and can balance that goal with other desired community goals.

In addition, by defining discrimination as various prohibited distinctions which cause nullification or impairment of the recognition, enjoyment, or exercise, *on an equal footing*, of human rights, Article 1 creates certain problems. Would this wording support the contention that the 'separate but equal' doctrine is consistent with the Convention? One could, of course, respond that separate facilities are never entirely equal and that they do not permit enjoyment of human rights on an equal footing. On another level, intangible considerations, such as the feeling of inferiority or the stigma which attaches to separate facilities for minority groups, are sufficient to render separate facilities and services unequal, or even inherently unequal.[35] The notion of equality advocated by the Convention, the concept of affirmative action, the preambular references to distinction and discrimination on the grounds of race, the reference to the right to equality before the law in Art. 5, and the prohibition in Art. 1(4) of the maintenance of separate rights for different racial groups after the objectives for which they were conferred have been achieved, all militate in favour of denial of the 'separate but equal' doctrine. But the text fails to make fully explicit this prohibition. The goal of affirmative action could have been assured through different wording. Art. 2 of the Universal Declaration of Human Rights,[36] which states that everyone is entitled to all the rights and freedoms set forth in the Declaration, without distinction of any kind, such as race, largely avoids this difficulty.[37] In practice, the problem

---

[35]   See *Brown* v. *Board of Education*, 347 U.S. 483 (1954).

[36]   GA Res. 217A, UN Doc. A/810, at 71 (1948) (hereinafter cited as Universal Declaration). See also Art. 2 of the International Covenant on Economic, Social and Cultural Rights (Economic Covenant), GA Res. 2200, 21 UN GAOR Supp. (No. 16) at 49, UN Doc. A/6316 (1966); Art. 2 of the International Covenant on Civil and Political Rights (Political Covenant), ibid. at 52. Art. 2 of the Economic Covenant employs the term 'discrimination', while Art. 2 of the Political Covenant employs the term 'distinction'. The use of the word 'discrimination' in the Economic Covenant was apparently intended to allow for preferential treatment of underprivileged groups. Ramcharan, above n. 18, at 258–9.

[37]   Ramcharan observes that during the drafting of the Covenants references to equality, equality before the law, equal protection of the law, non-discrimination, and non-distinction were used interchangeably. Ibid. at 251.

has not been troublesome, because members of the Committee appear to have treated distinctions on grounds of race as suspect[38] (except when justified in the context of affirmative action), without engaging in a serious inquiry into whether a particular distinction has the purpose or the effect of denying or impairing the enjoyment of human rights on an equal footing. Perhaps the Committee has been suggesting that distinctions on grounds of race constitute racial discrimination *per se*. Thus, the 'common law' of the Convention is based on the notion of equality, rather than on its definition of racial discrimination. This 'common law' has been developed by the Committee without any in-depth discussion of problems of interpretation or of the discrepancy between the definitional article of the Convention (Art. 1) and some of the operative provisions. This discrepancy was caused, at least in part, by the fact that the definitional article was drafted first[39] and was not adjusted to the operative provisions after they were prepared.

Distinctions made on the basis of race may be dangerous and subject to abuse for purposes of discrimination. 'Classifying persons according to their race is more likely to reflect racial prejudice than legitimate public concerns; the race, not the person, dictates the category.'[40] It would have been preferable, therefore, if the Convention had prohibited distinctions made on the basis of race, except in the context of affirmative action, without requiring a showing of their adverse effect on the enjoyment of human rights. The US Supreme Court subjects the classification of persons according to their race to the most exacting scrutiny.[41] While the Supreme Court has not ruled that all racial classification is inherently impermissible, it has moved in that direction (outside the context of affirmative action).[42]

On the equality before the law as a basic human right, see Partsch, above n. 17, at 196; Lillich, *Civil Rights*, in 1 Meron (ed.), above n. 17, at 115, 132-3. For a comparison of the concept of equality in the US Constitution and international human rights instruments, see Henkin, *International Human Rights and Rights in the United States*, ibid. at 25, 41-3. Regarding the definition of racial discrimination in other human rights instruments, see N. Lerner, above n. 4, at 31-2.

[38] See e.g., 38 UN GAOR Supp. (No. 18) paras. 168, 193, 280, UN Doc. A/38/18 (1983).

[39] Schwelb, above n. 4, at 1005.

[40] *Palmore* v. *Sidoti*, 104 S. Ct. 1879, 1882 (1984).

[41] Ibid.

[42] The Court decided, on the basis of the Equal Protection Clause of the Fourteenth Amendment, that '[t]he effects of racial prejudice, however real, cannot

III. PUBLIC AND PRIVATE REACH?

Whether the provisions of the Convention apply not only to public, but also to private, or partly private action presents particular difficulties of interpretation. Art. 1(1) defines racial discrimination as certain distinctions 'in the political, economic, social, cultural or any other field of *public life*' (emphasis added). This suggests that only public action is targeted by the Convention, including the activities of organizations which, though legally autonomous, perform functions of a public nature.[43] But without explicitly addressing the possible conflict with Art. 1(1), Art. 2(1) (d) obligates States Parties to 'prohibit and bring to an end, by all appropriate means, including legislation as required by circumstances, racial discrimination by any persons, group or organization'. The latter provision has been described as 'the most important and most far-reaching of all substantive provisions of the Convention'.[44] Interpreted in the context of Art. 1(1), Art. 2(1) (d) appears to mean that racially discriminatory action which occurs in public life is prohibited even if it is taken by any person, group, or organization.[45] But how does one determine what 'public life' is? To which area does the prohibition of discrimination apply? When does the duty to accord equal treatment prevail?

The Committee itself stated that national policies of States Parties 'must have as their aim the elimination of racial discrimination in all its forms — whether practised by public authorities, institutions or officials or by private individuals, groups or organizations'[46] and that they 'must entail the prohibition and the termination, by all appropriate means, of acts of racial discrimination perpetrated by any person or group against another'.[47] In this context the Committee emphasized the

justify a racial classification removing an infant child from the custody of its natural mother found to be an appropriate person to have such custody'. Ibid.

[43] N. Lerner, above n. 4, at 37 (in the context of Art. 2).

[44] Schwelb, above n. 4, at 1017.

[45] It may be noted that the Carter administration proposed an understanding to Art. 2(1) and to a number of other provisions stating that its obligations to enact legislation extended only to 'governmental or government-assisted activities and to private activities required to be available on a nondiscriminatory basis as defined by the Constitution and laws of the United States'. 1978 US Digest, above n. 12, at 443; 72 AJIL, above n. 12, at 622.

[46] 33 UN GAOR Supp. (No. 18) at 109, UN Doc. A/33/18 (1978).

[47] Ibid. at 110.

obligation of all States Parties, in accordance with Art. 6 of the Convention, to assure to everyone within their jurisdiction effective protection from and remedies for any acts of racial discrimination, including remedies for discriminatory acts by any person or group. But the Committee did not establish any parameters for the activities encompassed by the prohibition on discriminatory treatment. If the Convention goes beyond governmental action to encompass discriminatory action by non-governmental, private parties, what is the substantive area of public life which is covered or, conversely, of private life which is beyond the Convention's reach?[48] The problem of determining the reach of provisions prohibiting discrimination when non-governmental actors are involved arises also with regard to other human rights instruments, including Art. 26 of the Political Covenant,[49] but it is particularly difficult with regard to the Convention because of the contradictions inherent in its language.

Since Arts. 1(1) and 2(1) (d) offer no guidance on this difficult question, one must turn to other provisions of the Convention. Among the rights found in the catalogue of rights in Art. 5, one is of particular relevance: the guarantees under Article 5 (f) of equality before the law in '[t]he right of access to any place or service intended for use by the general public, such as transport, hotels, restaurants, cafés, theatres and parks'. While this

---

[48] One member of the Committee, noting that the Race Relations Act of Great Britain 'did not apply to personal and intimate relationships, said that it introduced a dangerous degree of flexibility which almost amounted to authorizing discrimination'. 38 UN GAOR Supp. (No. 18) para. 164, UN Doc. A/38/18 (1983). The British representative replied that such exceptions were necessary 'in the interest of striking a balance between individual freedoms and government restrictions'. Ibid., para. 172.

[49] Australia's acceptance of Art. 26 'on the basis that the object of the provision is to confirm the right of each person to equal treatment in the application of the law' (Multilateral Treaties, above n. 9, at 126), brought about an interesting exchange between the representative of Australia and some members of the Human Rights Committee established under Art. 28 of the Political Covenant. Some members of the Committee argued that Australia's interpretation of Art. 26 was not correct; that the article provided not only for equality of all before the law, but also for equal protection of all by the law against any discrimination. One member of the Committee disagreed and maintained that the article was concerned not with all types of discrimination, but only with the civil and political rights that States must guarantee. The representative of Australia maintained that the latter interpretation was 'more in keeping with the original intention of the framers'. 28 UN GAOR Supp. (No. 40) paras. 155, 175, UN Doc. A/38/40 (1973).

specification is certainly important and helpful, it is an exaggeration to claim, as Schwelb did, that 'Article 5 as a whole tells quite concretely what is meant by "public life" and probably answers most of the difficult questions of interpretation which might arise'.[50] For example, to what extent is housing (Art. 5 (e) (iii)) provided by private developers[51] covered by the Convention? The sanguine comment by Schwelb made in the context of a possible US ratification of the Convention is particularly striking when compared with his earlier acknowledgment that Art. 5 'lists several rights which certainly do not come within the sphere of public life, *e.g.*, the right to marriage and choice of spouse . . .'.[52] The wide sweep of the Convention is emphasized by the fact that members of the Committee have enquired whether discrimination can be found 'in the rental of a private apartment'[53] or admission to 'private clubs'.[54]

It is correct, however, to suggest that 'public life' is not synonymous with governmental action but is the opposite of 'private life',[55] which would thus not be reached by the Convention. But to apply this concept to concrete situations is difficult. The legislative history reveals concern that freedom of thought and expression may be jeopardized and the private life of individuals invaded.[56]

Perhaps a rationale for at least some distinction between public and private life can be developed by reference to the right of association.[57] That right is recognized in Art. 5 (d) (ix).

---

[50] Schwelb, *The International Obligations of Parties to the Convention*, in N. Nathanson and E. Schwelb, above n. 17, 1 at 7.

[51] Nathanson, *The Convention Obligations Compared with the Constitutional and Statutory Law of the United States*, ibid. 19 at 34 (suggesting that an owner renting an apartment within his own private dwelling may be more reasonably entitled to exercise personal preference in choice of tenants than the owner of a large apartment house or a substantial real estate developer).

[52] Schwelb, above n. 4, at 1005.

[53] 39 UN GAOR Supp. (No. 18) para. 238, UN Doc. A/39/18 (1984).

[54] Ibid. para. 256.

[55] Schwelb, above n. 50, at 6. See also Ramcharan, above n. 18, at 262 (on prohibited discrimination by individuals, other than in personal and social relationships, under Art. 26 of the Political Covenant).

[56] N. Lerner, above n. 4, at 38.

[57] On this right, see generally Humphrey, *Political and Related Rights*, in 1 Meron (ed.), above n. 17, at 171, 190-1; Partsch, *Freedom of Conscience and Expression, and Political Freedoms*, in Henkin (ed.), above n. 18, at 209, 235-7; Frowein, *Reform durch Meinungsfreiheit*, 105 Archiv des öffentlichen Rechts 169 (1980). Of particular importance is the case of Young, James, and Webster, Publications Eur.

It is widely acknowledged, however, that the catalogue of human rights in Art. 5 does not create those rights, but merely obligates a State Party to prevent racial discrimination in the exercise of those that it has recognized.[58] Art. 5 could have been drafted in a manner that clearly defined this limitation. But a more explicit formulation would have emphasized the liberty of States to deny some of the rights listed, which would possibly have weakened the authority of the Universal Declaration of Human Rights, on which the catalogue is based, and undermined the status of some rights as customary law. Although freedom of association is recognized in the Convention only in the limited context indicated above, that right is widely stated in other human rights instruments, including Art. 22 of the Political Covenant, which establishes, in its second paragraph, strict limits on any restrictions that may be imposed on its exercise. In accordance with the rule stated in Art. 31(3) (c) of the Vienna Convention on the Law of Treaties, the right of association — as a recognized principle of the international human rights law — may therefore be taken into account in the interpretation of the Convention so as to protect strictly personal relations from its reach.

The approach taken by the US Supreme Court in the recent case of *Roberts* v. *United States Jaycees*[59] is instructive in developing a rationale for the distinction between public and private life. This case involved gender-based discrimination, the constitutional freedom of association asserted by members of a private organization, and their First and Fourteenth Amendment rights. The Court suggested that in distinguishing 'public' and 'private' domains to determine the reach of the Constitution, account should be taken of the relative smallness of a relationship or an association, the degree of selectivity exercised, and the degree of seclusion from others.[60] Large

Ct. of Human Rights, 44 Judgments and Decisions (Series A, 1981), *reprinted in* 4 Eur. Human Rights Rep. 38 (Pt. 13, 1982); summarized in [1981] Y. B. Eur. Conv. on Human Rights 440 (Eur. Ct. of Human Rights) (1983).

[58]   28 UN GAOR Supp. (No. 18) para. 42, UN Doc. A/9018 (1973). See also ibid., paras. 53–6; 31 UN GAOR Supp. (No. 18) para. 56, UN Doc. A/31/18 (1976); 33 UN GAOR Supp. (No. 18) para. 21, UN Doc. A/33/18 (1978); Buergenthal, above n. 17, at 208–11.

[59]   104 S. Ct. 3244 (1984).

[60]   Ibid. at 3250-1.

business enterprises and their activities, for instance hiring practices, are not entitled to the same protection from intrusion as the more intimate associations. One must therefore carefully assess the objective characteristics of a particular relationship on a spectrum from the most intimate of personal attachments to the most attenuated, or from the least measure of public involvement to the most. While freedom to associate presupposes a freedom not to associate, the right to associate for expressive purposes is not absolute. With regard to large and unselective groups there is a compelling public interest in eliminating discrimination and assuring access for all to publicly available goods and services, which include not only tangible ones, but also privileges and advantages.

This or a similar approach should also be followed by States Parties and by the Committee. While certain private and inter-personal, associational relations would be insulated from the reach of the Convention, the activities of large private entities and of basically unselective organizations would be regarded as publicly available goods and services. Racial discrimination in the provision of these goods and services must be prohibited. In the absence of Convention guidelines for distinguishing the public from the private realm, this question will have to be answered through the case law of the Committee. One hopes that this will be done on the basis of criteria analogous to those applied by the Supreme Court in the *Roberts* case.

The dichotomy between the public and private realms also arises in the context of Art. 2(1)(b), which forbids States Parties to 'sponsor, defend or support racial discrimination by any persons or organizations'. Arguably, 'support' encompasses not only the extension of benefits as a positive action, but also the failure to impose obligations which are required of other persons or organizations. Granting tax-exempt benefits to a private organization which discriminates on the basis of race, for example, might be construed as a violation of Art. 2(1)(b). One commentator has concluded that any conflicts between the US Constitution and this provision would not be serious,[61] because of the reach of the state action doctrine; this position perhaps overly minimizes the points of conflict between the two. For

---

[61]   Nathanson, above n. 51, at 20-2.

example, if a routine grant of a liquor licence to a private club involved in racial discrimination is not state action in violation of the Fourteenth Amendment,[62] is it clear that this is also true under the Convention? Where the reach of the obligations arising under the Convention corresponds to the reach of the Fourteenth Amendment, as determined by the decisions of the Supreme Court involving the state action doctrine, significant conflicts between the Convention and the Constitution need not arise. But where governmental inaction, acquiescence, or tolerance[63] (for instance as through regulation, licensing, or enforcement) is deemed not to constitute state action and therefore to lie beyond the reach of government's authority to fight 'private' discrimination, conflicts would occur, were it not for the proposed US reservations, declarations, and understandings.[64] Moreover, the parameters of the state action doctrine, under which the acts of private organizations or individuals are subject to constitutional limitations if a sufficiently close relationship between those actions and governmental functions exists, are controversial and uncertain.[65] Since the degree to which government tolerance of private action will be considered state action is unclear, the possibility of conflict with the Convention remains.[66]

IV. THE SUPPRESSION OF RACIST THEORIZING AND RACIST ORGANIZATIONS

Art. 4 imposes the following obligations on States Parties: to penalize the dissemination of ideas based on racial superiority or hatred, incitement to racial discrimination, all acts of violence or incitement to such acts against any race or group of persons of another colour or ethnic origin, and the provision of any assistance to racist activities, including the financing of such activities (para. (a)); to declare illegal and prohibit organizations and all other propaganda activities which promote and incite

---

[62] Ibid. at 21 (discussion of *Moose Lodge* v. *Irvis*, 407 U.S. 163 (1972)). On state action doctrine, see also 3 T. Franck, Human Rights in Third World Perspective 463–6 (1982).
[63] L. Tribe, American Constitutional Law 1148 (1978).
[64] 1978 US Digest, above n. 12, at 443–4; 72 AJIL, above n. 12, at 621–2.
[65] See generally, L. Tribe, above n. 63, at 1147–74.
[66] Nathanson, above n. 51, at 21. But see ibid. at 22.

racial discrimination, and participation in such organizations or activities (para. (b)); and to prohibit public authorities or institutions from promoting or inciting racial discrimination (para. (c)).

In para. (a) 'assistance' is not defined. It might be extended to include providing financial support by purchasing the publications of racist groups,[67] or renting or leasing facilities such as public auditoriums to racist organizations.

Both racist groups as organizations and individuals who participate in such groups in violation of the prohibitions stated in Art. 4 are subject to criminal sanctions. The opening paragraph of Art. 4 identifies the eradication of all incitement to or acts of racial discrimination as the objective underlying the obligations enumerated. Paragraph (a) addresses the offence, rather than any particular offenders. Paragraph (b) covers not only organized, but also all other propaganda activities. It therefore appears that individuals who act alone in violation of the stated prohibitions are also subject to criminal sanctions.

The offences set forth in Art. 4 go beyond the definition of racial discrimination given in Art. 1(1). The latter encompasses only such prohibited distinctions as lead to the denial of human rights on an equal footing. The former prohibits certain organizations and activities, including the dissemination of opinion and thought (ideas and theories based on racial hatred or superiority), regardless of whether or not they lead to a denial of human rights. Does that prohibition encompass the publication of research aimed at proving the superiority of one race over another? The obligations stated in Art. 4 are also more extensive than those arising under Art. 20(2) of the Political Covenant, which penalizes only such racial hatred as constitutes incitement to discrimination, hostility, or violence. Given the tragic results of racist propaganda, for example in the Third Reich, the pain and suffering inflicted upon target groups, the tangible damage suffered, the vital community interest in the eradication of racial discrimination and its sources, and the conflict with the UN Charter goal of racial equality, the objectives of Art. 4 are commendable. Racist propaganda must never be taken with equanimity. Its destructive potential even

[67] N. Lerner, above n. 4, at 49–50.

in developed societies is a matter of history. However, it is not the objectives and goals of Art. 4 that create difficulties, but the relationship of the norms stated in it to other important values. While the article as a whole poses many problems, para. (a) gives rise to difficulties primarily in relation to freedom of expression and para. (b) challenges both freedom of expression and freedom of association.

Art. 4 explicitly mandates legislative action to implement its provisions. The Committee has insisted that reporting States have a duty to legislate irrespective of whether the prohibited activities actually occur in those States, except where legislation that fully satisfies the provisions of Art. 4 is already in existence.[68] When reporting States maintain that pre-existing law sufficiently implements Art. 4, the Committee engages in substantive analysis to determine the adequacy of those provisions.[69] In a study approved by the Committee, Inglés has argued that Art. 4 'is not self-executing. Despite the incorporation or transformation of the Convention as part of domestic law, article 4 may only be implemented if legislation is enacted to do what the article ordains.'[70] That States must take legislative action in compliance with Art. 4, irrespective of the actual existence of the prohibited activities or organizations, is consistent with the prophylactic purposes of the Convention as indicated by the definition of racial discrimination, the wide scope of the obligations of the parties, and the various educational measures mentioned in Art. 7. The Committee has emphasized, correctly, that '[f]ar from being concerned solely with combating acts of racial discrimination after they have been perpetrated, the national policies of the State Parties must also provide for preventive programmes, which seek to remove the sources from which those acts might spring — be they subjective prejudices or objective socio-economic conditions.'[71] A preventive penal policy is expressed through Art. 4, which requires all States Parties to make specified offences punishable

---

[68] General Recommendation I, Dec. 3(V), 27 UN GAOR Supp. (No. 18) at 37, UN Doc. A/8718 (1972); 34 UN GAOR Supp. (No. 18) para. 226, UN Doc. A/34/18 (1979); 31 UN GAOR Supp. (No. 18) para. 245, UN Doc. A/31/18 (1976); Buergenthal, above n. 17, at 193–4; Partsch, above n. 57, at 229.

[69] See e.g. 33 UN GAOR Supp. (No. 18) para. 320, UN Doc. A/33/18 (1978).

[70] Inglés, above n. 17, para. 216.

[71] 33 UN GAOR Supp. (No. 18) at 109, UN Doc. A/33/18 (1978).

regardless of whether racial discrimination is actually practised in their territories.[72] While mandating criminal sanctions, Art. 4 attempts to effect fundamental societal changes which should prevent the future occurrence of racial discrimination and violence. By creating prior restraints on freedom of expression and association, Art. 4 seeks to eradicate racist thought and racist organizations which generate racist acts. Thus, Inglés observes that 'Article 4 aims at prevention rather than cure; the penalty of the law is supposed to deter racism or racial discrimination as well as activities aimed at their promotion or incitement.'[73]

Organizations that promote racial discrimination, and not merely their specific activities which have that purpose or effect, are prohibited. During the drafting debates, an amendment inserting the words 'or the activities of such organizations' after the word 'organizations' in para. (b) was not adopted,[74] perhaps because the very existence of such organizations was felt to be destructive of the aims of the Convention. Would the language of that paragraph, as adopted, permit the prohibition of such groups as soon as it is clear that they intend to engage in promoting or inciting racial discrimination?[75] Members of the Committee have emphasized the need to outlaw certain organizations, which in fact engage in incitement to racial discrimination, even though they do not proclaim such incitement to be their objective.[76] They have inquired whether action has been taken with the intention of dissolving associations pursing goals which are illegal under Art. 4.[77] If the aims of an organization are clear even before its formation, does the language of Art. 4 permit its prohibition beforehand, rather than only its dissolution afterward? How are such aims determined? What is the level of activity necessary to constitute a violation? Inglés appears to answer the first of these questions in the affirmative by referring to legislation of States providing for the denial of permit or registration of organizations with an illegal

---

[72]   Ibid. at 110.
[73]   Inglés, above n. 17, para. 221.
[74]   N. Lerner, above n. 4, at 45.
[75]   Ibid. at 50.
[76]   32 UN GAOR Supp. (No. 18) para. 286, UN Doc. A/32/18 (1977).
[77]   39 UN GAOR Supp. (No. 18) para. 270, UN Doc. A/39/18 (1984). The Committee emphasized that it was not enough for the penal code to be applicable to

purpose, or their dissolution in the event that they have already been registered or granted permits.[78]

Art. 4 is potentially even broader than may at first be apparent from the text, because the initial paragraph employs the words '*inter alia*'. But even those measures which are enumerated pose problems. The drafting and application of laws giving effect to Art. 4 will be difficult, since the provision requires criminalization not only of acts and incitement to acts of racial discrimination and violence, but of the promulgation of racist theories and thought. With a few exceptions, traditional concepts of criminal liability require the commission of an act, or the failure to act when the law imposes a duty to do so, or incitement to action. But Art. 4 also requires States to impose criminal liability for 'dissemination of ideas' (freedom of expression) alone.

When compared with US law, this criminalization of speech and association (organizations) on the basis of racist content violates the content-neutral protection afforded by the First Amendment doctrine of freedom of expression.[79] But the different approach followed in the United States should not be explained on Constitutional grounds alone. It also reflects, at least in recent history, the feeling of confidence and security in a developed and relatively stable society which, while failing to eradicate racism, has found orderly means of dealing with its racial problems, as well as the traditional preference for individual freedoms over the regulatory power of the State. In some other countries, however, activities and organizations which in the United States would often be regarded as creating only a marginal possibility of violence and threat to public order might

---

individual members of an organization. The legislation should contain provisions prohibiting such organizations as required by Art. 4(b). Ibid., para. 509.

[78] Inglés, above n. 17, paras. 238–40.

[79] Greenberg points out that in the United States even groups which preach hatred, such as the Ku Klux Klan or the Nazis, benefit from the right of free expression and their activities based on racial, ethnic, or religious hatred are nearly uniformly permitted to continue. Greenberg, above n. 17, at 323–4. See *Collin* v. *Smith*, 578 F. 2d 1197, *cert. denied*, 436 U.S. 953 (1978). But see 'Smith Act', 18 USC § 2385 (1982). For the interpretation of the Act by the Supreme Court, see *Scales* v. *United States*, 367 U.S. 203 (1961); *Yates* v. *United States*, 354 U.S. 298 (1957); *Dennis* v. *United States*, 341 U.S. 494 (1951).

be regarded as a clear and present danger.[80] If certain provisions of the Convention are over broad when viewed against the United States' legal and social systems, it does not necessarily follow that they are over broad for some of the other countries. It is difficult, indeed, to find a common legislative policy for the Member States of the United Nations, in view of their diverse stages of development and their different cultures, traditions, conditions of social peace and security, and so on. The purpose of these comments is, of course, not to make a value judgment about which legal and social systems are superior, but simply to state some of the relevant factors.

Dissemination of racist thought and participation in organizations that engage in promotion of racial discrimination are prohibited under Art. 4 regardless of whether the communication of racist ideas leads to otherwise illegal conduct. Is there, then, a conflict between Art. 4 and the principles of freedom of expression and of association, as they are recognized in international law? The opening paragraph of Art. 4 reflects an effort to avoid such a conflict. The measures to be taken by States Parties are to be adopted 'with due regard to the principles embodied in the Universal Declaration of Human Rights and the rights expressly set forth in article 5 of this Convention'. The freedoms of expression and association are indeed embodied in Art. 5(d) (viii)–(ix), in the Universal Declaration of Human Rights and the Political Covenant, but in these and other international human rights instruments these principles are not absolute; they are subject to various limitations, the scope of

---

[80] *P. Hemalatha* v. *Govt. of A. P.* (SB), 1976 A.I.R. (A.P.) 375, paras. 19–24, reprinted in T. Franck, above n. 62, at 241; *The [Nigeria] Director of Public Prosecutions* v. *Chike Obi*, F.S.C. 56/1961, reprinted in ibid. at 229.

Even in the United States, however, racist invective was considered punishable as criminal libel, although it was not shown that it involved a clear and present danger to the target group. *Beauharnais* v. *Illinois*, 343 U.S. 250 (1952). The present status of *Beauharnais* is a matter of some doubt. In *Brandenburg* v. *Ohio*, 395 U.S. 444 (1969), the Supreme Court emphasized the principle that the Constitutional guarantees of free speech and free press do not permit a State to proscribe advocacy of the use of force or of law violation except where such advocacy is directed to inciting or producing imminent lawless action and is likely to incite or produce it. The indictment of a Ku Klux Klan leader was overruled as contrary to the First and the Fourteenth Amendments.

Regarding the 'Front National' in France and claims for defamation submitted by its leader Jean-Marie Le Pen, see *Le Monde*, 2 Nov. 1984, at 8, col. 3 (last edn.).

which is not clearly determined.[81] Under Art. 29(2) of the Universal Declaration, restrictions on the freedom of expression and association might be justified on the ground that the promulgation of racist ideas by individuals or groups would lead to the infringement of the rights of members of the targeted racial groups and adversely affect public order and the general welfare of society. This article has been invoked in support of limiting the dissemination of racist expression and the existence of racist organizations.[82] Of course, the promulgation of racist ideas may affect the rights of others. But, depending on the situation in a particular society, the argument that the promulgation of such ideas inherently endangers public order is usually persuasive only when such promulgation constitutes incitement to acts of discrimination or violence, which is already prohibited in any case.

The 'due regard' clause permits the invocation of another provision of the Universal Declaration, Art. 30, which states that '[n]othing in this Declaration may be interpreted as implying for any State, group or person any right to engage in any activity or to perform any act aimed at the destruction of any of the rights and freedoms set forth herein.' This article has been viewed as an injunction 'against interpreting the Declaration as implying for any State the right to destroy any of the rights and freedoms proclaimed therein'.[83] However, elsewhere, in discussing Art. 4 of the Convention, the same commentator expressed the view that Art. 30 of the Universal Declaration 'does not preclude or prohibit reasonable limitations as are expressly set forth in Article 29(2) which do not have the purpose or effect of destroying those rights and freedoms'.[84]

---

[81] Universal Declaration, above n. 36, Arts. 19, 20, 29, 30; Political Covenant, above n. 36, Arts. 4, 19–22.

[82] For statements referring explicitly or implicitly to the limitation clauses of the Universal Declaration in construing Art. 4, see e.g., 33 UN GAOR Supp. (No. 18) para. 279, UN Doc. A/33/18 (1978); 34 UN GAOR Supp. (No. 18) para. 227, UN Doc. A/34/18 (1979).

[83] J. Inglés, Study of Discrimination in Respect of the Right of Everyone to Leave Any Country, Including His Own, and to Return to His Country 37, UN Doc. E/CN.4/Sub.2/220/Rev.1 (1963).

[84] Inglés, above n. 17, para. 228. See generally E. Daes, The Individual's Duties to the Community and the Limitations on Human Rights and Freedoms under Article 29 of the Universal Declaration of Human Rights, UN Doc. E/CN.4/Sub.2/432/Rev.2 (1983).

Because it will be argued that the measures taken in implementation of Art. 4 do not have the purpose or effect of destroying the rights or freedoms stated in the Declaration, Art. 30 does not provide an effective protection against abuse. Despite its vagueness, Art. 30 could have perhaps been relied upon by the Committee more seriously to balance the prohibition of racial discrimination with the freedoms of association and expression stated in the Universal Declaration. It can, of course, be invoked by States in the course of their interpretation and application of the Convention.

The Committee has paid lip-service to the notion that the freedoms of expression and association 'are not irreconcilable' with the obligations created by Art. 4,[85] and to the 'due regard' clause of that Article, while expressing clear preference for the application of the norms stated in Art. 4:

The Committee is fully aware that the Convention — in laying down the obligations of States parties with regard to the prohibition of the dissemination of racist ideas, incitement to racial discrimination or violence, and racist organizations — allows for the fulfilment of those obligations to be accomplished 'with due regard' to the fundamental human rights to freedom of opinion, expression and association. However, it could not have been the intention of the drafters of the Convention to enable States parties to construe the phrase safeguarding the human rights in question as cancelling the obligations relating to the prohibition of the racist activities concerned. Otherwise, there would have been no purpose whatsoever for the inclusion in the Convention of the articles laying down those obligations.[86]

That a conflict arises has been acknowledged by some members of the Committee, for whom Art. 4 supersedes freedom of expression and association.[87] Indeed, since Art. 4 is premised on the belief that racist practices can be combated successfully only if the promulgation of racist ideas is curtailed and, perhaps, on the view that such ideas are inherently dangerous, such a conclusion follows logically. As a matter of fact, in construing Art. 20 of the Political Covenant, the Human Rights Committee has taken a position rather similar to that taken by the Committee on the Elimination of Racial Discrimination. It stated that the 'required prohibitions are fully compatible with the

---

[85] 33 UN GAOR Supp. (No. 18) at 113, UN Doc. A/33/18 (1978).
[86] Ibid. at 112.
[87] E.g., ibid. para. 51.

right of freedom of expression as contained in article 19, the exercise of which carries with it special duties and responsibilities'.[88] It thus emphasized categorically the duty of States to fulfil their obligations under Art. 20.

The wide sweep of Art. 4 has caused occasional resentment even within the Committee.[89] Western States have expressed some opposition to the restraints on freedom of expression and association created by the article[90] and the Committee itself has admitted that only a few States have taken the necessary measures to implement it.[91]

The obligations specified apply clearly to statements or acts of public officials within the territories of the States Parties. They must be deemed applicable also to the statements or acts of such officials in the United Nations and other international organizations.[92] Thus, racist remarks may violate the obligations of the States concerned under the Convention and should be scrutinized by the Committee. In an international forum the balancing of the various factors involved, such as the freedom of speech of governments against the Charter principles of racial

---

[88] General Comment 11, 38 UN GAOR Supp. (No. 40) at 110, UN Doc. A/38/40 (1983).

[89] Thus, one member of the Committee objected to the text of a questionnaire because the question concerning racist theorizing 'appeared to assume that Member States were required to penalize all dissemination of ideas based on racial superiority and not merely propaganda activities aimed at encouraging racial discrimination'. 30 UN GAOR Supp. (No. 18) para. 47, UN Doc. A/10018 (1975).

[90] Great Britain has interpreted the obligations of Art. 4 to be limited by the extent to which they may be fulfilled with due regard to the principles embodied in the Universal Declaration, in particular the right to freedom of opinion and expression and the right to freedom of peaceful assembly and association. Multilateral Treaties, above n. 9, at 107. Other governments, e.g., Belgium, ibid. at 101, have emphasized the need both to adopt the necessary legislation and to respect the freedoms of expression and association. The United States has made a general declaration limiting the scope of the obligations assumed under the Convention to those which would not restrict the right of free speech as guaranteed by the US Constitution and laws of the United States, and by Art. 5 of the Convention. 1978 US Digest, above n. 12, at 443. The government of the Federal Republic of Germany 'after careful consideration, reached the conclusion that dissemination of opinions of racial superiority should be punishable if it was intended to create racial discrimination or hatred', 32 UN GAOR Supp. (No. 18) para. 87, UN Doc. A/32/18 (1977). See also Inglés, above n. 17, at para. 225.

[91] 39 UN GAOR Supp. (No. 18) para. 303, UN Doc. A/39/18 (1984).

[92] On some other aspects of the extraterritorial reach of the Convention, see Buergenthal, above n. 17, at 211–18. See generally Meron, *Applicability of Multilateral Conventions to Occupied Territories*, 72 AJIL 542 (1978).

equality of all persons, and friendly relations among nations, may lead to results different from those which obtain internally in some States, where the freedom of speech of individuals, balanced against an all-powerful State and other community interests, is often an endangered value and deserves special protection. The prohibition of certain types of racist propaganda in the Convention and the Political Covenant should be observed first and foremost within the parent organization. Unfortunately, this is not always the case.[93]

Some of the obligations under the Convention apply, of course, to private individuals. But the Committee has never determined how far into private life the obligations of the Convention extend. Do they, for instance, cover racist remarks made between members of the same family or in a private letter not aimed at circulation or publication? According to some members of the Committee, insulting or defamatory racist remarks made to individuals should be included in the conduct to be penalized.[94] Some comments made by the members suggest that they have an extremely broad conception of the Convention's provisions. Thus, one State Party was criticized for legislation requiring that certain offences must be committed publicly in order to be punishable (for instance 'discriminatory measures which could be taken through correspondence' would not be covered by the legislation;[95] members or supporters of an association which advocated racial discrimination could be punished only when their activities 'took place publicly').[96]

---

[93] An egregious example of racist remarks can be found in the statement made in the UN General Assembly by the representative of the Libyan Arab Jamahiriya: 'It is high time for the United Nations and the United States in particular to realize that the Jewish Zionists here in the United States attempt to destroy Americans. Look around New York. Who are the owners of pornographic film operations and houses? Is it not the Jews who are exploiting the American people and trying to debase them?' UN Doc. A/38/PV. 88, at 19–20 (1983).

[94] 34 UN GAOR Supp. (No. 18) para. 157, UN Doc. A/34/18 (1979). Nevertheless, some members of the Committee noted with regard to a penal provision of Norway, which covered only public utterances and communications, that 'private utterances and communications lay outside the field in which the penal law could effectively be applied without an oppressive system of surveillance'. 32 UN GAOR Supp. (No. 18) para. 157, UN Doc. A/32/18 (1977).

[95] 39 UN GAOR Supp. (No. 18) para. 238, UN Doc. A/39/18 (1984) (in the case of Belgium).

[96] Ibid. The representative of Belgium responded that the Belgian Act 'would not apply in the case of a landlord who refused to rent a private apartment to a foreigner,

Another State reported to the Committee that, in implementing Art. 4, it had outlawed any form of racial discrimination, 'including verbal',[97] without specifying, however, whether this encompassed the private communication of ideas. If private as well as public communication of racist ideas is prohibited, it might invite state invasion of the right to privacy. In light of the harm caused by such behaviour, private civil actions might be a more appropriate remedy, reducing the scope of possible encroachment by the state into interpersonal relations. Nevertheless, civil actions would probably not effectively limit such conduct without the deterrent effect of criminal sanctions.

Concepts of criminal liability in US law usually link culpability with intent as closely as possible. But Art. 4 appears not to be based on the requirement of intent. Members of the Committee have interpreted the article accordingly and appeared to endorse the notion that it is based on absolute liability.[98] Inglés thus emphasizes 'that the mere act of dissemination is penalized, despite lack of intention to commit an offence and irrespective of the consequences of the dissemination, whether it be grave or insignificant'.[99] He criticizes States Parties whose legislation addresses only such dissemination or incitement as is intentional, or has the objective of stirring up hatred, or is threatening, abusive, or insulting: 'Obviously, these conditions are restrictive and ignore the fact that Art. 4 (a) declares

---

because it would be very difficult to present legal evidence of the grounds for the refusal, unless there were witnesses'. The requirement that the activities of racist associations be known to the public in order to be punishable resulted from the difficulty of proving any practice which was not a matter of public knowledge. Ibid. para. 244.

[97] Ibid. para. 276 (in the case of Denmark).

[98] 32 UN GAOR Supp. (No. 18) para. 84, UN Doc. A/32/18 (1977). In reviewing the adequacy under Art. 4 of Great Britain's Race Relations Act, members of the Committee approved a change in that legislation dispensing with the 'necessity to prove a subjective intention to stir up racial hatred'. Moreover, they implicitly endorsed absolute liability under Art. 4 in disapproving the provision of the Race Relations Act that in the publication or distribution of written matter 'it shall be a defence for the accused to prove that he was not aware of the content of the written material in question and neither suspected nor had reason to suspect it of being threatening, abusive or insulting'. 33 UN GAOR Supp. (No. 18) para. 339, UN Doc. A/33/18 (1978). One member of the Committee expressed the opinion 'that the question of [the offender's] good faith and intent did not enter into consideration in the implementation of Article 4 . . .". 35 UN GAOR Supp. (No. 18) para. 338, UN Doc. A/35/18 (1980).

[99] Inglés, above n. 17, para. 83.

punishable the mere act of dissemination or incitement, without any conditions.[100]

The point at which the culpability of a particular organization is sufficiently clear to warrant intervention by the state may be defined by States in a manner that restricts the freedom of expression and privacy more than is necessary to achieve the objectives of Art. 4.[101] But if the drafters had specified intent as an element of the offences listed, the difficulties attendant upon proving intent would have hampered the effectiveness of the article.

Given the prophylactic purposes of Art. 4, limitations on the exercise of free speech and on the right of association are unavoidable, while the reconciliation of the conflicting principles is artificial. If the drafters feared that the effectiveness of the provision would be hampered by introducing the requirement of intent,[102] they should at least have defined the offences more specifically and, perhaps, more narrowly. The Convention should have made punishable primarily individual conduct, or the conduct of individuals acting as a group, rather than the existence of organizations (unless they are involved in acts of violence, incitement to violence, or other illegal acts) and the promulgation of ideas, which would have limited the dangers of encroachment on the freedom of association and of arbitrary censorship. Finally, by reducing the scope of Art. 4 to public conduct, the drafters might have avoided conflict with the right to privacy in familial and intimate associational contexts, reduced the danger of intrusive state action, and lessened the conflict with the principle of freedom of opinion and expression. The overreach of Art. 4 creates difficulties for democratic States that take their obligations seriously and has prompted some of them to enter a relatively large number of reservations to that article.[103]

Neither Art. 4 nor the definitional provisions of the Convention address religious discrimination or invective. This poses problems when vilification occurs in the grey area between race

---

[100]   Ibid. para. 235.
[101]   See generally, N. Lerner, above n. 4, at 51.
[102]   Some States (e.g. the Federal Republic of Germany, above n. 90) insist, nevertheless, upon the requirement of intent.
[103]   See Multilateral Treaties, above n. 9, at 100–8.

and religion. The Norwegian Supreme Court dealt with an interesting case in point a few years ago; the judgment was included in the recent periodic report submitted by Norway to the Committee.[104] The case concerned an appeal against a conviction by a district court holding that the defendant had violated the penal code by circulating leaflets which violently attacked Norwegian policy on the immigration of 'Islamic foreign workers', the workers themselves, and the religion of Islam. In 'a weighing up process', Associate Justice Aasland compared utterances concerning Islam as a religion, conditions in the Islamic States, and Norwegian immigration policy, which were protected by the freedom of expression under the Constitution, with utterances which more directly attacked Islamic immigrants in Norway. The target of the leaflets was Islamic immigrants, their character, and their behaviour. Under the penal code, attacks on the characteristics of a population group and its behavioural pattern were punishable. Such attacks exposed that population group to hatred and contempt. Unless they were punished, it would be impossible to accord an exposed minority group the protection intended by the law.

This judgment was praised by some members of the Committee as a good example of the implementation of Art. 4 and as a balance between freedom of expression and the ban on incitement to racial discrimination: 'though the defendant was held entitled to express certain general views, she had broken the law when she had directed her remarks against specific ethnic groups.'[105] The judgment led the Committee to consider whether religious discrimination was covered by Art. 4. Some members believed that an attack on a particular religion would not breach the Convention, while an attack on an identifiable national or ethnic group would. Others said that good grounds could be found for extending the Convention to cover attacks against religion.[106] It remains to be seen whether the Committee will try to interpret the Convention as reaching incitement to hatred of groups that belong to a particular religious persuasion and have certain ethnic characteristics as well.

---

[104] Judgement No. 134 B/1981, reprinted in UN Doc. CERD/C/107/Add. 4 at 14 (1984).
[105] 39 UN GAOR Supp. (No. 18) para. 509, UN Doc. A/39/18 (1984).
[106] Ibid. para. 507.

V. AFFIRMATIVE ACTION

A. *Race-Conscious Policies under Affirmative Action Programmes.*

Art. 1(4) allows States Parties to take

[s]pecial measures . . . for the sole purpose of securing adequate advancement of certain racial or ethnic groups or individuals requiring such protection as may be necessary in order to ensure such groups or individuals equal enjoyment or exercise of human rights and fundamental freedoms . . ., provided, however, that such measures do not, as a consequence, lead to the maintenance of separate rights for different racial groups and that they shall not be continued after the objectives for which they were taken have been achieved.

This provision carves out an exception to the definition of racial discrimination. One consequence of the emphasis on racial equality is that the adverse effect upon a privileged racial group of the 'special measures' which may be taken pursuant to Art. 1(4), would not be considered racial discrimination[107] until and unless the measures led to 'the maintenance of separate rights for different racial groups' or 'continued after the objectives for which they were taken have been achieved'. Thus, bona fide affirmative action programmes cannot be challenged under the Convention, as they could be if the Convention mandated colour-blind policies.[108]

Because a violation of the exception stated in Art. 1(4) may become apparent only after the passage of time, there is a danger that States may use this provision to legitimize discriminatory practices. The Committee has been alert to this danger, however, and has scrutinized reports from States accordingly.[109]

---

[107] See generally N. Lerner, above n. 4, at 32-3.

[108] However, the government of Papua New Guinea justified its caution in protecting ethnic groups on the ground that 'protection of one group might be considered discrimination against others'. 39 UN GAOR Supp. (No. 18) para. 284, UN Doc. A/39/18 (1984).

[109] E.g., with regard to the provisions of the Constitution of India amended to extend the special reservation of seats in the Parliament and in the legislative assemblies for the scheduled castes and tribes and for the Anglo-Indian community for an additional period of 10 years. 38 UN GAOR Supp. (No. 18) para 280, UN Doc. A/38/18 (1983). The representative of India stated that 40 years was not a long period to bring to the level of the rest of the community groups which for centuries have been subjected to repression. Ibid., para. 285. For a discussion of these and other affirmative action provisions of the Indian Constitution in the context of

B. *Affirmative Action Measures: Their Necessity and Scope*

While Art. 1(4) excludes affirmative action from the definition of racial discrimination, Art. 2(2) actually obliges States Parties to take affirmative action. They shall 'when the circumstances so warrant, take, in the social, economic, cultural and other fields, special and concrete measures to ensure the adequate development and protection of certain racial groups or individuals belonging to them, for the purpose of guaranteeing them the full and equal enjoyment of human rights and fundamental freedoms'. This article as drafted fails to provide standards for determining which groups should benefit from special measures and when the political, economic, and social circumstances of those groups warrant the introduction of such measures. The words 'when the circumstances so warrant' suggest that a considerable measure of discretion is left to the States in deciding when remedial steps must be taken. Although the article mentions 'protection', it does not provide safeguards against the use of special measures which promote 'adequate development' of ethnic groups to achieve their assimilation into the society at large. Art. 2(2) does not concern individual rights but protects groups of persons[110] or individuals *qua* members of the group. Because of the wide acceptance of the Convention by States, the Convention and the Committee can play an important role in the protection of ethnic groups. Art. 27 of the Political Covenant protects various rights of persons belonging to certain minorities, but it does not explicitly provide for affirmative action.[111] While the Convention addresses racial

---

reservation of a certain percentage of seats in professional and technical colleges in favour of 'socially and educationally backward Classes', see *Singh* v. *Mysore*, 47 A.I.R. 338 (Mysore 1960), reprinted in T. Franck, above n. 62, at 428. It is of interest to contrast this case with *Regents of the University of California* v. *Bakke*, 438 U.S. 265 (1978). See also *Firefighters Local Union No. 1784* v. *Stotts*, No. 82-206, 104 S. Ct. 2576 (1984).

[110] 37 UN GAOR Supp. (No. 18) para. 468, UN Doc. A/37/18 (1982). Regarding group rights, see Humphrey, *Political and Related Rights*, in 1 Meron (ed.), above n. 17, at 171, 171-2.

[111] For a discussion of the scope of minority rights under Art. 27, see Sohn, *The Rights of Minorities*, in Henkin (ed.), above n. 18, at 270, 282-7. On minorities in general, see F. Capotorti, Study on the Rights of Persons Belonging to Ethnic, Religious and Linguistic Minorities, reprinted in UN Doc. E/CN.4/Sub.2/384 (Rev. 1, 1979), UN Sales Pub. No. E. 78. XIV. 1; Ermacora, *The Protection of Minorities Before the United Nations*, 182 Recueil des cours 247 (1983-IV).

'groups' (without specifying their percentage of the total population) rather than 'minorities', this may encompass protection of ethnic minorities as defined for purposes of Art. 27.[112]

The definition of racial groups gives rise to some questions. First, should the words 'certain racial groups' be interpreted to mean those groups not possessing majoritarian political status or adequate representation in the political and economic process or those constituting less than a majority of the total population? Unless the former interpretation is followed, the obligation to adopt special measures on behalf of ethnic groups with a limited share in the political and economic process[113] could be avoided by asserting that the groups in question comprise the largest percentage of the total population.[114] Conversely, racial groups that possess full political and economic rights do not qualify for special action under

In Communication No. R.6/24 (*Sandra Lovelace* v. *Canada*), the Human Rights Committee established under Art. 28 of the Political Covenant concluded that Sandra Lovelace, an ethnic Indian who because of her marriage to a non-Indian had lost her status as Indian under the provisions of the (Canadian) Indian Act, was entitled to be regarded as belonging to the Indian minority and claim the benefits of Art. 27 of the Political Covenant. Taking into account the fact that her marriage had broken up, and that she has been absent from the reservation for only a few years, the Committee concluded that to deny her the right to reside on the reservation was not reasonable and constituted an unjustified denial of her rights under Art. 27. 36 UN GAOR Supp. (No 40), Annex XVIII, UN Doc. A/36/40 (1981). See Bayefsky, *The Human Rights Committee and the Case of Sandra Lovelace*, 20 Can. Y.B. Int'l L. 244 (1982).

[112] For the meaning of 'minorities' in the context of Art. 27 of the Political Covenant, see Sohn, above n. 111, at 276–80.

The Commission on Human Rights recently asked the Sub-Commission on Prevention of Discrimination and Protection of Minorities to prepare a definition of the term 'minority', UN Doc. E/CN.4/Sub.2/1984/31. Such a definition would not focus on the interpretation of Art. 27 of the Political Covenant. By contrast, Capotorti's tentative definition (see above n. 111, at para. 568) was drawn up solely with the application of Art. 27 in mind. It spoke, in part, of '[a] group numerically inferior to the rest of the population of a State, in a non-dominant position, whose members . . . possess ethnic, religious or linguistic characteristics differing from the rest of the population and show, if only implicitly, a sense of solidarity, directed towards preserving their culture, traditions, religion or language'. Cited in UN Doc. E/CN.4/Sub.2/1984/31 at 2. See also definition of the term 'minority' by Jules Deschênes, UN Doc. E/CN.4/Sub.2/1985/31, at 30 (1985).

[113] The Committee has requested information on the machinery for drawing minorities into the political process in compliance with Articles 1(4) and 2(2) of the Convention (Vietnam). 39 UN GAOR Supp. (No. 18) para. 356, UN Doc. A/39/18 (1984).

[114] See generally J. Sigler, Minority Rights: A Comparative Analysis 5, 8 (1983).

Art. 2(2).[115] The obligations arising from Art. 2(2) may also prove difficult to implement in countries with populations consisting of a large number of discrete ethnic or tribal groups,[116] no single one of which constitutes a majority as a percentage of the total population.

How to identify racial groups presents a second set of definitional problems. A State may recognize a racial or ethnic group as distinct on the basis of linguistic, religious, economic, or social characteristics, or some combination of these features.[117] If a group is not identifiable as ethnically discrete, it is not entitled to the protection of Art. 2(2).[118] For example, a tribe which has traditionally been nomadic may not be otherwise distinguishable on the basis of physical characteristics, and if cultural and other non-racial characteristics are ignored,[119] a State might attempt to deny that group the protection of Art. 2(2). The degree to which a given group must be different from the remainder of the population to benefit from the provisions of Art. 2(2) is not clear.[120] States may attempt to evade their duties by refusing to acknowledge that a specific group should be defined as ethnically distinct.[121] States' obligations to resort to affirmative measures should be determined by the group's degree of access to political and economic resources, rather than by over-emphasis on the anthropological analysis of the group's relationship to the rest of the population. While Art. 2(2) does not provide standards for determining when circumstances warrant special

---

[115] Members of the Committee have inquired, rather suspiciously, about the extent of the separation and points of contact 'between the élite minority community' of Mauritius and the rest of the population. 39 UN GAOR Supp. (No. 18) para. 254, UN Doc. A/39/18 (1984).

[116] E.g., Tanzania, see 38 UN GAOR Supp. (No. 18) para. 330, UN Doc. A/38/18 (1983).

[117] See generally, Sigler, above n. 114, at 6–10.

[118] Sigler observes that '[m]ost nations avoid problems of group rights by simply not recognizing the status of the group'. Ibid. at 12–13.

[119] See generally ibid. at 10.

[120] E.g., should Spanish Basques be identified only as a linguistic minority, or do they constitute a discrete ethnic group? 37 UN GAOR Supp. (No. 18) para. 281, UN Doc. A/37/18 (1982).

[121] The representative of Niger argued that discrimination against nomadic groups in his country was economic, not ethnic. 38 UN GAOR Supp. (No. 18) para. 494, UN Doc. A/38/18 (1983).

measures,[122] the text suggests that the test is whether the group in question requires the protection and aid of the State to attain a full and equal enjoyment of human rights.[123] Article 2(2) uses the term 'racial groups', not races, which suggests perhaps a wider spectrum of beneficiaries. But the absence of clear definitions and the anthropological difficulty of defining[124] and identifying racial groups lead to the conclusion that this problem will continue to be troublesome.

To determine whether a State has complied with the obligations imposed by Art. 2(2), demographic statistics specifying the ethnic composition of the population may be essential, and a socio-economic profile of the various ethnic groups may be necessary as well.[125] Data based on religious[126] or linguistic affiliation are often irrelevant for these purposes.[127] But States

---

[122] Should Canadian Indians who have left the reservations no longer enjoy the same rights or protection as are afforded to those who remained on the reservations? Was the definition of membership in such groups too restrictive? Ibid. para. 394. See also above n. 111.

[123] Australia has recognized that its Aboriginal citizens constituted a group for which special and concrete measures were required to promote their development. 39 UN GAOR Supp. (No. 18) para. 328, UN Doc. A/39/18 (1984). Members of the Committee have inquired how the Aboriginal people could be helped to achieve in practice their full political and civil rights. Ibid. at para. 335.

[124] See generally UN Doc. E/CN.4/Sub.2/1984/31 at 4.

[125] The Committee has thus requested that Italy include in its next periodic report a comparative socio-economic analysis of the various minorities and ethnic groups so that it could be determined for which of those groups measures should be adopted to ensure their adequate development. 39 UN GAOR Supp. (No. 18) para. 300, UN Doc. A/39/18 (1984). The Committee has requested that the Government of the Central African Republic provide information not only on the demographic composition of the population, but also on the socio-economic situation of the various ethnic groups and about measures to improve the living conditions of the pygmies. Ibid. para. 117. In emphasizing its interest in the participation of ethnic groups in the economic and political processes, the Committee requested that the Government of Colombia provide information 'on the National Development Programme for Indigenous Peoples, measures to help disadvantaged groups and comparative figures for the various groups relating to education, per capita income, housing and medical care. Statistics should also be furnished . . . on the employment of members of the various racial groups in the public service and their representation among elected officials. The Committee would also like to have information on the enjoyment by members of the indigenous population of their political as well as cultural rights, their real situation . . .' Ibid. para. 131.

[126] In the case of Mauritius, which classifies its population on a religious rather than an ethnic basis, members of the Committee asked how a race relations act could be effective if information on the racial composition of the population was no longer kept. Ibid. paras. 252, 256.

[127] 37 UN GAOR Supp. (No. 18) para. 108, UN Doc. A/37/18 (1982).

may be unable to compile accurate demographic profiles, because census may not be frequently or effectively taken, or it may be considered improper to inquire about ethnicity, or the inhabitants may not be required to indicate their race.[128] Recognizing the difficulties, the Committee has agreed that demographic statistics need not be precise, but should at least indicate percentages of the total population and that it should press countries which have not been able to supply such information to do so when ethnic problems arise.[129]

C. *Towards Assimilation?*

Another problem already mentioned stems from the absence of safeguards against the use of measures which, in promoting the adequate development of racial groups in social, economic, cultural, and other fields, constitute assimilationist policies and may result in a group's loss of cultural identity. Art. 2(2) does not require States to aid in the preservation of cultural identity, but the reference to the cultural field and to 'protection', rather than only to 'development', suggests that at least the spirit of the Convention would be violated by such measures. Some States have shown considerable awareness of their obligations in this regard.[130] To some extent, the Committee has compensated for the deficiency by focusing inquiry upon the relevant issues. In examining specific programmes undertaken for the adequate development of certain racial groups, and the consequences of such measures, the Committee has recognized the tension between the need for social and economic equality and the need to preserve the integrity of discrete cultures. Thus, in discussing the report of New Zealand, the Committee stated that the 'one Nation: two peoples' approach followed by that

[128]   32 UN GAOR Supp. (No. 18) para. 87, UN Doc. A/32/18 (1977) (the Federal Republic of Germany). The Committee requested information on the demographic composition of the Algerian population. Its members asked for clarification regarding the assertion in Algeria's report that a census of the Algerian population on ethnic or racial grounds would be contrary to Islam. 39 UN GAOR Supp. (No. 18) para. 91, UN Doc. A/39/18 (1984).

[129]   38 UN GAOR Supp. (No. 18) paras. 513-14, UN Doc. A/38/18 (1983).

[130]   For the Italian government the problem was not the assimilation of the members of minorities, 'since they were completely integrated into the Italian society and had the same economic and political rights as the rest of the population, but the preservation of their cultural identity and languages'. 39 UN GAOR Supp. (No. 18) para. 307, UN Doc. A/39/18 (1984).

State 'in order to preserve the identity of the Maori . . . was within the context of article 2 and the Committee's policy on minorities'.[131] The Committee inquired both whether the Maoris lived in segregated areas and whether the Maori community living in urban areas was at risk of losing its identity.[132] If the concept of integration of ethnic groups into the mainstream of the society is carried too far, and traditions and customs are abandoned, could that constitute 'a form of racial discrimination'?[133] Would educational programmes instituted by the government to promote the use of the official language by the indigenous population result in the assimilation of diverse cultures? To avoid such a result, the use of the group's own language should be preserved and not eliminated by the official language.[134] One should be aware, however, of the danger that measures purportedly taken to preserve the language and the culture of a particular group, and which separate it from the community at large, may be used as a vehicle for continuing discrimination. In reviewing reports, the Committee has warned that, when governments take measures to promote the development of ethnic groups, they must guard against the assimilation which might result. On occasion, questions pertaining to claims of regional autonomy[135] or even self-determination[136] were raised by the Committee's members.

In States composed of various discrete racial or ethnic groups, the obligation to take special measures for their protection may

---

[131] Ibid. para. 78.

[132] Ibid.

[133] 29 UN GAOR Supp. (No. 18) para. 121, UN Doc. A/9618 (1974) (Norwegian Lapps and Gypsies). In response to comments from members of the Committee, the representative of Norway indicated that employment opportunities offered to the Lapps allowed them to retain their traditional way of life and that the government did not try to impose an alien way of life on gypsies. 31 UN GAOR Supp. (No. 18) paras. 207, 212, UN Doc. A/31/18 (1976).

[134] 38 UN GAOR Supp. (No. 18) para. 210, UN Doc. A/38/18 (1983) (measures taken by the government of Venezuela to promote the use of Spanish). The Committee requested information on whether the Government of the Central African Republic recognized and protected the rights of minorities to have their own language and develop their own culture (39 GAOR Supp. (No. 18) para. 117, UN Doc. A/39/18 (1984)) and on what was being done in Colombia to preserve the indigenous languages. Ibid. para. 131.

[135] 31 UN GAOR Supp. (No. 18) para. 70, UN Doc. A/31/18 (1976) (Iraqi Kurds).

[136] 37 UN GAOR Supp. (No. 18) para. 197, UN Doc. A/37/18 (1982) (ethnic groups in Ethiopia).

conflict with the perceived need to create a cohesive national identity,[137] because such measures may ultimately isolate rather than integrate the groups.[138] The traditional rights of groups to land[139] may conflict with the government's land use and redistribution policies, since the latter may stimulate the dispersal of racial groups and a consequent loss of cultural identity.[140] The conflict between guaranteeing economic rights and preserving traditional ways of life may often be irreconcilable.[141] Such forces as industrialization, population growth, depletion of resources, and the introduction of new agricultural techniques require adaptation which erodes cultural identity unless, perhaps, the government resorts to a policy of territorial grants.[142] If Art. 2(2) had been more carefully worded, it still might not have ensured the equalization of rights among ethnic groups

---

[137] The Committee inquired how the policy of Botswana of 'discouraging ethnocentrism among the different ethnic groups could be reconciled with the establishment of a separate house of chiefs in addition to the National Assembly' (39 GAOR Supp. (No. 18) para. 105, UN Doc. A/39/18 (1984)) and 'how the efforts being made to preserve racial harmony affected the traditions of various ethnic groups in the country, what provision was made to preserve their culture, and what were the consequences of fostering the process of nation-building while guaranteeing the identity of ethnic groups'. Ibid. para. 106.

[138] 37 UN GAOR Supp. (No. 18) para. 162, UN Doc. A/37/18 (1982) (an apparent inconsistency between Panamanian policies of integrating indigenous groups and of maintaining for them geographically distinct zones).

[139] In the case of Colombia, the Committee requested information 'regarding the indigenous population living in the reservation lands . . . the Government's land policy, the legal status of reservations, whether the indigenous population had the right to acquire real property elsewhere in Colombia and dispose of it at will, . . . development of reservation lands, . . . how the rights of the indigenous population were protected if a reservation was used for a national development project, whether the indigenous population was permitted to migrate from its reservation land, and, if so, whether it lost its rights to the land from which it had emigrated'. 39 UN GAOR Supp. (No. 18) para. 131, UN Doc. A/39/18 (1984).

[140] 31 UN GAOR Supp. (No. 18) para. 226, UN Doc. A/31/18 (1976) (with regard to the percentage of Ecuadorean Indians who had benefited from Ecuadorean agrarian reform); 37 UN GAOR Supp. (No. 18) para. 102, UN Doc. A/37/18 (1982) (has Fiji reserved for specific racial groups land leased by the government and what was the traditional or tribal basis for such leases?).

[141] The different policies followed by some Latin American governments on these questions: an amalgam of the various races v. integration of ethnic groups into the body politic while preserving their respective ethnic characteristics, were noted in 31 UN GAOR Supp. (No. 18) para. 234, UN Doc. A/31/18 (1976).

[142] 33 UN GAOR Supp. (No. 18) para. 300, UN Doc. A/33/18 (1978) (Brazilian policy of gathering the indigenous Amazon groups into certain areas of the country where they could live in conformity with their traditions or, if they so desired, strengthen their contacts with the outside culture).

without loss of cultural identity, but the present text exacerbates the difficulties through its lack of precision and standards.

VI. THE EXCEPTION BASED ON CITIZENSHIP

Art. 1(2) provides an exception to the applicability of the Convention which is overly broad. It allows States Parties to make 'distinctions, exclusions, restrictions or preferences . . . between citizens and non-citizens'. Art. 1(3) states that nationality, citizenship, or naturalization provisions of a particular State may not discriminate against any particular nationality, but no provision prohibiting discrimination against particular nationalities is made with regard to other matters. Under the wording of Art. 1(2), a State discriminating on the basis of race or ethnic origin may try to claim that the measures which it has taken are permissible because they are based upon alienage, since members of a given ethnic group may also be non-citizens. Such claims would be critically scrutinized by the Committee as to whether discrimination against any particular nationality on grounds of race[143] was involved. But, given the difficulty of establishing that racial factors were implicated (for instance in the case of a mass expulsion of aliens who happened to belong to a different ethnic or tribal group), a more careful formulation, placing upon the State the burden of demonstrating that its discriminatory action was based exclusively upon alienage, would have been preferable. The use of the citizenship exception as a pretext for discrimination could thus have been deterred.

The legal situation regarding the category of protected persons is further complicated by the broad statement in Art. 5 guaranteeing the rights of everyone, without distinction as to race, colour, or national or ethnic origin, to equality before the law, 'notably' in the enjoyment of certain enumerated rights. The drafting of the Convention and of Art. 5 has been criticized as inadequate even by the members of the Committee.[144] But Art. 5 — discussed in Section III above — must be interpreted in the context of the Convention as a whole, including Art. 1(2).

---

[143] See e.g., 28 UN GAOR Supp. (No. 18) para. 63, UN Doc. A/9018 (1973).
[144] Ibid. para. 61. For studies of Art. 5, see Partsch, above n. 17; Buergenthal, ibid. at 208–11.

Arguably, then, despite the broad language of Art. 5, States Parties may limit their obligations under Art. 5 to citizens if this limitation is not a pretext for racial discrimination. Other human rights instruments permit restriction of rights based upon citizenship, but the scope of permissible restrictions is circumscribed.[145] Could it thus be argued that distinctions applied to non-citizens are beyond the purview of the Convention and outside the competence of the Committee, even when the rights denied pertain to security of the person, protection by the State against violence, and civil rights generally,[146] rather than to political rights[147] or freedom of movement,[148] with regard to which aliens are in a different position?

Members of the Committee have tried to temper the severity of the restrictive interpretation, claiming that while political and economic rights may be limited on the basis of alienage, 'fundamental' or civil rights may not be so limited.[149] As regards economic rights, it can perhaps be argued that economic constraints may justify limiting some entitlements (such as welfare or health care) to citizens, but limiting employment-related benefits would not be supportable under this rationale. Some members of the Committee have gone further in arguing, for instance, that aliens should receive 'national invalidity and widows' pensions', on the same basis as citizens, whether or not there were bilateral agreements providing for such rights,[150] or questioning the adequacy of educational facilities for children of foreign workers.[151] On the other hand, some members have not regarded distinctions made among non-citizens pursuant to bilateral or regional economic agreements as violations of the Convention, if the agreements, and not race or ethnicity, are the

---

[145] Art. 21, Universal Declaration, above n. 36 (political rights and equal access to public service reserved to citizens); Art. 2(3), Economic Covenant above n. 36 (developing countries permitted to make distinctions with regard to economic rights of non-nationals).

[146] McKean observes that it is unfortunate that restrictions on aliens were not made more selective and that there is no redress under the Convention for restrictions based upon lack of citizenship. W. McKean, above n. 17, at 158. But see 34 UN GAOR Supp. (No. 18) para. 136, UN Doc. A/34/18 (1979).

[147] See 28 UN GAOR Supp. (No. 18) paras. 61–2, UN Doc. A/9018 (1973).

[148] See ibid. para. 59.

[149] Ibid. paras. 61–2.

[150] 34 UN GAOR Supp. (No. 18) para. 386, UN Doc. A/34/18 (1979).

[151] Ibid. para. 348.

basis for the differential treatment.[152] Despite the broad personal reach of Art. 5, differential treatment of citizens of different States, as when arising from the application of the most-favoured nation clause, has been seen as legitimate.[153]

VII. THE RIGHT OF INDIVIDUAL PETITION AND THE EXISTENCE OF COMPETENT INTERNAL BODIES

Art. 14 creates a right of petition for individuals or groups of individuals within the jurisdiction of a State Party which has made a declaration recognizing the competence of the Committee to receive and consider such communications. The Committee is authorized to make suggestions and recommendations concerning these communications and is not confined to making a statement of its views.[154] In accordance with Art. 14(9), upon the tenth declaration made by a State Party, the procedure outlined in Article 14 entered into force on 3 December 1982.[155]

In 1983 the Committee considered draft provisional rules of procedure governing the Committee's discharge of its responsibilities under Art. 14.[156] The meaning of that article has thus become an important matter. An interesting question of interpretation arises from the wording of Art. 14(2) and the relationship of that provision to other provisions of Art. 14. Art. 14(2) provides that

[a]ny State Party which makes a declaration as provided for in paragraph 1 of this article may establish or indicate a body within its national legal

---

[152]   28 UN GAOR Supp (No. 18) para. 64, UN Doc. A/9018 (1973). Regarding the relationship between the Convention and other human rights instruments, see ibid. para. 62. Buergenthal argues that 'if a state is under an international obligation, by virtue of its ratifications of the Covenants, to ensure the enjoyment of a right that is also listed in article 5 of the Convention, and if the state's failure to do so has more adverse consequences for individuals belonging to a racial minority than for the rest of its population, a violation of the Convention might be made out.' Above n. 17, at 211.

[153]   Partsch, above n. 17, at 228.

[154]   Art. 14(8) of the Convention is thus different from Art. 5(4) of the Optional Protocol to the International Covenant on Civil and Political Rights, Annex to GA Res. 2200, 21 UN GAOR Supp. (No. 16) at 59, UN Doc. A/6316 (1966).

[155]   38 UN GAOR Supp. (No. 18) para. 23, UN Doc. A/38/18 (1983). The Committee has already commenced considering communications under Art. 14. 39 UN GAOR Supp. (No. 18) para. 573, UN Doc. A/39/18 (1984).

[156]   38 UN GAOR Supp. (No. 18) at 7-13, 138-44, UN Doc. A/38/18 (1983).

order which shall be competent to receive and consider petitions from individuals and groups of individuals within its jurisdiction who claim to be victims of a violation of any of the rights set forth in this Convention and who have exhausted other available local remedies.

This wording would suggest that the existence of a body is optional. Art. 14(5), however, provides that '[i]n the event of failure to obtain satisfaction from the body established or indicated in accordance with paragraph 2 of this article, the petitioner shall have the right to communicate the matter to the Committee within six months.' How can the procedure be put into operation if a particular State, invoking the optional character of Art. 14(2) has neither established or indicated a 'body'? Art. 14(7) (a) which provides that the Committee shall not consider any communication from a petitioner unless it has ascertained that the petitioner has exhausted all available local remedies, except where the application of the remedies is unreasonably prolonged, makes no mention of either the 'body' or the six-months period. Because of concern that without the establishment of the 'body' the procedure outlined in Art. 14 could not be put in operation, an attempt has been made in the Committee to interpret Art. 14(2) as requiring the existence of a body.[157] There is, however, no merit in that interpretation.[158] It should obviously be left to States to decide how to handle complaints of racial discrimination in their domestic legal systems. Some countries may feel that the complexity of such complaints necessitates the involvement of various organs, depending upon the subject (for instance housing or employment) or the various competent levels of government (for instance federal, provincial, municipal).

The practical problems arising from the deficient drafting of

[157] It was thus argued that 'while it was true that the word "may" was used in that paragraph, it was the "establishment" or "indication" of that body that was optional, and not its existence'. 32 UN GAOR Supp. (No. 18) para. 124, UN Doc. A/32/18 (1977).

[158] This interpretation ignores the clear meaning of the text. The word 'may' was used to indicate the optional nature of the procedure. N. Lerner, above n. 4, at 84. Obviously, the 'body' cannot exist unless it is 'established' as a new entity, or it pre-existed and is identified or indicated by the State Party. The procedures outlined in paragraphs 4 and 5 are intended to ensure that local remedies have been exhausted, but the existence of such remedies need not depend upon the existence of the 'body'; other judicial or administrative forums providing such remedies may exist.

Art. 14 have been largely resolved by the Committee's Provisional Rules of Procedure. Rule 90(f) (now 91(f)) provides that the Committee or its Working Group shall ascertain '[t]hat the communication is, except in the case of duly verified exceptional circumstances, submitted within six months after all available domestic remedies have been exhausted, including, when applicable, those indicated in paragraph 2 of article 14'.[159] Rule 90(e) (now 91(e)) establishes the broader principle that the Committee should ascertain whether the individual has exhausted all available domestic remedies, including, when applicable, those mentioned in Art. 14(2), except when the application of the remedies is unreasonably prolonged. The Committee's Rules of Procedure by making it possible for the petition system to function without burdening States with obligations not dictated by the text of the Convention, provide a practical resolution of the problems created by the lack of textual clarity.

VIII. CONCLUDING OBSERVATIONS

The Convention is a primary international human rights instrument because of both the crucial nature of its subject and the exceptionally large number of States that have become parties to it. This study has explored only a limited number of questions; many other merit consideration, for instance whether Art. 9 has established a viable system of reporting or whether it has created a reporting burden which exceeds the administrative capacity of most States, especially if account is taken of reporting obligations under other human rights instruments.[160]

The work of the Committee has proved to be a useful lighthouse, illuminating some of the important issues that have emanated from implementation of the Convention. The Committee has often ventured into controversial areas in attempting to advance observance of the basic norms of the Convention. Composed of experts nominated and elected by States Parties

---

[159] Procedure for Considering Communications from Individuals under Article 14 of the Convention, 38 UN GAOR Supp. (No. 18) at 138, 141-2, UN Doc. A/38/18 (1983). For the current Rules of Procedure, see UN Doc. CERD/C/35/Rev.3 (1986).

[160] Meron, *Human Rights — Effective Remedies* (Remarks), 77 [1983] ASIL Proc. 397 at 400-3. See also UN Doc. A/39/484, paras. 16, 21-2 (1984).

in accordance with Art. 8, the Committee, not surprisingly, has reflected and given strong support to values held by the majority of the international community.

Like other human rights instruments, the Convention deserves praise for some of its provisions but only mixed reviews for others. Some provisions, such as the 'effect' clause of Art. 1(1) and the 'affirmative action' clauses, are important and appear to move in parallel directions to US civil rights law. In some areas, the Convention advances admirable objectives, for instance in seeking the elimination of racist theorizing. In many respects it establishes significant and desirable goals and objectives which merit the support of the international community. But a number of provisions suffer from a lack of textual clarity. Some provisions create serious conflicts with the rights of freedom of expression, association, and privacy. Indeed, the Convention reaches far into the area of private life. It creates substantial difficulties for democratic countries in which these rights are valued and protected by constitutions, legislation, and traditions. Unfortunately, such countries can comply with their Convention obligations only by resorting to reservations, rather freely allowed by Art. 20(2), which requires objections by two-thirds of the States Parties to determine that a reservation is 'incompatible or inhibitive'. It has been argued that '[i]n the absence of a definitive judicial ruling [by the International Court of Justice, under Art. 22 of the Convention] on the admissibility of the reservation in question, the State party concerned might be asked [by the Committee] to withdraw its reservation',[161] but if to 'ask' implies anything more than 'appeal', this appears to go beyond the Committee's powers under the Convention. Some States Parties, which could have availed themselves of the right to make reservations so as to remain legally within the framework of the Convention without actually having to implement some of its normative provisions, have not gone to the trouble of doing so, sometimes perhaps because of a desire to avoid highlighting their difficulties or because of a cynical attitude towards international human

---

[161] Inglés, above n. 17, para. 224. The UN Secretariat has advised the Committee, correctly, that even a unanimous decision by the Committee that a reservation is unacceptable would have no legal effect and that the Committee has no authority but to take into account the reservations made by States Parties. Ibid. para. 206.

rights commitments. Thus, although only a small minority of States Parties have made reservations to Art. 4, most States have not carried out their obligations under that article to adopt the necessary implementing legislation.

The tension between certain norms stated in the Convention and some of the rights with which they appear to conflict reflects divergent community priorities and important societal differences, especially when the reality and the immediacy of danger to the public peace posed by racist organizations and theories must be assessed and the rights of expression, association, and privacy are involved. The Convention requires that policies which perpetuate racial discrimination be changed, but it does not furnish adequate guidance about permissible restraints on implementation or balancing considerations which may properly be invoked by States Parties. Like other human rights instruments, the Convention is occasionally drafted in such general terms as to make its application to specific cases difficult.[162]

Several crucial provisions of the Convention suffer from deficient drafting. Some of these deficiencies result from the fact that the definition of racial discrimination was not adjusted to the operative provisions after the latter were drafted. The speed with which the Convention was considered and adopted, the robustness of the political forces which pushed its formulation and adoption, and perhaps a certain impatience with the niceties of legal drafting are among the factors that underlie some of the problems discussed in this study. The imperfect text that resulted reflects, of course, the political issues and realities of the United Nations. It would be simplistic therefore to expect that difficulties due to these factors could have been avoided through better legislative techniques. But some, if not all the Convention's weaknesses could have been avoided through better legislative techniques and skills, especially where there was no political reason for the language selected and the inadequate drafting.

The United States[163] and other governments have rightly

---

[162] See Greenberg, above n. 17, at 307, 318, 330; Lillich, *Civil Rights*, above n. 37, at 115, 121.

[163] Statement by Jerome J. Shestack in the Third Committee of the General Assembly, summarized in UN Doc. A/C.3/35/SR. 56 at 12–14 (1980).

criticized the UN human rights law-making process. A detailed critique of this process is, however, outside the scope of this chapter.[164] One can only speculate here whether, for a highly political subject and in a politicized environment, resort to the legislative techniques followed by the International Law Commission[165] (ILC), by the United Nations Commission on International Trade Law[166] (UNCITRAL), or by the International Labour Organisation (ILO)[167] would have produced a significantly better product.

In evaluating the Convention, it is ultimately necessary to distinguish between several different problems. One is deficient drafting. Another is policies with which we may disagree but which faithfully reflect the political wishes of the majority, for example with regard to the value of the freedom of speech, association, or private life in relation to other values. Third, there is the problem of the Convention's far-reaching goals, some of which do not lend themselves to a speedy and full implementation even in developed and sympathetic countries. It has already been observed that the Convention was intended to be, in its operative provisions, a 'maximalist'[168] instrument. Perhaps the majority of the United Nations wanted to adopt an ambitious set of goals, a programme, without worrying too much about the prospects for full implementation in the immediate future. *Demander le plus pour obtenir le moins.* Some observers would say that this breeds disrespect for the law. Others would maintain that laws not only should reflect the mores of the community, but should be a catalyst for progress, for ever higher standards, that they should lead, not follow. There is, of course, constant tension and interaction between the behaviour of the community and its norms of

---

[164] See generally Meron, *Norm Making and Supervision in International Human Rights: Reflections on Institutional Order*, 76 AJIL 754 (1982); Alston, *Conjuring up New Human Rights: A Proposal for Quality Control,* 78 AJIL 607 (1984). See Chapter VII, below.

[165] On the mandate and legislative techniques of the ILC, see 2 Review of the Multilateral Treaty-Making Process, UN Doc. ST/LEG/SER. B/21, at 183–223 (Provisional Version, 1982).

[166] On the mandate and legislative techniques of UNCITRAL, see ibid. at 224–36.

[167] On the mandate and legislative techniques of the ILO, see ibid. at 237–58.

[168] Schwelb, above n. 4, at 1057. A member of the Committee stated that 'the rights in the Convention were without limitation, whereas the rights and limitations in the International Covenants on Human Rights were more precisely defined'. UN Doc. CERD/C/SR. 624, at 3–4 (1983) (remarks by Mr Shahi).

conduct. Pollock has observed that, to be respected, law must express, on the whole, the conscience of the community.[169] Law can either lag behind public opinion or be in advance of it. Rules of law may elevate the standard of current morality: 'The moral ideal present to lawgivers and judges, if it does not always come up to the highest that has been conceived, will at least be, generally speaking, above the common average of practice; it will represent the standard of the best sort of citizens.'[170] Similarly, Schachter, discussing De Visscher's statement that custom is established not only through 'counting the observed regularities, but ... weighing them in terms of social ends considered desirable', observes that governmental law-making conferences do not operate only through an inductive process, but include 'as a necessary element a teleological factor which distinguishes the acceptance of certain patterns of conduct as law from the mere observation and recording of regularities of behaviour ... a collective judgement of states ... which implicitly recognizes the contemporary social value of the rules in the text'.[171]

Was the Charter of the United Nations adopted by a community that really practised the values stated in it? Or was it rather a code of *better* conduct of nations? To pave the way for greater respect for human rights and human dignity,[172] the human rights instruments must be more advanced than the mores of the community. But how far in advance should human rights instruments be? Idealism should not be confused with Utopia. Too great a distance will discourage acceptance and cause a proliferation of reservations. Whenever human rights instruments are drafted, this question deserves to be on the 'conceptual agenda' of the lawmakers.

---

[169]   F. Pollock, Jurisprudence and Legal Essays xlii (A. Goodhart ed., 1978).
[170]   Ibid. at 26.
[171]   Schachter, *The Nature and Process of Legal Development in International Society*, in The Structure and Process of International Law 745, 777 (R. Macdonald and D. Johnston eds., 1983).
[172]   See generally Schachter, *Human Dignity as a Normative Concept*, 77 AJIL 848 (1983).

II

The Convention on the Elimination of All Forms of Discrimination Against Women

I. INTRODUCTION

THE Convention on the Elimination of All Forms of Discrimination Against Women (the Convention) was adopted by the General Assembly of the United Nations on 18 December 1979 and entered into force on 3 September 1981.[1] As of 21 January 1985, the Convention had 65 States Parties.[2] While other conventions address particular aspects of women's rights, the Convention is the first universal instrument which focuses on the general prohibition of discrimination against women and contains a modest control machinery. The literature on the Convention is limited.[3] The Convention was signed on behalf of the United States of America on 17 July 1980 and, in one of the last Presidential acts of Jimmy Carter, transmitted to the Senate on 12 November 1980 with a view to obtaining its advice and consent, together with a detailed memorandum of law stating areas of concern which the Convention did not address

---

[1] GA Res. 34/180, 34 UN GAOR Supp. (No. 46) at 193, UN Doc. A/34/46 (1979); Multilateral Treaties Deposited with the Secretary-General: Status as at 31 December 1984, at 151, UN Doc. ST/LEG/SER.E/3 (1985).

[2] 40 UN GAOR Supp. (No. 40) at 1, UN Doc. A/40/45 (1985).

[3] See in particular Greenberg, *Race, Sex, and Religious Discrimination in International Law*, in 2 Human Rights in International Law: Legal and Policy Issues 307, 327–30 (T. Meron ed., 1984); Shapiro-Libai, *The Concept of Sex Equality: The UN Decade for Women*, 11 Israel Y.B. Human Rights 106 (1981); N. Hevener, International Law and the Status of Women (1983); Reanda, *Human Rights and Women's Rights: The United Nations Approach*, 3 Human Rights Q. 11 (1981); Loranger, *Convention on the Elimination of All Forms of Discrimination Against Women*, 20 Can. Y.B. Int'l L. 349 (1982); McDougal, Lasswell, and Chen, *Human Rights for Women and World Public Order: The Outlawing of Sex-Based Discrimination*, 69 AJIL 497 (1975); M. McDougal, H. Lasswell, and L. Chen, Human Rights and World Public Order 612–52 (1980).

or where conflict with US law was possible.[4] The Senate has held no hearings on the Convention to date. This chapter will examine the Convention with particular focus upon the differences between the obligations stated in the Convention and those existing in United States law, especially where such differences reflect constitutional restraints (other than federalism) on legislative authority. The expanding corpus of sex discrimination law in the United States is particularly useful for such a comparison.

While the norm outlawing discrimination on grounds of sex is among the principles of the United Nations stated in Art. 1(3) and Art. 55 of the Charter, as well as in other human rights instruments, unlike racial discrimination it has not become the focus for concerted international action and it is not listed as reflecting customary international law by the recent draft of the new Restatement of the Foreign Relations Law of the United States.[5] That discrimination against women is widespread and continuing is acknowledged in the Preamble to the Convention, which expresses concern that, despite the promulgation of various international instruments, 'extensive discrimination against women continues to exist'.[6] One half of the human race is thus still subjected to discrimination in fact, and often in law. In a candid statement, the representative of Panama, a State Party to the Convention, reported that '[c]urrently women's rights were respected to about 50 per cent'.[7] One expert insisted that 'traditional prejudice' was the

---

[4]   *Convention on the Elimination of All Forms of Discrimination Against Women: Message from the President of the United States Transmitting the Convention on the Elimination of All Forms of Discrimination Against Women, Adopted by the United Nations General Assembly on December 18, 1979, and Signed on Behalf of the United States of America on July 17, 1980*, S. Exec. R, 96th Cong., 2d Sess. (1980) (hereinafter cited as Memorandum of Law).

[5]   Restatement of Foreign Relations Law of the United States (Revised) § 702 (Tent. Draft No. 6, vol. i, 1985). Comment *a* states: . . . although discrimination against women is contrary to the Universal Declaration and to numerous provisions in international agreements, the status and treatment of women in the traditions and practices of many states militate against the conclusion that there has already developed a general principle of customary law forbidding discrimination on grounds of gender, or that a particular distinction or classification involving women is a violation of customary law. Such distinctions or classifications may constitute violations of some international agreements when practiced by parties to those agreements.

[6]   Convention on the Elimination of All Forms of Discrimination Against Women, Preamble, para. 6.

[7]   UN Doc. CEDAW/C/1985/L.1/Add.8, at para. 30 (1985).

'real obstacle'[8] to the attainment of equality for women in Panama. In no other area is the disparity between the formal or 'proclaimed' equality and the reality of discrimination at home, in society, and in the workplace so great. This is true even of the developed and enlightened countries which are members of the Council of Europe, whose legislation and practice do not always meet the goal of equality of women.[9] Deeply rooted societal and religious traditions have impeded progress.[10] The wide scope of continuing discrimination in many national traditions is illustrated by the following statement, remarkable for its candour, made by the representative of the Philippines in answer to questions raised by the Committee on the Elimination of Discrimination Against Women (the Committee):

Laws regarding the family had been introduced to protect women within the family. However, there were some which were still discriminatory to

---

[8] UN Doc. CEDAW/C/1985/L.1/Add.3, at para. 14 (1985).

[9] Recommendation No. R. (85) 2 of the Committee of Ministers to Member States on Legal Protection Against Sex Discrimination (1985); Recommendation No. R. (84) 17 of the Committee of Ministers to Member States on Equality Between Women and Men in the Media (1984); Recommendation No. R. (81) 6 of the Committee of Ministers to Member States on the Participation of Women and Men in an Equitable Proportion in Committees and Other Bodies Set Up in the Council of Europe (1981); Action Programme for the Promotion of Equality Between Sexes to be Implemented in the Context of the Second Medium-Term Plan, Council of Europe Doc. CAHFM (80) 9 (1980); Committee on the Status of Women, Situation of Council of Europe Staff with regard to Equality Between the Sexes, a Secretariat Memorandum, Council of Europe Doc. CAHFM (80) 7 (1980); Equality of Spouses in Civil Law, Resolution (78) 37 Adopted by the Committee of Ministers of the Council of Europe on 27 September 1978 and Explanatory Memorandum (Council of Europe 1979); Nationality of Spouses of Different Nationalities and Nationality of Children Born in Wedlock, Resolutions 77 (12) and 77 (13) Adopted by the Committee of Ministers of the Council of Europe on 27 May 1977 and Explanatory Memoranda (Council of Europe 1977); Equality Between Women and Men, Historical Development and Descriptive Analysis of National Machinery Set Up in Member States of the Council of Europe to Promote the Equality Between Women and Men, Comparative Study (Council of Europe, 1982); Equality Between Women and Men, Proceedings of the Seminar on the Contribution of the Media to the Promotion of Equality Between Women and Men, (Council of Europe 1984); 18th Council of Europe Teachers' Seminar on 'Sex Stereotypes in Schools — the Role and the Responsibility of the Teacher', Council for Cultural Co-Operation, Donaueschingen, 22–27 November 1982 (Council of Europe 1984); The Situation of Women In the Political Process, Part I, an Analysis of the Political Behaviour of Women in Europe, Part II, Women in the Political World in Europe, Part III, the Role of Women in Voluntary Associations and Organisations (Council of Europe 1984).

[10] McDougal, Lasswell and Chen, above n. 3, at 499–500; Loranger, above n. 3, at 349–50.

women. Examples of such laws were: a daughter above 21 but below 23 was not allowed to leave home without parental consent except to become a wife, or when she exercised a profession or calling or when the father or the mother had contracted a subsequent marriage. Sons of the same age did not face any such restriction. Another law was that which forbade a wife without the consent of the husband to receive any gift by gratuituous title, except from ascendants or collateral relatives. A husband might object to his wife's exercise of a profession or occupation, while a woman could not object to her husband's exercise of a profession. In addition, the wife's mobility was subordinate to her husband's choice of residence and the husband was considered the administrator of conjugal property.[11]

Another representative of the Philippines explained the severe penalties imposed in his country on the crime of rape not as a response to the violence against the victim herself, but as measures necessary because 'the honour of a husband, father or brother was affected if such a thing happened in the family'.[12]

Given the wide scope of discrimination against women in public and private life in most, if not in all countries, the Convention is a response to an urgent need and is potentially of great importance. This chapter will focus on some critical features of this Convention. Because the Convention is so recent, there will be only few references to the practice of the Committee which was established under Art. 17. That body consists of twenty-three experts elected by States Parties from a list of nominees proposed by the States. Under Arts. 20-1, the competence of the Committee is limited to the consideration of reports submitted by States Parties and to the making of suggestions and general recommendations based on the examination of reports and information received from States Parties. Unfortunately, the Convention does not provide for the examination of individual complaints or communications from victims of discrimination, or of complaints submitted by one State Party against another for failure to fulfil its obligations under the Convention.

The preceding chapter has already addressed the role, in the interpretation of the International Convention on the Elimination of All Forms of Racial Discrimination, of a committee of experts which is similar, in this respect, to that of the Committee established under Art. 17 of the Convention on the

---

[11]   39 UN GAOR 2 Supp. (No. 45) para. 109, UN Doc. A/39/45 (1984).
[12]   Ibid. at para. 103.

Elimination of All Forms of Discrimination against Women. Art. 29 provides for settlement of disputes pertaining to interpretation or application of the Convention by arbitration or, failing agreement on the organization of the arbitration, resolution by the International Court of Justice, subject to the right of any State Party to declare at the time of signature, ratification, or accession that it does not consider itself bound by that provision.

The instruments considered in Chapters I and III have been elaborated in the Sub-Commission on the Prevention of Discrimination and Protection of Minorities, the Commission on Human Rights, the Economic and Social Council (ECOSOC) and the General Assembly (principally, the Third Committee). Much of the drafting work of the Convention was carried out in the Commission on the Status of Women, and, of course, in the Third Committee, with some participation by ECOSOC. The Commission on the Status of Women is one of the functional commissions of ECOSOC. Its functions, initially set out in Res. 11(II) of ECOSOC,[13] were subsequently defined in ECOSOC Res. 48(IV).[14] The Commission is composed of representatives of States Members of the United Nations elected to serve on the Commission. The membership of the Commission has been expanded on several occasions and now comprises thirty-two members.[15]

The Convention has been considerably influenced not only by the Declaration on the Elimination of Discrimination Against Women[16] but by the International Convention on the Elimination of All Forms of Racial Discrimination, which is discussed in detail in Chapter I above. Discussion of problems common to these two Conventions therefore will be brief in this chapter.

II. OVERBREADTH AND OTHER PROBLEMS

The Convention is based on the twin obligations to prohibit discrimination and to ensure equality (for example Arts. 2, 3,

[13] E.S.C. Official Records, 1st Year, 2d Sess. at 405 (1946).
[14] E.S.C. Resolutions, 4th Sess. at 34 (1947).
[15] UN Action in the Field of Human Rights 290, UN Doc. ST/HR/2/Rev. 2 (1983).
[16] GA Res. 22/2263, 22 UN GAOR Supp. (No. 16) at 35, UN Doc. A/6716 (1967).

and 4). The Convention treats the principle of equality both as a binding obligation and as a goal. The equality contemplated is not merely *de jure*, but *de facto*, as emphasized, for example, in Art. 4. The Convention is characterized by substantial breadth and sometimes even overbreadth in the scope of the obligations created, which extend to political, economic, social, cultural, legal, familial, and personal fields of activity. Moreover, the Preamble itself contains a number of provisions which are not tailored to the proclaimed purposes of the instrument. For example, para. 10 states that the 'eradication of *apartheid*, all forms of racism, racial discrimination, colonialism, neo-colonialism, aggression, foreign occupation and domination and interference in the internal affairs of States is essential to the full enjoyment of the rights of men and women'. Para. 11 similarly lists conditions which, by promoting social progress and development, 'will contribute to the attainment of full equality between men and women', including 'general and complete disarmament, and in particular nuclear disarmament under strict and effective international control . . .'.

While the conditions referred to in paras. 10 and 11 may fairly be said to affect the role of women in society in some way, the text creates no convincing relationship between these conditions and the objectives of the Convention. The importance of the elimination of foreign domination may be clear, as is the desirability of achieving international agreement on disarmament, but the relevance of these matters to the efforts to end sexual discrimination cannot be assumed a priori. Without an indication of their relevance to the function of the Convention, these preambular paragraphs stand isolated from the remainder of the Convention and do not further the stated purposes of the instrument. Because the object of nuclear disarmament, for example, may be considered to reflect partisan values, its inclusion in the Preamble may discourage support for the Convention. Other statements in the Preamble, such as the goal of strengthening international peace, are so general as to be politically acceptable to the entire community of nations, but add nothing useful to the Convention.

These problems are not only of academic significance, for they may affect the reporting obligations of States under Art. 18, which requires that States report on measures adopted 'to give effect to the provisions of the present Convention and on the progress made in this respect'. From this language, it would appear that States need not report on matters such as those dealt with in paras. 10 and 11 of the Preamble. Nevertheless, in the 'General Guidelines Regarding the Form and Contents of Reports Received from States Parties under Article 18 of the Convention', the Committee specifically acknowledged the divergence of the content of certain preambular provisions from the remainder of the Convention and requested that '[t]he reports should also pay due attention to the role of women and their full participation in the solution of problems and issues which are referred to in the preamble and which are not covered by the articles of the Convention.'[17] In reviewing reports from States the Committee has raised questions concerning matters covered by the Preamble, for instance nuclear disarmament.[18] Since the Preamble creates no obligation upon States Parties to strive towards the solution of the problems mentioned, States should not be requested to report on such matters. Such requests may be regarded as a questionable expansion of the Committee's powers.

A. *Article 1 — Defining Discrimination*

Discrimination against women is defined in Art. 1 as follows:

For the purposes of the present Convention, the term 'discrimination against women' shall mean any distinction, exclusion or restriction made on the basis of sex which has the effect or purpose of impairing or nullifying the recognition, enjoyment or exercise by women, irrespective of their marital status, on a basis of equality of men and women, of human rights and fundamental freedoms in the political, social, cultural, civil or any other field.

While this definition replicates substantially the definition of racial discrimination contained in Art. 1(1) of the International Convention on the Elimination of All Forms of Racial Discrimination, the important phrase 'of public life', contained in the latter was deleted. As demonstrated in Chapter I, the operative provisions of the International Convention on the Elimination of All Forms of Racial Discrimination extend the reach of certain obligations beyond the action of public officials: racially

---

[17] UN Doc. CEDAW/C/7, at 3 (1983).
[18] 39 UN GAOR 2 Supp. (No. 45) para. 320, UN Doc. A/39/45 (1984).

discriminatory action which occurs in 'public life' is prohibited even when it is taken by 'any persons, group or organization' (Art. 2(1) (d)), without clearly delimiting the parameters of 'public life'. While ambiguity regarding the distinction between public and private life and tension between the principles of equality and freedom of association are integral to the latter Convention, the Convention on the Elimination of All Forms of Discrimination Against Women clearly extends the prohibition of discrimination to private life. Thus, one State Party was criticized for not reporting to the Committee 'explicitly enough . . . [on] the status of women in private life',[19] and another for not providing enough information on family relations and provisions governing equality between the sexes at home.[20] Because many of the relevant concepts have been explored with reference to racial discrimination in Chapter I, only brief comments on this definition of discrimination against women are necessary.

The provisions of the Convention on the Elimination of All Forms of Discrimination Against Women apply to a broad range of activities: unintentional as well as intentional discrimination is prohibited (as indicated by the 'effect' clause); private as well as public actions are regulated (as indicated by the phrase 'any other field'). By proscribing practices which have the effect of discriminating against women, the Convention guards against the use of facially neutral criteria as a pretext for discrimination, for instance the use of height and weight requirements which are not related to the requirements of the job and which tend to exclude women as a group. The 'effects' standard avoids the difficulties inherent in proving specific discriminatory motive. The prohibition of unintentional discrimination is necessary to achieve systemic change, because policies undertaken without discriminatory motive may perpetuate inequalities established by prior acts of purposeful discrimination. The inclusion of unintentionally discriminatory practices or policies within the prohibitions of the Convention appears to be therefore appropriate and necessary.

The definition of discrimination against women does not prohibit certain distinctions *per se*, but only when they have the purpose or the effect of denying women the enjoyment of

---

[19] 39 UN GAOR 1 Supp. (No. 45) para. 51, UN Doc. A/39/45 (1984).
[20] Ibid. at para. 139.

human rights and fundamental freedoms on a basis of equality with men. As discussed in Chapter I, the Committee on the Elimination of Racial Discrimination has tended to regard all ethnic distinctions as suspect, unless made in the context of affirmative action, without engaging in a substantive inquiry as to whether they have in fact had an adverse effect on the enjoyment of 'rights'. If the parties to the Convention on the Elimination of All Forms of Discrimination Against Women and the Committee established under Art. 17 follow a similar approach, a further expansion in the reach of the Convention would result. Moreover, the definition of discrimination against women encompasses discrimination with regard to all rights and fundamental freedoms, whatever their source. This can be compared with the more limited prohibition contained in Art. 3 of the International Covenant on Civil and Political Rights (discussed in Chapter III below) which addresses the obligation of States Parties to ensure the equal right of men and women to the enjoyment of all civil and political rights *set forth in the Covenant.*[21] Article 1 of the American Convention on Human Rights and Art. 14 of the European Convention on Human Rights and Fundamental Freedoms likewise prohibit discrimination on grounds of sex only with respect to the rights guaranteed therein. The Council of Europe's Committee on the Status of Women has thus pointed out that Art. 14 of the European Convention 'could not be relied on except in relation with other substantive provisions of the Convention'.[22] The Committee on the Status of Women recommended, therefore, that consideration be given to the possibility of enlarging the scope of Art. 14.[23] Art. 5 of the recently adopted Protocol No. 7 to the European Convention is aimed at creating one additional right to equality which is not stated in the European Convention itself. It states that spouses shall enjoy equality of rights and

---

[21] Art. 3 of the Political Covenant reads as follows: 'The States Parties to the present Covenant undertake to ensure the equal right of men and women to the enjoyment of all civil and political rights set forth in the present Covenant.'

[22] Council of Europe Doc. CAHFM (80) 9, at 6 (1980). For a discussion of the type of gender distinctions which the European Commission of Human Rights regards as discriminatory in its case-law, see Buquicchio-de Boer, *Sexual Discrimination and the Convention on Human Rights*, 6 Human Rights L.J. 1 (1985). See also Chapter III n. 114, below.

[23] Council of Europe Doc. CAHFM (80) 9, at 6.

responsibilities of a private law character between them and in their relations with their children, as to marriage, during marriage, and in the event of its dissolution.[24] The Explanatory Memorandum to Protocol 7 emphasizes that Art. 5 applies only to rights and responsibilities which are of a private law character and not to 'other fields of law, such as administrative, fiscal, criminal, social, ecclesiastical or labour laws'.[25]

It is not clear whether it was appropriate to extend the field of application of the Convention to encompass even private, interpersonal relations (except, of course, when the conduct which is challenged takes forms customarily regulated pursuant to the police power). It is certainly true that discrimination against women in personal and family life is rampant and may obviate equal opportunities which may be available in public life. There is danger, however, that state regulation of inter-personal conduct may violate the privacy and associational rights of the individual and conflict with the principles of free-dom of opinion, expression, and belief. Such regulation may require invasive state action to determine compliance, including inquiry into political and religious beliefs. Attempts to regulate discrimination in interpersonal conduct may invite abuse of the discretion vested in the State by the broad language of Art. 1.

A more restricted approach might have been preferable, limiting the definition of discrimination against women to distinctions on the basis of gender in the fields of activity listed in Art. 1 and 'in any other field of public life'. Such a definition, taken together, *mutatis mutandis*, with certain other provisions appearing in Art. 2 of the International Convention Against All Forms of Racial Discrimination, would have applied to discrimi-natory action which occurs in public life, even when taken by any person, group, or organization, but not to interpersonal, private acts. The approach adopted by the US Supreme Court in *Roberts* v. *United States Jaycees*[26] represents a reasonable balancing of the relevant values. The factors important in distinguishing between public and private life, analysed in the discussion of *Roberts* in Chapter I, are equally useful in this context. The need to modify cultural and social patterns of

[24]   Council of Europe Doc. H (84) 5 (1984).
[25]   Ibid. at 12.
[26]   104 S. Ct. 3244 (1984).

conduct with a view to eliminating prejudices and stereotyped notions of sex roles, emphasized in Art. 5 of the Convention, can best be advanced by education and appropriate governmental incentives, rather than by excessive encroachment by the State into interpersonal relations.

Art. 4 of the Convention provides that temporary special measures aimed at accelerating *de facto* equality between men and women (affirmative action) and measures aimed at protecting maternity shall not be considered discriminatory. Like the International Convention on the Elimination of All Forms of Racial Discrimination, the Convention on the Elimination of All Forms of Discrimination Against Women does not provide guidelines for determining when equality has been achieved and affirmative action must be discontinued. The problems regarding affirmative action explored in Chapter I above are also of concern in this context.

B. *Article 2 — Obligation to Eliminate Discrimination*

Para. (a) provides that States Parties shall embody the principle of equality of men and women in their national constitutions or other appropriate legislation and shall ensure, through law and other appropriate means, 'the practical realization of this principle ...'. In the United States the failure to ratify the proposed Equal Rights Amendment to the US Constitution makes it unlikely that 'the principle of equality between men and women' will be embodied in the US Constitution, as required by Art. 2(a), in the foreseeable future.[27] The final clause of this provision presents a question regarding the scope of the obligation created. The memorandum of the Department of State suggests that Art. 2(a) requires equal protection of men and women under the law[28] and imposes an affirmative obligation on Congress to initiate appropriate legislation to ensure equal protection of men and women under the law. But the language of Art. 2(a) may be interpreted to require States

[27] The Memorandum of Law, above n. 4, at 1, points out that the 14th and 5th Amendments to the US Constitution provide a basis to invalidate any federal or state classification or distinction based on sex if it is not substantially related to an important government objective (*Craig* v. *Boren*, 429 U.S. 190 (1976)), but proof of intent to discriminate may be required (*Personnel Administrator of Massachusetts* v. *Feeney*, 442 U.S. 256, 276–80 (1979)).

[28] Memorandum of Law, above n. 4, at 1–3.

Parties to ensure the practical realization of the principle of equality of men and women. The latter interpretation would reflect a duty of maximum breadth, but would be consistent with other provisions aimed at achieving *de facto* equality, such as Art. 4(1) and the various educational measures enumerated in Art. 10.

The remaining sections of Art. 2, paras. (b), (c), (e), and (f), reach interpersonal 'private' acts of discrimination, and are therefore characterized by the overbreadth discussed with regard to Art. 1. Para. (b) obligates States Parties to adopt measures, 'including sanctions where appropriate, prohibiting *all discrimination* against women' (emphasis added). Para. (c) requires States Parties to 'ensure through competent national tribunals and other public institutions the effective protection of women against *any act of discrimination*' (emphasis added). Para. (d) obligates States Parties to refrain from any act or practice of discrimination against women and to ensure that public authorities and institutions shall act in conformity with this obligation. Para. (e) mandates appropriate measures to eliminate discrimination against women by *'any person, organization or enterprise'* (emphasis added). This language, except for the addition of 'enterprise', replicates substantially that of Art. 2(1) (d) of the International Convention on the Elimination of All Forms of Racial Discrimination. Finally, para. (f) demands 'appropriate measures, including legislation, to modify or abolish existing laws, regulations, *customs and practices* which constitute discrimination against women' (emphasis added). States Parties are required by the language of these provisions to restrict privacy and associational rights if restrictions are necessary to prevent discrimination. Para. (f) may conflict not only with associational rights, but with rights of ethnic or religious groups. Measures taken pursuant to para. (f) may even give rise to claims that they constitute discrimination where the legislative measures designed to modify 'customs and practices' are applicable exclusively or primarily to certain ethnic or religious groups among whom such practices are traditional. Potential conflicts between the norm of non-discrimination of women and that of religious freedom will be discussed in Section IV of this chapter and in Section V of Chapter IV.

The memorandum of law of the Department of State expressed

concern regarding the conformity *vel non* of paras. (b), (c), (d) and (f) with existing federal statutes, and of para. (e) with statutes in the area of public accommodations which have not yet been amended to prohibit discrimination on the basis of sex. Congress has extended the prohibition of discrimination to activities of private organizations, through statutes prohibiting discrimination against women in areas such as employment, housing, credit, and education. Under United States law, however, it may be difficult to apply paragraph (e) to acts of discrimination by private clubs and organizations which are not supported in any way by federal financial assistance and are not subject to government regulation.[29] The discussion of state action in Chapter I above is also relevant in this context.

There is a certain overlap between paras. (f) and (g). While the former requires measures 'including legislation, to modify or abolish existing laws, regulations, customs and practices which constitute discrimination against women', the latter specifically addresses discriminatory national penal provisions only. Para. (f) is a truncated version of Art. 2(1) (c) of the International Convention on the Elimination of All Forms of Racial Discrimination, which requires change in laws and regulations 'which have the effect of creating *or perpetuating* racial discrimination wherever it exists'. While para. 2(1) (c) of the International Convention on the Elimination of All Forms of Racial Discrimination thus may affect general policies or laws which directly or indirectly aid in perpetuating racial discrimination, para. 2(f) of the Convention on the Elimination of All Forms of Discrimination Against Women more narrowly affects only such measures which themselves constitute discrimination against women. In this respect the latter Convention sets a more realistic goal than does the Convention against racial discrimination.

C. *Article 3 — Advancement of Women*

Art. 3 requires States Parties to 'take *in all fields*, in particular in the political, social, economic and cultural fields, all appropriate measures, including legislation, to ensure the full development and advancement of women, for the purpose of

---

[29] Ibid. at 3.

guaranteeing them the exercise and enjoyment of human rights and fundamental freedoms on a basis of equality with men' (emphasis added). The phrase 'all fields' extends the obligation of States to interpersonal and familial activities and thus poses the same problems discussed in regard to Art. 1. To a certain extent, the article may be an unnecessary repetition of principles stated in other provisions. The word 'appropriate' should be interpreted to mean necessary to the achievement of the stated objectives of the Convention, and not appropriateness under the national law of a State Party. According to general principles of international law, existing legal limitations on the State's ability to act pursuant to Art. 3 would not excuse the violation of its international obligations under the Convention.

D. *Article 5 — Modification of Patterns of Conduct*
Art. 5 provides that

States Parties shall take all appropriate measures:

(a) To modify the social and cultural patterns of conduct of men and women, with a view to achieving the elimination of prejudices and customary and all other practices which are based on the idea of the inferiority or the superiority of either of the sexes or on stereotyped roles for men and women;

(b) To ensure that family education includes a proper understanding of maternity as a social function and the recognition of the common responsibility of men and women in the upbringing and development of their children, it being understood that the interest of the children is the primordial consideration in all cases.

This provision mandates regulation of social and cultural patterns of conduct regardless of whether the conduct is public or private. Coupled with the broad and vague language of the preambular sentence discussed above ('all appropriate measures'), para. (a) might permit States to curtail to an undefined extent privacy and associational interests and the freedom of opinion and expression. Moreover, since social and cultural behaviour may be patterned according to factors such as ethnicity or religion, state action authorized by para. (a) which is directed towards modifying the way in which a particular ethnic or religious group treats women may conflict with the principles forbidding discrimination on the basis of race or religion.

The danger of intrusive state action and possible violation of the rights of ethnic or religious groups might have been mitigated by limiting state action to educational measures. Social and cultural patterns of conduct could be regulated by the substantive provisions which govern actual practices in a particular field, for example employment practices, without loss of substantive rights under the Convention.

E. *Article 6 — Exploitation of Prostitution*

Art. 6 provides that States Parties shall take all appropriate measures, including legislation, to suppress all forms of traffic in women and exploitation of prostitution of women. This provision should probably be interpreted as prohibiting the exploitation of prostitution, and not prostitution *per se*, although the term 'traffic in women' is not defined. While the Convention for the Suppression of the Traffic in Persons and of the Exploitation of the Prostitution of Others[30] did not define the term 'traffic in persons', it did define the specific offences which the contracting parties agreed to make punishable. Art. 6 of the Convention on the Elimination of All Forms of Discrimination Against Women fails to provide any definition whatsoever.

F. *Article 7 — Political Rights*

Art. 7 requires the elimination of sex discrimination in political and public life. Paras. (a) and (b) establish women's rights to vote and hold public office on a basis of equality with men. Para. (c) extends beyond public institutions to provide that women shall have the right to participate in non-governmental organizations and associations concerned with the public and political life of the country. Although the associational rights of members of non-governmental organizations may be restricted by para. (c) in so far as these groups are active in the public and political life of the country, such intrusion may be necessary in order to achieve political equality for women. Moreover, intrusion which might occur would not impinge upon interpersonal, 'private' relationships, but upon groups that have assumed a public role. The approach taken by the Convention

---

[30] Opened for signature 21 March 1950, 96 UNTS 272.

in this provision should be compared with that taken by the US Supreme Court in *Roberts* v. *United States Jaycees.*[31] While the Convention requires that women be allowed to participate in the work of associations concerned with the public and political life of the country, emphasizing the subject matter with which an association is concerned, criteria applied by the US Supreme Court in *Roberts* relate to the nature of the relationship among the association's members. The Court distinguishes private associations by such attributes as relatively small number of members, a high degree of selectivity in decisions to begin and maintain the affiliation, and seclusion from others in critical aspects of the relationship. That rationale would entitle women to participate in relatively open, 'public' associations even when their principal work is not 'concerned with the public and political life of the country'.

The memorandum of law of the State Department, written well before the *Roberts* decision, emphasized that, in general, the internal affairs of political parties — as distinguished from the electoral process — are not regulated by the federal government and proposed a statement of understanding clarifying the limited role of the federal government in non-governmental organizations and associations, including political parties.[32] Obviously, non-interference by the government in power with political parties and groups is an important principle.

G. *Article 9 — Nationality*

Art. 9 provides for equal rights for women regarding the status of their nationality (para. 1) and the nationality of their children (para. 2). These provisions properly affect the legal status of the persons concerned. Specific national, religious, and ethnic traditions and practices may, however, be implicated by this and other provisions of the Convention, as is apparent from the explanation given by Egypt of the reservation which it has made to Art. 9(2):

This is in order to prevent a child's acquisition of two nationalities where his parents are of different nationalities, since this may be prejudicial to his future. It is clear that the child's acquisition of his father's nationality is the procedure most suitable for the child and that this does not infringe

---

[31] *Roberts* v. *United States Jaycees*, 104 S. Ct. 3244, 3250-1 (1984).
[32] Memorandum of Law, above n. 4, at 5.

upon the principle of equality between men and women, since it is customary for a woman to agree, upon marrying an alien, that her children shall be of the father's nationality.[33]

H. *Article 10 — Education*

Art. 10 details measures to be taken in the field of education to ensure equality between women and men. This is a comprehensive and vital provision. States Parties are required not only to eradicate discrimination in the availability and in the quality of education (for instance para. (b) provides for '[a]ccess to the same curricula . . . [and] teaching staff with qualifications of the same standard . . .', and para. (d) provides for '[t]he same

---

[33] Multilateral Treaties, above n. 1, at 153.

The attitude reflected in Egypt's reservation can be found in other countries as well. In a recent Advisory Opinion sought by Costa Rica on a number of amendments proposed to the naturalization provisions of its Constitution, the Inter-American Court of Human Rights had an occasion to comment on the following text (Art. 14(4)): '[t]he following are Costa Ricans by naturalization: . . . [a] foreign woman who, by marriage to a Costa Rican loses her nationality or who after two years of marriage to a Costa Rican and the same period of residence in the country, indicates her desire to take on our nationality.' The Inter-American Ct. of Human Rights, *Proposed Amendments to the Naturalization Provisions of the Constitution of Costa Rica*, Advisory Opinion OC-4/84 of Jan. 19, 1984, ser. A: Judgments and Opinions No. 4, para. 44 (1984). The Court observed that the proposed amendment follows the formula 'adopted in the current Constitution, which gives women but not men who marry Costa Ricans a special status for purposes of naturalization. This approach . . . was based on the so-called principle of family unity and is traceable to two assumptions . . . [that] all members of a family should have the same nationality. The other derives from notions about paternal authority and the fact that authority over minor children was as a rule vested in the father and that it was the husband on whom the law conferred a privileged status of power, giving him authority, for example, to fix the marital domicile and to administer the marital property. Viewed in this light, the right accorded to women to acquire the nationality of their husbands was an outgrowth of conjugal inequality.'

Ibid. para. 64. The Court traced the development of 'a movement opposing these traditional notions', through Art. 1 of the Convention on Nationality of Women (Montevideo, 1933), Art. 6 of the Convention on Nationality (Montevideo, 1933), Art. II of the American Declaration of the Rights and Duties of Man (Bogota, 1948), Art. 1(3) of the Charter of the United Nations, Art. 3(j) of the Charter of the Organization of American States (Bogota, 1948), and Arts. 1(1), 17(4), and 24 of the American Convention on Human Rights (San José, 1969). Ibid. paras. 65–6. In its discussion of issues relating to nationality, but not in its discussion of issues of discrimination, the Court referred also to Art. 3 of the Convention on the Nationality of Married Women (New York, 1957) and to Art. 9 of the Convention on the Elimination of All Forms of Discrimination against Women, '[t]o the extent that they may reflect current trends in international law', Ibid. paras. 49–51. By unanimous vote, the Court expressed the opinion that the provision contained in Art. 14(4) 'which favours only one of the spouses, does constitute discrimination incompatible with Articles 17(4) and 24 of the Convention'. Ibid. at 113.

opportunities to benefit from scholarships . . .'), but also to offer education designed to eliminate sex discrimination in society (for instance para. (c) demands '[t]he elimination of any stereotyped concept of the roles of men and women at all levels . . . of education . . .').

The article does not mandate the introduction, but only the encouragement of coeducation (para. c). Separate but equal educational facilities satisfy the requirements of the Convention, as indicated by the reference in para. (b) to teaching staff with qualifications of the same standard and school premises and equipment of the same quality. Art. 10(g) provides for the same opportunities to participate actively in sports and educational facilities but apparently not the right to play on teams with men.[34] Obviously, even the obligation to encourage coeducation may give rise to conflict with religious freedom, especially when education is provided by religious organizations.

Art. 10 as a whole permits States to restrict the expression of religious belief to the extent that the practices and values propagated by a particular religious group deter equality in education between men and women. In view of the critical importance of education in altering social and cultural problems of gender discrimination, an appropriate balancing of the principles involved well justifies such restrictions. With regard to United States law, the memorandum of law of the State Department points out that Congress has acted to end discrimination in education by prohibiting sex discrimination in federally assisted education programmes or activities. These statutes apply only to public and private institutions that receive federal assistance, however.[35] While it is true that most educational institutions receive federal funds and are thus subject to Title IX Education Amendments of 1972,[36] the Supreme Court has recently held that only discrimination in the specific department receiving funds will be actionable.[37] The state action doctrine, discussed in Chapter I above, describes the limits of governmental authority to prohibit discrimination in private educational institutions. Because administration of public

---

[34] See Greenberg, above n. 3, at 330.
[35] Memorandum of Law, above n. 4, at 5–6.
[36] 20 USCA sections 1681–3, 1685–6 (1982).
[37] *Grove City College* v. *Bell*, 104 S. Ct. 1211, 1220–2 (1984).

elementary and secondary schools is a responsibility of the States, and no federal law requires coeducation or revision of textbooks to eliminate sexual stereotyping, the memorandum indicated that reservations to Art. 10 will be necessary.[38]

I. *Article 12 — Health Care*

Art. 12 mandates access to health services on a basis of equality for women and men. Para. (1) refers to 'health care services, including those related to family planning', and para. (2) requires States Parties to guarantee health care services during pregnancy and the post-natal period and to grant these services free of charge, if necessary. This article raises the question of the right to abortion, which arises also under Art. 16(e), to be considered below. Nowhere does the Convention refer expressly to abortion. In many countries family planning services (mentioned in Arts. 12(1) and Art. 14(2) (b)) and family planning information (mentioned in Art. 10(h)) include abortion. In requiring free health services only in connection with childbirth (Art. 12(2)), it is obvious that the Convention disfavours the alternative of abortion.

J. *Article 13 — Credit, Family Benefits*

Art. 13 requires States Parties to eliminate sex discrimination in economic life, including family benefits and financial credits, and in the right to participate in recreational activities, sports, and all aspects of cultural life. To the extent that these provisions fail to distinguish between public and private relationships, the problems of overbreadth already discussed are presented. Implementation of this obligation would be restricted in United States law by the fact that social relationships and the purely private activities of individual persons are beyond the scope of federal jurisdiction.[39]

K. *Article 16 — Domestic Relations and the Question of Abortion*

Art. 16 obligates States Parties to take 'all appropriate measures . . . in all matters relating to marriage and family relations' to ensure equality of men and women, with particular regard to

[38] Memorandum of Law, above n. 4, at 6.
[39] Ibid. at 7.

the enumerated rights, which include ownership of property, choice of spouse, and choice of occupation. It would appear that this provision regulates not only legal status but interpersonal conduct as well. Para. (c) refers to the 'same rights and responsibilities during marriage', and para. (d) to the 'same rights and responsibilities as parents . . .'. Read in conjunction with para. 13 of the Preamble and Art. 5(b), which promote change in the cultural patterns of sex role behaviour in the family, these provisions are apparently addressed to interpersonal relations and activities. Conflicts may thus arise with privacy interests of the individual, freedom of opinion and belief, and associational rights involved in marital and family relations.

The question of abortion has been mentioned previously, with regard to Art. 12. Art 16(e) guarantees men and women '[t]he same rights to decide freely and responsibly on the number and spacing of their children . . .'. It is doubtful whether the right to abortion is included within the family planning activities addressed by this article. Should the right to abortion be considered to be contemplated by implication, it would not be rooted in a woman's right of physical autonomy and individual privacy[40] but in the interest in familial and marital privacy. Because men have equal rights with women in matters of family planning, abortion under the Convention, if recognized at all, would not be a woman's individual right which she might exercise independently of consent of the father. Men claiming paternity could challenge, as a denial of their rights, a woman's decision to have an abortion.[41]

The practice of the Committee with regard to abortion is not yet clear. In reviewing reports submitted by States Parties, members of the Committee have inquired into the availability of abortions and thus presumably found abortion permissible, under the family planning provisions of the Convention.[42] In considering the report submitted by China, one member of the Committee asked whether China's family planning policy

[40] Such a principle is important in US law: see *City of Akron* v. *City of Akron Center for Reproductive Health*, 103 S. Ct. 2481 (1983); *Roe* v. *Wade*, 410 U.S. 113 (1973).

[41] Greenberg, above n. 3, at 330.

[42] See e.g., UN Doc. CEDAW/C/L.1/Add.5, at 4 (30 March 1984); UN Doc. CEDAW/C/L.1/Add.10, at 4 (4 April 1984).

did not contravene Art. 16 of the Convention, which ensures the freedom of choice regarding the number of children, but did not address the question of whether that choice was an individual right of the woman or a right of both parents.[43]

III. PROTECTING MATERNITY AND GUARANTEEING EMPLOYMENT

The Convention makes repeated reference to the role of women as childbearers and mothers (for example Preamble, para. 13, Arts. 4(2), 5(b), 11(1) (f), 11(2) (b), 11(2) (d), 12(2)). The Convention does include provisions intended to alter stereotypical concepts of women's role in society (Arts. 5(a) and 10(c)), and para. 14 of the Preamble specifically addresses the need to change the traditional roles of women and men in order to achieve equality between them. Art. 5(b) states that family education should include the recognition of the common responsibility of men and women in the upbringing and development of their children.

The Convention also contains, however, provisions granting States broad discretion to introduce legislation protecting maternity. Art. 4(2) states that adoption 'of special measures, including those measures contained in the present Convention, aimed at protecting maternity shall not be considered discriminatory'. The meaning of 'maternity' in this context is unclear. Does it refer to the capacity to bear children (fertility), to pregnancy, or to a woman's status as the mother of a child of young age or, indeed, of any age? There is danger that Art. 4(2) might be used as a pretext justifying discrimination against women, when a 'protective' purpose can be articulated. Art. 4(2) should have been drafted in a manner delimiting more precisely and more narrowly the authority granted to States, and should have included safeguards against abuse. Protective legislation which furthers legitimate health-related goals may serve an important purpose, but it is a mixed blessing. Commentators have argued that in the United States the effect of protective legislation has been to lower the economic status of women as a group, to deny them employment or force them

[43] 39 UN GAOR 2 Supp. (No. 45) para. 178, UN Doc. A/39/45 (1984).

into unskilled, low-paying positions, often in sex-segregated industries, and to deter their professional advancement.[44] The danger that 'over-protective legislation might easily lead to negative results . . . [such as] . . . prohibition of night work for women .   . . which may be counter-productive in terms of equality'[45] has been recognized by members of the Committee in their examination of reports submitted by States. Since pregnancy and motherhood bear no necessary relationship to individual ability, their recognition as permissible bases for denying equal treatment and opportunity to women would encourage sex discrimination. Although the Convention thus authorizes protective legislation which may be used to perpetuate or generate discrimination against women, in other provisions of the Convention the drafters correctly recognized that pregnancy and motherhood may not be utilized as a basis for discrimination against women if the goal of equality is ever to be achieved. The Convention explicitly proscribes discrimination on the grounds of marriage or maternity in the field of employment. Art. 11(2) (a) requires States Parties '[t]o prohibit, subject to the imposition of sanctions, dismissal on the grounds of pregnancy or of maternity leave and discrimination in dismissals on the basis of marital status . . .'. Art. 11(2) (b) requires the introduction of maternity leave 'with pay or with comparable social benefits without loss of former employment, seniority or social allowances . . .'. Although these provisions are important, they do not provide explicit protection to women in two principal areas: discrimination in hiring on grounds of maternity or pregnancy and discrimination in job assignment and promotion.

With regard to discrimination in hiring, Art. 11(1) (b) may appear at first glance to provide the necessary protection: States Parties must ensure '[t]he right to the same employment opportunities, including the application of the same criteria for selection in matters of employment . . .'. Because pregnancy

---

[44] See generally B. Babcock, A. Freedman, E. Norton, and S. Ross, Sex Discrimination and the Law: Causes and Remedies 247–82 (1975); J. Baer, The Chains of Protection: The Judicial Response to Women's Labor Legislation, Contribution in Women's Studies No. 1 (1978); A. Simmons, A. Freedman, M. Dunkle, and F. Blau, Exploitation from 9 to 5, at 65–82 (1975).

[45] 39 UN GAOR 2 Supp. (No. 45) para. 87, UN Doc. A/39/45 (1984). See also ibid. at para. 98.

or maternity status cannot be applied as a shared criterion in hiring of men and women, is there not a danger that criteria relating to pregnancy or maternity may be used as a pretext for gender discrimination in hiring?[46] Art. 11(1) (b) might not provide adequate protection against discrimination in this area.

Art. 11(1) (c) requires States Parties to guarantee 'the right to promotion, job security and all benefits and conditions of service', and Art. 11(2) (b) requires the introduction of maternity leave with pay without loss of former employment or seniority. Neither provision adequately guards against discrimination in job assignment or promotion *during pregnancy or maternity leave*. Art. 11(2) (b) protects only seniority, not promotion during maternity leave, and does not mention job assignment. Moreover, Art. 11(2) (d), which authorizes the provision of 'special protection to women during pregnancy in types of work proved to be harmful to them' may subordinate women's interests in job assignment to the asserted interest in safeguarding the reproductive and childbearing capacity of women. Explicit prohibitions of discrimination in promotion and job assignment on grounds of pregnancy or maternity leave should have been incorporated in Art. 11.

For example, Section 701(k) of Title VII of the Civil Rights Act of 1964 provides that all pregnancy-based distinctions constitute discrimination on the basis of sex and that pregnancy must be treated like other temporary disabilities for employment related purposes. This important provision states as follows:

The terms 'because of sex' or 'on the basis of sex' include, but are not limited to, because of or on the basis of pregnancy, childbirth, or related medical conditions; and women affected by pregnancy, childbirth, or related medical conditions shall be treated the same for all employment-related purposes, including receipt of benefits under fringe benefit programs, as other persons not so affected but similar in their ability or inability to work . . . .[47]

---

[46] See generally A. Simmons, A. Freedman, M. Dunkle, and F. Blau, above n. 44, at 99–100; *Phillips* v. *Martin Marietta Corporation*, 400 U.S. 542, 544 (1971); Comment, *Employment Rights of Women in the Toxic Workplace*, 65 Calif. L. Rev. 1113 (1977).

[47] 42 USC section 2000e(k) (1982).

Although Title VII of the 1964 Civil Rights Act, which prohibits discrimination on the basis of sex, including pregnancy
and related disabilities, is comprehensive in nature, it exempts
employers hiring fewer than fifteen employees and does not
apply to employees falling into certain categories.[48] Moreover,
it is not clear whether legislation requires equal pay for work of
comparable value. Appropriate reservations by the United
States would therefore be necessary.[49]

The goal of equal pay for work of comparable value has not
yet been attained even in enlightened and developed countries
which have acceded to the Convention. In Austria, for example, '[a]lthough the incomes in the public sector were
regulated through legislation, the wage difference between
women and men in the public sector still came to 19 per cent,
it amounted to about 40 per cent in the private sector.'[50] In

---

[48]   42 USCA sections 2000 (c) (a), and (f) (1982). See also *County of Washington*
v. *Gunther*, 452 U.S. 161, 166 (1981). Regarding maternity leave, see *Nashville Gas
Co.* v. *Satty*, 434 U.S. 136 (1977). Regarding sick leave for pregnant women, see
Zuniga v. *Kleberg County Hospital*, 692 F.2d 986 (5th Cir. 1982); *Burwell* v. *Eastern
Air Lines Inc.*, 633 F.2d 361 (4th Cir. 1980), *cert denied* 450 U.S. 965 (1981).

[49]   Memorandum of Law, above n. 4, at 6-7. The principle that women and men
should receive equal pay for equal work is stated in Art. 119 of the Treaty Establishing the European Economic Community (Treaty of Rome), 298 UNTS 11, but not in
the European Convention on Human Rights. See also Chapter IV, text accompanying
n. 105. Of central importance for the implementation of the principle of equal pay
in the European Economic Community is the following Directive of the Council of
10 Feb. 1975: Directive du Conseil (No. 75/117/CEE) concernant le rapprochement
des législations des États membres relatives à l'application du principe de l'égalité des
rémunérations entre les travailleurs masculins et les travailleurs féminins, 18 J. O.
Comm. Eur. (No. L 45/19) 1 (1975).

On some of the case law of the Court of Justice of the European Communities
(the Luxembourg Court) on the interpretation and application of Art. 19, see
Gabrielle Defrenne v. *Belgian State*, 1971 E. Comm. Ct. J. Rep. 445 (Preliminary
Ruling); *Gabrielle Defrenne* v. *Société Anonyme Belge. de Navigation Aérienne
Sabena*, 1976 E. Comm. Ct. J. Rep. 455 (Preliminary Ruling); *Gabrielle Defrenne* v.
Société Anonyme Belge de Navigation Aérienne Sabena, 1978 E. Comm. Ct. J. Rep.
1365 (Preliminary Ruling); *Macarthys Ltd.* v. *Wendy Smith*, 1980 E. Comm. Ct. J.
Rep. 1275 (Preliminary Ruling); *Susan Jane Worringham and Margaret Humphreys*
v. *Lloyds Bank Limited*, 1981 E. Comm. Ct. J. Rep. 767 (Preliminary Ruling); *J. P.
Jenkins* v. *Kingsgate (Clothing Productions) Ltd.*, 1981 E. Comm. Ct. J. Rep. 911
(Preliminary Ruling); *Eileen Garland* v. *British Rail Engineering Limited*, 1982 E.
Comm. Ct. J. Rep. 359 (Preliminary Ruling); *Arthur Burton* v. *British Railways
Board*, 1982 E. Comm. Ct. J. Rep. 555 (Preliminary Ruling); *Commission of the
European Communities* v. *Grand Duchy of Luxembourg*, 1982 E. Comm. Ct. J.
Rep. 2175; *Commission of the European Communities* v. *United Kingdom*, 1982
E. Comm. Ct. J. Rep. 2601.

[50]   UN Doc. CEDAW/C/1985/L.1/Add.8, at para. 15 (1985).

Canada, a female teacher earned only 62.7 per cent as much as a male teacher would earn[51] and females received on the average 65 per cent of the amount paid to males.[52]

IV. WOMEN'S EQUALITY AND RELIGIOUS FREEDOM

Greenberg has wisely drawn attention to potential conflicts between the Convention on the Elimination of All Forms of Discrimination Against Women and the Declaration on the Elimination of All Forms of Intolerance and of Discrimination Based on Religion or Belief.[53] 'If a religion', asked Greenberg, 'relegates women to a certain societal or familial status which would otherwise be deemed discrimination on the basis of sex, which convention governs?'[54] The Convention contains a resolution of conflicts provision in Art. 23:

Nothing in the present Convention shall affect any provisions that are *more conducive* to the achievement of equality between men and women which may be contained :

(a) In the legislation of a State Party; or

(b) In any other international convention, treaty or agreement in force for that State [emphasis added].[55]

Questions concerning normative conflicts generally will be discussed in Chapter IV below. Art. 23 opens the door to claims that other instruments or laws contain provisions which are more conducive to the achievement of equality. Moreover, it is unclear how the Convention purports to affect provisions in other international instruments which are *less conducive* to the achievement of equality. The problem of the relationship between these instruments cannot be resolved by a simplistic application of such provisions as Articles 30, 41, 58, and 59 of the Vienna Convention on the Law of Treaties.[56] However,

---

[51] UN Doc. CEDAW/C/1985/L.1/Add.7, at para. 17 (1985).

[52] UN Doc. CEDAW/C/1985/L.1/Add.1, at para. 22 (1985).

[53] GA Res. 36/55, 36 UN GAOR Supp. (No. 51) at 171, UN Doc. A/36/51 (1981); Greenberg, above n. 3, at 330.

[54] Greenberg, above n. 3, at 330.

[55] See generally, Meron, *Norm Making and Supervision in International Human Rights: Reflections on Institutional Order*, 76 AJIL 754, 758-9 (1982).

[56] Opened for signature 23 May 1969, UN Doc. A/CONF.39/27 (1969), reprinted in 63 AJIL 875 (1969), 8 ILM 679 (1969).

even without reference to conflicts with the Declaration on the Elimination of All Forms of Intolerance and of Discrimination Based on Religion or Belief, experience acquired in the implementation of the Convention points to major difficulties cast by the heavy shadow of religion on women's difficult road towards equality.

Egypt provides a case in point. Egypt ratified the Convention with a reservation to Art. 16 which provides that women and men shall have equality in all matters relating to marriage and family relations, including the same right to enter into marriage, and the same rights and responsibilities during marriage and at its dissolution. Egypt's reservation read as follows:

> Reservation to the text of article 16 concerning the equality of men and women in all matters relating to marriage and family relations during the marriage and upon its dissolution, without prejudice to the Islamic Sharia's provisions whereby women are accorded rights equivalent to those of their spouses so as to ensure a just balance between them. *This is out of respect for the sacrosanct nature of the firm religious beliefs which govern marital relations in Egypt and which may not be called in question* and in view of the fact that one of the most important bases of these rights is an equivalency of rights and duties so as to ensure complementarity which guarantees true equality between the spouses. The provisions of the Sharia lay down that the husband shall pay bridal money to the wife and maintain her fully and shall also make a payment to her upon divorce, whereas the wife retains full rights over her property and is not obliged to spend anything on her keep. The Sharia therefore restricts the wife's rights to divorce by making it contingent on a judge's ruling, whereas no such restriction is laid down in the case of the husband [emphasis added].[57]

Members of the Committee raised questions concerning some of the problems posed by this reservation. Because Arts. 2 and 16 establish the principle of equality which is fundamental to the Convention, and reservations incompatible with the object and purpose of the Convention are not permissible according to Art. 28, a legal opinion on reservations was requested.[58] Members of the Committee requested clarifications regarding several issues: 'complementarity' and the obligations of Islamic law; Islamic religious law and secular law, and the areas of law governed by each; polygamy and repudiation and the compatibility of these practices with the articles which stipulate that

---

[57] Multilateral Treaties, above n. 1, at 153.
[58] 39 UN GAOR 2 Supp. (No. 45) para. 190, UN Doc. A/39/45 (1984).

practices based on the idea of inferiority or superiority of either sex should be eliminated, and with Art. 16 of the Convention; how the Convention was incorporated into the judicial system of the country; whether harmony was being equated with equality; and the recourse which women had against discrimination.[59] The answers offered by the representative of Egypt to these questions did not elucidate these matters fully. While emphasizing the beneficial role of the Shari'a with regard to women's equality, she conceded that '[w]ith regard to rights and responsibilities during marriage and at its dissolution, a certain difference existed between the Convention and Islamic law'.[60] This, she implied, made the reservation to Art. 16 necessary.

These questions reflect difficulties created by religious practices in the field of marriage and family matters, and the status of women under religious law. Such difficulties, both with regard to substantive law and to evidence laws giving women's testimony less evidentiary weight (as in Rabbinic and in Islamic courts), are particularly grave in countries which do not follow strictly the principle of separation of Church and State, and where tribunals which have jurisdiction over family matters, marriage, divorce, custody, and so on, apply religious law rather than the Convention. While Art. 15 of the Convention addresses only women's capacity in civil matters, in some countries matters pertaining to family status, and so on, are considered to be within the domain of religion, and may even be within the exclusive jurisdiction of religious courts. It is therefore regrettable that the Convention does not address the question of the status of women in tribunals which adjudicate matters of family status on the basis of religious law and in religious courts, because such adjudication should be regarded as pertaining primarily to legal status rather than to religious beliefs. Religious beliefs are not, of course, the only values which conflict with women's equality. Other traditional social or ethnic practices are also implicated as is apparent from the statements of representatives of the Philippines before the Committee cited in Section I above.

---

[59] Ibid. at 26.
[60] Ibid. at 29.

V. RESERVATIONS

Art. 28 of the Convention provides that the Secretary-General shall receive and circulate to all States the text of reservations made by States Parties at the time of ratification or accession, and that a reservation incompatible with the object and purpose of the Convention shall not be permitted. In response to an inquiry by the Committee concerning the reservation by Egypt discussed in Section IV above, the Treaty Section of the Office of Legal Affairs of the United Nations Secretariat submitted a legal opinion interpreting Art. 28. The opinion noted the following points:

Firstly, in contrast to the Convention on the Elimination of Racial Discrimination which provides, in Art. 20, that a reservation is incompatible or inhibitive if at least two-thirds of the States Parties object to it, Art. 28 of the Convention on the Elimination of All Forms of Discrimination against Women does not establish any specific criteria of incompatibility. Secondly, as a consequence, Art. 29, which provides for arbitration or, failing agreement on the organization of the arbitration, for referral to the International Court of Justice, would be applicable if a dispute regarding the interpretation of Art. 28 arose. Thirdly, the Secretary-General has to receive and circulate the text of reservations and does not have the power to interpret the Convention. Fourthly, the functions of the Committee 'do not appear to include a determination of the incompatibility of reservations, although reservations undoubtedly affect the application of the Convention and the Committee might have to comment thereon in its reports in this context'.[61]

VI. THE ADEQUACY OF MEASURES FOR ENSURING IMPLEMENTATION

The functions of the Committee are described in Arts. 17, 18, and 21 of the Convention. Under Art. 18, the Parties undertake to submit reports on the legislative, judicial, administrative, or other measures which they have adopted to give effect to the provisions of the present Convention, and on the progress made

---

[61] Ibid. at 55–6.

in this respect one year after the Convention's entry into force for the State concerned and every four years thereafter. Under Art. 21 of the Convention the Committee may make 'suggestions and general recommendations based on the examination of reports and information received from the States Parties'. There is a serious inconsistency between the duty of the Committee, under Art. 21, to examine the reports submitted by States Parties under Art. 18, and the language of Art. 20, which states that '[t]he Committee shall normally meet for a period of not more than two weeks annually in order to consider the reports submitted in accordance with article 18 of the present Convention'. By 21 January 1985, 65 States were parties to the Convention and the Committee has been considering six reports in each of its sessions. One member of the Committee thus observed that at this pace 'the discussion of all reports would be completed by the year 2000'.[62] Although the language of Art. 20 is not categorical since the word 'normally' leaves a certain latitude to the Committee to meet more frequently or for longer periods, it is doubtful that a drastic and permanent extension of the annual sessions of the Committee would accord with the Convention.

Obviously, the narrow powers do not authorize the Committee to determine that violations of the Convention by a particular State Party have taken place. It is even doubtful whether the Committee may comment on violations of the Convention by a particular State Party.

Art. 21 limits the sources of information which the Committee may take into consideration in the preparation of suggestions and general recommendations. Provisions similar to those contained in Arts. 11-13 of the Convention on the Elimination of All Forms of Racial Discrimination, authorizing the Committee to consider complaints submitted by one State Party against another for failure to fulfil obligations under the Convention and to issue, in certain circumstances, 'a report embodying its findings on all questions of fact relevant to the issue between the parties and containing such recommendations as it may think proper . . .' would have been desirable. Because States are reluctant to submit complaints against each other in

---

[62] UN Doc. CEDAW/C/1985/L.1, para. 29 (1985); above n. 2.

matters pertaining to human rights, the Convention should also have provided for a procedure allowing the Committee to consider individual communications similar to the procedures created in the Optional Protocol to the International Covenant on Civil and Political Rights and Art. 14 of the Convention on the Elimination of All Forms of Racial Discrimination.

III

The International Covenant on Civil and Political Rights

I. INTRODUCTION

THE International Covenant on Civil and Political Rights[1] (Political Covenant), the most important universal instrument on civil and political rights, has been the subject of considerable literature and, most notably, of the important volume of essays edited by Henkin.[2] The Political Covenant was signed on behalf of the United States on 5 October 1977. On 23 February 1978, it was transmitted by President Carter to the US Senate, with far-reaching reservations, declarations, and understandings.[3] These reservations, declarations, and understandings have themselves been the subject of considerable discussion[4] and will not be addressed in this study. The Political Covenant has not been reported out of the Senate Committee on Foreign Relations and is not now under active consideration.

This chapter will not address all of the Political Covenants' provisions. The existing literature makes such a task unnecessary and the confines of the present study make it impracticable,

---

[1] For the text of the Political Covenant, see GA Res. 2200, 21 UN GAOR Supp. (No. 16) at 52, UN Doc. A/6316 (1966).

[2] The International Bill of Rights: The Covenant on Civil and Political Rights (L. Henkin ed., 1981). For bibliographies on the Political Covenant, see Vincent-Daviss, *Human Rights Law: A Research Guide to the Literature — Part I: International Law and the United Nations*, 14 N.Y.U. J. Int'l L. & Pol. 209, 269–73 (1981); A. Robertson, Human Rights in the World 74, n. 15 (1982); Lillich, *Civil Rights*, in 1 Human Rights in International Law: Legal and Policy Issues 115, 168–70 (T. Meron ed., 1984).

[3] [1978] Digest of United States Practice in International Law at 440–1, 450–7 (M. Nash ed., 1980).

[4] *International Human Rights Treaties: Hearings on Ex. C. D. E. and F. 95–2 — Four Treaties Relating to Human Rights Before the Senate Comm. on Foreign Relations*, 96th Cong., 1st Sess. (Comm. Print, 1980); Schachter, *The Obligation of the Parties to Give Effect to the Covenant on Civil and Political Rights*, 73 AJIL 462 (1979).

especially in light of the wide range of the provisions of the Political Covenant and the absence of a central focus, or even a limited number of discrete focal points. Instead, the chapter will consider a number of weaknesses of the Political Covenant, which cause problems in its interpretation, application, and efficacy. This chapter has benefited greatly from the past practice of the Human Rights Committee (Committee) established under Art. 28 of the Political Covenant and composed of eighteen experts serving in their personal capacity.

A few comments on the functions of the Committee may be appropriate at this point. Under Art. 40 of the Political Covenant, which is binding *ipso facto* on the States Parties, the Committee is charged with the duty of studying reports submitted by States and of making 'general comments', according to procedures to be developed by the Committee itself,[5] under Art. 39(2). This central function of the Committee will be further discussed in Section IX below. Under Art. 41 of the Political Covenant, the Committee has a conciliatory role with regard to interstate complaints, which may be entertained as between States that have recognized the competence of the Committee under that article. While more than the required ten declarations of acceptance have been received and the Art. 41 procedure is now in effect, this provision has not yet been invoked.

The Committee has an 'investigatory' role under the Optional Protocol to the International Covenant on Civil and Political Rights (Optional Protocol).[6] The Committee's competence under Art. 1 of the Optional Protocol is limited to receiving and considering communications from individuals subject to the jurisdiction of States Parties that have recognized its competence who claim to be victims of a violation by such a State Party of

---

[5] UN Doc. CCPR/C/3/Rev.1, Provisional Rules of Procedure, Rules 66–71 (1979).

It has been aptly observed that '[a]t present, the only formal obligation on the greater part of States parties to the Covenants was to submit regular reports to either the Economic and Social Council or the Human Rights Committee'. (Remarks by the Netherlands) UN Doc. E./CN.4/1985/SR.42/Add.1, at 2 (1985).

[6] 35 UN GAOR Supp. (No. 40) at 84, UN Doc. A/35/40 (1980).

For the text of the Optional Protocol to the International Covenant on Civil and Political Rights, see GA Res. 2200, 21 UN GAOR Supp. (No. 16) at 59, UN Doc. A/6316 (1966).

any of the rights set forth in the Political Covenant. Under Art. 5, the Committee is to forward its 'views' (not 'decisions' or 'determinations') to the State Party concerned and to the author of the communication. The Optional Protocol does not, however, address the question of the obligation of the State to comply with 'the views' of the Committee. The substance of the procedures to be followed by the Committee in the exercise of its functions under Art. 41 and the Optional Protocol is established by the Political Covenant or the Optional Protocol themselves.[7]

Unlike Art. 22 of the International Convention on the Elimination of All Forms of Racial Discrimination, considered in Chapter I above, the Political Covenant does not contain a provision on the settlement by the International Court of Justice of disputes between States Parties pertaining to the application or the interpretation of the Political Covenant. The conciliatory functions of the Committee under Art. 41 should not, however, in any way pre-empt the judicial functions of the Court under its Statute. The Committee's competence to interpret the Political Covenant appears to be implicitly confirmed in the 'Statement on the duties of the Human Rights Committee under article 40 of the Covenant', for instance in the reference by the Committee to general comments on the 'application and the content of individual articles of the Covenant . . .'.[8] The Political Covenant does not, however, explicitly confer on the Committee interpretative authority. As a treaty organ, the Committee is competent to interpret the Political Covenant in so far as is required for the performance of its functions. While the Committee's interpretation *per se* is not binding on States Parties, that interpretation (as discussed in Chapter I, Section I, and Chapter II, Section I) affects their reporting obligations and their internal and external behaviour. The Committee's interpretations shape the practice of States in the application of the Political Covenant and may establish and

---

[7] 35 UN GAOR Supp. (No. 40) at 84, UN Doc. A/35/40 (1980).
[8] 36 UN GAOR Supp. (No. 40) at 101, 102, UN Doc. A/36/40 (1981).
   In the context of committees composed of individual experts, the Soviet Union has made the strange claim that 'the interpretation of any international agreement came within the competence of States rather than of independent experts . . . UN Doc. E/CN.4/1985/SR.51/Add.1 at 2 (1985).

reflect the agreement of the parties regarding its interpretation.[9] Whether a particular interpretation or decision by the Committee serves such a function can, of course, be determined only *in concreto.*

II. DEROGATIONS

One of the principal weaknesses of the Political Covenant lies in the derogation provisions contained in Art. 4. Although the complex question of derogations will not be considered in detail,[10] some observations on the scope of that right are necessary. The right of derogation, it must be made clear at the very outset, is additional to the right given to States Parties to invoke various limitation clauses so as to restrict the application of certain articles of the Political Covenant.[11] Experience shows that it is in times of emergency, when the life of the nation is threatened, that cruel abuses of human rights are at their worst and claims of sovereignty and rejection of all foreign expressions of interest in events are especially strident. The role of national courts in trying to protect human rights in such

---

[9] Vienna Convention on the Law of Treaties, Art. 31, opened for signature 23 May 1969, UN Doc. A/CONF.39/27 (1969), reprinted in 8 ILM 679 (1969), 63 AJIL 875 (1969). See generally I. Sinclair, The Vienna Convention on the Law of Treaties 135-8 (1984).

[10] See generally Buergenthal, *To Respect and to Ensure: State Obligations and Permissible Derogations,* in Henkin (ed.), above n. 2, at 72; Higgins, *Derogations under Human Rights Treaties,* 48 Brit. Y.B. Int'l L. 281 (1976-7); Hartman, *Derogation from Human Rights Treaties in Public Emergencies,* 22 Harv. Int'l L.J. 1 (1981); Hartman, *Working Paper for the Committee of Experts on the Article 4 Derogation Provision,* 7 Human Rights Q. 89 (1985); Green, *Derogation of Human Rights in Emergency Situations,* 16 Can. Y.B. Int'l L. 92 (1978); States of Emergency: Their Impact on Human Rights (International Commission of Jurists 1983); Marks, *Principles and Norms of Human Rights Applicable in Emergency Situations: Underdevelopment, Catastrophes and Armed Conflicts,* in 1 The International Dimensions of Human Rights 175 (K. Vasak ed., P. Alston Eng. ed. 1982); Lillich, above n. 2, at 119-20.

[11] Kiss, *Permissible Limitations on Rights,* in Henkin (ed.), above n. 2, at 290. The UN Commission on Human Rights has been criticized for not paying enough attention 'to the effect of restriction clauses dealing with specific rights and invoking such grounds as public health, public order or national security. The way in which those restrictions were applied was of great importance to the enjoyment of guaranteed rights by the individual.' UN Doc. E/CN.4/1985/SR.42/Add.1 at 3 (1985) (remarks by the Netherlands). See also Siracusa Principles 1-38, UN Doc. E/CN.4/1985/4, Ann. at 3-6 (1985).

situations is often negligible.[12] The real value of human rights instruments should therefore be tested by examining their derogation clauses.

Derogation clauses, especially when they are drafted in terms as general as those of Art. 4 and give States such broad discretion to claim the existence of public emergency, have been used by States to justify the denial of human rights. The considerable potential for abuse is heightened by the inadequacy of Art. 4(3), which requires that any State Party availing itself of the right of derogation shall immediately inform the other States Parties, through the Secretary-General, of the provisions from which it has derogated and of the reasons advanced for the derogations. While there is a clear legal duty to issue such a notification, the violation of that duty does not appear to invalidate the derogation itself. These difficulties are amplified by the Committee's practice of denying its own competence to determine, in the course of the examination of reports from States under Art. 40 of the Political Covenant, that the reporting State has committed a breach of Art. 4 or of other provisions of the Political Covenant. This matter will be discussed in Section IX below.

Before turning to the question of the rights from which derogations are permissible, a short discussion of the procedural provisions pertaining to derogations may be appropriate. The important study prepared by Questiaux[13] groups 'deviations' from a 'reference model' of non-abusive derogations into several categories, including: (1) states of emergency not notified to other parties to an international instrument; (2) *de facto* states of emergency, where there is no proclamation or termination of a state of emergency or where the state of emergency subsists after it has been officially proclaimed and then terminated; (3) permanent states of emergency, where the institution of the state of emergency, with or without proclamation, is perpetuated either as a result of *de facto* systematic extension or because the constitution has not provided any time limit a priori. The very

---

[12] See Alexander, *The Illusory Protection of Human Rights by National Courts during Periods of Emergency*, 5 Human Rights L.J. 1 (1984).

[13] N. Questiaux, Study of the Implications for Human Rights of Recent Developments Concerning Situations Known as States of Siege or Emergency, UN Doc. E/CN.4/Sub.2/1982/15, at 26–32 (1982).

existence of Art. 4 thus opens wide the door to violations of human rights.

Members of the Committee have shown awareness of the danger of institutionalization of states of emergency. They have thus remarked, with regard to the report of Egypt:

> that little information was provided about the 'State of Emergency' introduced by Act No. 162 of 1958, which had been amended in 1981 and 1982 and had remained in force without interruption since its adoption, and noted that the increased powers which it conferred on the executive had been institutionalized to such an extent that it could be questioned whether the provisions of the Constitution were still applicable. Members also wondered, in the absence of notification by the Government of the state of emergency, whether the implementation of the Act implied no derogation from the obligations set forth in the Covenant.[14]

Members of the Committee also pointed out that 'since 1973 not one day had passed in Chile without a state of emergency being in force and that that situation could not be justified . . . [and questioned whether] Chile claimed the existence of a 'public emergency' within the meaning of [Art. 4] . . . [and] why the Government had not notified any derogation in accordance with paragraph 3 . . .'.[15]

In its general comments, the Committee has frankly admitted to encountering a number of problems with Art. 4: 'in the case of a few States which had apparently derogated from Covenant rights, it was unclear not only whether a state of emergency had been officially declared but also whether rights from which the Covenant allows no derogation had in fact not been derogated from and further whether the other States parties had been informed of the derogations and of the reasons for the derogations.'[16] Because of growing concern about this problem, several members of the Committee expressed the following views: that whenever a notification under Art. 4(3) was made, it should be transmitted forthwith to the members of the Committee; that the Committee had the power to request a special report on how a public emergency affected human rights; that the Committee should use all information available, or at least

---

[14] 39 UN GAOR Supp. (No. 40) at 56, UN Doc. A/39/40 (1984).
[15] Ibid. at 82.
[16] 36 UN GAOR Supp. (No. 40) at 110, UN Doc. A/36/40 (1981). See generally Walkate, *The Human Rights Committee and Public Emergencies*, 9 Yale J. World Public Order 133 (1982).

that available in the United Nations; and that such a situation or report should be considered, if necessary, at an extraordinary session of the Committee. To prevent *excès de pouvoir* by States Parties, the procedure for requesting such reports should be formalized.[17]

In opposition to the introduction of a regular procedure for requesting reports on emergency situations, certain members of the Committee invoked the broad discretion given to States by the language of Art. 4 which, they argued, did not confer on the Committee any competence to determine whether a situation threatening the life of a nation existed. The information submitted by a State declaring an emergency was not subject to third party approval or scrutiny as to whether derogations were limited to the extent strictly required by the exigencies of the situation. States Parties were not even required to report to the Committee, but only to notify other States Parties. The role of the Committee was thus limited to 'ascertaining whether other States Parties had been immediately informed, what rights were affected by the emergency measures and whether there had been derogations from the provisions mentioned in article 4(2) and determining what were the reasons by which the State had been actuated and when the derogations had been terminated'.[18]

In practice, on several occasions States Parties have supplied

[17] 37 UN GAOR Supp. (No. 40) at 75-6, UN Doc. A/37/40 (1982).

[18] Ibid. at 76. For the recommendations of the Siracusa Conference concerning the functions of the Human Rights Committee with regard to derogations, see UN Doc. E/CN.4/1985/4, Ann. at 12 (1985). See also Principles 39-70, ibid. at 7-12. Of particular importance is the Report [of the Enforcement of Human Rights Law Committee] on Mimimum Standards of Human Rights Norms in a State of Exception, in International Law Association, Report of the Sixty-First Conference at 56 (Paris, 1984). It may be of interest to contrast the practice of the Human Rights Committee with regard to derogations with that of the organs established by the European Convention for the Protection of Human Rights and Fundamental Freedoms (European Convention on Human Rights) 213 UNTS 221. The latter have exercised a stricter control over the use by member States of restrictions and limitations of human rights. Fifth International Colloquy About the European Convention on Human Rights, Report by T. Stein on Derogations from Guarantees Laid down in Human Rights Instruments, Council of Europe Doc. H/Coll (80) 6 (1980); Fifth International Colloquy About the European Convention on Human Rights, Report by J. Kelly on International Control of Restrictions and Limitations, H/Coll. (80) 3 (1980). See also European Commission of Human Rights, Applications No. 6780/74 and 6950/75, Cyprus Against Turkey, 1 Report of the Commission 157-62 (1976, declassified 1979). For the dissenting opinion of G. Sperduti and S. Trechsel on Art. 15 of the European Convention, see ibid. at 168-71 (1976).

the Committee with little or no information on how various provisions of the Political Covenant were being carried out under a state of emergency, so that the Committee has had to request States to provide additional information.[19] In examining reports from States under Art. 40, the Committee has taken a cautious attitude, refraining from suggestions that declarations of states of emergency were not justified by the terms of Art. 4 or that the derogations from various rights were excessive. Given the broad language of Art. 4, which grants an extremely wide discretion to the State, and the virtual absence of safeguards, this caution is understandable.

The Committee has gone considerably further, however, in exercising its competence under Art. 5(4) of the Optional Protocol.[20] In an important interpretation of the instruments concerned, the Committee stated:

Although the sovereign right of a State Party to declare a state of emergis not questioned, yet, in the specific context of the present communication, the Human Rights Committee is of the opinion that a State, by merely invoking the existence of exceptional circumstances, cannot evade the obligations which it has undertaken by ratifying the Covenant. Although the substantive right to take derogatory measures may not depend on a formal notification being made pursuant to article 4(3) of the Covenant, the State party concerned is duty-bound to give a sufficiently detailed account of the relevant facts when it invokes article 4(1) of the Covenant in proceedings under the Optional Protocol. It is the function of the Human Rights Committee, acting under the Optional Protocol, to see to it that States Parties live up to their commitments under the Covenant. In order . . . to assess whether a situation of the kind described in article 4(1) . . . exists in the country concerned, it needs full and comprehensive information. If the respondent Government does not furnish the required justification itself, as it is required to do under article 4(2) of the Optional Protocol and article 4(3) of the Covenant, the Human Rights Committee cannot conclude that valid reasons exist to legitimize a departure from the normal legal regime prescribed by the Covenant.[21]

Even on the assumption that there existed a situation of

---

[19] UN Doc. CCPR/C/SR.404 at para. 96 (1982) (these remarks did not identify the State concerned).

For examples of notifications of derogations, see UN Doc. CCPR/C/2/Add.8 at 5-32 (1985).

[20] Communication No. R.8/34, *Landinelli Silva* v. *Uruguay*, 36 UN GAOR Supp. (No. 40) at 130, UN Doc. A/36/40 (1981).

[21] Ibid. at 132-3.

emergency in the State concerned, Uruguay, no justification could be adduced for depriving all citizens who, as members of certain political groups, were candidates in previous elections of any political rights, for as long a period as 15 years. These deprivations amounted to an unreasonable restriction of their rights under Art. 25 of the Political Covenant.[22]

The 'views' adopted by the Committee in this case were commendable, for Uruguay clearly abused the right of derogation. The fact that Uruguay had not even gone through the motions of formulating a plausible case to defend measures so clearly excessive provided the basis for the position taken by the Committee. While such decisions are important, their influence is likely to be limited, because only a small number of States have accepted the Optional Protocol.[23]

The substantive scope of the right of derogation is very broad. The list of non-derogable rights stated in Art. 4 (Arts. 6, 7, 8(1), 8(2), 11, 15, 16, and 18) is clearly too limited to ensure the essential core of basic protections of the human person which must be respected at all times. For example, although in time of emergency the question of deportations is of particular importance, there is no prohibition of arbitrary deportations, even on a massive scale. Such deportations are prohibited by Art. 49 of Geneva Convention No. IV.[24] With regard to deportations, therefore, the human rights protections

---

[22] Ibid. at 133.

[23] While 80 States have become parties to the Political Covenant, only 35 States have become parties to the Optional Protocol to the International Covenant on Civil and Political Rights. 40 UN GAOR Supp. (No. 40) at 1, UN Doc. A/40/40 (1985).

[24] Convention Relative to the Protection of Civilian Persons in Time of War (Geneva Convention No. IV), Aug. 12, 1949, 6 UST 3516, TIAS No. 3365, 75 UNTS 287. See also Art. 17, Protocol Additional to the Geneva Conventions of 12 August 1949, and Relating to the Protection of Victims of Non-International Armed Conflicts (Protocol II), opened for signature 12 Dec. 1977, reprinted in 16 ILM 1442 (1977).

Individual expulsion of aliens is prohibited by Art. 13 of the Political Covenant which is derogable. The Political Covenant does not address collective expulsions.

See generally P. Sieghart, The International Law of Human Rights 174–8 (1983). Collective expulsion of aliens is prohibited under Art. 22(9) of the American Convention on Human Rights (for the official text, see Organization of American States, Handbook of Existing Rules pertaining to Human Rights in the Inter-American System 29, 40, OEA/Ser.L./V/II.60, doc. 28, rev.1 (1983)), and Art. 4 of Protocol No. 4 to the European Convention for the Protection of Human Rights and Fundamental Freedoms (Europ. T. S. No. 46), but not as a non-derogable protection. See

stated in the Political Covenant fall short of those granted by the Geneva Convention No. IV. On the other hand, the prohibition of imprisonment merely on the ground of inability to fulfil a contractual obligation, stated in Art. 11 of the Political Covenant, is not essential in times of emergency and its inclusion among the non-derogable provisions is bizarre. Among the criticisms which have been made of Art. 4 is not only that 'public emergency' is defined far too broadly and adequate safeguards are lacking, but that the provision fails to protect from derogation the rights stated in Art. 14 (due process) and many other important rights. The Political Covenant is further weakened by the limitation clauses contained in Arts. 12, 14, 18, 19, 21, and 22.[25]

Of course, in accordance with the conditions stated in Art. 4(1), derogations are not allowed which would be in conflict with other international obligations of the derogating State; this paragraph could be construed to encompass not only treaty commitments of that State, but also human rights which are categorical or absolute.[26] Derogations which are discriminatory, excessive (not strictly required by the exigencies of the situation), or arbitrary are not allowed. Far too many possibilities for violations of human rights remain, however. Art. 4 obviously falls short of the protections stated in Art. 27 of the American Convention on Human Rights,[27] which contains a longer catalogue of non-derogable rights. Most importantly, Art. 27 prohibits suspension of the judicial guarantees essential for the protection of the non-derogable rights which it states.

---

also Art. 1 of the recently adopted Protocol No. 7 to the European Convention, which contains a provision limiting the right of an alien not to be expelled before he has exercised certain legal rights, when such expulsion is necessary in the interests of public order or national security. Council of Europe Doc. H (84) 5 (1984). Art. 12(5) of the African Charter on Human and Peoples' Rights, which is not yet in force, prohibits mass expulsion of aliens. Mass expulsion is there defined as expulsion aimed at national, racial, ethnic, or religious groups. 21 ILM 58 (1982).

[25] See e.g. *Hearings*, above n. 4, at 250.

[26] See Meron, *On the Inadequate Reach of Humanitarian and Human Rights Law and the Need for a New Instrument*, 77 AJIL 589, 601 n. 69 (1983). *Jus cogens* is discussed in Chapter IV, Section VIII, below.

[27] Buergenthal, *The Inter-American System for the Protection of Human Rights*, in 2 Human Rights in International Law: Legal and Policy Issues 439, 448–51 (T. Meron ed., 1984).

III. THE EFFECT OF DEROGATIONS FROM DUE PROCESS ON NON-DEROGABLE RIGHTS: THE RIGHT TO LIFE

The protection of the right to life from arbitrary deprivation[28] is the first and naturally the most important of the non-derogable rights enumerated in Art. 4(1). The due process guarantees enumerated in Art. 14 are, however, not included among the non-derogable rights. Because the right to life under Art. 6 is not absolute, the effect of this crucial omission is, arguably, that in time of emergency, when protection of the right to life is most critical, death sentences can be imposed following summary procedures, provided that the more limited guarantees stated in Art. 6 itself are observed.

The protections afforded by the Political Covenant compare unfavourably with those in certain other human rights instruments. The American Convention on Human Rights[29] contains a better formulation. Art. 27(2) of that Convention prohibits

---

[28] Lillich, *Civil Rights*, in 1 Meron (ed.), above n. 2, at 115, 121–2; Dinstein, *The Right to Life, Physical Integrity, and Liberty*, in Henkin (ed.), above n. 2, at 114, 116. See also Inter-Am. Ct. Human Rights, Restrictions to the Death Penalty (Arts. 4(2) and 4(4) American Convention on Human Rights), Advisory Opinion OC-3/83, Sept. 8, 1983, ser. A: Judgments and Opinions No. 3. Regarding the work begun on the elaboration of a Second Optional Protocol to the International Covenant on Civil and Political Rights, Aiming at the Abolition of the Death Penalty, see UN Doc. A/39/535 (1984).

For examples of violations by States of the guarantees of the right to life stated in Art. 6 of the Political Covenant, see S. Wako, Report on Summary or Arbitrary Executions 21–4, UN Doc. E/CN.4/1985/17 (1985).

Wako's review of the national legislation 'made it clear that a number of exceptions, in the form of legislation, decisions or executive decrees, have been made to the national legislation applicable in normal situations in regard to safeguards of the right to life. The Special Rapporteur considers a disturbing trend with negative effects on the protection of the right to life, rendering the guarantees provided in the constitutions and other legislation meaningless. In such a context, summary or arbitrary executions can take place despite the safeguards of the right to life meticulously stipulated in national legislation in conformity with the International Covenant on Civil and Political Rights.'

Ibid. para. 74.

In a desire to strengthen the international instruments relating to the prevention of arbitrary or summary executions, which are continuing to take place, ECOSOC has recently approved 'Safeguards Guaranteeing Protection of the Rights of those Facing the Death Penalty', as recommended by the Committee on Crime Prevention and Control. ECOSOC Res. 1984/50, UN Doc. E/1984/INF/4, at 73 (1984). See also Ann., ibid. at 75.

[29] Above n. 24.

suspension of judicial guarantees essential to the protection of non-derogable rights. Common Article 3(1) (d) of the Geneva Conventions of August 12, 1949 for the Protection of Victims of War,[30] prohibiting 'the passing of sentences and the carrying out of executions without previous judgment pronounced by a regularly constituted court, affording all the judicial guarantees which are recognized as indispensable by civilized peoples', is also a better formulation. Although the due process provisions contained in Arts. 5 and 6 of the European Convention for the Protection of Human Rights and Fundamental Freedoms[31] are not included among the non-derogable provisions mentioned in Art. 15 of that Convention, the Council of Europe recently took an important step forward in adopting Protocol No. 6 to the European Convention, concerning the abolition of the death penalty.[32] Under Arts. 1 and 2 of that protocol, the death penalty shall be abolished, except that States may make provision in their laws for the death penalty with respect to acts committed in time of war or of the imminent threat of war. Any 'other public emergency threatening the life of the nation', mentioned in Art. 15 of the European Convention is thus excluded. Art. 3 provides that '[n]o derogation from the provisions of this Protocol shall be made under Article 15 of the Convention'.

A draft resolution proposed in the UN Commission on Human Rights, following the Questiaux Report, requested that ECOSOC:

authorize the Sub-Commission to appoint one of its members to undertake a closer study of the advisability of strengthening and extending the inalienability of the rights enumerated in article 4, paragraph 2 of the . . . Covenant . . ., with due consideration being given to national legislations as well as to relevant international and regional conventions . . . .[33]

Unfortunately, this language was greatly weakened in the revised draft resolution.[34] The UN General Assembly, however,

---

[30]   See e.g. Geneva Convention No. IV, above n. 24.
[31]   213 UNTS 221.
[32]   Council of Europe Doc. H. (83) 3 (1983).
[33]   UN Doc. E/CN.4/1983/L.29 (1983). For the Questiaux report, see above n. 13 and accompanying text.
[34]   UN Doc. E/CN.4/1983/L.29/Rev.1 (1983), which was adopted on 22 Feb. 1983, as Res. 1983/18, UN Doc. E/CN.4/1983/L.10/Add.2, at 6 (1983).

requested that the Commission on Human Rights consider elaborating a draft of a second optional protocol to the Political Covenant, aiming at the abolition of the death penalty.[35] The Commission has referred the matter to the Sub-Commission.[36]

As observed above, the effect of the derogability of Art. 14 is that in times of emergency, when due process rights are suspended, death sentences can arguably be imposed following summary procedures. The protection provided by Art. 6(2), which states that the death penalty can only be carried out pursuant to a final judgment rendered by a competent court, is illusory because the State can decide what a competent court is in a time of emergency. If the measures taken by the State can be viewed as 'arbitrary' under Art. 6(1), however, that provision would prohibit the imposition of death sentences under such circumstances. In an important report, Wako has thus argued that

[t]he term 'arbitrarily' in Article 6(1) of the Covenant coupled with the provision in Article 6(2) that the sentence of death may not be imposed 'contrary to the provisions of this Covenant,' can be interpreted to mean that the procedural safeguards of Article 14 cannot be derogated from even during public emergency in the hearing of a case where a death penalty can be imposed. Article 6(2) has the effect of bringing the procedural guarantees within the entrenched provisions as it relates to the death penalty.[37]

If the absence of Art. 14 from the list of non-derogable provisions meant that summary executions were permitted in states of emergency, '[t]his would be a paradoxical result since judicial guarantees are recognized in more serious conflicts by the Geneva Conventions'.[38] The matter is, however, far from simple. Proceedings which are in conflict with the due process norms of Art. 14 may also constitute a violation of Art. 6 if they lead to an arbitrary deprivation of life within the meaning of the latter article, or when they conflict with other guarantees

---

[35] GA Res. 37/192, 37 UN GAOR Supp. (No. 51) at 209–10, UN Doc. A/37/51 (1982).

[36] Res. 1984/19, UN Doc. E/1984/14, E/CN./4/1984/77, at 53. See generally UN Doc. E/CN.4/Sub.2/1984/17 (1984).

[37] S. Wako, Report on Summary or Arbitrary Executions, UN Doc. E/CN.4/1983/16, at 14 (1983).

[38] Ibid. at 13.

stated in Art. 6. But when a suspension of due process norms of Art. 14 is not in conflict with the guarantees stated in Art. 6, and when Art. 14 is 'suspended', in compliance with Art. 4 can the imposition of a death sentence in violation of due process provisions stated therein be really 'contrary to the provisions of the present Covenant'?

In a case arising under the Optional Protocol, the Human Rights Committee stated that the killing by police of a suspect without warning during a state of siege which was notified to the Secretary-General under Art. 4(3) was disproportionate to the requirements of law enforcement and constituted an arbitrary deprivation of life contrary to Art. 6(1) of the Political Covenant.[39] The Committee emphasized that the right to life is the supreme right of the human being and that deprivation of life by the authorities of the State may be effected only for the most serious crimes: '[t]he requirements [of Art. 6] that the right shall be protected by law and that no one shall be arbitrarily deprived of his life mean that the law must strictly control and limit the circumstances in which a person may be deprived of his life by the authorities of a State.' In this case, however, the summary execution of several suspects by the police was carried out without any court proceedings (Art. 14 was not even included among the articles of the Covenant mentioned in the notification sent to the Secretary-General), making inevitable the conclusion that the killing was arbitrary. The decision by the Human Rights Committee was especially significant in light of the fact that the Political Covenant does not contain provisions governing the use of force by law enforcement officials similar to those in Art. 2 of the European Convention.

[39] Communication No. R.11/45, *Pablo Camargo* v. *Colombia*, 37 UN GAOR Supp. (No. 40) at 137, 146, UN Doc. A/37/40 (1982). Similarly, in Communications No. 146/1983 and 148 to 154/1983, *Baboeram-Adhin* v. *Surinam*, the Human Rights Committee was of the view that the victims were arbitrarily deprived of their lives contrary to Art. 6(1) of the Political Covenant. The Committee emphasized that '[t]he requirements that the right [to life] shall be protected by law and that no one shall be arbitrarily deprived of his life mean that the law must strictly control and limit the circumstances in which a person may be deprived of his life by the authorities of a State. In the present case it is evident from the fact that 15 prominent persons lost their lives as a result of the deliberate action of the military police that the deprivation of life was intentional. The State party has failed to submit any evidence proving that these persons were shot while trying to escape.' UN Doc. CCPR/C/24/D/146/148–154/1983, Ann. at 9 (1985).

In general comments regarding Art. 6, made under Art. 40 of the Political Covenant, the Human Rights Committee expressed the view that States Parties 'should take measures . . . to prevent arbitrary killing by their own security forces . . . [and that] the law must strictly control and limit the circumstances in which a person may be deprived of his life by such authorities'.[40] The Committee thus appears to support the view that killings by the security forces must be neither arbitrary nor unlawful. The Committee has also called upon States to take effective measures 'to prevent the disappearance of individuals, something which unfortunately has become all too frequent and leads too often to arbitrary deprivation of life'.[41] These general comments by the Human Rights Committee referred not only to those procedural guarantees which are mentioned in Art. 6, but also to those stated in Art. 14:

[i]t also follows from the express terms of article 6 that . . . [the death penalty] can only be imposed in accordance with the law in force at the time of the commission of the crime and not contrary to the Covenant. The procedural guarantees therein prescribed must be observed, including the right to a fair hearing by an independent tribunal, the presumption of innocence, the minimum guarantees for the defence, and the right to review by a higher tribunal. These rights are applicable in addition to the particular right to seek pardon or commutation of the sentence.[42]

The general comments on Art. 14, though reflecting considerable concern about the existence in many countries of military or special courts which try civilians, did not attempt to limit significantly the derogations from that article in matters pertaining to the right to life: '[i]f States Parties decide in circumstances of a public emergency as contemplated by article 4 to derogate from normal procedures required under article 14, they should ensure that such derogations do not exceed those strictly required by the exigencies of the actual situation, and respect the other conditions in paragraph 1 of article 14.'[43] The Committee recognized that when military or special courts try civilians, serious problems arise 'as far as the equitable,

---

[40] 37 UN GAOR Supp. (No. 40) at 93, UN Doc. A/37/40 (1982).
[41] Ibid.
[42] Ibid. at 94.
[43] UN Doc. CCPR/C/21/Add.3 at 4 (1984); 39 UN GAOR Supp. (No. 40) at 144, UN Doc. A/39/40 (1984).

impartial and independent administration of justice is concerned. Quite often the reason for the establishment of such courts is to enable exceptional procedures to be applied which do not comply with normal standards of justice.'[44] While acknowledging that the 'Covenant does not prohibit such categories of courts', the Committee expressed the wish that trials of civilians by such courts 'should be very exceptional and take place under conditions which genuinely afford the full guarantees stated in article 14'.[45]

In general comments on Art. 6, the Committee has argued cogently that the expression 'inherent right to life' cannot properly be understood in a restrictive manner, that it should not be interpreted narrowly, and that States must adopt positive measures for the protection of the right to life.[46] The Committee emphasized that while States are not obliged to abolish the death penalty totally, they are obliged to limit the use of capital punishment and to abolish it for other than 'most serious crimes'[47] (Art. 6(2) of the Political Covenant). While the Committee's attempts to give the right to life a broad interpretation most favourable to the individual deserve praise, the question remains how far such attempts can reach, given both the vagueness of the language of Art. 6 and the limitations on authority of the Committee under Art. 40. The Committee can certainly insist on a restrictive reading of the phrase 'most serious crimes' or emphasize that the death penalty should be 'a quite exceptional measure'.[48] But concepts of criminal justice vary widely throughout the world. While some States have abolished the death penalty altogether and some impose it only for the crime of murder or wartime treason, other States impose death sentences for a broad range of other acts, such as drug-related offences, economic crimes against the State, theft, and adultery. The phrase 'most serious crimes' therefore gives a virtually unlimited discretion to the State. The Political Covenant should have established criteria or guidelines or, at a

---

[44] 39 UN GAOR Supp. (No. 40) at 144, UN Doc. A/39/40 (1984).
[45] Ibid.
[46] 37 UN GAOR Supp. (No. 40) at 93, UN Doc. A/37/40 (1982).
[47] Ibid. at 93–4.
[48] Ibid. at 94.

minimum, specified those crimes for which the death penalty could be prescribed or, conversely, could not be prescribed.

As already observed, the Political Covenant does not contain provisions regulating the use of force by law enforcement authorities, despite frequent use of excessive force by such authorities, especially in the suppression of disturbances and riots. The Sub-Commission on Prevention of Discrimination and Protection of Minorities has recently expressed concern at 'the numerous occurrences in many countries of excessive and/or completely unwarranted use of force by law enforcement officials and military personnel during public gatherings, resulting in civilian loss of life or injury . . .'.[49] In considering the protection of the right to life, the Human Rights Committee has raised questions concerning the use of arms by the security forces in such situations.[50] It is regrettable that the Political Covenant does not include provisions prohibiting the use of force by law enforcement officials unless such use is absolutely required,[51] based on the principle of proportionality between the objective to be attained and the degree of force used.[52]

Yet another problem arises in connection with Art. 6(5) of the Political Covenant, which prohibits the execution of a death sentence on a pregnant woman. The language of the provision suggests that pregnancy only postpones the execution until after the woman has given birth. The purpose of this provision is presumably to save the life of the unborn child.[53] The mother would be put to death at a time when the infant's survival and well-being would most depend on her, however. More liberal provisions are contained in humanitarian instruments. Article

[49] Res. 1983/24, UN Doc. E/CN.4/1984/3, E/CN.4/Sub.2/1983/43, at 91. See also Report on Restraints in the Use of Force prepared by the Secretary-General in accordance with Sub-Commission Resolution 1983/24, UN Doc. E/CN.4/Sub.2/1984/14 (1984).

[50] See, e.g. 33 UN GAOR Supp. (No. 40) at 49, UN Doc. A/33/40 (1978).

[51] See generally Code of Conduct for Law Enforcement Officials, GA Res. 34/169, 34 UN GAOR Supp. (No. 46) at 185, UN Doc. A/34/46 (1979).

[52] For a recent formulation of the principle of proportionality, see Arts. 51(5) (b) and 57(2) (a) (iii), Protocol Additional to the Geneva Conventions of 12 August 1949, and Relating to the Protection of Victims of International Armed Conflicts (Protocol I), opened for signature 12 Dec. 1977, reprinted in 16 ILM 1391 (1977). The use of weapons in violation of rules of international law applicable to the State concerned in international conflicts should be particularly prevented. Cf. Protocol I, Art. 36.

[53] Dinstein, above n. 28, at 117.

76(3) of Protocol I prohibits the execution of the death penalty on pregnant women or mothers of dependent infants, for an offence related to armed conflict, and Art. 6(4) of Protocol II prohibits the carrying out of a death sentence on pregnant women or mothers of young children.[54]

IV. PROTECTION *RATIONE PERSONAE*

Art. 1 of the European Convention on Human Rights and Fundamental Freedoms secures the rights and freedoms under the Convention (and its Protocols) to 'everyone within their jurisdiction'.[55] Regarding *jus standi*, Art. 25(1) states that the European Commission of Human Rights may receive petitions addressed to the Secretary-General of the Council of Europe from any person, non-governmental organization, or group of individuals claiming to be the victim of a violation. Various juridical persons have therefore been able to submit petitions under the European Convention.[56] Art. 1(1) of the American Convention on Human Rights assures 'to all persons' the rights

[54]   Concerning Protocol I, see above n. 52. Protocol Additonal to the Geneva Conventions of 12 August 1949, and Relating to the Protection of Victims of Non-International Armed Conflicts (Protocol II), opened for signature 12 Dec. 1977, is reprinted in 16 ILM 1442 (1977).

[55]   N. 31 above.

[56]   Buergenthal, above n. 10, at 73. See generally Frowein, *La Notion de victime dans la Convention Européenne des Droits de L'Homme*, in Studi in onore di Giuseppe Sperduti 586 (1984).

For examples of important proceedings before the organs of the European Convention instituted by companies, see The Sunday Times Case, Publications Eur. Ct. of Human Rights, ser. A: 30 Judgments and Decisions (1979); Sir William Lithgow and Others (Applications Nos. 9006/80 and others) against the United Kingdom, Rep. Eur. Comm. of Human Rights (7 March 1984).

Regarding 'representations' by industrial associations of employers or of workers, see Arts. 24–5 of the Constitution of the International Labour Organisation, Constitution of the International Labour Organisation and Standing Orders of the International Labour Conference (International Labour Office, 1982); Meron, *Violations of ILO Conventions by the USSR and Czechoslovakia*, 74 AJIL 206 (1980); ILO Doc. GB. 221/19/11 (1982); ILO Doc. GB. 222/18/23 (1983), reprinted in 66 ILO O. BULL. (ser. B, No. 1 (1983); ILO Doc. GB. 225/20/15 (1984); ILO Doc. GB. 228/9/19 (1984).

Regarding the work of the ILO Committee on Freedom of Association, see Outline of the Existing Procedure for the Examination of Complaints Alleging Infringements of Trade Union Rights (Issued by the International Labour Office, 1984); Reports of the Committee on Freedom of Association (234th and 235th Reports), 67 ILO O. BULL. (ser. B, No. 2, 1984).

and freedoms recognized in the Convention. In Art. 2(2) the Convention defines 'person' as 'every human being', thus excluding juridical persons from the protection of the Convention. However, Art. 44 recognizes the right of not only individual victims, but also of a 'group of persons or any non-governmental entity legally recognized in one or more member states of the Organization', to lodge complaints of violation.

The draft of the new *Restatement of the Foreign Relations Law of the United States* states that '[t]he contemporary international law of human rights, developed largely since the Second World War, is concerned with natural persons only, but deals with the obligations of states to all human beings, not to aliens alone.'[57] This statement, made perhaps in the context of the Political Covenant, may be over broad if account is taken of Art. 25(1) of the European Convention and Arts. 24-5 of the Constitution of the International Labour Organisation.

The Political Covenant is the least progressive of these three instruments in that it protects only the rights of natural persons and grants *jus standi* only to such persons. Yet, some rights ultimately benefiting individuals can best be protected by action taken by legal persons. In unambivalent language, Art. 2(1) states that each State Party undertakes to respect and to ensure to 'all individuals' the rights recognized in the Political Covenant. Similar language ('individuals') is employed in Art. 1 of the Optional Protocol with regard to *jus standi*. Buergenthal suggests that, these provisions notwithstanding, measures taken by a State Party against a juridical person may amount to a violation of the Political Covenant if they infringe upon rights of individuals, for example the right of association.[58] This interpretation is certainly sound, despite difficulties that may arise in the context of *jus standi*, and should be adopted by the Committee.

The case law of the Human Rights Committee is not yet sufficiently developed to determine whether Buergenthal's suggestion will be accepted. Thus far the Committee appears to have taken a rather negative position on communications submitted by entities, rather than by individuals. In the case of a

[57] Restatement of Foreign Relations Law of the United States (Revised) 446 (Tent. Draft No. 6, vol. i, 1985). See also above n. 56.
[58] Buergenthal, above n. 10, at 73.

communication submitted by 'an unincorporated political party' and by its leader, the Committee concluded that since the party was an association and not an individual, 'as such [it] cannot submit a communication to the Committee under the Optional Protocol'.[59]

The Committee has also rejected as inadmissible the communication of a group of associations for the defence of the rights of disabled and handicapped persons in Italy, Coordinamento (an NGO), and of the representatives of those associations who claimed that they were themselves disabled or handicapped or that they were parents of such persons.[60] The authors of the communication argued that an Italian decree violated the right of disabled and handicapped persons to work, thereby infringing upon Art. 26 of the Political Covenant. Invoking Art. 1 of the Optional Protocol, the Committee stated that '[t]o the extent, therefore, that the communication originates from the Coordinamento, it has to be declared inadmissible because of lack of personal standing'.[61] To the extent that the communication had been submitted on their own behalf by representatives of the associations forming the Coordinamento, the Committee found that it failed to satisfy other requirements set forth in Arts. 1 and 2 of the Optional Protocol. Under these provisions the author of the communication must himself make a substantiated claim to be the victim of a violation. The Committee noted that it is not its task to review *in abstracto* national legislation for compliance with obligations imposed by the Political Covenant.[62]

---

[59] Communication No. 104/1981, *J.R.T. and the W.G. Party* v. *Canada*, 38 UN GAOR Supp. (No. 40) at 231, 236, UN Doc. A/38/40 (1983).

[60] Communication No. 163/1984, *A Group of Associations* v. *Italy*, 39 UN GAOR Supp. (No. 40) at 197-8, UN Doc. A/39/40 (1984).

[61] Ibid. at 198.

[62] Ibid. The Committee insisted that 'individuals may not criticize national laws in the abstract, since the Optional Protocol gives them the right to bring the matter before the Committee only where they claim to be victims of a violation of the Covenant'. Communication No. 91/1981, *A.R.S.* v. *Canada*, International Covenant on Civil and Political Rights, Human Rights Committee, Selected Decisions under the Optional Protocol (Second to sixteenth sessions), UN Doc. CCPR/C/OP/1 at 29, 30 (1985) (thereinafter cited as Selected Decisions).

In another case, the Committee stated that '[i]t cannot review in the abstract whether national legislation contravenes the Covenant, although such legislation may, in particular circumstances, produce adverse effects which directly affect the individual, making him thus a victim in the sense contemplated in articles 1 and 2 of the

The Committee has rejected as inadmissible communications from a non-governmental organization, but based this decision not on the inadmissibility of communications from NGOs *per se*, but on the ground that 'a communication submitted by a third party on behalf of an alleged victim can only be considered if the author justifies his authority to submit the communication'.[63] In this case, the Committee was not persuaded that the author had the necessary authority to submit the communication on behalf of the alleged victim. When the existence of the proper power of attorney has been established, would the Committee admit communications submitted by an NGO on behalf of an individual victim? In principle, a victim should be able to select any representative before the Committee. When the author of a communication does not even claim authorization from the victim to submit the communication on the victim's behalf, and justifies action on the grounds that 'every prisoner treated unjustly would appreciate further investigation of his case by the Human Rights Committee',[64] a finding of inadmissibility is, perhaps inevitable. Difficulties may arise should the Committee insist on a clear power of attorney in all cases, because in certain situations a victim may be unable to communicate freely with an NGO. The interest in effective protection of individuals sometimes requires that NGOs be permitted to submit complaints on their behalf. Let us hope, therefore, that the Committee adopts a flexible approach on this issue when it comes up again.

The Committee's statement of policy on the standing of the author does not address the question of the standing of NGOs in their capacity as representatives of individual claimants:

Article 1 of the Optional Protocol provides that the Committee can receive communications from individuals who claim to be victims of violations of rights set forth in the Covenant. In the Committee's view this does not

Optional Protocol'. Communication No. 61/1979, *Hertzberg* v. *Finland*, Selected Decisions, above, at 124, 126.

It may be of interest to compare the above decisions with United States jurisprudence on the question of standing of claimants.

[63] Communication No. 136/1983, *X* v. *Uruguay*, 38 UN GAOR Supp. (No. 40) at 245, UN Doc. A/38/40 (1983). See also Communication No. 137/1983, *X* v. *Uruguay*, ibid. at 247.

[64] Communication No. 128/1982, *L. A.* v. *Uruguay*, 38 UN GAOR Supp. (No. 40) at 239, UN Doc. A/38/40 (1983).

mean that the individual must sign the communication himself in every case. He may also act through a duly appointed representative and there may be other cases in which the author of the communication may be accepted as having the authority to act on behalf of the alleged victim. For these reasons, rule 90, paragraph (1) (b), of the Committee's provisional rules of procedures [*sic*] provides that normally the communication should be submitted by the alleged victim himself or by his representative (for example, the alleged victim's lawyer), but the Committee may accept to consider a communication submitted on behalf of an alleged victim when it appears that he is unable to submit the communication himself. The Committee regards a close family connexion as a sufficient link to justify an author acting on behalf of an alleged victim. On the other hand, it has declined to consider communications where the authors have failed to establish any link between themselves and the alleged victims.[65]

The Committee has seen no difficulty in entertaining complaints submitted under the Optional Protocol by *several* individuals, or a group of individuals, or by one individual on behalf of a number of individuals, provided that each is a victim of a violation of a right set forth in the Political Covenant.[66]

In some cases it may be difficult to determine whether a particular person can properly be considered a victim. When presented with a communication concerning Mauritian statutes which imposed only upon the foreign husband of a Mauritian woman and not upon the foreign wife of a Mauritian man the obligation to apply for a residence permit in order to enjoy the same rights as before the enactment of the statutes, and which subjected only the husband to the possibility of deportation, the Committee decided that only the three co-authors of the communication who were married to foreign husbands could claim to be victims. Seventeen co-authors who were unmarried women were not considered to be victims of the alleged violations. The Committee stated that '[a] person can only claim to be a victim in the sense of article 1 of the Optional Protocol if he or she is actually affected'.[67] The Committee acknowledged that it was a 'matter of degree how concretely this requirement should be taken', adding that, '[h]owever, no individual can in

---

[65]   34 UN GAOR Supp. (No. 40) at 122, UN Doc. A/34/40 (1979).
For the text of Rule 90, see Selected Decisions, above n. 62, at 156.

[66]   See, e.g. Communication No. 16/1977, *Monguya Mbenge v. Zaire*, 38 UN GAOR Supp. (No. 40) at 134, 135-6, UN Doc. A/38/40 (1983). See also Communication No. R.9/35, *Aumeeruddy-Cziffra v. Mauritius*, 36 UN GAOR Supp. (No. 40) at 134, UN Doc. A/36/40 (1981).

[67]   Communication No. R. 9/35, above n. 66, at 139.

the abstract, by way of an *actio popularis*, challenge a law or practice claimed to be contrary to the Covenant. If the law or practice has not already been concretely applied to the detriment of that individual, it must in any event be applicable in such a way that the alleged victim's risk of being affected is more than a theoretical possibility.'[68] In the case concerned, there was, in the Committee's view, neither an actual interference with any person's rights, nor any evidence that any person's enjoyment of any right was likely to be affected. This conclusion was not inevitable. The Committee could have reasoned that the statutes affected the right of women to marry persons of their choice and that, therefore, these women could claim to be affected by a violation of Art. 23 when considered in conjunction with the provisions of the Political Covenant prohibiting discrimination. This question will be discussed further in Section VIII below.

[68] Ibid. In another case, the Committee stated that '[t]here are of course circumstances in which one individual must be regarded as having the necessary standing to act on behalf of another. But with regard to the present communication the Committee cannot accept . . . that there is a sufficient link to enable the signatories of the communication to act on behalf of the alleged victims who are not signatories to the communication. The Protocol grants to all the individuals concerned the right to submit communications, but does not, on the other hand, allow for an *actio popularis*.' Communication No. 1/1976, *A* v. *S*, Selected Decisions, above n. 62, at 17.

In a recent decision, the Human Rights Committee deemed inadmissible a communication submitted against Sweden on its author's behalf and on behalf of Arabs and Muslims who allegedly have been targets of discrimination in Sweden because 'the communication does not in any manner substantiate the author's claim that he is personally a victim of any alleged violation of the International Covenant on Civil and Political Rights [or] . . . that the author has any authority to speak on behalf of other persons . . .' Communication No. 183/1984, UN Doc. CCPR/C/24/D/183/1984, Ann. at 3 (1985).

In another recent decision, the Human Rights Committee deemed inadmissible a communication submitted against Canada by a retired member of the Canadian armed forces, alleging discrimination on the basis of language in the Canadian armed forces in violation of Art. 2(1) of the Political Covenant, on the ground that he failed 'to put forward any facts to indicate that he has himself been a victim of discrimination in violation of the . . . Covenant. An allegation to the effect that past or present promotion policies are generally to the detriment of English-speaking members of the Canadian Armed Forces is not sufficient in this respect.' The Committee noted that Arts. 1–2 of the Optional Protocol require that the author of a communication 'must himself claim, in a substantiated manner, that he is or has been a victim of a violation . . . of any of the rights set forth in the Covenant [and that it was not the Committee's task] to review *in abstracto* national legislation or practices as to their compliance with obligations imposed by the Covenant'. Communication No. 187/1985, *J. H.* v. *Canada*, UN Doc. CCPR/C/24/D/187/1985, Ann. at 3 (1985).

The place of residence of the individual author of a communication submitted under the Optional Protocol is of no relevance to the competence of the Committee. The Committee has thus considered as admissible complaints against Zaire by Zairian citizens residing in Belgium for violations of the Covenant committed in Zaire.[69]

V. PROTECTION *RATIONE LOCI*

A serious problem arises concerning the territorial scope of applicability of the Political Covenant. Art. 2(1) provides that each State Party undertakes to respect and to ensure to all individuals within its territory and subject to its jurisdiction the rights recognized in the Political Covenant. Thus, even if a State Party does not derogate from the Political Covenant by invoking Art. 4, the Political Covenant as interpreted by some scholars would not apply to occurrences beyond the territory of the State concerned.[70] This would be a serious limitation in situations .in which agents of the State operate in foreign territories and, notably, in time of armed conflict, when whole armies are present on foreign soil. According to this view, individuals in such territories would not be protected by the Political Covenant. Difficulties may also arise with regard to the applicability of human rights instruments to the population of occupied territories.[71]

A better interpretation is that suggested by Buergenthal, who argues that the word 'and' in the phrase 'within its territory and subject to its jurisdiction', 'should be read as a disjunctive conjunction, indicating that a State Party must be deemed to have assumed the obligation to respect and to ensure the rights recognized in the Covenant "to all individuals within its territory" *and* "to all individuals subject to its jurisdiction"'.[72]

There is a striking difference between the language of Art. 2(1) of the Political Covenant and that of Art. 1(1) of its

---

[69]   Communication No. 16/1977, above n. 66, at 134, 135-6.

[70]   Schindler, *Human Rights and Humanitarian Law*, 31 Am. U. L. Rev. 935, 939 (1982).

[71]   See generally Meron, *Applicability of Multilateral Conventions to Occupied Territories*, 72 AJIL 542 (1978).

[72]   Buergenthal, above n. 10, at 74.

companion instrument, the Optional Protocol. The latter states that a State Party to the Political Covenant that becomes a party to the Protocol recognizes the competence of the Human Rights Committee to receive and consider communications from individuals 'subject to its jurisdiction', without any reference to 'territory'. It is distressing that this discrepancy should have been allowed to occur. The language of the Optional Protocol, formulated after the language of Art. 2(1) of the Political Covenant had been completed, supports Buergenthal's interpretation.

A similar position was taken by the Committee in general comments on Art. 2, made under Art. 40 of the Political Covenant, in which the Committee mentioned the undertaking of States Parties to ensure the enjoyment of rights 'to all individuals under their jurisdiction',[73] without any reference to the phrase 'within its territory'. The language of Art. 2(1) of the Political Covenant has been explicitly addressed by the Committee in its consideration of communications under Art. 5(4) of the Optional Protocol. One such case concerned the

---

[73] 36 UN GAOR Supp. (No. 40) at 109, UN Doc. A/36/40 (1981).
It should be noted that a similar interpretative approach was adopted in the case law of the European Commission of Human Rights. Thus, with regard to the applicability of the European Convention on Human Rights in the parts of Cyprus occupied by Turkey, and the Commission's competence *ratione loci*, the Commission stated: 'In Art. 1 of the Convention, the High Contracting Parties undertake to secure the rights and freedoms defined in Section 1 to everyone 'within their jurisdiction' (in the French text: 'relevant de leur juridiction'). The Commission finds that this term is not, as submitted by the respondent Government, equivalent to or limited to the national territory of the High Contracting Party concerned. It is clear from the language, in particular of the French text, and the object of this Article, and from the purpose of the Convention as a whole, that the High Contracting Parties are bound to secure the said rights and freedoms to all persons under their actual authority and responsibility, whether that authority is exercised within their own territory or abroad. . . .
The Commission further observes that nationals of a State, including registered ships and aircrafts [*sic*] are partly within its jurisdiction wherever they may be, and that authorised agents of a State, including diplomatic or consular agents and armed forces, not only remain under its jurisdiction when abroad but bring any other persons or property 'within the jurisdiction' of that State, to the extent that they exercise authority over such persons or property. Insofar as, by their acts or omissions, they affect such persons or property, the responsibility of the State is engaged.' Application No. 6780/74 & 6950/75, *Cyprus* v. *Turkey*, Eur. Comm. of Human Rights, 2 Decisions and Reports 125, 136 (1975), reprinted in [1975] Y.B. Eur. Conv. on Human Rights 82, 118. See also Application No. 8007/77, *Cyprus* v. *Turkey*, Eur. Comm. of Human Rights, 13 Decisions and Reports 85, 148-9 (1979), reprinted in [1978] Y.B. Eur. Conv. on Human Rights 100, 230-4.

abduction of the victim by agents of the respondent State and his forcible transfer to the latter's territory. The Committee observed that although the arrest and the initial mistreatment of the victim allegedly took place on foreign territory, neither the language of Art. 2(1) of the Political Covenant nor that of Art. 1 of the Optional Protocol barred the Committee from considering the case 'inasmuch as these acts were perpetrated by Uruguayan agents acting on foreign soil'.[74] The Committee construed Art. 1 of the Optional Protocol to refer 'not to the place where the violation occurred, but rather to the relationship between the individual and the State in relation to a violation of any of the rights set forth in the Covenant, wherever they occurred'.[75] With regard to the more difficult problem posed by Art. 2(1), the Committee stated that it 'does not imply that the State party concerned cannot be held accountable for violations of rights under the Covenant which its agents commit upon the territory of another State, whether with the acquiescence of the Government of that State or in opposition to it'.[76] Invoking Art. 5(1) of the Political Covenant, the Committee emphasized that 'it would be unconscionable to so interpret the responsibility under article 2 of the Covenant as to permit a State party to perpetrate violations of the Covenant on the territory of another State, which violations it could not commit on its own territory'.[77] In an individual opinion, one member of the Committee, Tomuschat, explained that the words 'within its territory' should not be given a strict literal meaning as this would lead to absurd results. This language was intended to confine the obligations of States to their own territory, when enforcing the Political Covenant outside of the national territory would be likely 'to encounter exceptional obstacles',[78] as in the case of the inability to ensure the effective protection of rights to citizens residing abroad. 'Never was it envisaged, however, to grant States parties unfettered

---

[74] Communication No. R.12/52, *Saldías de López* v. *Uruguay*, 36 UN GAOR Supp. (No. 40) at 176, 182, UN Doc. A/36/40 (1981). See also Communication No. 56/1979, *Celiberti de Casariego* v. *Uruguay*, Selected Decisions, above n. 62, at 92, 94.

[75] Communication No. R.12/52, above n. 74.

[76] Ibid.

[77] Ibid. at 183.

[78] Ibid. at 184.

discretionary power to carry out wilful and deliberate attacks against the freedom and personal integrity against [*sic*] their citizens living abroad.'[79]

In a case involving the claim of a citizen residing abroad to a passport, the Committee has considered *sua sponte* whether the fact that the victim resides abroad 'affects the competence of the Committee to receive and consider the communication under article 1 of the Optional Protocol, taking into account the provisions of article 2(1) of the Covenant'.[80] In this rather obvious case, the Committee stated that

[t]he issue of a passport to a Uruguayan citizen is clearly a matter within the jurisdiction of the Uruguayan authorities and [the citizen] is 'subject to the jurisdiction' of Uruguay for that purpose. . . . It . . . follows from the very nature of the right that, in the case of a citizen resident abroad it imposes obligations both on the state of residence and on the State of nationality. Consequently, article 2(1) of the Covenant cannot be interpreted as limiting the obligations of Uruguay under article 12(2) [the right to leave any country, including his own] to citizens within its own territory.[81]

Similarly, when a State claimed that a communication was not admissible because the victim had left the country and was therefore no longer subject to its jurisdiction, the Committee stated that the Optional Protocol was clearly intended to apply to individuals subject to the jurisdiction of the State Party concerned at the time of the alleged violation.[82]

VI. THE PROHIBITION OF TORTURE

Torture is prohibited by laws and constitutions of States and by international human rights instruments, and condemned by statements of governments and public opinion.[83] The prohibition of torture is generally recognized as constituting not only a customary, but even a peremptory rule of international

---

[79] Ibid.

[80] Communication No. R.13/57, *Vidal Martins v. Uruguay*, 37 UN GAOR Supp. (No. 40) at 157, 160, UN Doc. A/37/40 (1982).

[81] Ibid.

[82] Communication No. 110/1981, *Viana Acosta v. Uruguay*, 39 UN GAOR Supp. (No. 40) at 169, 171, UN Doc. A/39/40 (1984).

[83] Draft Restatement, above n. 57, § 702, Reporters' note 5.

law (*jus cogens*).[84] Nevertheless, torture is practised in many States in one form or another. States deny, however, that they practise or tolerate acts of torture, and join in the condemnation of such acts. Their laws and statements, as well as their actions such as support for the international instruments prohibiting torture, reflect both practice and *opinio juris*. The frequent acts of torture should, therefore, be considered as violations of the law and not detract from the customary nature of the prohibition of torture.

Art. 7 of the Political Covenant duplicates, except for the added reference to medical or scientific experimentation, the language of Art. 5 of the Universal Declaration of Human Rights.[85] Admirable as it is for its brevity, Art. 7 states a prohibition without a definition: 'No one shall be subjected to torture or to cruel, inhuman or degrading treatment or punishment. In particular, no one shall be subjected without his free consent to medical or scientific experimentation.' The absence of a definition and of criteria for distinguishing torture from cruel, inhuman, or degrading treatment (under the *Ireland* v. *United Kingdom* judgment of the European Court of Human Rights, the distinction derives principally from the intensity of the suffering inflicted)[86] and the high level of generality with which the prohibition is formulated gives rise to difficulties with regard to its application to concrete cases, for instance how is it to be applied to the many situations which fall outside the traditional conception of torture or cruel, inhuman, or degrading treatment or punishment? The same criticisms could also be made of Art. 3 of the European Convention and Art. 5(2) of the American Convention, which contain virtually identical prohibitions. The substantive norm must, however,

---

[84] Dinstein, *The Right to Life, Physical Integrity, and Liberty*, above n. 28, at 122; Lillich, above n. 2, at 127 and nn. 69–70; Frowein and Kühner, *Drohende Folterung als Asylgrund und Grenze für Auslieferung und Ausweisung*, 43 Zeitschrift für ausländisches öffentliches Recht und Völkerrecht 537, 539–43 (1983). See also *Filartiga* v. *Peña-Irala*, 630 F. 2d at 884, 890.

[85] GA Res. 217A, UN Doc. A/810, at 71 (1948); Lillich, above n. 2, at 126.

[86] 25 Pub. Eur. Ct. Human Rights, ser. A. para. 167 (1978), summarized in [1978] Y.B. Eur. Conv. on Human Rights 602, 606. For discussion of the difference between the position taken by the European Court of Human Rights in its judgment and the European Commission of Human Rights in its report (summarized in [1976] Y.B. Eur. Conv. on Human Rights 512, 792–4) on acts which amount to torture as distinguished from inhuman or degrading treatment, see Lillich, above n. 2, at 128–30; Frowein and Kühner, above n. 84, at 544–6.

be considered in the context of the character, functions, and competence of the control organs which have been established under the several instruments. The European Commission of Human Rights and the European Court of Human Rights have developed a rich jurisprudence on Art. 3 of the European Convention (which provides that '[n]o one shall be subjected to torture or to inhuman or degrading treatment or punishment').[87] The case law of the Commission and the Court has given a meaningful and workable definition and interpretation to the concepts of torture and inhuman or degrading treatment or punishment, thus supplementing the imperfect text of Art. 3. In contrast, and as discussed further in Section IX below, except under the Optional Protocol, the Human Rights Committee has no competence to determine that a particular State Party has committed torture. The 'views' adopted by the Committee under Art. 5(4) of the Optional Protocol and containing findings of inhuman treatment or torture (mostly by Uruguay) and, thus, of violations of Art. 7 of the Political Covenant, while important, have failed to elaborate on the concept of the prohibition stated in Art. 7 and to develop a definition of torture or of cruel, inhuman, or degrading treatment or punishment.[88] In 1982, the Committee attempted to fill the void.

[87] For discussion of the jurisprudence of the European Court of Human Rights and the European Commission of Human Rights, see Duffy, *Article 3 of the European Convention on Human Rights*, 32 Int'l & Comp. L.Q. 316 (1983); Spjut, *Torture under the European Convention on Human Rights*, 73 AJIL 267 (1979); O'Boyle, *Torture and Emergency Powers under the European Convention on Human Rights: Ireland* v. *The United Kingdom*, 71 AJIL 674 (1977); Higgins, *The European Convention on Human Rights*, in 2 Meron (ed.), above n. 2, at 495, 511-15.

[88] See Communication No. 4/1977, *Torres Ramírez* v. *Uruguay*, Selected Decisions, above n. 62, at 49; Communication No. 5/1977, *Hernández Valentini de Bazzano* v. *Uruguay*, ibid. at 40; Communication No. 8/1977, *Garcia Lanza de Netto* v. *Uruguay*, ibid. at 45; Communication No. 11/1977, *Grille Motta* v. *Uruguay*, ibid. at 54; Communication No. 28/1978, *Weinberger Weisz* v. *Uruguay*, ibid. at 57; Communication No. 30/1978, *Bleier Lewenhoff* v. *Uruguay*, ibid. at 109; Communication No. 33/1978, *Buffo Carballal* v. *Uruguay*, ibid. at 63; Communication No. 52/1979, *Saldías de López* v. *Uruguay*, ibid. at 88; Communication No. 63/1979, *Setelich* v. *Uruguay*, ibid. at 101; Communication No. 37/1978, *Soriano de Bouton* v. *Uruguay*, ibid. at 72; Communication No. 73/1980, *Teti Izquierdo* v. *Uruguay*, ibid. at 132; Communication No. 49/1979, *Marais* v. *Madagascar*, 38 UN GAOR Supp. (No. 40) at 141; UN Doc. A/38/40 (1983); Communication No. 74/1980, *Estrella* v. *Uruguay*, ibid. at 150; Communication No. 80/1980, *Vasilskis* v. *Uruguay*, ibid. at 173; Communication No. 88/1981, *Larrosa* v. *Uruguay*, ibid. at 180; Communication No. 110/1981, *Viana Acosta* v. *Uruguay*, 39 UN GAOR Supp. (No. 40) at 169, UN Doc. A/39/40 (1984); Communication No. 124/1982, *Muteba* v. *Zaire*, ibid. at 182.

The interpretation of Art. 7 of the Political Covenant advanced by the Human Rights Committee in general comments made under Art. 40 of the Political Covenant does not provide clear criteria for distinguishing *in abstracto* between torture and other prohibited acts of cruel, inhuman, or degrading treatment or punishment. The Committee limits itself to observing that such distinctions 'depend on the kind, purpose and severity of the particular treatment'.[89] Thus, the Committee follows, in effect, the criteria established in the case of *Ireland* v. *United Kingdom* and takes a broad and realistic view of the scope of the prohibition stated in Art. 7. It thus regards Art. 7 as extending to corporal punishment, 'including excessive chastisement as an educational or disciplinary measure',[90] as well as to solitary confinement, especially when the person is kept incommunicado. The Committee interprets this provision as protecting pupils in educational institutions and patients in medical institutions and not only persons arrested or imprisoned. It emphasizes also that it is the duty of public authorities to ensure legal protections against such treatment, even when imposed by persons acting outside or without any official authority.[91] The meaning of the words 'outside . . . official authority' in the Committee's comments is unclear, however. These general comments, while important, could hardly compensate for the normative inadequacy of the prohibition of torture and of cruel, inhuman, or degrading treatment or punishment and for the institutional weakness inherent in the inadequate powers given to the Human Rights Committee.

The need for greater specificity, and for a special control organ endowed with wider authority than the Human Rights Committee, were demonstrated by the decision of the General Assembly of the United Nations, in 1984, to adopt a special instrument: a Convention Against Torture and Other Cruel, Inhuman or Degrading Treatment or Punishment.[92] It is of interest to observe that, rather than aim at amending the

---

[89]   37 UN GAOR Supp. (No. 40) at 94, UN Doc. A/37/40 (1982).
[90]   Ibid. at 94–5.
[91]   Ibid.
[92]   UN Doc. E/1984/14, E/CN.4/1984/77 at 13 (1984); UN Doc. E/CN.4/1983/ L.2 (1983); UN Doc. E/CN.4/1983/63 (1983); UN Doc. E/CN.4/1984/72 (1984). For the text of the Convention, see GA Res. 39/46, opened for signature 10 Dec. 1984, 39 UN GAOR Supp. (No. 51) at 197, UN Doc. A/39/51 (1985).

Political Covenant under Art. 51, the void was filled by a new special instrument against torture, indicating perhaps the future direction for supplementing the weaknesses of the Political Covenant by the adoption of special instruments. Even in the Council of Europe, with its superior control institutions, work aimed at the elaboration of a new convention against torture has begun (discussed in Chapter IV, Section II (C)), but the goal of the Council's law-making project is the establishment of a system of visits to all persons deprived of their liberty, rather than the elaboration of a new definition of torture or of inhuman or degrading treatment or punishment. In contrast, the new UN Convention is a comprehensive instrument, providing, *inter alia*, for a more effective control machinery (a Committee against Torture, established under Art. 17 and functioning in accordance with Arts. 18–24) and for a detailed definition of torture contained in Art. 1(1), which provides as follows:

For the purposes of this Convention, the term 'torture' means any act by which severe pain or suffering, whether physical or mental, is intentionally inflicted on a person for such purposes as obtaining from him or a third person information or a confession, punishing him for an act he or a third person has committed or is suspected of having committed, or intimidating or coercing him or a third person, or for any reason based on discrimination of any kind, when such pain or suffering is inflicted by or at the instigation of or with the consent or acquiescence of a public official or other person acting in an official capacity. It does not include pain or suffering arising only from, inherent in or incidental to lawful sanctions.

The Convention's principal definitional article thus does not encompass acts of cruel, inhuman, or degrading treatment or punishment. These 'lesser' acts are addressed in Art. 16(1), which states that

[e]ach State Party shall undertake to prevent in any territory under its jurisdiction other acts of cruel, inhuman or degrading treatment or punishment which do not amount to torture as defined in article 1, when such acts are committed by or at the instigation of or with the consent or acquiescence of a public official or other person acting in an official capacity.

The Convention as a whole and, particularly its definition of torture, responds to an urgent need of the international community, which is amplified by the weaknesses of the Political Covenant, to attempt to suppress more effectively acts of torture and of cruel, inhuman, or degrading treatment or punishment. This is not to suggest, however, that the Convention is a perfect instrument. While it is not our intention to subject this Convention to a critical analysis, it may be observed, in passing, that in defining torture, the Convention takes a fairly narrow, 'classical' approach to that concept, focusing on acts by public officials who intentionally inflict severe pain or suffering, whether physical or mental, in order to punish, intimidate, coerce, or extort. In certain situations, mentioned in the above general comments made by the Human Rights Committee on Art. 7 of the Political Covenant, it may be difficult to determine whether a person is a public official or is acting in an official capacity. The Convention separated the definition of torture from the provision concerning lesser types of ill-treatment. It remains to be seen whether this separation was wise. Moreover, the Convention did not define acts which constitute 'cruel, inhuman or degrading treatment or punishment'. While no gap is allowed between torture and other acts of cruel, inhuman, or degrading treatment or punishment which do not amount to torture, the absence of the definition of the latter acts (the drafting of such a definition would be extremely difficult) is likely to exacerbate the difficulties inherent in distinguishing permissible from impermissible treatment.

VII. FREEDOM OF EXPRESSION

Despite its being recognized in constitutions and laws and proclaimed in international human rights instruments, freedom of expression is not regarded as constituting international customary law.[93] Indeed, in many countries freedom of expression is subjected to far-reaching limitations, whether temporary or permanent, for instance in the Soviet Union, whose Constitution allows the rights of freedom of speech and of the press to be exercised in the interests of the people and in order to strengthen and develop the socialist system.[94] Given the suppression of the freedom of expression in many countries, it is not surprising that the drafters of the Political Covenant have

---

[93] Restatement, above n. 57, § 702.
[94] Partsch, *Freedom of Conscience and Expression, and Political Freedoms*, in Henkin (ed.), above n. 2, at 209, 222.

made that freedom vulnerable to encroachments by the State. Freedom of expression is thus one of the 'weakest' rights in the Political Covenant, but this weakness is not a result of inadequate drafting or of insufficient research but rather of the lack of political support for a better protected right.

Freedom of expression is stated in Art. 19(2) of the Political Covenant as follows:

Everyone shall have the right to freedom of expression; this right shall include freedom to seek, receive and impart information and ideas of all kinds, regardless of frontiers, either orally, in writing or in print, in the form of art, or through any other media of his choice.

This is an important and fairly comprehensive statement of freedom of expression,[95] which is unfortunately emasculated by other provisions of the Political Covenant. Freedom of expression is thus subject to challenge from three possible directions: the derogation provision of the Covenant (Art. 4), already discussed in Section II above; the limitation clause contained in Art. 19 itself (Art. 19(3)); and the prohibition, in Art. 20, of certain types of propaganda.

Art. 19(3) reads as follows:

The exercise of the rights provided for in paragraph 2 of this article carries with it special duties and responsibilities. It may therefore be subject to certain restrictions, but these shall only be such as are provided by law and are necessary:

(a) For respect of the rights' and reputations of others;

(b) For the protection of national security or of public order (*ordre public*), or of public health or morals.

The limitation clauses contained in Art. 19(3) and in certain other articles of the Political Covenant have already been discussed in the literature.[96] While the need for some reasonable limitations on the freedom of expression may be conceded in the drafting of international human rights instruments for States with diverse regimes and cultures, it is obvious that Art. 19(3) (especially 19(3)(b)) states vague standards, defined far too broadly, which lend themselves to an almost unlimited abuse by States bent on repressing the freedom of expression. Not surprisingly, these clauses have caused considerable concern,

---

[95] For a discussion of Art. 19(2), see Partsch, ibid. at 217–19.
[96] See Partsch, ibid. at 219–22; Kiss, above n. 11.

especially in the United States, where they are far below the standard of protection established by the guarantee of freedom of speech contained in the First Amendment to the US Constitution,[97] as interpreted and applied through the jurisprudence of the Supreme Court.

The Committee has interpreted the limitation clause of Art. 19(3) in an interesting manner. In general comments made under Art. 40 of the Political Covenant, the Committee stated that restrictions on the freedom of expression may only be imposed subject to the following conditions: the restrictions must be provided by law; they may only be imposed for one of the purposes set out in Art. 19(3) (a) and (b); and they must be justified as being necessary for that State Party for one of those purposes. Since the purposes for which restrictions may be imposed are stated in broad and vague terms, the potential for abuse is great. The Committee ventured somewhat beyond the language of Art. 19, however, in stating that 'when a State party imposes certain restrictions on the exercise of freedom of expression, these may not put in jeopardy the right itself'.[98] It is doubtful whether that interpretation will limit the many restrictions on freedom of expression which may be permissible under the language of Art. 19(3), for instance when a State invokes vague terms such as public order or morals or claims that certain 'rights . . . of others' take precedence over freedom of expression.

In one of the cases arising under the Optional Protocol, the Committee acknowledged that 'public morals differ widely. There is no universally applicable common standard. Consequently, in this respect, a certain margin of discretion must be accorded to the responsible national authorities.'[99] The Committee thus refused to question the decision of the Finnish Broadcasting Corporation that radio and television are not appropriate forums to discuss issues related to homosexuality.

As already mentioned, the Committee's general comments mentioned the duty of States to provide justification of limitations made under Art. 19(3). Given the broad and vague terms

[97]   *Hearings*, above n. 4, at 250, 465.
[98]   38 UN GAOR Supp. (No. 40) at 109, UN Doc. A/38/40 (1983).
[99]   Communication No. 61/1979, *Hertzberg* v. *Finland*, Selected Decisions, above n. 62, at 124, 126.

of the limitation clauses of Art. 19(3), States can easily provide such justifications. But what is the situation when a State nevertheless fails to provide such justification? In a case arising under the Optional Protocol, the Committee pointed out, in the context of Art. 19, that the government of Uruguay submitted no evidence regarding the nature of the political activities in which the victims were alleged to have been involved and which led to their arrest, detention, and trial.[100] The Committee stated that information that they were charged with subversive association was not in itself sufficient and that the Committee was unable to conclude that the arrest, detention, and trial were justified on any of the grounds mentioned in Art. 19(3).[101] The failure of the government to carry the burden of justifying the invocation of Art. 19(3) did not lead to a finding of a violation of Art. 19. In other cases, however, the Committee has concluded that Art. 19(2) was violated because the victim was detained for having disseminated information relating to trade union activities,[102] or because he was arrested detained, and tried for his political and trade union activities,[103] or that there was violation of 'Article 22(1) [which provides for freedom of association] in conjunction with article 19(1) [which provides for the right to hold opinions without interference] and (2)', because the victim suffered persecution for his trade union activities.[104] All of these cases involved Uruguay.

Given the fact that Uruguay had not made great efforts to justify its acts by supplying the Committee with more ample information and by utilizing to the utmost the provisions allowing the imposition of restrictions on the freedom of expression, the readiness of the Committee to find that State guilty of breach of Art. 19(2) is understandable and important. It must, however, be emphasized that such findings are only possible in cases arising under the Optional Protocol, and not in the course of examination of reports submitted by States under Art. 40 of the Political Covenant.

---

[100] Communication No. 8/1977, *Garcia Lanza de Netto* v. *Uruguay*, ibid. at 45, 49.

[101] Ibid. The Committee has taken a similar approach in Communication No. 11/1977, *Grille Motta* v. *Uruguay*, ibid. at 54, 57.

[102] Communication No. 28/1978, *Weinberger Weisz* v. *Uruguay*, ibid. at 57, 60.

[103] Communication No. 44/1979, *Pietraroia* v. *Uruguay*, ibid. at 76, 80.

[104] Communication No. 52/1979, *Saldías de López* v. *Uruguay*, ibid. at 88, 91.

The challenge to freedom of expression advocated by the Political Covenant arises also from its Art. 20, which requires that any propaganda for war and any advocacy of national, racial, or religious hatred that constitutes incitement to discrimination, hostility, or violence shall be prohibited by law. The question of prohibition of racist propaganda is considered in greater detail in Chapter I. There is a clear conflict between Art. 20 and the First Amendment's guarantee of freedom of speech. This conflict made it necessary for the United States to formulate the following reservation to Art. 20 :

The Constitution of the United States and Article 19 of this Covenant contain provisions for the protection of individual rights, including the right of free speech, and nothing in this Covenant shall be deemed to require or to authorize legislation or other action by the United States which would restrict the right of free speech protected by the Constitution, laws and practices of the United States.[105]

In general comments on Art. 20 made under Art. 40 of the Political Covenant, the Committee did not contribute towards the protection of freedom of expression, simply stating that in its opinion 'these required prohibitions are fully compatible with the right of freedom of expression as contained in article 19, the exercise of which carries with it special duties and responsibilities'.[106]

The fragility of the normative provisions of the Political Covenant is thus amplified by the institutional inadequacy of its control organ. In an important essay on the freedom of expression, Partsch drew an analogy between the right and the duty of the control organs established under the European Convention and the control organ established under the Political Covenant to examine whether limitations imposed on the freedom of expression were permissible.[107] He concluded that '[w]ith all due regard to the differences between the organs of the European Convention and those established by the Covenant, the principle is the same. The latter, too, have the right and duty to review the state's decision that a restriction is necessary

---

[105] [1978] Digest of United States Practice in International Law 456 (M. Nash ed. 1980).
[106] 38 UN GAOR Supp. (No. 40) at 110, UN Doc. A/38/40 (1983).
[107] Partsch, above n. 94, at 220.

. . .'[108] This conclusion appears somewhat sanguine, especially if account is taken of the broad powers of the European control organs and the democratic form of government of the relatively homogenous States Parties to the European Convention as distinguished from the limited powers of the Human Rights Committee under the Political Covenant and the undemocratic regimes which prevail in many of the States Parties to the Political Covenant.

VIII. PROHIBITION OF DISCRIMINATION IN THE EXERCISE OF RIGHTS UNDER THE POLITICAL COVENANT OR EQUAL PROTECTION OF THE LAW?

Art. 2(1) states the obligation of every State Party to respect and to ensure to all individuals within its territory and subject to its jurisdiction the rights recognized in the Political Covenant without distinction of any kind, such as race, colour, or sex. Art. 3, while addressing only sex discrimination, similarly obligates States Parties to ensure equal rights of men and women in the enjoyment of all civil and political rights set forth in the Political Covenant. The prohibition of discrimination would thus appear not to cover matters which are beyond the scope of the rights set forth in the Political Covenant. Thus, under these provisions a national statute discriminating against women with regard to rights not stated in the Political Covenant would not be prohibited. The prohibition of discrimination would not apply to rights guaranteed by another human rights instrument or by custom unless those rights are also granted by the Political Covenant. Art. 26, however, states that all persons are entitled without any discrimination to the equal protection of the law. More importantly, it provides that the law shall prohibit any discrimination and shall guarantee to all persons equal and effective protection against discrimination on grounds such as race, colour, or sex.

One difference between Art. 2(1) and Art. 26 is the use of the term 'discrimination' in the latter rather than the word 'distinction', which is used in the former. Ramcharan has, however, demonstrated that, in the drafting of the Covenants, references to equality, equality before the law, non-discrimination, and

[108] Ibid. at 220–1.

non-distinction were used interchangeably.[109] These terms are discussed in greater detail in Chapter I above.

The difficulty in the interpretation of the Political Covenant lies in the fact that Art. 26 mandates equal protection of the law and requires that the law prohibit any discrimination, even in matters not protected by rights set forth in the Political Covenant. Ramcharan attempts to reconcile the apparent conflict between Arts. 2(1) and 26 by suggesting that because equal protection of the law is guaranteed in the latter article, equal protection can be regarded as a right recognized in the Political Covenant for the purposes of Art. 2(1).[110] This argument is attractive, but, perhaps, not entirely convincing. The prohibition of discrimination stated in Art. 2(1) encompasses all substantive rights granted by the Political Covenant, whether normative or procedural in nature. Art. 26 addresses, however, an unlimited spectrum of national laws *en dehors* the Political Covenant. If Art. 2(1) states that rights a, b, and c are covered by the prohibition of discrimination, Art. 26 would, according to Ramcharan's interpretation, add a prohibition of discrimination with regard to all the national laws, whatever their subject, thus outlawing discrimination in general. Obviously, there is a clear conflict between Arts. 2(1) and 26, which can be explained by the fact that Art. 26 was adopted much later than Art. 2(1) and by a considerably different composition of States.[111] The preparatory work by the drafters provides no guidance regarding the interpretation of these provisions and their possible reconciliation.[112] Obviously, these provisions should have been redrafted before the adoption of the Political Covenant in order to avoid this conflict. As no evidence appears to be available concerning the intent of the drafters and both provisions have the same authority, the interpretative policy of the Committee is of the greatest importance. This policy determination clearly involves not only legal, but also political considerations. The general comments made by the Committee

---

[109] Ramcharan, *Equality and Nondiscrimination*, in Henkin (ed.), above n. 2, at 246, 251.

[110] Ibid. at 256.

[111] Ibid. at 251. On the conflict between Arts. 1(2) and 47 with regard to expropriation of property, see Cassese, *The Self-Determination of Peoples*, ibid. at 92, 104–5.

[112] Ramcharan, above n. 109, at 256.

under Art. 40 on Arts. 2 and 3 do not address the relevant questions.[113] In considering one case under the Optional Protocol involving discrimination, the Committee focused on Arts. 2(1) and 3 and gave only limited weight to Art. 26. In the case brought by Mauritian wives, discussed in Section IV above, Mauritius argued that since the Political Covenant does not guarantee the general right to enter, to reside in, and not be expelled from a particular country, exclusion or restriction upon entry or residence of some individuals and not others cannot constitute discrimination in respect of a right or freedom guaranteed by the Political Covenant, and can therefore not be a violation of, *inter alia*, Articles 2, 3, 4, or 26 thereof.[114] The Constitution of Mauritius did not prohibit discrimination on grounds of Sex.[115] The Committee found, however, a violation of Arts. 2(1) and 3 'in conjunction with' Art. 17(1)[116] and violations of Arts. 2(1), 3, and 26 in relation to Art. 23(1).[117] Regarding the significance of Art. 26, the Committee stated that:

the principle of equal treatment of the sexes applies by virtue of articles 2(1), 3 and 26, of which the latter is also relevant because it refers particularly to the 'equal protection of the law.' Where the Covenant requires a

---

[113] 36 UN GAOR Supp. (No. 40) at 109-10, UN Doc. A/36/40 (1981).

[114] Communication No. R.9/35, above n. 65, at 136. For a similar case arising under Art. 14 of the European Convention and a Report of the European Commission of Human Rights in favour of the applicants, see Application Nos. 9214/80, 9473/81, and 9474/81, *Mmes X, Cabales and Balkandali* v. *United Kingdom*, Report of the Commission (12 May 1983). See also European Court of Human Rights, Case of Abdulaziz, Cabales and Balkandali (15/1983/71/107-109), Judgment of May 28, 1985 (to be published as 94 Pub. Eur. Ct. Human Rights, Ser. A). The Court found a violation of Art. 14 taken together with Art. 8 of the European Convention. Ibid. para. 83. Art. 14 of the European Convention for the Protection of Human Rights and Fundamental Freedoms prohibits only discrimination in the enjoyment of the rights and freedoms set forth in that Convention. See generally Buquicchio-de Boer, *Sexual Discrimination and the European Convention on Human Rights*, 6 Human Rights L.J. 1 (1985); European Court of Human Rights, Rassmussen Case (9/1983/65/100), Judgment of Nov. 28, 1984 (to be published as 87 Pub. Eur. Ct. Human Rights, Ser. A); European Court of Human Rights, Case of *X and Y v. The Netherlands* (16/1983/72/110), Judgment of March 26, 1985 (to be published as 91 Pub. Eur. Ct. Human Rights, Ser. A).

Art. 1 of the American Convention on Human Rights follows a similar approach. Art. 24 of the American Convention concerning equal protection of the law does not contain a provision parallelling the second sentence of Art. 26 of the Political Covenant.

[115] Communication No. R.9/35, above n. 66, at 140.

[116] Ibid. at 141.   [117] Ibid.

substantial protection as in article 23, it follows from those provisions that such protection must be equal, that is to say not discriminatory, for example on the basis of sex.[118]

Art. 26 was interpreted to require equal protection of the law where a particular substantial protection is mandated by the Political Covenant, as it is in Arts. 17 and 23. If Art. 26 necessitates no more than this, then it is redundant, because with regard to rights guaranteed by the Political Covenant the obligation to ensure equal protection before the law is already clearly subsumed in the general prohibition of discrimination stated in Arts. 2(1) and 3. It remains to be seen whether the Committee will continue to focus on Art. 2(1) in future practice. Because of the emphasis placed upon the principle of equality in the United Nations, a shift of the centre of gravity towards Art. 26 may yet occur.

Such a tendency may be intimated by the tenor of the discussion which took place in the Committee in 1983 concerning the report of Australia.[119] This discussion turned on the second sentence of Art. 26. Members of the Committee expressed the view that the provision required equal protection of the law 'against any discrimination',[120] and thus, presumably, also against discriminatory practices by individuals, firms, and organizations. One member of the Committee disagreed and, invoking the intent of the authors of the Political Covenant, argued 'that Article 26 did not require that States should combat all types of discrimination, and that the Covenant was concerned only with the civil and political rights that States must guarantee'.[121] The representative of Australia insisted that his government's interpretation of Art. 26 'was more in keeping with the original intention of the framers of that provision'.[122]

The debate on the meaning and significance of Art. 26 will no doubt continue. An intriguing subject for further discussion would be a communication under the Optional Protocol complaining of discrimination violating Art. 26 of the Political

---

[118] Ibid.
[119] 38 UN GAOR Supp. (No. 40) at 27, UN Doc. A/38/40 (1983).
[120] Ibid. at 32.
[121] Ibid. On prohibited discrimination by individuals other than in personal and social relations under Art. 26 of the Political Covenant, see Ramcharan, above n. 109, at 262-3.
[122] 38 UN GAOR Supp. (No. 40) at 37-8, UN Doc. A/38/40 (1983).

Covenant in conjunction with a right which is not mentioned in the Political Covenant, but which is stated in the International Covenant on Economic, Social and Cultural Rights. The latter instrument does not include a procedure for the consideration of individual communications.

The emerging jurisprudence of the Committee on this question is not yet entirely clear. In one recent case, the author of a communication, who occasionally worked as a TV-repairman without the required licence from the Chamber of Commerce, claimed that he was 'discriminated against by Dutch legislation which prevents him from gainful employment and which punishes him for seeking an alternative to being unemployed'.[123] He argued that he was a victim of a violation of Art. 26 of the Political Covenant and invoked also Art. 6 (the right to work) of the Economic Covenant. Not surprisingly, the Human Rights Committee concluded 'that no facts have been submitted in substantiation of the author's claim that he is a victim of a violation of any of the rights guaranteed by the International Covenant on Civil and Political Rights'.[124]

IX. THE COMPETENCE OF THE HUMAN RIGHTS COMMITTEE WITH REGARD TO REPORTS FROM STATES

Art. 40(4) of the· Political Covenant provides that the Committee shall study the reports submitted by States Parties and that it 'shall transmit its reports, and such general comments as it may consider appropriate, to the State Parties'. Since Art. 40 is binding on all States Parties to the Political Covenant *ipso facto* as of the date of their acceptance of the Political Covenant and applies without any further actions on their part, the functions of the Committee under that article are central. Yet the article is poorly drafted and the powers of the Committee are ill-defined. Does the reference to 'general comments' mean that the Committee may not focus attention on specific violations by a particular reporting State and bring influence to bear on remedying those violations? The discussion of this

---

[123] Communication No. 178/1984, *J. D. B.* v. *The Netherlands*, UN Doc. CCPR/C/24/D/178/1984, Ann. at 2 (1985).
[124] Ibid. at 2.

question by the Committee in 1980 revealed considerable divergencies of opinion on the meaning of Art. 40(4).[125]

The majority maintained that since the Political Covenant imposed on the Committee a duty to study the reports, there must be a purpose to that study: namely to determine whether the State Party had performed its reporting obligations (for example whether its reports were complete and comprehensive) and, most importantly, 'whether it had implemented or was implementing the Covenant as it had undertaken to do'.[126] This practice would lead to the adoption of separate reports by the Committee on each State Party's report, for separate transmission to the State concerned, which could then submit its own observations under Art. 40(5). This view found some support in Art. 70(3) of the provisional rules of procedure which refers to a possible determination by the Committee that some of the obligations of a State Party have not been discharged.[127] The general comments would concern the results of an overall study of the reports, highlighting matters of common interest, such as possible amendments of the Political Covenant, the general nature of reporting obligations, the nature and scope of the rights set forth in the Political Covenant, and methods of implementation. According to the minority view, the study of the reports did not include any element of assessment or evaluation. Rather, the primary function of the Committee under Art. 40 was to assist States in the promotion of human rights, not to pronounce 'on whether the State parties were or were not implementing their undertaking under the Covenant . . . The Committee was not empowered under the Covenant to interfere in this manner in the internal affairs [*sic*] of States parties.'[128]

The 'Statement on the duties of the Human Rights Committee under article 40 of the Covenant'[129] adopted by the Committee in 1980 and the subsequent annual reports of the Committee suggest that the general comments of the Committee have not been specific in nature and have not

---

[125] 35 UN GAOR Supp. (No. 40) at 83–7, UN Doc. A/35/40 (1980).
[126] Ibid. at 85.
[127] Ibid. at 85 n. 7.
[128] Ibid. at 86.
[129] 36 UN GAOR Supp. (No. 40) at 101, UN Doc. A/36/40 (1981).

referred to particular violations by a particular State Party. The minority view, pressed adamantly by experts from Socialist States, thus appears to have prevailed. The Committee does not consider itself competent to evaluate whether a report by a particular State reveals violations of the Political Covenant. This unfortunate result could have been avoided had the Political Covenant conferred on the Committee a clearer authority to evaluate each report for compliance with the obligations under the Political Covenant. The new Convention Against Torture contains a better formulation. That Convention authorizes the Committee Against Torture established under Art. 17 to make comments and suggestions on the reports submitted by States Parties and to forward these to the States concerned. The Committee may also decide to include such comments and suggestions with the observations thereon received from the State Party concerned in its annual report made in accordance with Art. 24.

The Human Rights Committee has to a certain extent filled the gap left by Art. 40 of the Political Covenant by questioning the representatives of reporting States regarding matters about which the reports appear incomplete. These inquiries and comments by Committee members and the dialogue with representatives of the reporting State are recorded in the Summary Records and in the annual reports of the Committee. These exchanges may reflect satisfaction or disapproval with the situation prevailing in a particular State and are, therefore, significant. This practice, however, cannot be an adequate substitute for a statement in published reports of the Committee's considered opinions as to whether or not the reports by a certain State indicate compliance. The Committee has, however, taken a vigorous stand on formulating often important and useful general comments on problems of policy, implementation, and the interpretation of the Political Covenant.

Art. 40(5) provides that States may submit to the Committee observations on any comments that the Committee may have made. No requirement of compliance with the Committee's comments is stated. Had the Committee adopted the majority view regarding the nature of the comments which it should make, this provision would have been of major importance. In the present state of the Committee's practice, it reflects only one further weakness in a flawed, but extremely important, instrument.

The general comments of the Committee have proven to be important for the interpretation of the Political Covenant and for focusing attention on common problems in the observance of the Political Covenant and in reports from States. The Committee has adopted guidelines which give it a broad discretion in formulating such general comments.[130] The language of Art. 40(4), while not entirely clear, suggests that the general comments should be related to the reports. Nevertheless, the general comments made by the Committee, with regard to the prohibition of nuclear weapons,[131] for example, are not clearly related to the reports from States, and might expose the Committee to accusations of politicization.

One comment about the Optional Protocol is called for. Art. 5(4) provides that the Committee 'shall forward its views [not decision] to the State Party concerned and to the individual'. Although the acceptance in good faith of the Optional Protocol implies the duty to comply with the 'views' of the Committee, it would have been preferable to state *expressis verbis* their binding character.

X. CONCLUDING OBSERVATIONS

In this chapter, a number of important weaknesses of the Political Covenant have been discussed. While some result from a technically deficient drafting process, others reflect the more fundamental failure of the drafters to agree on better and comprehensive norms and on a more advanced measure of control of implementation. Yet other difficulties are due to the extremely general terms in which some provisions were formulated, and which were perhaps necessary for reaching a consensus. Not surprisingly, the technical and political problems met with regard to the more specialized human rights instruments, discussed in Chapters I and II above, are also to be found, sometimes amplified, in the case of the more general Political Covenant, with its wide range of provisions whose drafting has necessitated accommodation between different, and

---

[130]   39 UN GAOR Supp. (No. 40) at 106-7, UN Doc. A/39/40 (1984).
[131]   See, e.g. UN Doc. CCPR/C/21/Add.4 (1984).

often antagonistic political, economic, and cultural constituencies. The attention focused in this study on the difficulties should not, however, detract from the cardinal importance of the Political Covenant for the advancement and protection of human rights.

Some of these difficulties can be partially remedied by the Human Rights Committee in the course of its interpretation and application of the Political Covenant. Others would require amendments of the Political Covenant in accordance with Art. 51, but political consensus for the amendment of the Political Covenant is improbable in the near future. Perhaps rather than attempt to amend the Political Covenant, the international community will attempt to adopt more specialized instruments responding to its most urgent needs, as in the case of the already adopted Convention against Torture and Other Cruel, Inhuman or Degrading Treatment or Punishment or, hopefully, of the elaboration of a Second Optional Protocol to the International Covenant on Civil and Political Rights, Aiming at the Abolition of the Death Penalty, which is being considered.[132] Other subjects, such as the protection of rights of the human person in situations of internal strife[133] and for the elaboration of certain minimum non-derogable due process rights, also merit concern.

This trend to adopt more specific instruments may result in better instruments, as the range of subjects involved in political trade-offs is reduced, greater expertise is available, and public opinion plays a more focused and effective role. A consensus as to the 'existence' or the need for the 'progressive development' and effective protection of a particular human right is, of course, necessary to further the law-making process. The academic community can and should identify areas where more law-making is needed, and act as a catalyst for public opinion, thus encouraging the formation of consensus.

[132] See UN Doc. A/39/535 (1984). See also above n. 92.
[133] See Meron, above n. 26, at 589; Meron, *Towards a Humanitarian Declaration on Internal Strife*, 78 AJIL 859 (1984).

PART II

Relations Between Human Rights Instruments and Organs

IV

Normative Relations Between Human Rights Instruments

I. INTRODUCTION

HUMAN rights instruments are elaborated and adopted by many international organizations, including universal and general organizations (for instance the United Nations), universal and specialized organizations (for instance ILO, UNESCO, WHO) and regional organizations (for instance the Council of Europe, the Organization of American States, the Organization of African Unity).

The dispersal of law-making activities gives rise to instruments which may be inconsistent or mutually incompatible, which may overlap (not always undesirable for effective protection of human rights), or which may fail to address subjects that merit regulation. Jenks has observed, correctly, that conflict between law-making treaties is inherent in the nature of the law-making process, an imperfection which cannot be wholly eliminated[1] in the present stage of development of 'international legislative technique'.[2] In the situation now prevailing in the field of law-making co-ordination, one may agree with the notion of inevitability of conflicts among instruments adopted by different and autonomous organizations. Conflicts also arise among instruments adopted within the same organization, and even among various provisions of the same instrument, however, as demonstrated in preceding chapters. These conflicts are neither a necessary result of the decentralized nature of the international law-making process, nor are they always compelled by political or other 'objective' factors. Such conflicts are often caused by the failure to introduce effective and well co-ordinated law-making techniques in the organization. This is a weakness which

---

[1] Jenks, *The Conflict of Law-Making Treaties*, 30 Brit. Y. B. Int'l L. 401, 402 (1953) (hereinafter cited as Jenks, *The Conflict*).
[2] Ibid. at 416.

can be remedied. In comparing the law-making process followed
by the ILC with politicized multilateral negotiations, commentators have suggested that the latter 'often result in legal
inconsistencies both within the instrument [and] with other
norms of international law'.[3] A UN Secretariat study of the
multilateral treaty-making process has candidly observed that:

As the body of international law created by multilateral treaties increases,
greater and greater problems arise about possible conflict between treaties
already in force, whether on a world-wide or regional or otherwise restricted basis, and new proposed instruments. Naturally, identification of
the existing instruments that bear on the subject matter of a proposal is
always part of the research performed at some stage of the treaty-making
process by the secretariat of the organization concerned. This task is
particularly important in fields such as international labour legislation because of the large number of treaties that ILO and other bodies have
already originated in this area. The ILO secretariat has therefore developed
a particularly careful practice of identifying such treaties, including both
those within its own organization and those concluded or under consideration outside . . .[4].

The risk of conflict between various norms and instruments is
intensified by the fact that in the United Nations the policy has
been for each normative instrument to create its own system of
supervision and for each organ of supervision to apply only
those norms adopted in the specific founding instrument.

The development of an integrated and rational system of
international instruments governing human rights has a number
of goals. Unnecessary duplication, conflicts between instruments, and variations in the interpretation and implementation
of instruments adopted by different organizations would be
avoided. An integrated system would ensure that statutory
provisions regarding complex technical subjects are established
and supervised by the most competent organizations.[5] Given

---

[3] M. El Baradei, T. Franck, and R. Trachtenberg, The International Law Commission: The Need for a New Direction 22 (UNITAR Policy and Efficacy Studies
No. 1, 1981).

[4] 1 Review of the Multilateral Treaty-Making Process 25, UN Doc. ST/LEG/Ser.
B/21 (Provisional Version, 1982).

[5] See Annual Report of the Administrative Committee on Co-ordination for
1973–1974, UN Doc. E/5488, at 51–2 (1974).

The 1973 report of the *Ad Hoc* Inter-Agency Meeting of Legal Experts on Co-
ordination of Legislative Work of Organizations within the UN system suggested that
the concept of 'legislative work' should be interpreted 'in the widest sense as including all international and regional norms and standards designed to be applied by

the improbability that conflicts can be avoided completely, the object must be not only to try to avoid, reduce, or minimize differences by rational law-making procedures, but also to consider procedures and principles for resolving conflicts which may arise despite procedural reforms.[6]

II. THE RELEVANCE OF THE COMPETENCE OF CONTROL ORGANS

Conflicts may arise between rights recognized in the same instrument, or between instruments of the same universal and hierarchical order, for instance the International Covenant on Civil and Political Rights[7] (Political Covenant) and the International Covenant on Economic, Social and Cultural Rights (Economic Covenant).[8] The order of priority of classic human rights, such as civil and political rights, and social human rights, such as economic, social and cultural rights, presents particularly difficult problems.[9] While classic rights lend themselves, in principle, to immediate implementation, social rights can only be implemented progressively. This does not imply, of course, that classic rights are more important than social rights. It has been argued, not always bona fide, that developing States cannot be expected to implement the classic freedoms fully as long as they have not reached a level of economic development which enables them to implement social rights, and that those States must therefore give priority to social rights and to economic and social development in order to facilitate the

the member States of the various organizations, whether they were in the form of Conventions, Declarations, Recommendations, Resolutions and Regulations such as the International Health Regulations or Codex Alimentarius Standards, or model codes and other guides to national legislative activity.' Report of the *Ad Hoc* Inter-Agency Meeting of Legal Experts on Co-ordination of Legislative Work of Organizations, UN Doc. Co-ordination/R.1003, at 1 (1973) (hereinafter cited as Co-ordination Report).

[6] Jenks, *The Conflict,* above n. 1, at 405.
[7] GA Res. 2200, 21 UN GAOR Supp. (No. 16) at 52, UN Doc. A/6316 (1966).
[8] Ibid. at 49.
[9] For the distinction between classic human rights and social human rights, see Ministry of Foreign Affairs of the Netherlands, Human Rights and Foreign Policy 93-4 (1979); Trubek, *Economic, Social and Cultural Rights in the Third World: Human Rights Law and Human Needs Programs,* in 1 Human Rights in International Law: Legal and Policy Issues 205, 224-7 (T. Meron ed., 1984). The distinction between classic and social human rights should not be equated with that between individual and collective rights. See Humphrey, *Political and Related Rights,* in ibid. at 171, 171-3.

realization of civil and political rights. However, the two Covenants themselves attach equal weight to classic rights and to social rights.[10] Indeed, among international human rights instruments this accordance of equal weight is both admirable and rare. Furthermore, the UN General Assembly and the UN Commission on Human Rights have stressed the principle that human rights are indivisible and interdependent and have emphasized that civil and political rights should receive the same level of attention as economic, social, and cultural rights.[11] This guidance should be legally significant, despite its generality, not only to States but also to control organs which in the course of their work must often balance the different normative provisions and the community values underlying them. On the political level, however, this problem will continue to be troublesome..[12]

The problem is further complicated by the fact that the supervision of the two Covenants is entrusted to different organs: the Human Rights Committee for the Political Covenant and ECOSOC (acting through its Sessional Working Group) for the Economic Covenant.[13] When a particular control organ is competent to consider issues arising from a possible conflict

---

[10] See e.g. the Preamble to the Economic Covenant, the Preamble to the Political Covenant.

[11] GA Res. 32/130, 32 UN GAOR Supp. (No. 45) at 150, UN Doc. A/32/45 (1977), discussed in Donnelly, *Recent Trends in UN Human Rights Activity: Description and Polemic*, 35 Int'l Org. 633 (1981); Commission on Human Rights Res. 36 (XXXVII), operative para. 2, UN Doc. E/CN.4/L.1561/Add.4, at 22, 24 (1981).

[12] See generally Alston, *Development and the Rule of Law: Prevention Versus Cure as a Human Rights Strategy*, in Development, Human Rights and the Rule of Law 31, 47-54 (Int'l Comm'n of Jurists 1981); Trubek, above n. 9, at 224-5 and nn. 79-80.

[13] Sohn, *Human Rights: Their Implementation and Supervision by the United Nations*, in 2 Human Rights in International Law: Legal and Policy Issues 369, 376-7 (T. Meron ed., 1984). The working group originally established by ECOSOC decision 1978/10, and modified by decision 1981/158, was renamed by Resolution 1982/33 as the 'Sessional Working Group of Governmental Experts on the Implementation of the International Covenant on Economic, Social and Cultural Rights'. In 1985, ECOSOC decided to rename the Committee 'Committee on Economic, Social and Cultural Rights.' The Committee was to consist of eighteen experts. ECOSOC Resolution 1985/17. Regarding the co-operation of the ILO in the reporting procedure under the Economic Covenant and the assignment, within the ILO, of the reporting function to the existing Committee of Experts on the Application of Conventions and Recommendations, see ILO Doc. GB.201/IO/3/1 (1976). See also Meron, *Violations of the ILO Conventions by the USSR and Czechoslovakia*, 74 AJIL 206 (1980).

between various norms, whether in the context of one or two instruments, that organ should act much as national courts or other control bodies do in balancing different provisions of national law and different policies. In the international context, such balancing should take into account the accepted principles of interpretation of treaties[14] and other provisions of the Vienna Convention on the Law of Treaties (particularly Art. 30 governing application of successive treaties relating to the same subject-matter), as well as any other principles of law which may be appropriate. There is nothing unusual in the balancing of norms and priorities by control organs. Differences between provisions are thus often resolved through interpretation and application, and conflicts are avoided or reduced. This process is exemplified by the following cases.

A. *One Instrument — One Control Organ*

In a communication submitted by Sandra Lovelace against Canada, the Human Rights Committee had to balance not only the Political Covenant's provisions on non-discrimination and on protection of minorities, but also the provision on the right to choose one's residence and those rights aimed at protecting the family and children.[15] In examining the communication, the Human Rights Committee considered 'the extent to which the general provisions in articles 2 and 3 [of the Political Covenant] as well as the rights in articles 12(1), 17(1), 23(1), 24, 26 and 27, may be applicable . . .'[16]. The Committee concluded that Article 27, concerning the protection of minorities, was most directly applicable to the complaint. But taking into account also the limitation clauses to Art. 12 (regarding choice of residence), the Committee stated that certain restrictions on the right to choose one's residence, such as the government's right to define the category of persons entitled to live on a reserve in order to protect its resources and preserve the identity of its people, could not be ruled out under Art. 27. Such restrictions, however, must have both a reasonable and objective

---

[14] Vienna Convention on the Law of Treaties, Arts. 31-3, opened for signature 23 May 1969, UN Doc. CONF.39/27 (1969), reprinted in 63 AJIL 875 (1969), 8 ILM 679 (1969).
[15] *Sandra Lovelace* v. *Canada*, Communication No. R.6/24, 36 UN GAOR Supp. (No. 40) at 166, UN Doc. A/36/40, discussed also in Chapter I n. 111, above.
[16] Communication No. R.6/24, above n. 15, at para. 11.

justification and be consistent with the other provisions of the Political Covenant read as a whole. The Committee concluded that to deny Sandra Lovelace the right to reside on the reserve was not reasonable or necessary to preserve the identity of the tribe and, viewed in the context of the other provisions of the Political Covenant, constituted an unjustifiable denial of her rights under Art. 27. In light of this finding, the Committee concluded that an examination of the facts to determine whether separate breaches of the other rights invoked had occurred was unnecessary.

Thus, by limiting its findings to a breach of Art. 27 while recognizing the existence of some statutory restrictions affecting the right of a member of the minority concerned to residence on a reserve, the Committee could avoid addressing the conflict between the several provisions of the Political Covenant relevant to the Lovelace situation.

B. *Two Instruments — One Control Organ*

(i) Art. 2(1) of the Political Covenant provides that each State Party 'undertakes to respect and to ensure to all individuals within its territory and subject to its jurisdiction' the rights recognized in the Political Covenant. This language raises the question of whether the State is responsible for breaches of the Political Covenant occurring outside its national territory. The language of Art. 2(1) of the Political Covenant differs strikingly from that of Art. 1 of the companion instrument, the Optional Protocol. The latter addresses communications from individuals 'subject to its jurisdiction', (the jurisdiction of a State Party which recognizes the competence of the Human Rights Committee to receive and consider such communications) without any reference to 'territory'. The interpretation by the Human Rights Committee of these two provisions, in a manner emphasizing the obligation of States to respect and to ensure to all individuals subject to its *jurisdiction* the rights stated in the Political Covenant, was discussed in Chapter III, Section V above. The development of such a uniform interpretation of the two instruments and the resulting reduction of conflict between the instruments was possible because the Political Covenant and the Optional Protocol have the same control organ, that is the Human Rights Committee.

(ii) An interesting case arising outside the UN system of organizations is that of the difference between the language of Art. 1 of the American Declaration of the Rights and Duties of Man[17] (the American Declaration) and that of Art. 4(1) of the American Convention on Human Rights[18] (the American Convention). While the former states that '[e]very human being has the right to life, liberty and the security of his person', the latter adds that the right to life 'shall be protected by law and, in general, from the moment of conception'. It should be emphasized that the American Declaration has a normative character and is binding on all the Member States of the Organization of American States[19] (OAS), including the United States, which is not a party to the American Convention. The Inter-American Commission on Human Rights (the Commission) has certain control powers with regard to the observance of both the norms stated in the American Convention and the American Declaration. These powers of the Commission under the regime of the American Convention and the revised OAS Charter include the examination of individual petitions.[20]

In a petition submitted to the Commission by United States anti-abortionists against the United States, the petitioners alleged that the United States had violated the right to life granted by the American Declaration, as clarified by the American Convention, because the US Supreme Court had reversed the manslaughter conviction of a doctor who had performed an abortion in a Boston hospital.[21] The petitioners claimed that while the Declaration did not specifically state when life begins, the *travaux préparatoires* of the Declaration evidenced the intention of the Conference to protect the right to life from the moment of conception. Moreover, the petitioners

[17] For the official text, see Organization of American States, Handbook of Existing Rules Pertaining to Human Rights in the Inter-American System 19, OEA/SER.L./V/II.60, Doc. 28, rev. 1 (1983).

[18] For the official text *see id.* at 29. See also OAS TS No. 36, reprinted in 9 ILM 673 (1970).

[19] Buergenthal, *The Inter-American System for the Protection of Human Rights*, in 2 Meron (ed.), above n. 13, at 439, 475.

[20] Ibid. at 454–60; 470–9. See generally Organization of American States, Inter-American Commission on Human Rights, Ten Years of Activities: 1971–1981, at 82, 99–247 (1982).

[21] Res. No. 23/81, Case No. 2141, IACHR, Annual Report 1980–81, at 6, OEA/SER.L/V/II.54, Doc. 9, rev. 1 (1981).

asserted, the American Convention defined the right to life as beginning with conception and was 'to be read as a corollary document'. The United States government argued that the *travaux préparatoires* of the American Declaration suggested that it was incorrect to read that document as incorporating the notion that the right to life exists from the moment of conception. The United States conceded that the vagueness of the rights stated in the Declaration left substantial room for the Commission's interpretation, but maintained that that interpretation must be consistent with the intentions of those who adopted the Declaration.

The Commission concluded that the *travaux préparatoires* did not support the petitioners' claim that the Declaration incorporated the notion that the right to life exists from the moment of conception. The Bogotá Conference had chosen, in fact, not to adopt language which would clearly have stated that notion. As regards the American Convention, the Commission observed that the *travaux préparatoires* of the Convention indicated that to avoid conflict with Art. 6(1) of the Political Covenant it had been proposed to delete the phrase 'in general, from the moment of the conception', but that that proposal was rejected. The addition of these words did not, however, indicate an intention to modify the concept of the right to life that prevailed in Bogotá. Moreover, even had the American Convention established an absolute concept of the right to life from the moment of the conception, 'it would be impossible to impose upon the United States Government . . . by means of "interpretation," an international obligation based upon a treaty that such State has not duly accepted or ratified'.[22]

The Commission, as an organ competent to consider both the American Declaration and the American Convention, was thus able to interpret these instruments so as to avoid conflicts between the two. Whether consciously or not, the Commission acted in accordance with the presumption, well known in statutory interpretation, that '[w]here the interpretation of a treaty provision is doubtful, there is a presumption that the provision was not intended to be in conflict with the provisions of another law-making treaty of a general character'.[23] In situations

---

[22] Ibid. at 24.
[23] Jenks, *The Conflict*, above n. 1, at 451.

in which each organ is charged with the supervision of implementation of only one instrument, such a result might not have been obtained. International human rights law does not incorporate conflict of laws rules, and in a typical situation each organ tends to act in isolation.

The American Convention contains an interesting provision governing its interpretation in relation to the American Declaration and certain similar instruments. Art. 29(d) states that '[n]o provision of the Convention shall be interpreted as: excluding or limiting the effect that the American Declaration . . . and other international acts of the same nature may have.' Whether or not the provision on the right to life in the Convention has a more restrictive effect than in the Declaration is unclear. A conflict, which is not resolved by the texts of the Convention and the Declaration, occurs in the situation in which the protection of the right to life of the foetus endangers the right to life of the mother. In such situations state practice appears generally to accord priority to the latter. A conflict may also arise, however, between the former right and the freedom of choice of the mother. Some observers may view the latter freedom as precluded by the language of the Convention, but not by that of the Declaration. If the Convention's provision on the right to life is regarded as a restriction on women's freedom of choice (right to abortion) under the Declaration, Art. 29(d) should have constituted a mandate for the Commission to adopt the type of interpretation which it has in fact supported. As noted in a commentary, the Commission failed to mention this provision, although 'where the Convention appears to adopt a more restrictive formulation than that contained in the Declaration, the Convention itself arguably gives priority to the broader language of the Declaration'.[24]

If, however, Art. 1 of the American Declaration is viewed as protecting the life of the foetus, then Art. 29(d) would not necessarily be relevant, because the rights of the foetus are probably broader under Art. 4(1) of the American Convention (the ambiguity of the 'in general' clause notwithstanding). The explicit application of Art. 29(d) would have compelled

---

[24] Sheldon, *Abortion and the Right to Life in the Inter-American System: the Case of 'Baby Boy'*, 2 Human Rights L. J. 309, 315 (1981).

the Commission to discuss the scope of the right to life provision in the Declaration in relation to the Convention with greater specificity than the Commission may have wished. Given the ambiguity inherent in the provisions concerned and the sensitivity of the subject, the caution exercised by the Commission is not surprising.

C. *One Instrument or Two Instruments with the same Normative Basis — Two Control Organs*

Inspired by a proposal launched in the United Nations by the government of Costa Rica for the adoption of a Draft Optional Protocol (prepared by the International Commission of Jurists) to the (then) Draft International Convention against Torture and other Cruel, Inhuman or Degrading Treatment,[25] the Parliamentary Assembly of the Council of Europe adopted, on 28 September 1983, Recommendation 971 (1983), which recommended that the Committee of Ministers adopt the draft European Convention on the Protection of Detainees from Torture and from Cruel, Inhuman or Degrading Treatment or Punishment, the text of which was appended to the Recommendation. The proposed Convention which, at the time of this writing, is being discussed by the Committee of Experts for the Extension of Rights Embodied in the European Convention on Human Rights, provides for a system of visits to all persons deprived of their liberty, whatever the reason for the deprivation of liberty may be, by members of a special expert commission or by other persons acting for the commission. These visits to places of detention would include both periodic visits and such other visits as may be required. An interesting feature of the proposed system is that its aim is essentially to prevent violations, rather than to establish, after the fact, that violations have taken place. The operation of the system would not depend on the initiative taken by a person claiming to be a victim of violations. While the European Commission of Human Rights and the European Court of Human Rights 'could only be activated after the fact and after local remedies had been exhausted . . . . [the new Commission] could be brought into action without

---

[25]   For the proposal of Costa Rica, see UN Doc. E/CN.4/1409 (1980).

the exhaustion of local remedies being required'.[26] Although the proposed Commission would not have quasi-judicial powers, and its reports, findings, and recommendations would be confidential as a rule, if the government concerned fails to co-operate or refuses to comply with its recommendations, the Commission could, by way of exception, make public its findings and recommendations. Since the new Convention could result in an assessment of whether conditions of detention met the required standards, the normative terms of reference of the Commission are of particular importance. The draft proposed by the Consultative Assembly articulates in Art. 3 the principle of the most advantageous treatment applicable to detainees under domestic legislation or under other international instruments, such as the European Convention for the Protection of Human Rights and Fundamental Freedoms (the European Convention), but does not contain a clear definition of the normative basis which would guide the Commission. Art. 3, however, suggests that the European Convention would provide the normative framework for the work of the Commission. It states that '[i]n order better to ensure respect for and observe Article 3 of the European Convention . . . the Contracting Parties agree to supplement the procedure provided for in the European Convention . . . by creating a procedure for the protection of detainees from torture and cruel, inhuman or degrading treatment or punishment.'

The danger therefore arises of conflicting interpretations of the provisions of the European Convention on Human Rights by two or three different organs, the new expert Commission and the European Commission, or Court, of Human Rights. Various ideas have been advanced to avoid such a conflict. These include the creation of normative terms of reference which would not be related to the European Convention on Human Rights but to other standards, such as principles regulating

---

[26] Memorandum submitted by the government of the Netherlands to the European Ministerial Conference on Human Rights, Vienna, 19-20 March 1985, Council of Europe Doc. MDH (85) 6, at 3 (1985). Res. No. 2 adopted by the European Ministerial Conference on Human Rights urged the Committee of Ministers to have the work on the draft instrument on torture completed as rapidly as possible with a view to its adoption. European Ministerial Conference on Human Rights (Vienna, 19-20 March 1985): Texts Adopted at 4, 6, Council of Europe Doc. H (83) 7 (1985).

treatment of detainees, including the Standard Minimum Rules for the Treatment of Prisoners, adopted by the First United Nations Congress on the Prevention of Crime and the Treatment of Offenders, held in Geneva in 1955 and approved by the Economic and Social Council by its Resolutions 663C (XXIV) of 31 July 1957 and 2076 (LXII) of 13 May 1977, general principles of international human rights law concerning torture, inhuman or degrading treatment or punishment, and so on. Another possibility which has been suggested is to maintain the proposed normative relationship with the European Convention on Human Rights but avoid conflict by means of institutional measures. This would involve the establishment of functional links between the new Commission and the European Commission of Human Rights. The links would enable the latter body to assure conformity between its jurisprudence and the practice of the new Commission. Additionally, the European Court of Human Rights could be given the power to give rulings on the interpretations of the European Convention on Human Rights by the new Commission.

III. CONFLICT AND DIVERGENCE: IS THE DISTINCTION SIGNIFICANT?

Jenks has suggested that a distinction be made between a conflict and a divergence:

A divergence between treaty provisions dealing with the same subject or related subjects does not in itself constitute a conflict. Two law-making treaties with a number of common parties may deal with the same subject from different points of view or be applicable in different circumstances, or one of the treaties may embody obligations more far-reaching than, but not inconsistent with, those of the other. A conflict in the strict sense of direct incompatibility arises only where a party to the two treaties cannot simultaneously comply with its obligations under both treaties.[27]

According to Jenks, there is no conflict, but only a divergence, if the obligations arising under one instrument are stricter than, but not incompatible with those under another instrument, or if it is possible to comply with the obligations arising under one instrument by refraining from exercising a privilege or

---

[27] Jenks, *The Conflict*, above n. 1, at 425–6.

discretion accorded by another.[28] He acknowledges, however, that such a divergence may none the less defeat the object of one of the instruments and make it inoperative.

While the difference between a conflict and a divergence may be important in theory, the practical significance of this distinction is limited. It is indeed difficult to determine *in abstracto* whether a difference between norms contained in two instruments constitutes a conflict or merely a divergence. This determination can only be made *in concreto* taking into account the entire complex of relevant legal provisions, the reservations made, and the factual circumstances, including the identities of the particular States involved.

Even differences which do not result in a conflict, as defined by Jenks, are undesirable in the field of human rights, where the goals of uniformity and of the creation of customary law are important. As discussed further in Section IV below, human rights have an objective character as norms governing, for the most part, relations between governments and the governed. Human rights should not be viewed as mere separable contractual obligations arising between particular States. Differences among the standards set may prevent the attainment of normative uniformity in the scope of human rights, a goal which is especially important in the context of universal human rights law. Somewhat different considerations may arise when universal and regional human rights are contrasted because of differences in the stages of social, economic, and political development and in the types of universal and regional organizations which have been established. Moreover, there is always a danger that a State may take advantage of a dissimilarity in norms stated in two instruments to acknowledge only the lower standard of protection.

In discussing differences between standards set forth in various instruments pertaining to the international labour law, Valticos suggests that a conflict can only arise if two 'formal conditions' are met. First, the instruments involved must give rise to international obligations, that is the instruments must be treaties rather than recommendations. Second, a State must be actually bound by two separate instruments which mandate

[28] Ibid. at 451.

contradictory standards.[29] Beyond the field of international labour law, the first condition would appear, perhaps, to be somewhat formalistic. In an area of fluid and rapidly developing, often still 'soft' law, declarations and recommendations play an important role. Can it be said *in abstracto* that recommendations never impose legal obligations?[30] Cannot conflicts arise, for example, between one normative declaration, such as the Declaration on the Elimination of All Forms of Intolerance and of Discrimination Based on Religion or Belief,[31] and another normative declaration, and perhaps even between normative provisions stated in a declaration and in a convention? The form of an instrument is an important factor in determining the legal significance and force of the norms stated but it is only one of the factors to be considered. Indeed, the ILO itself has been exerting considerable efforts to avoid differences between UN draft declarations and existing ILO conventions, as is demonstrated in Section IX below.

As regards the second condition, Valticos suggests that a conflict does not arise when one of the two instruments provides for a higher standard of protection than the other, since the implementation of the higher standard necessarily entails the implementation of the lower one.[32] In international labour law this statement is based on the principle that, in the event of a conflict between standards, preference should be given to the standard which is more favourable to the workers. The principle that conflicts should be resolved by giving preference to the standard more advantageous to the individual concerned is commendable, not only in international labour law, but in international human rights area as a whole.[33] With regard to conflicts arising between non-ILO instruments, however, it cannot be assumed that this principle would be respected,

---

[29]   N. Valticos, International Labour Law 72 (1979).

[30]   On the importance of declarations, see Schachter, *The Nature and Process of Legal Development in International Society*, in R. Macdonald and D. Johnston, The Structure and Process of International Law 745, 787–95 (1983).

[31]   GA Res. 36/55, 36 UN GAOR Supp. (No. 51) at 171, UN Doc. A/36/51 (1981).

[32]   N. Valticos, above n. 29, at 73.

[33]   Ibid. Regarding the 'favourable to the individual' interpretation by the Inter-American Court of Human Rights, see Buergenthal, *The Advisory Practice of the Inter-American Human Rights Court*, 79 AJIL 1, 19–20 (1985).

except in situations where one organ (or two hierarchically related organs such as the European Commission of Human Rights and the European Court of Human Rights) is charged with the control of implementation of several instruments, or where the principle of the most favourable standard is stated in the governing instrument, as in Art. 29 of the American Convention and in Art. 60 of the European Convention. In other situations, States might argue that the principle of the most favourable treatment constitutes a principle *de lege ferenda* and try to benefit from the existence of two different standards by observing the lower of the two. They might insist on the application of the principle stated in the instrument which has established the control organ, even if it provides for a lower standard of protection than that stated in another instrument which is binding on the State concerned.

IV. POTENTIAL FOR CONFLICTS

Jenks has observed that multipartite instruments may give rise to the following classes of conflicts:

[conflicts] between multipartite instruments which, although concluded between identical groups of parties, operate in different functional orbits and sometimes within the framework of different international organizations, conflicts between a multipartite instrument and another instrument (multipartite or bilateral) to which some but not all of the parties to the first instrument are parties (*inter se* instruments), and conflicts between multipartite instruments the parties to which consist of groups which contain some, and in some cases a large majority of, common members but which do not coincide (a typical situation in connexion with the revision of multipartite instruments).[34]

A common difficulty arises where there are differences between an original and a revised instrument or between successive revisions of an instrument which are in force for nonidentical groups of States.[35] Jenks has lamented 'the imperfect development of the law governing the revision of multipartite instruments and defining the legal effect of such revision'.[36] Since the date of his writings the international community has, however,

---

[34] Jenks, *The Conflict*, above n. 1, at 404.
[35] Ibid. at 418.
[36] Ibid. at 403.

agreed upon a framework of rules to govern the interpretation of differences between an original and a revised instrument.

This framework is provided by Art. 30 and, to a lesser extent, by Arts. 41, 58, and 59 of the Vienna Convention on the Law of Treaties. Whether these articles provide adequate guidance for the resolution of conflicts arising between human rights instruments is, however, doubtful.

In the human rights field, a typical conflict situation arises when a State undertakes different obligations pursuant to several multilateral instruments. Since these obligations pertain to human rights, their contractual (interstate) element is less important than the normative protections which they contain. Human rights instruments differ in this respect from international agreements on other subjects. The European Court of Human Rights has observed aptly in the case of *Ireland* v. *United Kingdom* that

[u]nlike international treaties of the classic kind, the Convention [European Convention for the Protection of Human Rights and Fundamental Freedoms] comprises more than mere reciprocal engagements between Contracting States. It creates, over and above a network of mutual, bilateral undertakings, objective obligations which in the words of the Preamble, benefit from a 'collective enforcement'. By virtue of Article 24, the Convention allows Contracting States to require the observance of those obligations without having to justify an interest deriving, for example, from the fact that a measure they complain of has prejudiced one of their own nationals . . . the drafters of the Convention also intended to make clear that the rights and freedoms set out in Section I would be directly secured to anyone within the jurisdiction of the Contracting States . . .[37]

A similar position was taken by the European Commission of Human Rights in the case of *Austria* v. *Italy*, Application no. 788/60.[38] The special status of treaties of humanitarian character is recognized also in Art. 60(5) of the Vienna Convention, which provides that '[p]aragraphs 1 to 3 do not apply to

---

[37] 25 Judgments and Decisions, para. 239, Publications of the Eur. Ct. of Human Rights, ser. A (1978).

[38] [1961] Y. B. Eur. Convention on Human Rights 116, 138, 140.

Mendelson has pointed out that it is arguable that human rights treaties fall into a special category which is 'not susceptible of derogation by later treaties (at least in the absence of express indication of an intention so to derogate)' (footnote omitted), M. Mendelson, The Impact of European Community Law on the Implementation of the European Convention on Human Rights 13 (Council of Europe, Directorate of Human Rights, 1984).

provisions relating to the protection of the human person contained in treaties of a humanitarian character, in particular to provisions prohibiting any form of reprisals against persons protected by such treaties'. Thus, as pointed out by Sinclair, 'material breach by one of the parties to a treaty does not operate as a ground for termination or suspension where the breach concerns provisions relating to the protection of the human person contained in treaties of a humanitarian character, in particular provisions prohibiting reprisals against persons protected by such treaties.'[39]

A similar approach was taken by the International Law Commission's special rapporteur Riphagen, when he proposed the text of Art. 11(1) (c) of Part Two of draft articles on State Responsibility,[40] which states that

The injured State is not entitled to suspend the performance of its obligations towards the State which has committed the internationally wrongful act to the extent that such obligations are stipulated in a multilateral treaty to which both States are parties and it is established that:
. . .
(c) Such obligations are stipulated for the protection of individual persons irrespective of their nationality.[41]

Furthermore, different human rights instruments cannot always be regarded as successive treaties relating to the same subject matter and therefore as appropriate for regulation by Art. 30[42] of the Vienna Convention. The relevance of Art.

---

[39] See I. Sinclair, The Vienna Convention on the Law of Treaties 190 (2nd edn., 1984).

[40] UN Doc. A/CN.4/389 (1985).

[41] Ibid. at 21–2.

[42] Art. 30 reads as follows:

1. Subject to Article 103 of the Charter of the United Nations, the rights and obligations of States parties to successive treaties relating to the same subject-matter shall be determined in accordance with the following paragraphs.

2. When a treaty specifies that it is subject to, or that it is not to be considered as incompatible with, an earlier or later treaty, the provisions of that other treaty prevail.

3. When all the parties to the earlier treaty are parties also to the later treaty but the earlier treaty is not terminated or suspended in operation under article 59, the earlier treaty applies only to the extent that its provisions are compatible with those of the later treaty.

4. When the parties to the later treaty do not include all the parties to the earlier one:
(a) as between States parties to both treaties the same rule applies as in paragraph 3;

41[43] of the Vienna Convention (concerning agreements to modify multilateral treaties between certain of the parties only) to multilateral human rights instruments is not absolutely excluded. However, such instruments do not seem to lend themselves as a general proposition to modification by two or more parties as between themselves only, as distinguished from the revision or amendment of a multilateral treaty by all the parties in accordance with Art. 40 of the Vienna Convention. Moreover, as the ILO has observed, many of the instruments adopted within the framework of international organizations create legal ties not only between States Parties but also between such States and the organization concerned. The ILO has stated that 'one cannot conceive of an international labour convention relating to one of the fundamental human rights . . . being modified in respect of the mutual relations of some of the parties thereto by an *inter se* agreement among them.'[44]

It is entirely possible, therefore, that the provisions of the Vienna Convention will not provide the answers to the conundrums related to human rights which may come up in practice and that the reach and, sometimes, the very applicability to human rights treaties of some provisions of the Vienna Convention may be questioned. The question of the reach of the

(b) as between a State party to both treaties and a State party to only one of the treaties, the treaty to which both States are parties governs their mutual rights and obligations.

5. Paragraph 4 is without prejudice to article 41, or to any question of the termination or suspension of the operation of a treaty under article 60 or to any question of responsibility which may arise for a State from the conclusion or application of a treaty the provisions of which are incompatible with its obligations towards another State under another treaty.

[43] Article 41 reads as follows:

1. Two or more of the parties to a multilateral treaty may conclude an agreement to modify the treaty as between themselves alone if:

(a) the possibility of such a modification is provided for by the treaty; or
(b) the modification in question is not prohibited by the treaty and:
    (i) does not affect the enjoyment by the other parties of their rights under the treaty or the performance of their obligations;
    (ii) does not relate to a provision, derogation from which is incompatible with the effective execution of the object and purpose of the treaty as a-whole.

2. Unless in a case falling under paragraph 1(a) the treaty otherwise provides, the parties in question shall notify the other parties of their intention to conclude the agreement and of the modification to the treaty for which it provides.

[44] Co-ordination Report, above n. 5, Ann. II, at 10.

Vienna Convention to human rights treaties merits further study. In an advisory opinion ('The Effect of Reservations on the Entry into Force of the American Convention (Arts. 74 and 75)'),[45] the Inter-American Court of Human Rights viewed Art. 20, paras. 2–3, of the Vienna Convention, which concern reservations, as being inapplicable to the American Convention

inter alia, because the object and purpose of the Convention is not the exchange of reciprocal rights between a limited number of States, but the protection of the human rights of all individual human beings within the Americas, irrespective of their nationality. Moreover, the Convention is not the constituent instrument of an international organization. Therefore, Article 20(3) is inapplicable.

. . . the Court notes that the principles enunciated in Article 20(4) reflect the needs of traditional multilateral international agreements which have as their object the reciprocal exchange, for the mutual benefit of the States Parties, of bargained for rights and obligations.

The Court must emphasize, however, that modern human rights treaties in general, and the American Convention in particular, are not multilateral treaties of the traditional type concluded to accomplish the reciprocal exchange of rights for the mutual benefit of the contracting States. Their object and purpose is the protection of the basic rights of individual human beings, irrespective of their nationality, both against the State of their nationality and all other contracting States. In concluding these human rights treaties, the States can be deemed to submit themselves to a legal order within which they, for the common good, assume various obligations, not in relation to other States, but towards all individuals within their jurisdiction.[46]

International law does not contain general rules governing conflict of laws between different instruments and control organs. The question of whether such rules could be introduced as a part of general principles of law is an interesting one. In circumstances in which provisions governing the applicable law in case of conflict are not made in the instruments themselves, and the Vienna Convention on the Law of Treaties does not

---

[45] The Inter-American Ct. of Human Rights, The Effect of Reservations on the Entry into Force of the American Convention (Arts. 74 and 75), Advisory Opinion OC-2/82 of Sept. 24, 1982, ser. A: Judgments and Opinions No. 2 (1982). For a discussion of the special character of human rights treaties, see Buergenthal, above n. 33, at 20–3. See also Schwelb, *The Law of Treaties and Human Rights*, 16 Archiv des Völkerrechts 1 (1974–5).

[46] Advisory Opinion, above n. 45, at paras. 27–9. See generally, Reservations to the Convention on Genocide, 1951 I.C.J. 15; Imbert, *Reservations and Human Rights Conventions*, 6 Human Rights Rev. 28 (1981).

suggest a clear approach to resolving the conflict, a danger arises that particular norms will be applied without any consideration of norms stated in other instruments. A proposed framework of techniques for the elimination, reduction, and resolution of conflicts will be discussed later in this chapter.

Since the differences among the norms contained in various international human rights instruments are numerous, the potential for conflicts is virtually unlimited.[47] Normative differences commonly encountered include the following: (*a*) differences between two universal instruments dealing with the same or other subject-matters; (*b*) differences between a universal and a regional instrument; (*c*) differences between instruments protecting the same category of persons, especially when one instrument is broadly orientated and general and the other deals with a specific subject matter which may well be within the competence of a specialized agency or may embody protective standards of social legislation;[48] (*d*) differences between an instrument protecting a particular category of persons and an instrument protecting a particular right or freedom or dealing with particular subjects or problems.[49]

For example, important differences exist with regard to the scope of rights of persons in situations of non-international armed conflict under the derogation provisions of the Political Covenant and under common Article 3 of the Geneva Conventions of August 12, 1949 for the Protection of Victims of War[50] ((*a*), above). Important differences may also be found between the Economic Covenant and certain international labour

---

[47] For examples of possible conflicts, see Jenks, *The Conflict*, above n. 1, at 408–20.

[48] Jenks, *The Conflict*, above n. 1, at 415.

[49] Ibid.

[50] Convention for the Amelioration of the Condition of the Wounded and Sick in Armed Forces in the Field (Geneva Convention No. I), Aug. 12, 1949, 6 UST 3114, TIAS No. 3362, 75 UNTS 31. Convention for the Amelioration of the Condition of the Wounded, Sick and Shipwrecked Members of Armed Forces at Sea (Geneva Convention No. II), Aug. 12, 1949, 6 UST 3217, TIAS No. 3363, 75 UNTS 85. Geneva Convention Relative to the Treatment of Prisoners of War (Geneva Convention No. III), Aug. 12, 1949, 6 UST 3316, TIAS No. 3364, 75 UNTS 135. Convention Relative to the Protection of Civilian Persons in Time of War (Geneva Convention No. IV), Aug. 12, 1949, 6 UST 3516, TIAS No. 3365, 75 UNTS 287.

See Meron, *On the Inadequate Reach of Humanitarian and Human Rights Law and the Need for a New Instrument*, 77 AJIL 589, 599–602 (1983).

conventions[51] ((a), above). A State Party to the Political Covenant and to one of the regional human rights instruments in force (for instance the European Convention[52] or the American Convention[53]) is bound by significantly different normative provisions and even by different derogation clauses under the universal instrument and under the regional instrument ((b), above).[54] There are important differences, to be further discussed below, between the Convention on the Elimination of All Forms of Discrimination Against Women[55] and the existing ILO conventions on the work of women ((c), above). The Declaration on the Elimination of All Forms of Intolerance and of Discrimination Based on Religion or Belief[56] may contravene norms stated in the Convention on the Elimination of All Forms of Discrimination Against Women ((d), above).

Jenks has observed aptly that it is difficult to avoid inconsistency and conflict between statements of general principles, which cannot contain the various qualifications and exceptions necessary to make them workable in practice, and the detailed instruments which embody such qualifications.[57] Nevertheless, Jenks saw a lesser potential for conflict in the social field because the ILO was, in his opinion, the only specialized agency engaged in legislative social action on a large scale.[58] Since the time at which Jenks presented these views, however, the United

---

[51] The ILO has prepared a comprehensive study of these differences. See *Comparative Analysis of the International Covenants on Human Rights and International Labour Conventions and Recommendations*, 52 ILO O. BULL. 181 (1969).

[52] Convention for the Protection of Human Rights and Fundamental Freedoms, 213 UNTS 221.

[53] Above n. 18.

[54] Meron, above n. 50, at 601-2. For an interesting discussion of the possible impact of Art. 15 (the derogation clause) of the European Convention on the scope of obligations of the parties to both the European Convention and the International Convention on the Elimination of All Forms of Racial Discrimination (660 UNTS 195), see Buergenthal, *International and Regional Human Rights Law and Institutions: Some Examples of their Interaction*, 12 Tex. Int'l L. J. 321, 324-5 (1977).

[55] GA Res. 34/180, 34 UN GAOR Supp. (No. 46) at 193, UN Doc. A/34/46 (1979).

[56] Above n. 31. For a discussion of the use of the term 'declaration' in UN practice, see United Nations Action in the Field of Human Rights, UN Doc. ST/HR/2/Rev.2, at 318-9 (1983).

[57] Jenks, *The Conflict*, above n. 1, at 409-10.

[58] Ibid. at 417.

Nations has encroached on the field of competence of the ILO, at least in so far as migrant workers are concerned.[59]

The objective difficulties are aggravated by the lack of co-ordination within national governments, the differing political interests of various governments within various organizations, the special interests of international organizations, particularly the interests of their secretariats, and the overlap between certain provisions of the Charter of the United Nations and some of the broad constitutional provisions of the specialized agencies particularly concerned with human rights, for instance ILO, UNESCO, and WHO, as discussed in Chapter VI, Section III below.

Overlap occurs between comprehensive UN conventions and instruments of more limited scope adopted within the specialized agencies. Comprehensive UN conventions are often expressed in terms of general principles, and the selection of means for their implementation is sometimes left to the States' discretion[60] or to specialized agencies, particularly the ILO. The ILO has argued that these comprehensive conventions might well result in erosion, even without formal contradiction, of the more precise international obligations created by the more limited or specialized instruments.[61] Jenks, who was in part responsible for the general language of the Economic Covenant, has observed that the Economic Covenant and the Political Covenant afford substantially less protection for certain stipulated rights than do the relevant labour conventions.[62] Moreover, since each organization has its own machinery of supervision and many areas of human rights fall within the shared or concurrent competence of several organizations, governments may receive varying or conflicting guidance.[63]

---

[59] For a discussion of these developments, see Meron, *Norm Making and Supervision in International Human Rights: Reflections on Institutional Order*, 76 AJIL 754, 760 and at n. 39 (1982).

[60] Co-ordination Report, above n. 5, Ann. II, at 3.

[61] Ibid.

[62] Jenks, *Human Rights, Social Justice and Peace: The Broader Significance of the I.L.O. Experience*, in International Protection of Human Rights 227, 252 (A. Eide and A. Schou eds., 1968).

[63] Co-ordination Report, above n. 5, Ann. II, at 3.

V. WOMEN'S EQUALITY v. FREEDOM OF RELIGION: REFLECTIONS ON NORMATIVE CONFLICTS

Because the status as customary law of the norm prohibiting religious discrimination is not, as yet, entirely clear, the Declaration on the Elimination of All Forms of Intolerance and of Discrimination Based on Religion or Belief (the Declaration), adopted by the General Assembly of the United Nations on 25 November 1981, is of crucial importance.[64] Although not a treaty, the Declaration is not merely hortatory, but has a normative character, reflected in Arts. 4 and 7. Art. 4 requires States to 'make all efforts to enact or rescind legislation where necessary to prohibit' discrimination on the grounds of religion or belief and take measures to combat intolerance on such grounds. Art. 7 goes beyond the duty, stated in Art. 4, to 'make efforts' and requires that '[t]he rights and freedoms set forth in the present Declaration shall be accorded in national legislations in such a manner that everyone shall be able to avail himself of such rights and freedoms in practice'. While conflicts between this normative instrument and several other instruments can be foreseen, the normative relationship between the Declaration and the Convention on the Elimination of All Forms of Discrimination Against Women (Discrimination Against Women Convention), adopted by the General Assembly of the United Nations on 18 December 1979,[65] presents a particularly interesting example of potential conflicts.

Several conflicts between the norm prohibiting discrimination against women and the norm of freedom of religion were discussed in Chapter II. Although the saving clauses of the

---

[64] Above n. 31. § 702 of the Restatement of the Foreign Relations Law of the United States (Revised) (Tent. Draft No. 6, 1985) does not list religious discrimination among violations of customary international law. But a case for treating systematic religious discrimination as a violation of customary international law is made in Comment *j* and in Reporters' Note 8. Comment *j* states: 'The UN Charter (articles 1, 13, 55) links and places religious discrimination on the same plane with racial discrimination, and to the extent that racial discrimination violates the Charter religious discrimination does too. Religious discrimination is also treated identically with racial discrimination in the principal covenants and in the constitutions and laws of many states. While there is as yet no convention on the elimination of religious discrimination, and there has been no concerted attack on such discrimination comparable to that on apartheid, there is a strong case that systematic discrimination on grounds of religion as a matter of state policy is also a violation of customary law.'

[65] Above n. 55.

Declaration and of the Discrimination Against Women Convention are discussed in greater detail in Section IX below, some brief comments on these clauses are necessary here. The saving clause of the Convention, Art. 23, does not 'protect' the provisions of the Declaration from the reach of the Convention, not only because the Declaration is not an 'international convention, treaty or agreement in force' for a particular State, but because it does not state norms 'more conducive to the achievement of equality between men and women'. Similarly, the saving clause of the Declaration, Art. 8, does not protect the Convention from the reach of the provisions of the Declaration. Only those instruments expressly mentioned, the Universal Declaration of Human Rights and the two International Covenants, are so protected. Due to the failure of the lawmakers to provide deterrents to conflict between these instruments, the potential is great for unregulated conflicts between religious freedom and other norms, such as women's equality. This potential is particularly serious given the intensity of religious belief, the conviction of the supremacy of religious law over secular law which prevails in some countries (for instance as regards the Islamic Shari'a), and the far-reaching impact of religion on social, cultural, and political life. This potential is reflected in the discussion by the UN Commission on Human Rights of Arcot Krishnaswami's 'Study of Discrimination in the Matter of Religious Rights and Practices':[66]

One view was that these difficulties [of the subject matter] stemmed mainly from the existence in the world of conflicting attitudes towards the question of freedom of thought, conscience and religion, and in part from the absolute character which religion had for the believer and the passions which it aroused. According to some members, religion was not merely an individual and a social phenomenon, but it also, by its very nature, pervaded all the thought, endeavours and activities of its adherents . . .

Another view was that the difficulties stemmed from the fact that conditions concerning religion in different States varied in the extreme: in every State there were to be found not only followers of numerous religions or beliefs, among whom there were conflicting convictions, but also atheists, who maintained non-religious convictions. While religion had a sacred character for its followers, those who held non-religious

---

[66] A. Krishnaswami, Study of Discrimination in the Matter of Religious Rights and Practices, UN Doc. E/CN.4/Sub.2/200/Rev.1 (1960), UN Publication Catalogue No. 60. XIV. 2.

beliefs were equally entitled to maintain their beliefs and to be protected against discrimination, since to them their convictions were no less sacred. It was thus necessary to establish a balance between those who professed a religion and those who did not. According to this view there could be no freedom of conscience in a State in which adherents of one religion or belief held a privileged position and there was discrimination against adherents of other religions or beliefs. Nor could there be freedom of conscience in a State in which there was discrimination against persons holding atheistic views. Separation of the Church and the State, and of the Church and the schools, was an essential guarantee of freedom of conscience.[67]

Given the force of religion in many societies, it is entirely possible that, in the future, States Parties to the Discrimination Against Women Convention will invoke the principles embodied in the Declaration as grounds for evading obligations under the Convention which are incompatible with specific religious practices. Reconciliation of conflicts between these two sets of principles may prove difficult. Regardless of whether certain discriminatory religious practices are intended to discriminate against women or not, the continuation of those practices may bar or impair the achievement of the equality of sexes. The attainment of the goal of equality of women may therefore require encroachment upon religious freedom. The following discussion will focus upon two principal areas of conflict.

A. *Legal Status of Women under Religious Laws*

Art. 1 of the Declaration provides for the right of everyone to freedom of thought, conscience, and religion. 'This right shall include freedom to have a religion or whatever belief of his choice, and freedom, either individually or in community with others and in public or private, to manifest his religion or belief in worship, observance, practice and teaching.' Although the establishment and maintenance of tribunals for the purpose of administering religious laws is not explicitly stated in Art. 6, that article's enumeration of various freedoms is not intended to be comprehensive, as evidenced by the introductory phrase: 'shall include, *inter alia*'. For some religions, the 'observance' and 'practice' of religion 'in community with others' and 'in public' includes the freedom to establish and maintain tribunals

---

[67] Commission on Human Rights, Report of the 18th Sess., 34 UN ESCOR Supp. (No. 8) paras. 108-9, UN Doc.3616/Rev.1, E/CN.4/832/Rev. 1 (1962).

for the purpose of administering religious laws. The application of religious laws may itself constitute the observance and practice of religion.

Assuming that the freedom of religious groups to administer religious law is protected by the principles of the Declaration, restrictions placed by the State upon that freedom would be permissible only if they complied with Art. 1(3), which provides that '[f]reedom to manifest one's religion or beliefs may be subject only to such limitations as are prescribed by law and are necessary to protect public safety, order, health, or morals or the fundamental rights and freedoms of others'.

In light of the unsystematic manner in which human rights instruments are drafted, the usage of 'fundamental rights and freedoms' in Art. 1(3) of the Declaration would not, in itself, be particularly significant were it not for two considerations: (*a*) the fact that Art. 1(3) departs from the 'model' clause of Art. 29(2) of the Universal Declaration; (*b*) the fact that the Declaration in several other places employs the term 'human rights and fundamental freedoms' (twice in the Preamble, and Arts. 2, 3, and 4) and in one context (Art. 7), the phrase 'rights and freedoms'. The formulation of Art. 1(3) may, therefore, have been deliberately selected in order to impose greater limitations on possible encroachments by the State upon freedom of religion. Arguably, the effect of this language may be to limit the State's right to regulate religious courts even when such regulation may be justified by the advancement of the goal of women's equality.[68]

Should the distinction between 'human rights' and 'fundamental human rights' be accepted in the context of Art. 1(3) of the Declaration, despite the conceptual difficulty in defining that distinction, the question would thus arise whether the women's right which is implicated constitutes a fundamental right and freedom. This question cannot be answered *in abstracto*, without reference to conditions and concepts prevailing in particular societies. In some societies, the conditions required for the application of Art. 1(3) might not be satisfied.

The norm of prohibition of discrimination against women would not be implicated where women themselves select

---

[68]   For further discussion, see below, text accompanying notes 141-3.

religious tribunals as the forum for adjudication, and where women have full access to secular courts. But where religious tribunals assert the power to adjudicate the legal rights of women or where national legislation embodies religious law, the status of the rights guaranteed by the Discrimination Against Women Convention may be implicated. In particular, the following provisions of the Convention affecting women's legal status may conflict with the freedom to administer religious law where the latter mandates sex discriminatory practices: Art. 2(c), 2(f), 9, 13, 15, and 16.

The most significant of these, Art. 15, provides for the equality of women and men before the law, and grants women legal capacity identical to that of men in civil matters. Religious tribunals adjudicating civil matters would thus be required to accord women legal status and capacity equal to that of men despite any religious doctrine to the contrary. For example, where Islamic and Jewish religious laws give less evidentiary weight to testimony by women in civil matters and the State allows those laws to be administered in this discriminatory manner, a violation of Art. 15 occurs. Adjudication purporting to affect only women's rights within the religious community or group, but not their rights in civil matters, would not, however, violate Art. 15. Thus, for example, the refusal to grant a woman a religious divorce for reasons involving sex discrimination would not violate Art. 15 unless that refusal affected her ability to obtain a civil divorce. Nevertheless, toleration of such practices may call into question a State's compliance with Art. 5 of the Convention, which requires States Parties to take all appropriate measures to modify social and cultural patterns based on the idea of inferiority or superiority of either of the sexes or on stereotyped roles for men and women. The Convention would forbid the application and require the repeal of national laws codifying religious measures which deny or impair women's ability to exercise rights guaranteed by the Convention (Arts. 2 (c), (d), (f), (g)).

Conversely, state-imposed restrictions upon the operation of religious tribunals for the purpose of preventing sex discrimination might be challenged as impermissible interference with the exercise of religious freedom. Restrictions 'necessary to protect ... the fundamental rights and freedoms' of women would be valid if the fundamental nature of those rights were conceded. The denial of equal treatment before the law, or the application of sex discriminatory religious laws affecting women's legal status or their legal right to equal treatment, are not only repugnant in themselves, but are particularly dangerous because they deny or impair the ability to enforce other rights. Even if the distinction between human rights and fundamental human rights is admitted, a strong case can be made for regarding such discriminatory practices as affecting the fundamental rights and freedoms of women and therefore as appropriate subjects for state intervention.

B. *Religious Practices concerning Marriage and Family Matters*

Art. 5(1) of the Declaration provides that 'parents . . . have the right to organize the life within the family in accordance with their religion or belief . . .'. Where religious doctrine prescribes sex discriminatory practices within the family life (for instance the choice of spouse for a female child), the observance of such customs may constitute breach of obligations not to discriminate in those specific practices under certain provisions of the Convention: for instance Art. 9, regarding the nationality of children[69] (mentioned in Chapter II, Section II(G) above), and Art. 16, concerning rights and responsibilities in marriage. Such practices within marriage also implicate provisions concerning the legal capacity of women.

To the extent that religious doctrine is embodied in social customs, discriminatory practices based upon that doctrine may violate Art. 5 of the Convention, which requires that States take appropriate measures to modify 'social and cultural patterns of conduct of men and women, with a view to achieving the elimination of prejudices and customary and all other practices which are based on the idea of the inferiority or the superiority of either of the sexes or on stereotyped roles for men and women . . .'. Art. 5 also requires the inclusion in family education of an 'understanding of maternity as a social function and the recognition of the common responsibility of men and women in the upbringing and development of their children . . .'.

[69] See Tinker, *Human Rights for Women: The UN Convention on the Elimination of All Forms of Discrimination Against Women*, 3 Human Rights Q. 32, n. 36 and 12 (1981).

Because the perpetuation of socio-cultural sexism prevents the achievement of *de facto* equality, the obligations stated in Art. 5 are as necessary to the elimination of sex discrimination as are the duties to refrain from specific acts of discrimination.

None the less, because no restrictions on the means to be utilized are imposed, Art. 5 of the Convention creates the potential for abuse of the State's authority to regulate socio-cultural activities and for conflict with principles forbidding religious discrimination. In implementing Art. 5, a State must, of course, refrain from taking measures involving religious or racial discrimination. Moreover, the interests in preserving the privacy of the family and respecting, in so far as is possible without eviscerating the Convention, religious freedom suggest that a balancing of the interests involved should be attempted. Thus, religious practices within the family which have relatively less significance for women's ability to function as full human beings in society might be permitted even though those practices perpetuate stereotyped roles, while practices which impair women's ability to exercise their rights and foreclose opportunities to function outside stereotyped roles (for instance a prohibition on women working outside the home) must not be allowed.

Art. 5(2) of the Declaration states that children shall have the right to have access to education in the matter of religion or belief in accordance with the wishes of their parents. Children thus have the right to instruction in religious doctrine even if that doctrine mandates or encourages sex discrimination. If the custom in a particular religious group is to offer religious instruction to male children only, and if the parents so wish, there probably would be no violation of Art. 5 of the Convention in discriminating against female children in granting access to religious education. Where instruction in religious doctrine includes encouragement of sex discrimination, Art. 5(2) of the Declaration appears to be in conflict with Art. 10(c) of the Convention which requires States Parties to take all appropriate measures to eliminate 'any stereotyped concept of the roles of men and women at all levels and in all forms of education . . .'. However, to require the elimination of sex-role stereotyping in the teaching of religious doctrine would constitute coercion to alter religious practice or belief, in violation of Art. 1(2) of the

Declaration, to the extent that such stereotyping is a genuine doctrinal feature of the religion.

VI. RAISING STANDARDS

Although normative conflicts may threaten to eviscerate rights, the multiplicity of norms may at times be advantageous, allowing the individual to seek the most favourable provision. Such benefit may occur especially when different instruments supplement each other. In certain cases it may be possible to apply in system *a* the most favourable norm even if the norm originates in system *b*. Through a gradual and rather indirect process, the Court of Justice of the European Communities has applied some of the substantive provisions of the European Conventon on Human Rights when those provisions were more favourable to the individual concerned.[70] While noting with satisfaction

---

[70] The Luxembourg Court has applied not only the norms described in the Treaty of Rome, but also fundamental human righs contained in the general principles of Community law. See *Stauder* v. *Ulm*, 1969 ECR 419, [1970] Comm. Mkt. L. R. 112. The Court has also recgonized that basic constitutional rights common to the member States of the Communities are part of the general principles of law that it protects. See *Nold* v. *Commission*, 1974 ECR 491, [1974] 2 Comm. Mkt. L. R. 338. In *Rutili* v. *Minister of the Interior*, 1975 ECR 1219, [1976] 1 Comm. Mkt. L. R. 140, the Court of Justice reached the question of the application of the provisions of the European Convention on Human Rights. The Court stated: '[T]hese limitations placed on the powers of Member States in respect of control of aliens are a specific manifestation of the more general principle, enshrined in Articles 8, 9, 10 and 11 of the [European Convention on Human Rights], . . . which provide[s] . . . that no restrictions in the interests of national security or public safety shall be placed on the rights secured by the above-quoted articles other than such as are necessary for the protection of those interests 'in a democratic society.' 1975 ECR at 1232, [1976] 1 Comm. Mkt. L. R. 155.

In *Hauer* v. *Land Rheinland-Pfalz*, 1979 ECR 3727, [1980] 3 Comm. Mkt. L. R. 42, which concerned a complaint that regulations promulgated by the Council of the European Communities prohibiting new plantings of vines violated Hauer's property rights, the Court of Justice referred to human rights treaties on which the member States of the European Communities had collaborated or to which they were parties, and discussed and interpreted Art. 1 of Protocol No. 1 to the European Convention on Human Rights. In this further and more specific application to the law of the European Communities of human rights norms established outside of the framework of the European Communities, the Court of Justice stated that it had 'also emphasized in [Internationale Handelsgesellschaft, 1970 ECR 1125], and later in . . . *Nold* . . ., that fundamental rights form an integral part of the general principles of the law, the observance of which it ensures; that in safeguarding those rights, the Court is bound to draw inspiration from constitutional traditions common to the Member States, so that measures which are incompatible with the fundamental rights recognized by the constitutions of those States are unacceptable in the Community; and that, similarly, international treaties for the protection of human rights on which the Member States have collaborated or of which they are signatories, can supply guidelines which should be followed within the framework of Community law.' 1979 ECR at 3744-5, [1980] 3 Comm. Mkt. L. R. at 64. The Court of Justice considered the right to property to be guaranteed in the Community legal order in accordance with the ideas common to the constitutions of the Member States, which are also reflected in the first Protocol to the European Convention for the Protection of Human Rights.

. . .

. . . [T]he second paragraph of Article 1 of the Protocol provides an important indication in so far as it recognizes the right of a State 'to enforce such laws as it deems necessary to control the use of property in accordance with the general interest.' Thus the Protocol accepts in principle the legality of restrictions upon the use of property, whilst at the same time limiting those restrictions to the extent to which they are deemed 'necessary' by a State for the protection of the 'general interest.' 1979 ECR at 3745-6, [1980] 3 Comm. Mkt. L. R. at 64-5.

The Court of Justice then considered the constitutional rules and practices of the (then) nine member States, and particularly the legislative measures that have given concrete expression to the social function of the right to property, such as restrictions on the use of agricultural or forest land. It concluded that the relevant regulation could not be challenged in principle since it 'is a type of restriction which is known and accepted as lawful, in identical or similar forms, in the constitutional structure of all the Member States'. 1979 ECR at 3747, [1980] 3 Comm. Mkt. L. R. at 66.

See generally Lecourt, *Interferences Between the European Convention on Human Rights and the Community Law Concerning the Community and National Judicial Control*, in Proc. of the Colloquy About the European Convention on Human Rights in Relation to Other International Instruments for the Protection of Human Rights, Athens, 21-22 September 1978, at 81, 92-4 (1979); E. Stein, P. Hay, and M. Waelbroeck, European Community Law and Institutions in Perspective 136-40, 274-302 (1976); Dowrick, *Overlapping International and European Laws*, 31 Int'l & Comp. L. Q. 59, 81-2 (1982); Brown and McBride, *Observations on the Proposed Accession by the European Community to the European Convention on Human Rights*, 29 Am. J. Comp. L. 691 (1981).

Mendelson, above n. 38; Mendelson, *The European Court of Justice and Human Rights*, 1 Y.B. Eur. L. 125 (1982); Frowein, *Human Rights in International Law and Community Law*, in House of Lords, Papers and Bills, 362d Sess. at 73 (1979-80); Frowein, *Die Europäische Menschenrechtskonvention und das Europäische Gemeinschaftsrecht*, 2 Schriftenreihe des Arbeitskreises Europäische Integration e. V.: Die Grundrechte in der Europäischen Gemeinschaft (1978). Imbert, Le Consentement des états en droit international: réflections à partir d'un cas pratique concermant la participation de la CEE aux traités du Conseil de l'Europe, 89 Rev. générale de droit international public 353 (1985). See also below n. 82. Art. 4 of the Draft Treaty Establishing the European Union provides that within the period of five years the Union shall take a decision on its accession to, *inter alia*, the European Convention for the Protection of Human Rights and Fundamental Freedoms. European Parliament, Draft Treaty Establishing the European Union at 11-12 (1984). The 'Colombo Commission' of the Council of Europe has recently recommended 'the study of ways and means to prevent the emergence of two different bodies of case-law (that of the European Court of Human Rights and that of the Court of Justice of the European Communities) on the interpretation of the same rights, one such means being accession by the Community to the Convention.)

Council of Europe, Report of the Colombo Commission at 7 (1985). See also ibid. App. at 10-11.

the decisions of the Court of Justice of the European Communities in the field of human rights, the Parliamentary Assembly of the Council of Europe has expressed concern that 'complications could result from the simultaneous interpretation of the articles of the European Convention on Human Rights by both the Commission and Court of Human Rights on the one hand, and by the Court of Justice of the European Communities on the other'.[71] The Parliamentary Assembly recommended that the Committee of Ministers introduce a system of consultation between the Court of Justice and the two human rights control organs of the Council of Europe, 'possibly by concluding an additional protocol to the European Convention on Human Rights'.[72]

---

[71] Recommendation 791 (1976) of the Parliamentary Assembly of the Council of Europe, paras. 7–8, 28th Ordinary Session (2nd Pt.) (1976).

It is not clear whether the practice of control organs to consider only the norms stated in the specific 'founding' instrument is always compelled by the language of the governing instrument or by considerations such as whether the other relevant instruments have been ratified by the State concerned. Compare this trend with the unified system of implementation and supervision followed by the ILO. See generally, Wolf, *Human Rights and the International Labour Organisation*, in 2 Meron (ed.), above n. 13, at 273; Wolf, *Aspects judiciaires de la protection internationale de droits de l'homme par l'O.I.T.*, 4 Rev. Droits de l'Homme 773 (1971). See also Buergenthal's discussion of the incorporation by reference in Art. 15 of the European Convention, above n. 52, of norms originating in human rights instruments established outside the framework of the Council of Europe. Buergenthal, *International and Regional Human Rights Law and Institutions: Some Examples of their Interaction*, 12 Tex. Int'l L. J. 321, 324–5 (1977). See also below n. 229.

It should be observed, however, that the UN Commission on Human Rights and fact-finding bodies established by resolutions of organs of the United Nations often invoke 'broadly recognized normative standards'. Franck and Fairley, *Procedural Due Process in Human Rights Fact-Finding by International Agencies*, 74 AJIL 308 (1980). Thus, the *Ad Hoc* Working Group of Experts on Human Rights in Southern Africa of the Commission on Human Rights, when investigating allegations of infringements of trade union rights in South Africa, considered the applicable South African legislation in light of a number of international human rights instruments to which South Africa was not a party. UN Doc. E/CN.4/1986, at 3–5 (1982). For a list of human rights standards invoked by fact-finding bodies, see Ramcharan, *Substantive Law Applicable*, in International Law and Fact-Finding in the Field of Human Rights 26, 31–9 (B. Ramcharan ed., 1982). This practice of fact-finding bodies to invoke instruments to which the 'defendant' State is not a party has not been based on an articulated distinction between norms that have attained the status of customary international law and other norms. Have such instruments been invoked primarily as the applicable political rules or as the common law of mankind? These questions merit a study which falls outside the confines of this book.

[72] Recommendation 791 (1976) of the Parliamentary Assembly of the Council of Europe, para. 12 (b), 28th Ordinary Session (2nd Pt.) (1976).

The position taken by the Court of Justice of the European Communities is atypical of other human rights organs, however. Most supervisory organs apply only those norms stated in their founding instruments. Where the scope of the applicable norms cannot be extended by the case law or rules of procedure of a particular organ, the use of a special protocol for this purpose should be considered. Such extension requires, of course, that the State concerned accept the relevant norms through the special protocol. Additional protocols have been regularly employed by the Council of Europe in its law-making process as a means of extending rights (see Section VII below).

In drafting a special protocol, conflicts with the founding or constitutent instrument should be avoided. In some cases, reconciliation of the terms of the two instruments may be difficult. Such a problem arose over proposals to entrust the Human Rights Committee, established under the Political Covenant, with the implementation of the norms of the (then proposed) convention against torture and other cruel, inhuman, or degrading treatment or punishment.[73] The Legal Counsel of the United Nations advised that the 'legal validity [of this solution] could be challenged on the ground that it constitutes a modification of the terms of the Covenant which has established the Human Rights Committee and defined its terms of reference. Such modification can only be effected by the procedure specified in article 51 of the Covenant.'[74] The Legal Counsel appeared to be suggesting that, as a treaty organ, the

---

[73] UN Doc. E/CN.4/1982/L.40, para. 54 (1982). It may be recalled that Art. 9 of the International Convention on the Suppression and Punishment of the Crime of *Apartheid*, GA Res. 3068, 28 UN GAOR Supp. (No. 30) at 75, UN Doc. A/9030 (1973), provides that reports by States Parties be considered by a group appointed by the Chairman of the Commission on Human Rights consisting of three members of the Commission who are also representatives of States Parties to the Convention, which avoids establishing a new organ. It is more difficult to follow such a solution where members of a body (e.g. the Human Rights Committee under the Political Covenant) are elected in their personal capacity and not as representatives of States. It has been proposed that the Committee against Torture consisting of experts elected in their personal capacity, should be composed, so far as possible, of persons who are also members of the UN Human Rights Committee. UN Doc. E/CN.4/1982/ L.40, Ann. II, Art. 17(2) (1982). This proposal is reflected in Art. 17(2) of the Convention Against Torture and Other Cruel, Inhuman or Degrading Treatment or Punishment. GA Res. 39/46, opened for signature 10 Dec. 1984, 39 UN GAOR Supp. (No. 51) at 197, UN Doc. A/39/51 (1985).
[74] UN Doc. E/CN.4/WG.2/WP/6 (1981).

Human Rights Committee may function according to the terms of the Political Covenant only, and that it is 'not sufficient . . . that there is a general concordance in purpose between the proposed convention and article 7 of the Covenant'.[75]

A distinction can be made between modifying the powers of the Human Rights Committee as a Covenant organ and conferring authority to apply other norms on the Committee by means of another instrument concluded by members of the United Nations. Arguably, the Human Rights Committee should be allowed to exercise such authority with regard to States that have so agreed through a special protocol or other instrument, especially since the Committee is financed under the UN budget and is serviced by officials of the UN Secretariat.

An argument might be raised that the United States and other countries would face a constitutional problem if such a special protocol incorporated other human rights instruments by specific reference and such a country became a party to the protocol but not to the other instruments. Would the United States have to ratify the several incorporated instruments separately before becoming legally bound by them?[76] If the special protocol set out *de novo* the relevant norms, the constitutional issue might be avoided, but then drafting the special protocol and obtaining for it the necessary measure of political agreement would become even more difficult.

In the elaboration of new instruments, the new norms stated should raise the substantive international standards and the instruments should improve the efficiency of the control procedures[77]

---

[75]   Ibid. Art. 7 of the Political Covenant spells out the prohibition of torture.

[76]   See generally US Const. Art. II, § 2, cl. 2.

[77]   For an interesting proposal to reform and raise the standards of the Council of Europe's system of control and implementation of human rights, see Functioning of the Organs of the European Convention on Human Rights, Report Submitted by the Swiss Delegation to the European Ministerial Conference on Human Rights, Vienna, 19–20 March 1985, Council of Europe Doc. MDH (85) 1 (1984). The reforms proposed by Switzerland include conferring on the individual the right to bring his case before the European Court of Human Rights, making the system of control completely independent by reducing the intervention of the Committee of Ministers, concentrating on preventive measures, such as preliminary rulings by the European Court of Human Rights at the request of national courts, and the merging of the existing Commission and Court in a single full-time European Court of Human Rights, assisted by full-time Advocates General. See generally European Ministerial Conference on Human Rights (Vienna, 19–20 March 1985): Texts Adopted, Resolutions Nos. 1–2, Council of Europe Doc. H (85) (7) (1985).

or at least not adversely affect the existing control procedures. The purpose of new instruments is not always to develop higher standards, however. If an organization has overreached and States are not willing to ratify a treaty that establishes high standards, the organization may have to be less ambitious and prepare a treaty with lower substantive standards or less demanding implementation provisions.[78] This problem has occurred with respect, *inter alia*, to international labour conventions which are not subject to reservations.[79] The ILO has attempted to enable developing States to become parties to these conventions by adopting more flexible revised conventions and by including in new conventions so-called flexibility clauses.[80] An organization involved in human rights law-making must, therefore, determine in each case which is more important, higher standards or more ratifications.

VII. REGIONAL INSTRUMENTS

The attempt to achieve legislative co-ordination and the integration of systems of supervision of human rights must not prevent or impede the raising of standards. Homogenous regional organizations sometimes improve upon the standards set by world-wide conventions. For example, the regulations of the European Communities regarding the social security of migrant

---

[78] An example of lowering of standards with regard to implementation is found in the Protocol relating to the Status of Refugees (1967), Arts. IV and VII, which allow reservations to the settlement of disputes clause. 19 UST 6223, TIAS No. 6577, 606 UNTS 267. The Convention relating to the Status of Refugees (1951), Arts. 38 and 42, did not allow such reservations. 189 UNTS 137. An example of raising of standards with regard to implementation may be found in Art. 20 of the Convention Against Torture and Other Cruel, Inhuman or Degrading Treatment or Punishment, above n. 73. The investigative powers of the Committee under this Convention go beyond those of the Human Rights Committee under the Political Covenant. At the time of signature, ratification, or accession, each State may (Art. 28(1)), however, declare that it does not recognize the competence of the Committee provided for in Art. 20.

[79] See Valticos and Wolf, *L'Organisation internationale du Travail et les pays en voie de développement: Techniques d'élaboration et mise en œuvre de normes universelles*, in Pays en voie de développement et transformation du droit international 127, 131 (Société Française pour le Droit International, 1974).

[80] For a discussion of these techniques, see Valticos, above n. 29, at 51–5; Meron, above n. 59, 773 and n. 100.

workers offer greater protection than the general standards established in the relevant international labour conventions.[81]

The danger remains, however, that regional agreements dealing with human rights also covered by universal agreements may perpetuate disparities where a common standard is desirable.[82] Such danger is probably more than compensated for by some of the advantages of regional agreements. Jenks has summarized those advantages as follows:

> There are cases in which a larger measure of agreement can be secured through regional co-operation than would be possible on a broader international basis. Regional instruments may deal with problems which are peculiar to or take a particular form in a particular region; they may deal with problems which it is premature or of little practical importance to deal with on a world-wide scale; they may prescribe a higher standard, more extensive facilities, a greater degree of unification of previous law or practice, or a fuller measure of reciprocity than can be secured internationally; they may provide for greater uniformity in a particular region than is practicable on a wider basis in the application of provisions in a general instrument leaving certain matters to national discretion . . .[83]

The American Convention on Human Rights exemplifies a regional human rights instrument which contains broader protections than those recognized by a universal instrument (the Political Covenant). The American Convention contains a longer catalogue of human rights than does either the European Convention of Human Rights or the Political Covenant.[84] The provision on derogations (Art. 27) states a longer list of non-derogable rights than do the derogation provisions of the latter two instruments. The right of individual communication to the Inter-American Commission on Human Rights without the need for a special declaration by the State concerned is recognized; by becoming a party to the Convention, a State accepts *ipso*

---

[81] Co-ordination Report, above n. 5, Ann. II, at 3; Jenks, *Human Rights*, above n. 62, at 248. See generally Forde, *The European Convention on Human Rights and Labor Law*, 31 Am. J. Comp. L. 301 (1983).

[82] Jenks, *The Conflict*, above n. 1, at 412. Additionally, a certain possibility of conflicts exists even among different regional instruments, such as the Treaty of Rome, establishing the European Economic Community, and the European Convention on Human Rights. See also Mendelson, above n. 38.

[83] Jenks, *The Conflict*, above n. 1, at 412.

[84] Buergenthal, above n. 19, at 442.

See generally Tardu, *The Protocol to the United Nations Covenant on Civil and Political Rights and the Inter-American System: A Study of Co-existing Petition procedures*, 70 AJIL 778 (1976).

facto the jurisdiction of the Commission to receive private complaints against that State.[85] No policy reasons restrict a regional organization's power to confer rights broader than those recognized by universal organizations. The goal of uniformity must not lead to the acceptance of the lowest possible common denominator.

The two Covenants and the Optional Protocol to the Political Covenant were adopted by the UN General Assembly on 16 December 1966, and the American Convention was signed nearly three years later, on 22 November 1969. Not surprisingly, in the course of work leading to the elaboration of the Convention, the question of compatibility with the Political Covenant was considered. A rapporteur appointed by the Inter-American Commission on Human Rights prepared a 'Comparative Study of the United Nations Covenants on Civil and Political Rights and on Economic, Social and Cultural Rights, and of the Draft Inter-American Convention on Human Rights'.[86] On the basis of that study and other documents the Commission adopted an important opinion which included the following points:

I. It is perfectly possible for the United Nations International Covenant on Civil and Political Rights, with the Optional Protocol thereto, and its International Covenant on Economic, Social and Cultural Rights and the Inter-American Convention on Human Rights to coexist.
. . .
III. The need for, and the desirability of, a regional convention for the Americas are based on the existence of a body of American international law built up in accordance with the specific requirements of the countries of this hemisphere. That need and desirability also follow from the close relationship that exists between human rights and regional economics development and integration . . .

IV. Consequently the Inter-American Convention on the Protection of Human Rights should be autonomous rather than complementary to the United Nations covenants, although it should indeed be coordinated with those covenants.

V. To this end, the substantive part of the Inter-American Convention could coincide in certain respects with the United Nations Covenants on Civil and Political Rights with such additions as are necessary and it could, in addition, include other rights that are not contemplated in that covenant, but the international protection of which is demanded because of conditions peculiar to the Americas.[87]

[85] Buergenthal, above n. 19, at 454–60, 484–7.
[86] [1968] Inter-American Y. B. Human Rights 89 (1973).   [87] Ibid. at 89–91.

On the basis of the above opinion, the Council of the Organization of American States adopted a resolution instructing the Inter-American Commission to prepare a revised text which should 'be in harmony with the International Covenants of the United Nations . . .'[88]

This position, taking the Covenant into account without requiring adherence to its guidance, allowed the Convention to have the effect of broadening the scope of the available protections. The provisions of the Political Covenant on occasion influenced the drafting of the Convention.[89] On other occasions, however, suggestions to revise the proposed wording so as to ensure compatibility with the Political Covenant were rejected, as with regard to the formulation of the right to life in Art. 4(1) (discussed in relation to Art. 6(1) of the Political Covenant, above).[90] When the formulation of the right to life was discussed at the Conference of San José which adopted the Convention, the United States proposed 'that the text be accommodated with Article 6, paragraph 1, of the [Political] Covenant'. This proposal was not accepted after Brazil objected on the ground that 'the Conference should not follow the text of the Pact of the United Nations in a servile manner'.[91]

One should not, however, assume that the rights recognized under regional instruments are necessarily more comprehensive than those recognized in the UN Covenants. It has thus been observed that the European Convention on Human Rights of 4 November 1950, which preceded by sixteen years the adoption of the Covenants, and the European Convention's first five protocols[92] safeguard nineteen different rights, while the Political Covenant safeguards twenty-three.[93] A number of additional rights have now been adopted through Protocols 6 and 7, to which further reference will be made. Of these seven protocols, additional rights are granted by Protocols 1, 4, 6, and 7, all of which except for Protocol 7 are now in force. The

---

[88]   Ibid. at 93.
[89]   E.g. ibid. at 107.
[90]   Ibid. at 97; above n. 21, at 23.
[91]   T. Buergenthal and R. Norris, 2 Human Rights: The Inter-American System 31-2 (1982).
[92]   Reprinted in Basic Documents on Human Rights 257-65 (2nd edn. I. Brownlie ed. 1981).
[93]   Council of Europe Doc. CAHMP (80) 1, at 5 (1980).

European Convention and the Political Covenant protect a number of the same rights, defined in a generally similar manner. Yet there is a risk of conflict between the regimes, resulting either from disparity between the definitions of the rights or from dissimilarities in international procedures to protect the rights, particularly as interpreted by the control bodies.[94] The risk of substantive conflict may also be increased by divergencies in the interpretation and application of limitations which may be imposed on various rights, for instance in the name of public order or national security. It is in the development of control institutions and procedures, which involve adjudication and legally binding decisions, that the European system for protection of human rights is far in advance of the universal system.[95] The institutional inferiority (control procedures) of the Covenants was partly compensated for by their normative superiority (number and content of rights) in some respects.[96]

The method followed by the Council of Europe for raising human rights standards and sometimes for limiting the deviations from standards set in the global instruments is to adopt additional protocols to the European Convention on Human Rights. Eight such protocols have by now been adopted,[97] the first six of which are in force. One of the factors which led to the extension of rights within the Council of Europe was the

---

[94] Contra Eissen, *The European Convention on Human Rights and the United Nations Covenant on Civil and Political Rights: Problems of Coexistence*, 22 Buffalo L. Rev. 181, 209 (1972).

[95] The European Convention on Human Rights, which essentially covers rights which can be described as civil and political, is endowed with a machinery for judicial control, whereas the European Social Charter, Eur. T.S. No. 35, reprinted in Brownlie, above n. 92, at 301, which covers essentially economic and social rights, provides only for a supervisory machinery that may lead to adoption of recommendations. Recommendation 839 (1978) on the revision of the European Social Charter, adopted by the Parliamentary Assembly of the Council of Europe, contains not only proposals for the extension of the norms stated in the Charter, but also for the strengthening of the supervisory machinery. A preliminary draft of a First Additional Protocol to the European Social Charter was prepared by the Steering Committee for Social Affairs, UN Doc. E/CN.4/1985/42, at 29 (1985).

[96] Eissen, above n. 94, at 184.

[97] Protocol No. 8 to the Convention for the Protection of Human Rights and Fundamental Freedoms (Council of Europe Doc. H (85) 6 (1985), opened for signature 19 March 1985. This Protocol contains measures primarily designed to accelerate the petition procedure before the European Commission of Human Rights, but also would accelerate cases before the European Court of Human Rights. Explanatory Memorandum, ibid. at 5.

recognition that the European Convention had a narrower normative scope than the Political Covenant. In October 1967, the Committee of Ministers of the Council of Europe instructed the Committee of Experts on Human Rights (CDDH) to investigate the problems of 'coexistence' with the Political Covenant.[98] The CDDH prepared a detailed study of 'Differences as regards the Rights Guaranteed'.[99] This study served as one of the conceptual bases for the work on the extension of rights. On 23 October 1972, the Parliamentary Assembly of the Council of Europe adopted Recommendation No. 683 (1972), calling for a study of the question of extending the rights guaranteed by the European Convention.[100] By Recommendation No. 791 (1976) of 17 September 1976, the Parliamentary Assembly recommended that the Committee of Ministers 'endeavour to insert as many as possible of the substantive provisions of the UN Covenant in the European Convention on Human Rights'.[101]

On 27 April 1978, the Committee of Ministers adopted a Declaration on Human Rights, deciding to give priority to exploring the possibility of extending the lists of rights of the individual, notably rights in the social, economic, and cultural fields. By Recommendation No. 838 (1978) of 27 September 1978, the Parliamentary Assembly formulated important guidelines for the work being undertaken for the extension of rights: 'in order to be incorporated in the convention, any right must be fundamental and enjoy general recognition, and capable of sufficiently precise definition to lay legal obligations on a state, rather than simply constitute a general rule'.[102] The CDDH took these guidelines into account in the preparation of the new Protocol No. 7 and 'kept in mind the need to include in the Convention only such rights as could be stated in sufficiently specific terms to be guaranteed within the framework of the

---

[98] Council of Europe Doc. H (84) 5, at 5 (1984).

[99] Report of the Committee of Experts on Problems Arising from the Co-existence of the United Nations Covenants on Human Rights and the European Convention on Human Rights: Differences as Regards the Rights Guaranteed, Council of Europe Doc. H (70) 7 (1970).

[100] Council of Europe Doc. H (84) 5, at 5 (1984).

[101] Res. 791, para. 12(c) (ii), Council of Europe, Parliamentary Assembly, 28th Ordinary Sess. (2d Pt.), Texts Adopted by the Assembly (1976).

[102] Res. 838, para. 12, Council of Europe, Parliamentary Assembly, 30th Ordinary Sess. (2d Pt.), Official Report of Debates 311 (1979).

system of control instituted by the Convention'.[103] Thus, the three criteria applied by the CDDH were that, to qualify for possible extension in a protocol, a right must be fundamental, universal, and justiciable.[104]

By applying these criteria, experts of the Council of Europe identified a number of economic, social, and cultural rights for possible inclusion in an additional protocol, but have failed to reach unanimous agreement on some of them, apparently because the rights contemplated for inclusion did not satisfy the criterion of justiciability and were not suited to the control machinery established by the Convention. Underlying such legal objections were, of course, concerns regarding economic problems, especially on the part of some States Members of the Council of Europe. The following rights were proposed for inclusion in an additional protocol: the right to compensation for expropriation; the right of men and women to equal pay for the same work; the equality of rights of men and women with regard to employment and occupation and the right to free elementary education.[105] It has been suggested that, for rights not found to be suitable for protection under the European Convention, 'a more flexible control machinery could be envisaged. . . . for instance . . . by an extension of the Social Charter, which would, however, necessitate an improvement of its control machinery'.[106]

Work on the extension of civil and political rights has been far more successful. Following the submission of a final draft by the Steering Committee for Human Rights, the Committee of Ministers approved and opened for signature, on 28 April 1983, the text of Protocol No. 6 to the Convention for the Protection of Human Rights and Fundamental Freedoms

---

[103] Council of Europe Doc. H (84) 5, at 6 (1984).
[104] Council of Europe Doc. H/ONG (82) 3, at 3 (1982). For additional information on the work of the Council of Europe on extension of rights, see UN Doc. E/CN.4/1450, at 19–20 (1981); Reply from the Committee of Ministers to Recommendation 838 (1978), Council of Europe Doc. H/Inf. (79) 4, App. III, at 21 (1979); Report of the Committee of Experts, above n. 99. Concerning the European Convention on Human Rights in relation to other international instruments for the protection of human rights, see Proc. of the Colloquy above n. 70, at 21-2.
[105] Report Submitted by the Austrian delegation to the European Ministerial Conference on Human Rights, Vienna, 19-20 March 1985, Council of Europe Doc. MDH (85) 2, at 9 (1984).
[106] Ibid.

concerning the Abolition of the Death Penalty.[107] The Protocol provides for abolition of the death penalty in peacetime. A State may make provision in its law for the death penalty only in respect to acts committed in time of war or of imminent threat of war. No derogations under Art. 15 of the Convention or reservations under Art. 64 thereof in respect of the provisions of the Protocol may be made.

A number of additional civil and political rights were identified as suitable for inclusion in another protocol: due process guarantees for aliens in the event of expulsion from the territory of a contracting State; the right of everyone convicted of a criminal offence by a tribunal to have his conviction or sentence reviewed by a higher tribunal; compensation for the victim of a miscarriage of justice; the principle of *non bis in idem*; equality of rights and responsibilities between spouses with regard to marriage, during marriage, and in the event of dissolution of marriage; the right of access for every citizen, on general terms of equality, to the civil service of his country.[108] All of these rights, except for the last mentioned, are included in the text of Protocol No. 7 to the Convention for the Protection of Human Rights and Fundamental Freedoms, which was opened for signature on 22 November 1984.[109] Like its predecessor (Protocol No. 6), Protocol No. 7 does not only enlarge upon the scope of ordinary normative protection, but adds to the core of non-derogable provisions: Art. 4 (*non bis in idem*) provides that no derogation from that article may be made under Art. 15 of the Convention.

As urged in Chapter VII below, the United Nations should emulate the example of the Council of Europe and approach the task of law-making not as an activity designed only to produce a particular instrument, but as a continuing process, which includes extension, elaboration, consolidation, and revision. The work begun on the possible formulation of a Second Optional Protocol to the International Covenant on Civil and Political Rights, Aiming at the Abolition of the Death Penalty points in the right direction.

[107] Council of Europe Doc. H (83) 3 (1983).
[108] Council of Europe Doc. H/ONG (82) 3, at 2 (1982).
[109] Council of Europe Doc. H (84) 5 (1984).

VIII. OBSERVATIONS ON A HIERARCHY OF NORMS

The quest for a hierarchy among international human rights continues unabated, despite the impressive challenge raised by Professor Weil to the notion of 'relative normativity' of international legal norms.[110] To illustrate, in *Tel-Oren* v. *Libyan Arab Republic*,[111] a suit brought under the (First) Judiciary Act of 1789,[112] Judge Harry T. Edwards discussed whether torture, as distinguished from terrorism, 'is among the handful of crimes to which the law of nations attributes individual [civil] responsibility'.[113]

The International Court of Justice gave currency to the idea of a hierarchy in the *Barcelona Traction*[114] case in a famous dictum, by suggesting that 'basic rights of the human person' ('droits fondamentaux de la personne humaine') create obligations *erga omnes*.[115] This dictum was construed by the International Law Commission (ILC) to mean that there are 'a number, albeit a small one, of international obligations which, by reason of the importance of their subject-matter for the

---

[110] Weil, *Towards Relative Normativity in International Law?* 77 AJIL 413 (1983).

[111] 726 F. 2d 774 (DC Cir., 1984).

[112] 28 USC § 1350 (Alien Tort Statute, which provides Federal Courts with jurisdiction over actions by an alien for a tort committed in violation of the law of nations or a treaty of the United States).

[113] Above n. 111, at 795 (Edwards J., concurring).

[114] *Barcelona Traction, Light and Power Company, Limited* (*Belgium* v. *Spain*), 1970 I.C.J. 3 (Judgment of Feb. 5).

[115] Ibid. at 32. In the Case Concerning United States Diplomatic and Consular Staff in Tehran (*United States of America* v. *Iran*), the Court referred to the 'fundamental principles enunciated in the Universal Declaration of Human Rights'. 1980 I.C.J. 3, 42 (Judgment of May 24). In the Advisory Opinion on Legal Consequences for States of the Continued Presence of South Africa in Namibia (South West Africa) notwithstanding Security Council Resolution 276 (1970), the Court stated that the 'denial [by South Africa] of fundamental human rights is a flagrant violation of the purposes and principles of the Charter'. 1971 I.C.J. 16, 57 (Advisory Opinion of June 21).

In a statement on human rights, Secretary of State Kissinger declared that while there will 'always be differences of view as to the precise extent of the obligations of government . . . there are standards below which no government can fall without offending fundamental values, such as genocide, officially tolerated torture, mass imprisonment or murder, or the comprehensive denial of basic rights to racial, religious, political, or ethnic groups. Any government engaging in such practices must face adverse international judgment.' Statement by Sec'y of State Kissinger before the OAS General Assembly, 75 Dep't of State Bull. No. 1932, at 1, 3 (1976).

international community as a whole, are — unlike the others — obligations in whose fulfilment all States have a legal interest'.[116] Extrapolating from *Barcelona Traction* into the field of international criminal responsibility, the ILC adopted[117] on first reading the controversial Article 19(3) (*c.*) of the draft articles on State responsibility — proposed by Special Rapporteur Professor (now Judge) Ago. Article 19(3) (*c*) provides that an international crime may result, *inter alia*, from 'a serious breach on a widespread scale of an international obligation of essential importance for safeguarding the human being, such as those prohibiting slavery, genocide and *apartheid*'. For international crimes, the ILC thus introduced a twofold test relating to the seriousness both of the violation and of the norm.

More recently, in discussing derogations from human rights, a United Nations document spoke of the 'intangibility of certain fundamental rights'.[118] The UN Secretary-General complained of the denial by South Africa of the 'most fundamental human rights'.[119] And the authoritative draft *Restatement of the Foreign Relations Law of the United States (Revised)* considers the rules of customary law of human rights listed in Section 702 (discussed below) to constitute *jus cogens*.[120]

Claims of hierarchical status are also raised as to the relationship among rights belonging to the so-called first generation (civil and political rights), second generation (economic, social, and cultural rights), and third generation (solidarity rights, for example the rights to peace, development, and a protected environment).[121] Perhaps because, as Professor Brownlie aptly observes, 'there is no Rubicon between law and morality',[122] in

[116] [1976] 2 Y.B. Int'l L. Comm'n 99, UN Doc. A/CN.4/Ser.A/1976/Add.1 (pt. 2).

[117] Ibid. at 73. For the text of Art. 19(3) (*c*), see ibid. at 95.

[118] UN Doc. E/CN.4/Sub.2/1985/19, at 6.

[119] UN Press Release (Geneva) SG/SM/617, July 24, 1985.

[120] Restatement of Foreign Relations Law of the United States (Revised) § 702, Comment *l* (1 Tent. Draft No. 6, 1985) (hereinafter cited as Draft Restatement).

[121] See generally Sohn, *The New International Law: Protection of the Rights of Individuals rather than States*, 32 Am. U. L. Rev. 1, 61-2 (1982). Regarding the interdependence and equal status of human rights, see ibid. at 63. See also Alston, *Conjuring up New Human Rights: A Proposal for Quality Control*, 78 AJIL 607, 612 (1984).

[122] Brownlie, *Causes of Action in the Law of Nations*, [1979] 50 Brit. Y. B. Int'l L. 13, 40 (1981).

the largely political controversy over the ranking of the several generations of rights (the first two generations represent *lex lata*, the third still largely *lex ferenda*), little attention is paid to the distinction between rights and claims. Yet another priority claim arises in distinguishing between individual and collective rights: the Canadian expert on the UN Sub-Commission on Prevention of Discrimination and Protection of Minorities (Deschênes) recently called for an end to the suppression of individual rights in the name of collective rights.[123]

The increasing use of a hierarchical terminology in international human rights merits attention. In addition to its conceptual interest, this development is of practical importance in resolving conflicts between norms. The object of this section is to examine the significance and the implications of the trend towards a graduated normativity in international human rights in regard to two sometimes overlapping notions: fundamental (or basic) human rights and peremptory (*jus cogens*) human rights.

A. *Aspects of the Notion of a Hierarchy of Norms in International Law*

National legal systems are characterized by a well-established hierarchy of norms. Constitutional provisions prevail over ordinary statutes, the latter prevail over secondary legislation or administrative regulations, and so on. It is therefore only natural that international lawyers, trained in national legal systems, should try to seek hierarchical principles in the international legal system as well. But in its present stage of development, the international community has no single and supreme legislature whose decrees would prevail over those of subordinate

[123] UN Press Release (Geneva) HR/1735, Aug. 7, 1985, at 2.
See generally, Schachter, *International Law in Theory and Practice* 178 Recueil des Cours 12, 331-2 (1982-V); Humphrey, *Political and Related Rights*, in 1 International Law of Human Rights: Legal and Policy Issues 171, 171-4 (T. Meron ed., 1984); Shestack, *The Jurisprudence of Human Rights*, ibid. at 69, 99-101; van Boven, *Distinguishing Criteria of Human Rights*, in 1 The International Dimensions of Human Rights 43, 53-7 (K. Vasak ed., P. Alston Eng. ed., 1982); Marks, *Emerging Human Rights: A New Generation for the 1980s?*, in International Law: A Contemporary Perspective 501 (R. Falk, F. Kratochwil, and S. Mendlovitz eds., 1985); Vasak, *Pour une troisième génération des droits de l'homme*, in Studies and Essays on International Humanitarian Law and Red Cross Principles in Honour of Jean Pictet 837 (C. Swinarski ed., 1984); Alston, above n. 121.

law-making bodies. Moreover, such an institution is not likely to be established in the foreseeable future. Nor has customary law filled the gap (consider the various constitutional conventions in the United Kingdom). Except for the emerging rules of *jus cogens* to be discussed later in this section, only in Article 103 of the Charter of the United Nations (which provides that in the event of a conflict between the obligations of member States under the Charter and their obligations under any other international agreement, their obligations under the Charter shall prevail) is a hierarchical principle of general international law made explicit. Its binding character is to be explained, as Lord McNair does, by the 'constitutive or semi-legislative character' of the Charter.[124]

The supremacy of the Charter, of course, carries implications for other instruments concerned, wholly or partly, with human rights. Thus, in one of its earliest resolutions, the UN Economic and Social Council (ECOSOC) has expressed the wish that, '[p]ending the adoption of an international bill of rights, the general principle shall be accepted that international treaties involving basic human rights, including to the fullest extent practicable treaties of peace, shall conform to the fundamental standards relative to such rights set forth in the Charter'.[125] The generality of these standards and the resultant difficulty in realizing this *voeu* should in no way detract from its salutary purpose, that is the avoidance of normative conflicts, which is particularly important where they cannot be resolved by invoking generally agreed hierarchical principles.

This is not to suggest that, apart from Article 103 of the Charter, hierarchical principles are totally absent from international law. Some such rules have been developed in international organizations and administrations. In the European

[124] A. McNair, The Law of Treaties 217 (1961). For a recent discussion of the hierarchical character of Article 103, see Flory, *Article 103*, La Charte des Nations Unies 1371 (J. Cot and A. Pellet eds., 1985).

In the Advisory Opinion on Reparation for Injuries Suffered in the Service of the United Nations the Court stated that the member States of the United Nations, representing the vast majority of the international community, had the power to bring into being an entity possessing objective international personality and the capacity to bring international claims against States not members of the United Nations. 1949 I.C.J. 174, 185 (Advisory Opinion of April 11). See also Art. 6(2) of the Charter.

[125] ECOSOC Res. 9(II), 2 UN ESCOR 400, at 401 (1946).

Economic Community, for example, the Treaty establishing the European Community (Treaty of Rome) is supreme law;[126] in the United Nations, Staff Rules promulgated by the Secretary-General are subordinate to Staff Regulations (Resolutions of the General Assembly); and the latter, of course, are subordinate to the Charter. Nevertheless, despite occasional claims to the contrary,[127] the reach of hierarchically superior instruments adopted within a particular regional or specialized institution is limited to the legal system of the parent organization and should not be confused with *jus cogens*.

Apart from *jus cogens*, whose application in particular cases is made difficult not so much by the continuing doctrinal controversy about the concept itself as by the lack of consensus about the identity of most peremptory norms, some human rights are obviously more important than other human rights. But, except in a few cases (for instance the right to life or to freedom from torture), to choose which rights are more important than other rights is exceedingly difficult. It is fraught with personal, cultural, and political bias, and, to make matters worse, has not been addressed by the international community as a whole, perhaps because of the improbability of reaching a meaningful consensus. The prevailing differences in the social, cultural, political, and economic values of States have made it easier to arrive at an agreement on a set of rights than on the order of priority to govern them. As Professor Schachter cogently argues, setting up a hierarchy of goals has an attractive simplicity, but '[e]ven the attempt to impose guidelines . . . for relatively well-defined specific situations involves choices among competing values which states are reluctant to make in advance or to abide by in practice'.[128] Except, perhaps, in cases where the same control organ is competent to interpret and balance two potentially conflicting norms, the practical consequences of the assessment that right x is more important than right y are not clear.[129] The

[126] See, e.g. Arts. 228 and 234, Treaty Establishing the European Economic Community (Treaty of Rome), 298 UNTS 11.

[127] For instance, Gormley, *The Right to Life and the Rule of Non-Derogability: Peremptory Norms of Jus Cogens*, in The Right to Life in International Law 120, 125–6 (B. Ramcharan ed., 1985).

[128] Schachter, *The United Nations and Internal Conflict*, in Dispute Settlement through the United Nations 301, 305 (K. Raman ed., 1977).

[129] See Meron, above n. 59, at 774.

intrinsic value of a particular norm, a necessarily subjective notion, should not be confused with recognized hierarchical principles that have clearly established legal significance.

B. *Fundamental Rights*

Examination of the Charter of the United Nations (Preamble, Articles 1(3), 13(b), 55(c), 62(2), 76(c)), the Universal Declaration of Human Rights (Preamble, Articles 2, 29(2) and 30), the International Covenant on Civil and Political Rights (Political Covenant) (Articles 2(1), 3, 5(1), 5(2)), the International Convention on the Elimination of All Forms of Racial Discrimination (Preamble, Article 1(1)), and the Convention on the Elimination of All Forms of Discrimination Against Women (Preamble, Articles 1, 3) reveals that the terms 'human rights', 'freedoms', 'fundamental human rights', 'fundamental freedoms', 'rights and freedoms', and, most commonly, 'human rights and fundamental freedoms' appear, in general, to be used interchangeably. This practice suggests that there is no substantive or definable legal difference between these terms. In these instruments at least, 'human rights' are not inferior to 'fundamental' rights and freedoms. They are the same.

The Tentative Proposals for a General International Organization submitted by the United States to the Dumbarton Oaks Conference (1944) referred to 'basic human rights', a term that was subsequently replaced by 'human rights and fundamental freedoms'.[130] Interpreting the latter term, Kelsen found that '"freedoms" are human rights'.[131]

The regional instruments on human rights also do not show

---

[130] L. Goodrich, E. Hambro, and A. Simons, Charter of the United Nations 373 (1969).

In an important study, Professor Sohn has pointed out that the reference to 'basic human rights' in the US Tentative Proposals of 1944 was preceded by other references, for instance by President Roosevelt in his 1941 'Four Freedoms' message to 'four essential freedoms'. The United States Bill of Rights of 1942 and theDeclaration of 1943 spoke of 'human rights'. Sohn, *A Short History of United Nations Documents on Human Rights*, in Commission to Study the Organization of Peace, the United Nations and Human Rights: 18th Report 44–7 (1968). For discussions at San Francisco, see ibid. at 48–56 and documents cited therein.

[131] H. Kelsen, The Law of the United Nations 29 (1966). Professors Cot and Pellet have observed that little importance should be attached to the distinction between references in the Charter to fundamental human rights and to human rights *tout court*. Cot and Pellet, *Preambule*, in Cot and Pellet (eds.), above n. 124, at 1, 14.

that the international community has defined fundamental rights or placed them ahead of ordinary rights. The European Convention for the Protection of Human Rights and Fundamental Freedoms[132] (European Convention) names in its body various rights and freedoms *tout court*, though the title and Preamble refer to 'fundamental freedoms'. The American Convention on Human Rights (American Convention) speaks of the obligation of the States Parties to respect various rights and freedoms, rather than fundamental rights.[133] The African Charter on Human and Peoples' Rights,[134] which has not yet entered into force, mentions fundamental human rights that 'stem from the attributes of human beings', in its Preamble, but in its body, simply rights and freedoms.

Nevertheless, the literature of international human rights demonstrates that some observers believe that there is a substantive difference between fundamental human rights and other human rights. One of these observers, Professor van Boven, alluding to the term 'fundamental human rights' in the Charter, emphasizes the 'supra-positive' character of such rights,[135] suggesting, perhaps, that they are based in natural law. However, whether this term brings any significance to bear on the question of a hierarchy of norms in positive international law is not clear. The author states that the principle of non-discrimination on grounds of race has been 'upgraded on the hierarchical scale of human rights norms', but he qualifies this claim by adding 'in so far as there is any such scale'.[136] Because it is not certain that the prohibition of some forms of racial discrimination would prevail over other human rights, in case of a conflict,[137] can one really speak here of a true hierarchical relationship?

The draft *Restatement* contains an important instance of a distinction between fundamental rights and other rights:

---

[132]   213 UNTS 221.
[133]   For the official text, see Organization of American States, Handbook of Existing Rules Pertaining to Human Rights in the Inter-American System 29, OEA/Ser.L./V/II.60, doc. 28, rev. 1 (1983).
[134]   Reprinted in 21 ILM 58 (1982).
[135]   Above n. 123, at 44.
[136]   Ibid.
[137]   Consider, for example, the relationship between freedoms of association and expression, and the suppression of racist theorizing discussed in Chapter I above.

Section 702(g) mentions 'consistent patterns of gross violations of internationally recognized human rights' as a violation of customary international law. This formulation results from the grafting of language from United States legislation[138] on to that of ECOSOC Resolution 1503 (XLVIII).[139] Comment *k* to Section 702 states that 'while all the rights proclaimed in the Universal Declaration and protected by the . . . Covenants . . . are internationally recognized human rights, some rights are fundamental and intrinsic to human dignity, and consistent patterns of violation of such rights as state policy may be deemed "gross" *ipso facto.*' Comment *k* thus suggests that when a pattern of violations of certain rights has reached a critical mass, it may be regarded as a breach of customary international law. But would this proposition not hold true also if applied to all internationally recognized human rights, rather than to 'fundamental rights' only?

The lack of generally agreed standards makes it extremely difficult to select such fundamental rights. To illustrate: among the fundamental rights listed in comment *k* to Section 702 is the right to leave one's country. Nevertheless, this right, considered *ut singuli*, is not listed among the customary human rights in the black-letter text of Section 702. This writer agrees with the drafters of the Restatement that the right to leave is fundamental. Yet the relativity of our perceptions is emphasized by the fact that in a recent study prepared for the UN Sub-Commission on Prevention of Discrimination and Protection of Minorities, Rapporteur Mubanga-Chipoia, discussing the effect of limitation clauses such as that contained in Article 12(3) of the Political Covenant, asks whether the right to leave one's country, which is stated in Article 12(2) thereof, constitutes a right 'or is rather a mere human attribute'.[140]

In a certain sense, all human rights can be regarded as fundamental, but the inconsistent use of the terms 'human rights' and 'fundamental human rights' may give rise to difficulties in

[138] Draft Restatement, above n. 120, § 702, Reporters' Note 9 (listing examples of relevant US statutes); Schachter, *International Law Implications of US Human Rights Policies*, 24 N.Y.L. Sch. L. Rev. 63, 75 (1978); Meron, *Teaching Human Rights: An Overview*, in 1 Meron (ed.), above n. 123, at 1, 20 and nn. 98-100.

[139] 48 UN ESCOR, Supp. (No. 1A) at 8-9, UN Doc. E/4832/Add. 1 (1970).

[140] UN Doc. E/CN.4/Sub.2/1985/9 at 5. On the right to leave, see generally Lillich, *Civil Rights*, in 1 Meron (ed.), above n. 123, at 115, 151-2.

the interpretation of international human rights instruments.

For example, Article 2 of the Declaration on the Elimination of All Forms of Intolerance and of Discrimination Based on Religion or Belief[141] prohibits discrimination on grounds of religion or other beliefs by any State, institution, group of persons, or person, and it defines intolerance and discrimination based on religion or belief as 'any distinction, exclusion, restriction or preference based on religion or belief and having as its purpose or as its effect nullification or impairment of the recognition, enjoyment or exercise of human rights and fundamental freedoms on an equal basis'. Assuming that the freedom of religious groups to administer religious law is protected by the principles of the Declaration, restrictions placed by the State upon that freedom would be permissible only if they complied with Article 1(3), which provides: '[f]reedom to manifest one's religion or belief may be subject only to such limitations as are prescribed by law and are necessary to protect public safety, order, health, or morals or the *fundamental* rights and freedoms of others.' (Emphasis added.) Any limitation not prescribed by law and not considered necessary to protect one of the stated goals would be 'discrimination based on religion or belief'.

The catalogue of limitations tracks the language of Article 18(3) of the Political Covenant and differs significantly from that in Article 29(2) of the Universal Declaration of Human Rights,[142] which served as the original model for this type of clause: while the latter also allows limitations for the purpose of securing due recognition and respect for the rights and freedoms of others and of meeting the requirements of the general welfare in a democratic society,[143] Article 1(3) is addressed only to the *'fundamental rights and freedoms* of others.' (emphasis added). Was this formulation of Article 1(3) deliberately selected to impose greater limitations on the State's ability to encroach upon freedom of religion? Arguably, this language

---

[141] GA Res. 36/55, 36 UN GAOR Supp. (No. 51) at 171, UN Doc. A/36/51 (1981).

[142] GA Res. 217A, UN Doc. A/810, at 71 (1948).

[143] See generally E. Daes, The Individual's Duties to the Community and the Limitations on Human Rights and Freedoms under Article 29 of the Universal Declaration of Human Rights, UN Doc. E/CN.4/Sub.2/432/Rev.2 (1983).

may limit the State's right to regulate the exercise of freedom of religion, even when such regulation may be justified by other human rights, for instance the advancement of women's equality, unless, of course, the latter is considered a fundamental right, rather than a right *tout court*. Thus, as a matter of literal construction, invocation of the human rights of others will not suffice; only 'fundamental human rights' will do. Does the determination that a right is fundamental *vel non* depend on international conceptions or on the mores and traditions of a particular national society? If the latter, account must be taken of the deplorable fact that some societies will not yet accept the goal of women's equality as a fundamental right.

The term 'fundamental rights', which inspired the development of international human rights, originated in national constitutions,[144] where it continues to be commonly employed. It is in this sense that the Court of Justice of the European Communities spoke of 'fundamental rights [which] form an integral part of the general principles of the law' and of 'the fundamental rights recognized by the constitutions [of Member States]'.[145] In national legal systems, fundamental or constitutional rights are characterized by the especially rigorous procedures required for their adoption, amendment, or termination, and by their superior position in the hierarchy of legal norms. In case of conflict, a subordinate norm must yield to a constitutional norm and its legal validity may even perhaps be questioned.

None of these characteristics can be found in the notion of fundamental human rights. In its Commentary on Article 17 of the draft articles on State Responsibility, the ILC has already warned that

only by erroneously equating the situation under international law with that under internal law . . . some lawyers have been able to see in the 'constitutional' or 'fundamental' principles of the international legal order an independent and higher 'source' of international obligations. In reality there is, in the international legal order, no special source of law for creating 'constitutional' or 'fundamental' principles. The principles which

---

[144] See generally Schindler, *The International Committee of the Red Cross and Human Rights*, Int'l Rev. Red Cross, No. 208, Jan.-Feb. 1979, at 3, 6.
[145] *Hauer* v. *Land Rheinland-Pfalz*, 1979 ECR 3727, 3744–5, [1980] 3 Comm. Mkt. L.R. 42, 64.

come to mind when using these terms are themselves customary rules, rules embodied in treaties, or even rules emanating from bodies or procedures which have themselves been established by treaties. Consequently, the view that international responsibility generated by a breach of certain obligations established by those principles is more grave, cannot be justified on the basis of their 'origin', but rather by taking account of the undeniable fact that the international community has a greater interest in ensuring that its members act in accordance with the specific requirements of the obligations in question.[146]

While it is true, as the ILC suggested, that the determination of the 'greater importance' of some obligations should be the function of the international community, in absence of effective institutional procedures for making such a determination and given the continued elusiveness of international consensus, the characterization of some rights as fundamental results largely from our own subjective perceptions of their importance. Perhaps they possess a special *erga omnes* character, as suggested by the Court in *Barcelona Traction*. We shall see, however, that the *erga omnes* character is no longer the exclusive attribute of fundamental rights. Moreover, being *erga omnes* is a consequence, not the cause, of a right's fundamental character. The *erga omnes* criterion is, therefore, unhelpful for characterizing rights as fundamental or ordinary.

For those fundamental rights which overlap with *jus cogens*, of course, Articles 53 and 64 of the Vienna Convention on the Law of Treaties[147] suggest certain analogies with higher, constitutional norms in national legal systems, but this is because of their being 'peremptory' rather than fundamental. While it is true, as the ILC pointed out in its Commentary on Article 50 (now 53) of the Vienna Convention on the Law of Treaties, that '[i]t is not the form of a general rule of international law but the particular nature of the subject-matter with which it deals that may . . . give it a character of *jus cogens*',[148] it is more difficult to accept the ILC's suggestion, made in the Commentary on Article 17 of the draft articles on State Responsibility, that

---

[146] [1976] 2 Y.B. Int'l L. Comm'n 73, 85-6, UN Doc. A/CN.4/Ser.A/1976/ Add. 1 (pt. 2).
[147] Opened for signature 23 May 1969, UN Doc. A/CONF. 39/27 (1969); reprinted in 63 AJIL 875 (1969), 8 ILM 679 (1969).
[148] [1966] 2 Y.B. Int'l L. Comm'n 169, 248, UN Doc. A/CN.4/Ser. A/1966/ Add. 1 (1967).

the 'process by which they [such rules] were created' is irrelevant.[149] Process is relevant for the acceptance of a rule of *jus cogens*, which requires a very large majority of the States ('the international community as a whole'), and even more for the establishment of a subsequent norm of general international law having the character of *jus cogens* and modifying an earlier rule of *jus cogens* (*jus cogens superveniens*). Can a subsequent rule of *jus cogens* modifying an earlier rule of *jus cogens* be established through practice and customary law that is in conflict with the earlier rule, or by a general multilateral treaty as suggested by the ILC?[150] What would the significance be of practice or of customary law which is being crystallized in·conflict with existing rules of *jus cogens*? Neither the scant international practice nor the richer doctrine has given fully satisfactory answers to this question.

If a fundamental right may constitute a peremptory right, the difficulty of identifying fundamental rights gives way to the even greater difficulty of qualifying certain rights as peremptory. Because invalidity of a norm may result from its conflict with *jus cogens*, this qualification is a formidable, even awesome task. For the scholar as well as the practitioner, it requires discharging a heavy burden of proof.

A catalogue of 'fundamental human rights' can, of course, be established by a future agreement or, perhaps, developed through international practice and jurisprudence. Such a catalogue should not be confused with lists of non-derogable rights and their relationship with *jus cogens*, to be discussed later in this section.

Account must be taken, however, of the following important, but ambivalent, dictum by the International Court of Justice in its judgment in the *Barcelona Traction* case:[151]

33. When a State admits into its territory foreign investments or foreign nationals, whether natural or juristic persons, it is bound to extend to

---

[149] Above n. 146, at 85.

[150] Above n. 148. Sir Ian Sinclair has questioned the status of a new multilateral treaty which, at the time of its conclusion, would be in conflict with an earlier rule of *jus cogens* (Sinclar, above n. 39, at 226). But would such a conflict arise where the international community has accepted, through a very large majority support for a new general multilateral treaty, the formulation of a new rule of *jus cogens*? Would such acceptance not indicate the emergence of a new rule of *jus cogens* and the modification of the previous rule of *jus cogens* even before the entry into force of the new treaty?

[151] Above n. 114.

them the protection of the law and assumes obligations concerning the treatment to be afforded them. These obligations, however, are neither absolute nor unqualified. In particular, an essential distinction should be drawn between the obligations of a State towards the international community as a whole, and those arising vis-à-vis another State in the field of diplomatic protection. By their very nature the former are the concern of all States. In view of the importance of the rights involved, all States can be held to have a legal interest in their protection; they are obligations *erga omnes*.

34. Such obligations derive, for example, in contemporary international law, from the outlawing of acts of aggression, and of genocide, as also from the principles and rules concerning the basic rights of the human person, including protection from slavery and racial discrimination. Some of the corresponding rights of protection have entered into the body of general international law . . .; others are conferred by international instruments of a universal or quasi-universal character. [152]

The above pronouncement does not make clear, however, whether 'basic rights of the human person', which give rise to obligations *erga omnes*, are synonymous with human rights *tout court*, or are limited to rights intimately associated with the human person and human dignity and generally accepted, such as the protection from slavery and racial discrimination. Moreover, the distinction between basic rights of the human person and 'ordinary' human rights is not self-evident. If the Court intended to set apart the basic rights of the human person, the inclusion of some human rights among them would perhaps depend on their acceptance into the corpus of general international law or on their incorporation into instruments of a universal or quasi-universal character, but a more subjective and difficult characterization would also have to be made, such as the nature of their association with the human person and human dignity.

Elsewhere in the judgment, an indication can, indeed, be found that the Court intended to distinguish between human rights in general and the basic rights of the human person. The Court emphasized that, in contrast to the European Convention, 'which entitles each State which is a party to the Convention to lodge a complaint against any other contracting State for violation of the Convention, irrespective of the nationality of the victim',[153] 'on the universal level, the instruments which

---

[152] Ibid. at 32.
[153] Ibid. at 47.

embody human rights do not confer on States the capacity to protect the victims of infringements of such rights irrespective of their nationality'.[154] The Court seems to suggest that, while basic rights of the human person give rise to obligations *erga omnes* and are appropriate for protection by States regardless of the nationality of the victim, other human rights, or ordinary human rights, can be espoused under the agreements embodying such rights, only by the State of the nationality of the victims.

This pronouncement of the Court will obviously create some perplexity when the need arises to characterize human rights as either ordinary or basic. Most observers would probably agree that protection of the right to life from arbitrary taking and protection of the human person from torture or egregious racial discrimination are fundamental rights. Perhaps they would also agree that the small number (irreducible core) of rights that are deemed non-derogable under both the International Covenant on Civil and Political Rights (Political Covenant)[155] and the European and American Conventions constitutes fundamental, and perhaps even peremptory norms. But that irreducible core comprises four rights only : the right to life and the prohibitions of slavery, torture, and retroactive penal measures. The prospects for a consensus reaching beyond these few rights are not immediate. For instance, while for some observers, including this writer, due process rights are fundamental and indispensable for ensuring any other right, for others, the rights to food and other basic needs take precedence. Superficially seductive formulas such as the notion of rights protecting the physical and mental well-being of the human person are not helpful either, because they involve clusters of rights whose components require scrutiny. Would the prohibition of indefinite preventive detention, for example, be considered fundamental?

One point is clear, however. The Court's reference to the body of general international law and to universal or quasi-universal agreements suggests that a fundamental right must be firmly rooted in international law and that mere claims or goals, important as they may be, would not qualify.

---

[154] Ibid.
[155] GA Res. 2200, 21 UN GAOR Supp. (No. 16) at 52, UN Doc. A/6316 (1966).

Protection from slavery and racial discrimination, the examples of basic human rights mentioned by the Court, may well reflect its conception of norms of *jus cogens*, which it did not explicitly spell out; but rights characterized by an *erga omnes* reach are not necessarily identical with *jus cogens*. Despite a certain overlap, the latter is narrower than the former.

Since the judgment of the Court, and perhaps under the impact of that judgment, there has been a growing acceptance in contemporary international law of the principle that, apart from agreements conferring on each State party *locus standi* against the other States Parties, all States have a legitimate interest in and the right to protest against significant human rights violations wherever they may occur, regardless of the nationality of the victims. This crystallization of the *erga omnes* character of human rights, rooted in Articles 55 and 56 of the Charter, is taking place despite uncertainty as to whether a State not directly concerned (for example in the protection of its nationals), *ut singuli*, may take up claims against the violating State[156] and demand reparation for a breach of international law. However, the general principle establishing international accountability and the right to censure can be regarded as settled law.[157] Thus, while doubts may persist about the appropriate remedies that can be demanded by a third State that does not have a direct interest in the matter, subject to the acceptance by the States concerned of the jurisdiction of a competent tribunal the *locus standi* of such a third State, in principle, is not questioned.

But the most interesting feature of this development is that the growing acceptance of the *erga omnes* character of human rights has not been limited to the basic rights of the human person only. Thus, Section 703(2) of the Draft Restatement[158] provides that any State may pursue international remedies against any other State for a violation of customary international law of human rights. In their notes, the reporters elaborate as follows:

[t]he customary law of human rights . . . protects individuals subject to

---

[156] Sinclair, above n. 39, at 213, Schachter, above n. 123, at 196-9; 341-2.
[157] See generally Schachter, above n. 138, at 66-74; Schachter, above n. 123, at 200.
[158] Draft Restatement, above n. 120.

each state's jurisdiction, and the international obligation runs equally to all other states, with no one state a victim of the violation more than any other. If there is to be any remedy at all, it must be available equally to all states.[159]

The *erga omnes* character of human rights is also suggested by Article 5(d) (iv) of the draft articles on State Responsibility (Part Two), proposed by the ILC's special rapporteur, Professor Riphagen, which states as follows:

For the purposes of the present articles 'injured State' means:
. . .
(d) if the internationally wrongful act constitutes a breach of an obligation imposed by a multilateral treaty, a State party to that treaty, if it is established that:
. . .
(iv) the obligation was stipulated for the protection of individual persons, irrespective of their nationality.[160]

While the above provision concerns obligations imposed by treaties[161] it is noteworthy that the distinction between basic rights of the human person and ordinary human rights is not addressed.

In a recent statement, the UN Assistant Secretary-General for Human Rights, Dr Kurt Herndl, has emphasized that one of

---

[159] Ibid, § 703, Reporters' Note 3.

[160] Report of the International Law Commission on the work of its thirty-sixth session, 39 UN GAOR Supp. (No. 10) at 237 n. 299, UN Doc. A/39/10 (1984); Report of the International Law Commission on the work of its thirty-seventh session, 40 UN GAOR Supp. (No. 10) at 39, UN Doc. A/40/10 (1985).

[161] UN Doc. A/CN.4/389, at 9 (1985). In 1985, the ILC amended Art. 5(d) (iv) of the Riphagen draft, emphasizing that the principle stated in it applied to international customary law as well. The relevant part of Art. 5 as provisionally adopted by the ILC reads as follows:
'2. In particular, 'injured State' means
. . .
     (e) if the right infringed by the act of a State arises from a multilateral treaty or from a rule of customary international law, any other State party to the multilateral treaty or bound by the relevant rule of customary international law, if it is established that:
. . .
     (iii) the right has been created or is established for the protection of human rights and fundamental freedoms;'
Report of the International Law Commission on the work of its thirty-seventh session, 40 UN GAOR Supp. (No. 10) at 54, UN Doc. A/40/10 (1985). The Commentary explained that '[t]he term "human rights and fundamental freedoms" is here used in the sense which is current in present-day international relations'. Ibid. at 58.

the accomplishments of the United Nations has been to consolidate the principle that human rights are a matter of international concern that the international community is entitled to discuss.[162] Scholarly writings point in the same direction. Thus, in an important study of international accountability and the right to censure human rights violations, Professor Schachter does not distinguish between the basic rights of the human person and human rights *tout court*. He points out, rightly, that in the absence of specific interests of their own, States tend to focus on censuring violations of 'fundamental norm[s] of humanity'.[163] This tendency, however, appears to reflect considerations of foreign policy and an assessment of the significance of the breach, rather than a formal distinction between fundamental rights and ordinary rights.

In sum, international practice and scholarly opinion seem to have moved well beyond the *erga omnes* dictum of *Barcelona Traction*: perhaps the distinction between basic human rights and human rights *tout court*, as regards their *erga omnes* character, can no longer be supported.

We shall see, however, that despite the acknowledged vagueness of the term,[164] the Institute of International Law has carried the notion of basic rights of the human person even further into the uncertain terrain of *jus cogens*.

C. *Jus Cogens*

The notion of the peremptory norms of international law (*jus cogens*) is stated in Articles 53 and 64 of the Vienna Convention on the Law of Treaties. Article 53 provides as follows:

---

[162] UN Press Release (Geneva) HR/1733, Aug. 6, 1985, at 2. See also UN Doc. A/40/348, at 6–7 (1985).

[163] Schachter, above n. 138, at 70. Principle 2 of the Principles for the International Law of the Future emphasized the duty of each State to 'treat its own population in a way which will not violate the dictates of humanity and justice or shock the conscience of mankind'. 38 AJIL Supp. 72, 74 (1944). These terms can be traced to the preambular Martens clause to (Hague) Convention (No. IV) Respecting the Laws and Customs of War on Land, with Annex of Regulations, Oct. 18, 1907, 36 Stat. 2277, TS No. 539. See Meron, above n. 50, at 593 and n. 24.

[164] See e.g. Suy, *Droit des traités et droits de l'homme*, in Völkerrecht als Rechtsordnung, internationale Gerichtsbarkeit, Menschenrechte: Festschrift für Hermann Mosler 935, 936–7 (R. Bernhardt, W. Geck, G. Jaenicke, and H. Steinberger eds., 1983); I. Brownlie, Principles of Public International Law 512 (3rd edn., 1979).

A treaty is void if, at the time of its conclusion, it conflicts with a peremptory norm of general international law. For the purposes of the present Convention, a peremptory norm of general international law is a norm accepted and recognized by the international community of States as a whole as a norm from which no derogation is permitted and which can be modified only by a subsequent norm of general international law having the same character.

The literature on *jus cogens* is rich.[165] For our purposes, only a few observations narrowly focused on human rights are called for.

The principle of *jus cogens*, which restricts the freedom of States to contract and voids instruments that conflict with peremptory norms, has unquestionable ethical underpinnings and unimpeachable antecedents. It may be traced to the distinction in Roman law between *jus strictum* and *jus dispositivum* and to Grotius's references to *jus strictum*.[166] Its moral and deterrent effect is of particular importance in our era, characterized as it is by internal and international violence and frequent breaches of most human rights. But even for those who accept it, as this author does, this principle gives rise to difficult questions.

First, what is, in the contemporary reality, the relevance of *jus cogens* for agreements implicating human rights? As a matter of fact, States do not conclude agreements to commit torture or genocide or enslave peoples. Many of the examples of *jus cogens* commonly cited in legal literature are really *hypothèses d'école*. Moreover, States are not inclined to contest the absolute illegality of acts prohibited by the principle of *jus cogens*. When such acts do take place, States deny the factual allegations or justify violations by more subtle or ingenious arguments. Thus, while the principle of *jus cogens* has a moral and potential value, its immediate practical importance to the validity of agreements is still limited. However, when it comes to balancing one human right which has assumed the status of *jus cogens*

---

[165] See I. Sinclair, above n. 39, at 203–6, and the literature mentioned in ibid. at 236 n. 8; Weil, above n. 110; Whiteman, *Jus Cogens in International Law, With a Projected List*, 7 Ga. J. Int'l & Comp. L. 609 (1977); Domb, *Jus Cogens and Human Rights*, 6 Israel Y.B. Human Rights 104 (1976); Schwelb, *Some Aspects of International Jus Cogens as Formulated by the International Law Commission*, 61 AJIL 946 (1967); Gros Espiell, *Self-Determination and Jus Cogens*, in UN Law/Fundamental Rights 167 (A. Cassese ed., 1979).

[166] Frowein, *Jus Cogens*, [Instalment] 7 Encyclopedia of Public International Law 327, 328 (R. Bernhardt ed., 1984).

against another human right which has not gained such an exalted status, the concept may be relevant.

A second set of questions stems from the continuing lack of agreement about the identity of the peremptory rules themselves. The International Law Commission, which prepared the draft of the Vienna Convention, has prudently refrained from suggesting a catalogue of peremptory rules. Few attempts have been made to identify such rules in the field of human rights. Invoking the authority of Professors McDougal, Lasswell, and Chen,[167] Comment 1 to § 702 of the Draft Restatement[167] states that the prohibitory rules of customary international law carefully listed in that section constitute *jus cogens* and that an international agreement that would violate them would be void. The following prohibitions are so listed: genocide, slavery or slave trade, the murder or causing the disappearance of individuals, torture or other cruel, inhuman, or degrading treatment or punishment, prolonged arbitrary detention, systematic racial discrimination, and consistent patterns of gross violations of internationally recognized human rights, all of which constitute

---

[167] M. McDougal, H. Lasswell, and L. Chen, Human Rights and World Public Order 338–50 (1980). The authors state that 'many of the policies about human rights would appear to be so intensely demanded that they are acquiring . . . not merely the status of "international concern," but in addition that of *jus cogens* or of a global bill of rights.' Ibid. at 185. They regard the Universal Declaration of Human Rights 'as established customary law, having the attributes of *jus cogens*'. Ibid. at 274. They suggest that 'the great bulk of the contemporary human rights prescriptions' are identifiable as *jus cogens*. Ibid. at 345. The view of the learned authors finds support in the statement of Judge Tanaka that 'the law concerning the protection of human rights may be considered to belong to the *jus cogens*'. South West Africa Cases (*Ethiopia* v. *South Africa*; *Liberia* v. *South Africa*), Second Phase, 1966 I.C.J. 250, 298 (Judgment of July 18) (Tanaka J., diss. op.). Also Verdross argues that 'all rules of general international law created for a humanitarian purpose' constitute *jus cogens*. Verdross, *Jus Dispositivum and Jus Cogens in International Law*, 60 AJIL 53, 59 (1966).

Sinclair, who disagrees with the attempts to regard all human rights as *jus cogens*, asks whether rights subject to progressive realization under Article 2(1) of the International Covenant on Economic, Social and Cultural Rights (Economic Covenant) can constitute *jus cogens*. Sinclair, above n. 39, at 217. For the text of the Economic Covenant, see GA Res. 2200, 21 UN GAOR Supp. (No. 16) at 49, UN Doc. A/6316 (1966). For a view that not all human rights are *jus cogens*, see also Schachter, above n. 123, at 339; Higgins, *Derogations under Human Rights Treaties*, [1976–77] 48 Brit. Y.B. Int'l L. 281, 282 (1976–7).

[168] Draft Restatement above n. 120, Reporters' Note 10; See also 2 ibid. § 331(2), Comment *e* and Reporters' Note 4. See generally Schachter, above n. 123, at 333–8.

violations if practiced as a matter of State policy.[169] To this list one should perhaps add certain norms of international humanitarian law. Considering the difficulties inherent in this subject, it is not surprising that in a study prepared in 1977 Whiteman compiled a significantly different and shorter list of peremptory human rights.[170] Because the prohibition of prolonged arbitrary detention is not mentioned among the non-derogable rights in Article 4 of the Political Covenant, the Restatement's identification of that prohibition as a rule of *jus cogens* creates a particularly difficult problem.[171]

The relationship between *jus cogens* and derogability is an interesting one. The principal human rights instruments (the Political Covenant, the American Convention, the European Convention) contain the same hard core of non-derogable rights, yet different lists of non-derogable rights. Rights that are non-derogable under such instruments are not necessarily *jus cogens* (for example the right not to be imprisoned merely on the ground of inability to fulfil a contractual obligation, which is stated in Article 11 of the Political Covenant, or perhaps the more important non-derogable right to participate in government, which is stated in Article 23 of the American Convention) and some of them may not even have attained the status of customary law. Conversely, can a right whose derogation is permitted by a primary international human rights agreement (the Political Covenant) be regarded as *jus cogens* in light of the statement of the principle of *jus cogens* in Article 53 of the Vienna Convention (a norm from which no derogation is permitted)?

---

[169] A later draft omitted 'consistent patterns of gross violations of internationally recognized human rights' from the list of peremptory norms. Restatement of the Foreign Relations Law of the United States (Revised), § 702, Comment *n*, Reporters' Note 10 (Tent. Final Draft, 1985) (hereinafter cited as Tent. Final Draft).

[170] Whiteman, above n. 165, at 625–6.

[171] It has been suggested that detentions occurring during time of emergency and which comply with the requirements of Art. 4 of the Political Covenant are not arbitrary. § 702, Reporters' Note 10, Tent. Final Draft Restatement, above n. 169. But the requirements of Article 4 are addressed primarily to the conditions for the proclamation of an emergency, not the standards governing detention procedures (due process). The notion of arbitrariness must refer to the character of the procedures of detention themselves, rather than only to the legality of the state of emergency under which they are authorized. Is there not a danger that the suggestion made in Reporters' Note 10 might be invoked to support the claim that every detention which takes place in a time of emergency in compliance with Article 4 is non-arbitrary, despite the prevalence of arbitrary detentions in such situations?

The existence of non-derogable rights is cited by some writers as evidence for the existence of 'at least a minimum catalogue of fundamental or elementary human rights'.[172] In an important essay, Professor Suy carries this argument further into the field of the public order of the international community, which is somewhat analogous to *jus cogens*, and to which we shall return later in this essay:

L'interdiction formelle de toute dérogation nous paraît en effet être un critère objectif permettant d'identifier une règle relevant de l'ordre public de la communauté internationale. En appliquant ce critère, non seulement on sera amené à exclure du champ de cet ordre public tous les droits de l'homme auxquels il est expressément permis de déroger, mais on y fera aussi rentrer toutes les normes auxquelles il n'est pas permis de déroger qu'elles aient trait ou non aux droits de l'homme.[173]

While the first part of Professor Suy's suggestion is perfectly correct, the second is true only with regard to States contractually bound to a particular list of non-derogable rights. Since the reference to the public order of the international community is to general international law, the fact that a particular right is stated in a particular instrument, even one as important as the Political Covenant, is not necessarily conclusive.

While most non-derogable rights are of cardinal importance, some derogable rights may be of equal importance (for example due process of law under Article 14 of the Political Covenant). The international community as a whole has neither established a uniform list of non-derogable rights nor ranked non-derogable rights ahead of derogable rights. If a derogable right conflicts with a non-derogable right, the latter will not necessarily prevail, unless, of course, its status as a peremptory norm of general international law is recognized. We shall return to certain additional problems of derogability in our discussion of international public order.

Even a well-established right such as the prohibition of systematic racial discrimination, mentioned in section 702 (f) of the Draft Restatement, presents difficulties when regarded as *jus cogens*. Apartheid, which is mentioned in Comment *i* to section 702, is easy to characterize because of its governmental nature and systematic administration as well as its egregious

---

[172] Van Boven, above n. 123, at 46.
[173] Suy, above n. 164, at 938.

character. Even apart from apartheid, there is little disagreement with the overall prohibition of racial discrimination, but the consensus narrows as one moves from the general principle to specific manifestations of discrimination.

These comments are not meant to disparage the ethically important contribution made by the Draft Restatement to the crystallization, through a proposed list, of the still fluid notion of *jus cogens*. In the long run, such a list may influence the development of the law of *jus cogens*, whose contents will be established through general custom or by universal or quasi-universal agreements.

A recent advisory opinion of the Inter-American Court of Human Rights deals with another important aspect of *jus cogens*: the relationship between derogability and reservations. The Court emphasized that 'a reservation which was designed to enable a State to suspend any of the non-derogable fundamental rights must be deemed to be incompatible with the object and purpose of the Convention and, consequently, not permitted by it.'[174] Judge Buergenthal comments that this opinion

constitutes the first unambiguous international judicial articulation of a principle basic to the application of human rights treaties, that non-derogability and incompatibility are linked. The nexus between non-derogability and incompatibility derives from and adds force to the conceptual interrelationship which exists between certain fundamental human rights and emerging *jus cogens* norms.[175]

While the possibility of conflicts between *jus cogens* norms in the field of human rights and other human rights is largely academic, conflicts may arise between human rights and rules, and especially the implementation of rules, embodied in international agreements governing other matters such as extradition. The *jus cogens* nature of human rights is thus implicated as the deliberations of the prestigious Institute of International Law (Cambridge, 1983) reveal to interesting effect.

Under the item 'New problems of the international legal

---

[174] Restrictions to the Death Penalty (Arts. 4(2) and 4(4) American Convention on Human Rights), Advisory Opinion No. OC-3/83, Sept. 8, 1983, Inter-American Ct. of Human Rights, ser. A: Judgments and Opinions No. 3, para. 61 (1983).

[175] Buergenthal, *The Advisory Practice of the Inter-American Human Rights Court*, 79 AJIL 22, 25 (1985) (footnote omitted). On reservations and *jus cogens*, see generally Sinclair, above n. 39, at 211–12.

system of extradition with special reference to multilateral treaties', the rapporteur, Professor Doehring, proposed a draft resolution which provided (Article III(1)) that '[t]he invocation of the duty to protect human rights should in any case justify non-extradition, in particular [sic! The word 'even' would have been preferable] in cases where political persecution does not exist and where thus the granting of asylum cannot be based on that ground'.[176] Rather than merely recommend that States include in extradition agreements provisions stating that if any of their obligations under the agreements conflict with human rights, the latter shall prevail, Professor Doehring's proposal would in effect, have conferred a hierarchically superior status on human rights *tout court*.

In proposing that the expression 'human rights' in the draft resolution be replaced by 'basic rights of the human person', Judge Mosler explained that the latter, 'though lacking a well-defined content, took account of the dignity of the human person and the needs closely linked with the development of man as a human being'. He added that it would not be an exaggeration to state that 'the protection that this basic human position justified might prevail over treaties as a norm of *jus cogens*'.[177] On the other hand, the expression 'human rights' could be interpreted as meaning the United Nations Covenants on Human Rights, at least that on civil and political rights, and even regional conventions. Judge Mosler considered that it was clear that 'obligations to protect human rights as *jus cogens* did not go [so] far. Many of these law-making conventions defined human rights in a precise manner and prevented a wide interpretation of them by making exceptions, for example, for domestic jurisdiction or for measures "necessary in a democratic

---

[176] 60 Y.B. Institute of International Law 214 [1983 II] (1984).

In opposing Doehring's proposal, Briggs argued that 'the concepts of asylum and human rights were introduced as a sort of unilateral *jus cogens* justifying violation of obligations'. Ibid. at 230. McDougal, in supporting the proposal, argued that 'for some two hundred years there had been decisions to the effect that the responsibility of the State in respect of the protection of aliens overrode national laws. States could not unilaterally, and *a fortiori* bilaterally, override human rights'. Ibid at 230.

It is of interest to note that Frowein and Kühner single out the danger of torture as justifying non-extradition. Frowein and Kühner, *Drohende Folterung als Asylgrund und Grenze für Auslieferung und Ausweisung*, 43 Zeitschrift für ausländisches öffentliches Recht und Völkerrecht 537 (1983).

[177] 60 Y.B. Institute of International Law, above n. 176, at 234.

society".' Judge Mosler concluded by recommending that the latter type of provisions should be excluded from Professor Doehring's draft resolution.[178]

Judge Schwebel proposed that the English text of Article III(2) should employ the (synonymous) word 'fundamental' rather than 'basic' to modify human rights,[179] as in the French text (*droits fondamentaux*) of the judgment in the *Barcelona Traction* case. The text that was eventually adopted by the Institute as Article IV of the resolution reads as follows: 'In cases where there is a well-founded fear of the violation of the fundamental human rights of an accused in the territory of the requesting State, extradition may be refused . . .'[180]

The Institute appears therefore to support the proposition that 'fundamental human rights' are *jus cogens* and prevail over extradition agreements. We have already discussed the difficulties inherent in defining the content of fundamental human rights. These difficulties are neither resolved nor alleviated by the resolution. If fundamental human rights already constitute *jus cogens*, why does the resolution not employ the term 'shall' rather than 'may', which would imply a clear duty to accord priority to the norms of *jus cogens*?

To be sure, some human rights that can well be regarded as fundamental have become *jus cogens*. Yet can a whole block of fundamental human rights lacking a well-defined content, as Judge Mosler himself admits, constitute norms that the international community of States as a whole accepts and recognizes as permitting no derogations? Nevertheless, the Institute's resolution promotes valuable ethical considerations and may yet contribute to the crystallization of human rights into *jus cogens* and the development of the notion of fundamental human rights.

Another question crucial to international human rights is whether the concept of *jus cogens* applies only to the law of treaties or whether it extends to other fields of international law, including the unilateral action of States. Since violations of human rights almost always result from the unilateral acts of States, rather than from international agreements, the

---

[178] Ibid.
[179] Ibid. at 259.
[180] Ibid. at 306.

non-treaty aspect of the problem is far more important than the treaty aspect. Even scholars who reserve *jus cogens* to treaty law tend to agree with the elementary proposition that international public order, public order of the international community, and international public policy do not allow States to violate severally such norms as they are prohibited from violating jointly with other States.[181]

The International Law Commission appears to have applied the term 'peremptory norms' outside the law of treaties to unilateral state action when it adopted the draft articles on State responsibility.[182] Article 33(2) (*a*) provides that 'a state of necessity may not be invoked by a State as a ground for precluding wrongfulness . . . if the international obligation with which the act of the state is not in conformity arises out of a peremptory norm of general international law'.[183] In this context, however, peremptory norms may refer to categorical rules of international law, or of international public policy, rather than *jus cogens*, (which contrasts with the bulk of the rules of international law, the *jus dispositivum*, from which States are permitted, *inter partes*, to contract out) a concept that resides primarily in the law of treaties. Judge Mosler, who deserves credit for coining the phrase 'public order of the international community', characterized such order as

consist[ing] of principles. and rules the enforcement of which is of such vital importance to the international community as a whole that any unilateral action or any agreement which contravenes these principles can have no legal force. The reason for this follows simply from logic; the law

---

[181] H. Mosler, The International Society as a Legal Community 19-20 (1980). *Contra* Stein, *The Approach of the Different Drummer: The Principle of the Persistent Objector in International Law*, 26 Harv. Int'l L.J. 457, 481 (1985).

[182] [1980] 2 Y.B. Int'l L. Comm'n 30, UN Doc. A/CN.4/Ser.A/1980/Add.1 (pt. 2) (1981).

The ILC's commentary to draft Art. 12(b) on State responsibility (Part Two) mentions the reluctance of some members to apply the concept of *jus cogens* outside of the framework of the Vienna Convention on the Law of Treaties. Other members, however, supported the retention of that article. The view was expressed that 'a provision relating to *jus cogens* required . . . a procedural provision along the lines of that provided for in the Vienna Convention'. Report of the International Law Commission on the Work of its Thirty-seventh session, 40 UN GAOR Supp. (No. 10) at 41, 48, UN Doc. A/40/10 (1985).

[183] [1980] 2 Y.B. Int'l L. Comm'n 33, UN Doc. A/CN.4/Ser.A/1980/Add.1 (pt. 2). See generally Gaja, *Jus Cogens beyond the Vienna Convention*, 172 Recueil des cours 271, 296-7 (1981-III).

cannot recognise any act either of one member or of several members in concert, as being legally valid if it is directed against the very foundation of law.[184]

Obviously, the rationale underlying the concepts of *jus cogens* and public order of the international community is the same: because of the decisive importance of certain norms and values to the international community, they merit absolute protection and may not be derogated from by States, whether jointly by treaty or severally by unilateral legislative or executive action. It is in this sense that the International Court of Justice, in the case *Concerning United States Diplomatic and Consular Staff in Tehran*,[185] treated the 'imperative character of the legal obligations incumbent upon the Iranian Government'.[186]

Elsewhere, we have suggested that even States that are not parties to the Political Covenant may not derogate from categorical or absolute human rights and that derogations cannot be clearly excessive or arbitrary, or in conflict with other international obligations of the State concerned.[187] Comment *h* to § 711 of the Draft Restatement contains the intriguing proposition that the derogations permissible during an emergency under the Political Covenant are presumably also permissible under customary law in relation to nationals of other States.[188] Perhaps there is, indeed, some overlap in international law between derogations permitted by Article 4 of the Political Covenant and the customary rules of exception to the law governing State responsibility, such as those based on *force majeure*, state of necessity, or self-defence (draft Articles 31, 33, and 34 of the draft articles on State Responsibility). It is not certain, however, that the match of these customary rules with derogations permissible under Article 4 is perfect, or that the scope of the derogations allowed is identical.

If human right *x* is binding on a State not party to the Political Covenant in relation to its nationals or aliens, the derogating State would have to discharge the burden of establishing justifications such as state of necessity, just as if it had

---

[184] Mosler, above n. 181, at 18.
[185] 1980 I.C.J. Reports 3 (Judgment of May 24).
[186] Ibid. at 41.
[187] Meron, above n. 50, at 601-2 and n. 69.
[188] Draft Restatement, above n. 120.

breached any other international legal obligation. Where a State cannot successfully discharge such a burden, the principle applies, as pointed out by Professor Marek (who cites Professor Verdross),[189] that a single State is not permitted to derogate from any rule of international law, peremptory or not. The significance of the *jus dispositivum* character of most rules of international law lies in the fact that a group of States, strictly in their mutual relations, may substitute a rule of conventional law for a rule of customary law. The difference between peremptory and other rules of international law is that, in the case of the former, the prohibition of derogations is absolute.

If the rationale underlying the concepts of *jus cogens* and public order of the international community is the same, are the legal consequences of violation also the same? An affirmative answer is suggested by Judge Mosler, who insists that an agreement or unilateral action that conflicts with the public policy of the international community can have no legal force and presumably is void *ipso jure*.

This thesis requires scrutiny. Of course, a conflict between an international agreement and a rule of *jus cogens* nullifies the former. Judge Mosler would find a unilateral act similarly void. A treaty, however, is a creature of international law, while a unilateral state act may be rooted in the national legal system. Depending on the relationship between international law and internal law in the State concerned, it cannot be taken for granted that the unilateral act would have no internal legal force. (Indeed, the possibility of nullity is not even mentioned in Article 33 of ILC's draft Articles on state of necessity.) The violating State would incur international responsibility (or perhaps even international criminal responsibility if the principle stated in Article 19(3) of the ILC's draft Articles were applied), but the unilateral act itself would probably not be void, at least as regards its consequences under internal law. Professor Marek properly warns against 'l'oblitération de la différence entre acte illicite et acte nul'.[190]

The appropriate remedy for such a violation of a peremptory norm may therefore be annulment of the unilateral act, rather

---

[189] Marek, *Sur la notion de progrès en droit international*, in 38 Annuaire suisse de droit international 28, 35 (1982).
[190] Ibid.

than nullity *ipso jure*. Third States would have the right and the duty to question the illegal act, and to refrain from recognizing it or giving it legal effect. On the international legal plane, the principle *ex injuria jus non oritur* would thus be followed. Judge Mosler's statement that the unilateral act would have no legal force may have been intended to suggest that the act would not be recognized by third States as valid under international law. It is in this sense that Professor Jaenicke perceives the ramifications of international public order.[191]

These observations may become clearer if viewed against a specific case. The United Nations Report on Protection of Human Rights in Chile (Ermacora report) discussed a Chilean amnesty decree-law, which had been applied to protect governmental agents responsible for the deaths of detainees.[192] The report argued that Chile was responsible under Articles 29 and 146 of the Convention Relative to the Protection of Civilian Persons in Time of War (Geneva Convention No. IV) of Aug. 12, 1949.[193] It is not our present object to discuss whether this position was correct in law. Suffice it to observe that rather than insist on the nullity of the decree-law, the report recommended that the 'amnesty decree-law should not be applied in such a way as to run counter to Chile's international responsibilities, especially in regard to the Geneva Convention'.[194]

D. Concluding Observations

The use of hierarchical terms in discussing human rights reflects the quest for a normative order in which higher rights could be invoked as both a moral and a legal barrier to derogations from and violations of human rights. Their introduction into international law was inspired by the national law analogy with its firmly established hierarchical structure. The trend towards the characterization of certain rights as hierarchically superior may also be seen as a response to the proliferation of human rights instruments, sometimes of poor quality and uncertain legal value. When some rights proclaimed by such instruments are

---

[191] Jaenicke, *International Public Order*, in Encyclopedia, above n. 166, at 314, 317.

[192] UN Doc. A/34/583/Add.1, at 96 (1979).

[193] Ibid. For the text of Geneva Convention No. IV, see 6 UST 3516, TIAS No. 3365, 75 UNTS 287.

[194] Above n. 192, at 98.

questioned, it is not surprising that attempts are made to up-grade other rights by giving them various quality labels, on the assumption that the authority of the higher right will not be impugned.

One cannot deny that the quality labels are a useful indication of the importance attached to particular rights. They strengthen the case against violation of such rights. Hierarchical terms constitute a warning sign that the international community will not accept any breach of those rights. Historically, the notions of 'basic rights of the human person' and 'fundamental rights' have helped establish the *erga omnes* principle, which is so crucial to ensuring respect for human rights. Eventually, they may contribute to the crystallization of some rights, through custom or treaties, into hierarchically superior norms, as in the more developed national legal systems.

Yet the balance of pros and cons does not necessarily weigh clearly on the side of the pros. Resort to hierarchical terms has not been matched by careful consideration of their legal significance. Few criteria for distinguishing between ordinary rights and higher rights have been agreed upon. There is no accepted system by which higher rights can be identified and their content determined. Nor are the consequences of the distinction between higher and ordinary rights clear. Rights not accorded quality labels, that is the majority of human rights, are relegated to inferior, second-class, status. Moreover, rather than grapple with the harder questions of rationalizing human rights law-making[195] and distinguishing between rights and claims, some commentators are resorting increasingly to superior rights in the hope that no state will dare — politically, morally, and perhaps even legally — to ignore them. In these ways, hierarchical terms contribute to the mystification of human rights, rather than to their greater clarity. Caution should therefore be exercised in resorting to a hierarchical terminology. Too liberal an invocation of superior rights such as 'fundamental rights' and 'basic rights', as well as *jus cogens*, may adversely affect the credibility of human rights as a legal discipline.

Removal of the underbrush that clutters the landscape of

---

[195] See generally Chapter VII, below; Alston, above n. 121, at 607.

concepts and nomenclature may make it possible to build a sounder, less amorphous structure of human rights, which should be based on an enlarged core of non-derogable rights. To these ends, the international community should direct its efforts to defining the distinction between ordinary and higher rights and the legal significance of this distinction, steps which would contribute significantly to resolving conflicts between rights. It should also intensify the effort to extend the list of non-derogable rights recognized by the international community of States as a whole. In addition, the ethically important concepts of *jus cogens* and public order of the international community should be allowed to develop gradually through international practice and growing consensus. General acceptance of these concepts would go far towards deterring violations. Finally, the new human rights structure should eventually be secured by international acceptance of binding provisions for the adjudication of disputes implicating *jus cogens* and public order of the international community.

IX. TECHNIQUES FOR AVOIDANCE OR REDUCTION OF NORMATIVE CONFLICTS

In 1973 the ILO proposed certain techniques for the avoidance or reduction of conflicts.[196] To avoid duplication and conflict, the ILO suggested that, whenever possible, those organizations which had previously left a matter to other organizations should desist from any new legislative action. If the existing standards are unsatisfactory, or contain lacunae, the organization which adopted the original 'legislation' should undertake its revision. When a subject already addressed requires further legislative action, the new text should contain cross-references to the existing provisions, rather than establishing a new text as if dealing with a *tabula rasa*. One approach would be to refer in a preambular or other clause of the new instrument to the existing provision and to refrain from 'legislating' anew on the subject. Thus, no question would arise about the relationship between the obligations created by the two instruments. Another variant of the same cross-reference technique would be

---

[196] Co-ordination Report, above n. 5, Ann. II, at 5–9.

to state explicitly in the operative part of the new instrument that the existing provisions would continue to apply. Yet another technique would be to employ a saving clause which would provide that the obligations arising from an earlier instrument or instruments would not be affected by the adoption of the new instrument.

Saving or cross-reference clauses, when properly formulated, may be the equivalent for human rights instruments of provisions providing for the governing law or choice of law in private international law (conflict of laws). This function is described in Art. 30(2) of the Vienna Convention on the Law of Treaties which provides that '[w]hen a treaty specifies that it is subject to, or that it is not to be considered as incompatible with, an earlier or later treaty, the provisions of that other treaty prevail'. A saving clause or an avoidance of conflict clause would normally determine that situation a, which in the absence of a saving clause could be governed by norm x (contained in a new instrument) or by norm y (contained in an existing instrument), would be governed by the latter norm only. Such clauses are needed particularly where there are normative differences between the various instruments. The best technique for conflict avoidance, however, is not the formulation of such clauses but mutual legislative restraint leading either to abstention from legislating anew on a subject already regulated by an existing instrument, or to the formulation of norms which are parallel, similar, and complementary to existing provisions. Legislative co-ordination requires, of course, awareness and responsibility on the part of the lawmaking bodies and research leading to the identification of the existing instruments dealing with the subject matter of a new law-making proposal.[197] Since it is extremely difficult to ensure absolutely even by proper legislative co-ordination, that conflicts will not arise between a new instrument and an existing provision, saving clauses are always desirable.

As observed in Section I of this chapter, the International Labour Office has been effective in bringing to the attention of UN lawmakers potential conflicts with existing ILO instruments and has suggested, on occasion, specific language aimed

---

[197] Above n. 4.

at the elimination of such conflicts. The following examples of such efforts are of interest.

(*a*) In the case of the draft Convention on the Rights of the Child, the ILO submitted a number of comments to the Commission on Human Rights, highlighting problems and proposing the necessary amendments, for instance with regard to eligibility for social security and the employment of children, specifically in order to eliminate inconsistency between the proposed draft and the ILO Minimum Age Convention, 1973 (No. 138).[198]

(*b*) In the case of the draft declaration on the human rights of individuals who are not citizens of the country in which they live,[199] the ILO pointed out to the working group of the General Assembly charged with the elaboration of the draft that the draft declaration left unresolved the question of whether the declaration should apply to all aliens who are in a State or only to those who are present lawfully.[200] In contrast, the ILO Migrant Workers (Supplementary Provisions) Convention, 1975 (No. 143),[201] provides certain guarantees even for migrants in an 'irregular situation'. The ILO also pointed out that the draft convention on the protection of the rights of all migrant workers and their families, under consideration in another working group of the General Assembly, also established a number of guarantees to be enjoyed even when their beneficiaries are not in a 'regular situation'. Consistency in the standards to be established by the two drafts under preparation therefore had to be achieved. Furthermore, restrictions of some rights in the interest of national development were under consideration, which would make enjoyment of some economic and social rights subject to national law and the rights of aliens to join trade unions and to participate in their activities subject not only to the rules of the organizations concerned, but also to

[198] UN Doc. E/CN.4/1984/WG.1/WP.1 (1983); Convention (No. 138) concerning Minimum Age for Admission to Employment, International Labour Conventions and Recommendations 1919–1981, at 730 (International Labour Organisation (1982) (hereinafter cited as International Labour Conventions).

[199] GA Res. 37/169, 37 UN GAOR Supp. (No. 51) at 196, UN Doc. A/37/51 (1982); GA Res. 38/87, UN Doc. A/RES/38/87 (1983); UN Doc. A/C.3/39/9 and Corr. 1 (1984).

[200] UN Doc. A/38/147 at 6 (1983).

[201] Convention (No. 143) concerning Migrations in Abusive Conditions and the Promotion of Equality of Opportunity and Treatment of Migrant Workers, International Labour Conventions, above n. 198, at 821.

national laws in force. These restrictions exceeded those permitted by the ILO Freedom of Association and Protection of the Right to Organise Convention, 1948 (No. 87).[202] The ILO further argued that certain provisions of the draft pertaining to health protection, medical care, and social security appeared to be inconsistent with both the Economic Covenant and the relevant ILO Conventions.

(*c*) In the case of the draft declaration of the rights and responsibilities of youth, the ILO expressed reservations regarding the provisions which sought to establish the duty of young people to contribute actively to economic development.[203] The draft declaration was not to be merely hortatory, but was to be a basis for legal standards to be adopted through legislative and administrative measures. A legally enforceable duty to work might be created, which would conflict with Art. 8 of the Political Covenant and with Art. 1(b) of the ILO Abolition of Forced Labour Convention, 1957 (No. 105),[204] which provides for suppression of forced or compulsory labour as a method of mobilizing labour for purposes of economic development.

(*d*) The ILO has been particularly active during the last few years in trying to prevent conflicts between the existing ILO conventions and the proposed convention on the rights of all migrant workers and their families.[205] In this context, the ILO has prepared a comprehensive comparison between the provisions of the draft convention and the existing ILO instruments.[206]

To summarize, whenever legislative abstention is not possible, legislative cross-references or saving clauses should be employed.[207] In some cases, legislative abstention may be ac-

---

[202] Convention (No. 87) concerning Freedom of Association and Protection of the Right to Organise, International Labour Conventions, above n. 198, at 4.

[203] From unpublished correspondence.

[204] Convention (No. 105) concerning the Abolition of Forced Labour, International Labour Conventions, above n. 198, at 39.

[205] For recent drafts prepared by a working group of the General Assembly, see UN Doc. A/C.3/39/1 (1984) and UN Doc. A/C.3/39/4 (1984). The following are among the principal documents pertaining to the position of the ILO: UN Doc. E/1980/16 at 7 (1980), UN Doc. A/C.3/35/1 (1980), UN Doc. A/C.3/35/WG.1/CRP.2 (1980), UN Doc. A/C.3/35/WG.1/CRP.8 (1981); ILO Doc. GB.212/15/28 (1980); ILO Doc. GB.215/IO/1/5 (1981), ILO Doc. GB.219/IO/1/6 (1982), ILO Doc. GB.221/IO/17 (1982), ILO Doc. GB.222/IO/1/4 (1983), ILO Doc. GB.222/IO/5/4 (1983), ILO Doc. GB.225/IO/1/1 (1984), ILO Doc. GB.225/IO/3/3 (1984).

[206] ILO Doc. GB.225/IO/1/1/, App. I (1984).

[207] Co-ordination Report, above n. 5, Ann. II, at 6–8.

companied by a cross-reference or a saving provision in the new instrument. The latter technique provides double protection against conflicts and greater certainty that conflict will be avoided. An early example of both legislative restraint and a normative cross-reference, admirable in its simplicity, is Art. 21 of the Regulations annexed to the Fourth Hague Convention with respect to the Laws and Customs of War on Land of 1907.[208] That article provides that '[t]he obligations of belligerents with regard to the sick and wounded are governed by the Geneva Convention'. One of the most recent examples of a provision reflecting both legislative restraint and a normative cross-reference was an amendment to Art. 138 (General conduct of States in relation to the Area) of the United Nations Convention on the Law of the Sea,[209] which would have created a second paragraph reading as follows:

2. Signatories to this treaty agree to enforce internationally recognized labor standards regarding working conditions and maritime safety. Internationally recognized labor standards are defined as those standards specified in the conventions and the recommendations of the International Labour Organisation, with special reference to the Minimum Standards in the Merchant Ships Convention (Number 147) . . .[210]

This amendment was, however, withdrawn together with a number of other amendments as part of a compromise designed to enable the Conference to complete its work.[211]

Another important example of a legislative cross-reference or saving clause appears in Art. 46 of the Political Covenant and its counterpart, Art. 24 of the Economic Covenant. Art. 46 provides that '[n]othing in the present Covenant shall be interpreted as impairing the provisions of the Charter of the United Nations and of the constitutions of the specialized agencies which define the respective responsibilities of the various organs of the

---

[208]   36 Stat. 2277, TS No. 539.

[209]   The Law of the Sea: United Nations Convention on the Law of the Sea with Index and Final Act of the Third United Nations Conference on the Law of the Sea 43, UN Publication Sales No. E.83.V.5 (1983).

[210]   UN Doc. A/CONF.62/L.121, at 2 (1982).

[211]   Wolf and Kellerson, *Les Problèmes de droit du travail et la Convention sur le Droit de la Mer*, in Colloque de Rouen, perspectives du droit de la mer à l'issue de la 3e Conférence des Nations Unies 224, 235 (Société Française pour le Droit International, 1984).

United Nations and of the specialized agencies in regard to the matters dealt with in the present Covenant'.

Recent clauses designed to avoid conflicts have not been uniform. Some aim at saving only the more advantageous provisions of other instruments. Thus, the saving clause of the Discrimination Against Women Convention, Art. 23, provides that nothing in the Convention shall affect for a State Party any provisions in any other international convention, treaty, or agreement 'that are more conducive to the achievement of equality between men and women . . .'.[212] Whether a particular provision is in fact more conducive to the achievement of equality may not always be easy to determine.[213] Whether one right is more advantageous than another depends very much on the perspective from which the problem is examined and, certainly, on the character and mandate of the organ concerned. Organs established under two human rights instruments may well arrive at different and conflicting conclusions. A related problem arising from Art. 29 of the American Convention was discussed in Section II above. Art. 29 of the American Convention and Art. 60 of the European Convention reflect the principle that the more favourable treatment should be accorded to the individual. This principle is also reflected in Art. 1(2) of the Convention against Torture and Other Cruel, Inhuman or Degrading Treatment or Punishment.[214] These Conventions yield to agreements stating more extensive rights. They allow for the raising of standards and preclude their lowering.

An ambiguous saving clause may itself generate difficult questions of interpretation and may not effectively prevent conflicts with other instruments. A case in point is the above-mentioned Art. 23 of the Discrimination Against Women Convention. The Director-General of the ILO objected that an earlier version of that article (draft Art. 16(2)) posed legal difficulties which could have adversely affected the standard-setting activities of the United Nations and the specialized agencies.[215] The text of Art. 16(2), which does not differ

---

[212] Above n. 55.

[213] As shown by the discussion of an earlier version of Art. 23. UN Doc. E/5938 at 2 (1977).

[214] GA Res. 39/46, opened for signature 10 Dec. 1984, 39 UN GAOR Supp. (No. 51) at 197, UN Doc. A/39/51 (1985).

[215] UN Doc. E/5938 (1977).

significantly from Art. 23, read as follows: 'Similarly, nothing in this convention should affect existing conventions adopted under the auspices of the United Nations or its specialized agencies and having as their object the regulation of various aspects of the status of women if they provide for more extensive rights for women.'[216]

The Director-General acknowledged that no substantial conflict existed between the proposed convention and existing ILO Conventions; in 1975, the ILO submitted detailed comments and suggestions on the then existing draft convention against discrimination of women.[217] Invoking Arts. 24 and 8 of the Economic Covenant, which safeguard the constitutional authority and the instruments adopted within the specialized agencies, the Director-General warned that the provision implied that 'the new convention will supersede existing conventions adopted under the auspices of the United Nations or its specialized agencies unless these provide for more extensive rights for women'. Moreover, the term 'more extensive' was vague: did it mean 'more detailed, or more favourable, and by reference to what standard would this be determined'?[218] He therefore proposed that the qualifying phrase 'if they provide for more extensive rights for women' be deleted. The problems mentioned would thus be circumvented and a government 'could ratify the new convention in the knowledge that, if any conflict with an existing obligation were found to exist, it was expressly entitled to continue to comply with the existing obligation'.[219]

The qualifying clause was retained despite these considerations. Since Art. 11 of the Discrimination Against Women Convention prohibits unequal treatment for men and women, with the exception of measures for the protection of maternity under Art. 4(2), the potential for conflict with such ILO Conventions as that concerning Night Work (Women) (revised) (No. 89) (1948)[220] and that concerning Underground Work

---

[216] Ibid. at 2.

[217] From unpublished correspondence.

[218] UN Doc. E/5938, at 2 (1977).

[219] Ibid. at 4.

[220] Convention (No. 89) concerning Night Work of Women Employed in Industry (Revised 1948), International Labour Conventions, above n. 198, at 706. Art. 3 of this Convention prohibits the employment of women 'without distinction of age' during the night, in any public or private industrial undertaking, as defined in the Convention.

(Women) (No. 45) (1935),[221] exists. These Conventions cannot be said to establish rights more conducive to the achievement of equality between men and women and do not benefit, therefore, from the protection of Art. 23. Moreover, since the ILO Conventions include special protective measures for women which are not maternity-related *strictu sensu* and which may lessen women's competitiveness on the labour market, they may be in conflict with the substantive provisions of the Convention. The question arises, therefore, whether a State Party to the Discrimination Against Women Convention, which creates general standards, and to the above-mentioned ILO Conventions, which establish specific standards on more limited subjects, therefore may be unable to fulfil simultaneously its obligations under these Conventions.[222]

Certain other saving clauses refer only to specific instruments, leaving open the possibility of unregulated conflict with other instruments. Art. 8 of the Declaration on the Elimination of All Forms of Intolerance and of Discrimination Based on Religion or Belief states that nothing in it 'shall be construed as restricting or derogating from any right defined in the Universal Declaration of Human Rights and the International Covenants on Human Rights'.[223] Should a similar provision be included in a future convention on religious discrimination, normative conflicts might occur between rights guaranteed under that future convention and those conferred by other conventions. Assume, for example, that the future convention against religious discrimination permits a certain type of discrimination against women to continue because it is based on religious beliefs, and assume further that the Discrimination against Women Convention prohibits this type of discrimination, but that such a prohibition is not adequately delineated in either of the two Covenants. Which of the two Conventions would prevail if a suitable control organ is asked to consider the order of priority of these rights?

---

[221] Convention (No. 45) concerning the Employment of Women on Underground Work in Mines of All Kinds, International Labour Conventions, above n. 198, at 709. Art. 1 prohibits the employment of any female, 'whatever her age' in any mine, as defined in the Convention.

[222] For a detailed discussion of this question, see ILO Doc. GB.228/24/1 (1984).

[223] Above n. 31.

Some instruments may contain jurisdictional, but not normative, avoidance of conflict provisions. An example of such a provision is Art. 16 of the International Convention on the Elimination of All Forms of Racial Discrimination. That Convention contains, in addition, a more narrowly focused normative avoidance of conflict clause, Art. 4. Art. 4 prohibits racist organizations and racist propaganda and states that the obligations of States to eradicate such organizations and activities should take place 'with due regard to the principles embodied in the Universal Declaration of Human Rights and the rights expressly set forth in article 5 of this Convention . . .'. The ineffectiveness of this avoidance of conflict clause was discussed in Chapter I, Section IV above.

The recently adopted Convention against Torture and Other Cruel, Inhuman or Degrading Treatment or Punishment[224] contains a saving clause, Art. 16(2), which provides that '[t]he provisions of this Convention are without prejudice to the provisions of any other international instrument or national law which prohibits cruel, inhuman or degrading treatment or punishment or which relates to extradition or expulsion'. An example of a particularly well-drafted and unambiguous normative saving clause is Art. 8(3) of the Economic Covenant, which provides that '[n]othing in this article shall authorize States Parties to the International Labour Organisation Convention of 1948 concerning Freedom of Association and Protection of the Right to Organize to take legislative measures which would prejudice, or apply the law in such a manner as would prejudice, the guarantees provided for in that Convention.'

The drafting of pro forma avoidance-of-conflict clauses is not an adequate response. The clauses must be formulated so as to avoid or resolve conflicts. If the difficulty is not resolved by drafting, that failure is to be explained largely by substantive or political, rather than technical, considerations. Some factors adversely affecting co-ordination in law-making are discussed in Chapter VI below. In light of the experience with Art. 23 of the Discrimination Against Women Convention, and in order to avoid adverse effects on obligations under other international agreements or uncertainty as to the legal position, the ILO

---

[224] Above n. 214.

proposed to the United Nations in 1983 a model saving clause, reading as follows: 'Nothing contained in this Convention shall affect the obligations assumed by a State under any other convention, treaty or agreement to which it is a party.'[225]

Each of these various techniques has pros and cons and may or may not prove helpful in specific situations. A legislative cross-reference in the operative part of a new instrument may not be suitable if the existing provisions have not been widely accepted, because the resulting indirect acceptance of the earlier instrument may make the acceptance of the new instrument more difficult. Beyond devising such technical solutions,[226] we must identify the desired goal of the international community. Since the acceptance of various human rights instruments is as yet far from complete and some States have subscribed to some instruments but not to others, maximizing accession by States is a desirable goal of the international community,[227] even at the cost of risking a certain overlap between instruments.

Legislative rationalization would be enhanced by the creation of an interorganizational committee for co-ordination of human rights law-making, composed of legal advisers and directors of human rights divisions of the various international organizations and other experts. The committee would be charged with establishing an 'early warning system' to identify possible normative and jurisdictional conflicts and with formulating proposals to avoid or reconcile such conflicts. A means would have to be found to confer adequate influence upon such a group, especially when one of the organizations wished to expand its 'legislative' reach. A possible solution would be for the UN Secretary-General and the executive heads of the specialized agencies[228] to circulate the committee's reports to the legislative or governing bodies of all the organizations as official documents. Those bodies would thus at least be made aware of the problem studied. Some progress in the right direction is reflected in interagency meetings on human rights which are convened

---

[225] From unpublished correspondence.

[226] E.g. Co-ordination Report, above n. 5, Ann. II, at 5–9.

[227] See generally Weissbrodt, *A New United Nations Mechanism for Encouraging the Ratification of Human Rights Treaties*, 76 AJIL 418 (1982).

[228] On the machinery for inter-organizational co-ordination, see Meron, *Status and Independence of the International Civil Servant*, 167 Recueil des cours 289, 295 and n. 6 (1980-II).

annually by the UN Centre for Human Rights. In these meetings, which are attended by a number of intergovernmental organizations, including regional bodies, and the International Committee of the Red Cross, information on human rights activities of the various organizations is exchanged.

In addition, means should be found to permit judicial or other supervisory organs to take into account a spectrum of human rights broader than those stated in their constitutive instruments and with regard to which they possess a special expertise.[229] When new instruments are drafted, this objective should be taken into consideration. As regards existing instruments, where their language compels the conclusion that the scope of applicable norms cannot be extended by the case law or rules of procedure of a particular organ, the possibility of doing so by a special protocol should be considered.

A desirable long-range solution would be to establish through a special agreement a United Nations human rights tribunal which would be empowered *ratione materiae* to supervise the application not only of the International Bill of Human Rights but of the entire *corpus juris* of international human rights adopted under the aegis of the United Nations, or at least of such enumerated instruments as each State Party to the agreement would accept. The (optional) *ratione personae* jurisdiction of the tribunal would extend to States that become parties to the special protocol. By consistently and rationally applying and interpreting human rights instruments, and by proper balancing of the norms therein contained, as national tribunals routinely do, such a tribunal would reduce immensely the risk of normative conflicts and would enlarge the range of norms

---

[229] See e.g. Arts. 60 and 61, African Charter on Human and Peoples' Rights, reprinted in 21 ILM 58 (1982), regarding the broad principles that may be taken into consideration by the future African Commission on Human and Peoples' Rights. See also above n. 71.

A salutary example of 'judicial restraint' based on taking into account other human rights instruments is demonstrated by the position taken by the European Commission of Human Rights in 1 Report on Applications Nos. 6780/74 and 6950/75, *Cyprus* v. *Turkey*, at 109 (1976, declassified in 1979). Because of the applicability of the Geneva Convention Relative to the Treatment of Prisoners of War (Geneva Convention No. III), Aug. 12, 1949, 6 UST 3316, TIAS No. 3364, 75 UNTS 135, the Commission 'has not found it necessary to examine the question of a breach of Article 5 of the European Convention on Human Rights with regard to persons accorded the status of prisoners of war'.

which could be applied to specific violations. The tribunal would have such competence as would be accepted by each State that becomes a party to the special protocol.[230] It could be given authority, *inter alia*: to entertain complaints from individuals or groups, against States Parties; to decide, on the basis of reciprocity or unconditionally, disputes between States relating to the interpretation or application of particular human rights instruments; to give advisory opinions; or, hopefully, the greatest combination of such powers. Although the poltiical will to establish such a tribunal may still be lacking, the concept merits serious consideration. The advance achieved by the new United Nations Convention on the Law of the Sea in establishing tribunals and fostering third-party settlement should create an auspicious climate for attempts to promote such institutions also in the field of human rights.

---

[230] Cf. the important proposals made by Das for the establishment of an international court of human rights. Das, *Some Reflections in Implementing Human Rights*, in Human Rights: Thirty Years After the Universal Declaration 131, 152-5 (B. Ramcharan ed. 1979).

V

Jurisdictional Relations Between Human Rights Instruments and Organs

1. INTRODUCTION

THE purposes of rationalizing and co-ordinating the systems of supervision of human rights are similar to the goals of integrating the treaty law of human rights, as described in Chapter IV. Some of the matters discussed in Chapter IV are therefore relevant to the present chapter as well.

Supervision of compliance should be entrusted to those organizations with the greatest technical competence in the field. Duplication and conflicts of interpretation should be avoided. Conflicts which nevertheless occur, be they in the area of complaints submitted by one State against another or in the area of applications by individuals, should be resolved. The latter task is of growing importance because of the multiplicity of existing procedures.

The UN General Assembly, the UN Commission on Human Rights, the UN Secretariat, and other international organs are committed to improving the co-ordination of their activities, but thus far no significant reforms appear to have been made.[1]

---

[1] See GA Res. 33/54, 33 UN GAOR Supp. (No. 45) at 144, UN Doc. A/33/45 (1978); GA Res. 34/25, 34 UN GAOR Supp. (No. 46) at 164, UN Doc. A/34/46 (1979); Comm'n on Human Rights Res. 22 (XXXV), 35 UN ESCOR Supp. (No. 6) at 128, UN Doc. E/1979/36 (1979). For an analysis of some of the existing UN procedures for dealing with communications concerning violations of human rights, see UN Doc. E/CN.4/1317 (1979). Regarding co-ordination of systems of compliance, see UN Doc. E/CN.4/1193 (1976); UN Doc. E/CN.4/1433 (1980). A useful description of the practical measures of co-ordination and collaboration between international organizations in the area of human rights is contained in F. Wolf, Building the Law of the World: A Look at the Process (World Association of Lawyers of the World Peace Through Law Center, Washington, DC 1976).

On multiplicity of procedures of international investigation of human rights violations, see generally Samson, *Procedural Law*, in International Law and Fact-Finding in the Field of Human Rights 41 (B. Ramcharan ed., 1982); Buergenthal, *International and Regional Human Rights Law and Institutions: Some Examples*

II. POTENTIAL FOR CONFLICTS

The potential for conflicts in supervision and implementation of human rights is virtually unlimited. Conflicts can arise when two organizations claim to have competence over a particular matter, and when one organization which lacks competence over a particular matter encroaches upon the domain of the competent organization or of a State. An attempt to avoid such interference on the part of the United Nations in matters within the competence of an occupying power and, perhaps, of the International Committee of the Red Cross, was made by the Legal Counsel of the United Nations.[2]

It should not be assumed that jurisdictional conflicts arise only between the United Nations and the specialized agencies or between the global and regional organizations. Such conflicts can also arise between two overlapping, or partly overlapping, regional systems, such as the Council of Europe and the European Economic Community,[3] or within the United Nations itself. Thus, in 1979 the Government of Chile asserted that the procedures of the Ad Hoc Working Group on the Situation of Human Rights in Chile, established pursuant to resolutions of the General Assembly and the Commission on Human Rights, conflicted with the procedures on Chile established under ECOSOC Resolution 1503 (XLVIII),[4] and that the

---

of Their Interaction, 12 Tex. Int'l L. J. 321 (1977); Eissen, *The European Convention on Human Rights and the United Nations Covenant on Civil and Political Rights: Problems of Coexistence*, 22 Buffalo L. Rev. 181 (1972); Tardu, *The Protocol to the United Nations Covenant on Civil and Political Rights and the Inter-American System: A Study of Co-existing Petition Procedures*, 70 AJIL 778 (1976); Meron, *Norm Making and Supervision in International Human Rights: Reflections on Institutional Order*, 76 AJIL 754 (1982).

[2] UN Doc. A/SPC/37/SR. 44, at 11–12 (1982) (remarks by E. Suy).

[3] M. Mendelson, The Impact of European Community Law on the Implementation of the European Convention on Human Rights 12–16, 30 (Council of Europe, Directorate of Human Rights 1984); see generally Mendelson, *The European Court of Justice and Human Rights*, 1 Y.B. Eur. L. 125 (1981).

[4] 48 UN ESCOR Supp. (No. 1A) at 8, UN Doc. E/4832/Add.1 (1970). Under this resolution, the Sub-Commission on Prevention of Discrimination and Protection of Minorities of the Commission on Human Rights was empowered to appoint a working group that would consider communications 'which appear to reveal a consistent pattern of gross and reliably attested violations of human rights and fundamental freedoms'. Ibid. Consideration of such communications does not depend on whether the concerned State is a party to any of the instruments on human rights. See Restatement of the Foreign Relations Law of the United States (Revised) § 702, Reporter's Note 9 (1 Tent. Draft No. 6, 1985).

situation in the country should be considered exclusively under the Political Covenant, to which Chile was a party.[5]

In response to these claims, the special rapporteur on human rights in Chile, Abdoulaye Diéye, took the position that a government cannot stipulate the procedure under which its domestic human rights situation should be examined. He stated that the procedure established under ECOSOC Resolution 1503 (XLVIII) was complementary to other pre-existing and subsequent procedures established by the United Nations, just as the procedure established under ECOSOC Resolution 1235 (XLII)[6] complemented that established under ECOSOC Resolution 1503 (XLVIII).[7] Special Rapporteur Diéye further pointed out that Chile had neither made a declaration under Art. 41 of the Political Covenant nor ratified the Optional Protocol to the International Covenant on Civil and Political Rights. The Human Rights Committee could only examine reports submitted by the Chilean Government, rather than communications from another party under Art. 41 of the Political Covenant or from individuals alleging violations by Chile of Covenant obligations under the Optional Protocol. Therefore, '[t]he Government cannot . . . plead that the procedures established under the International Covenant on Civil and Political Rights should be applied to the situation in Chile in exclusion of other procedures which the United Nations may consider appropriate to deal with that situation.'[8] The special rapporteur thus strongly defended the multiplicity of investigatory procedures.[9]

Golsong has illustrated the complexity of these issues:

If you take the possible overlapping of procedures . . . [of] supervision over states vis-à-vis freedom of association, the following provisions may

---

[5] See UN Doc. A/34/503, paras. 1–3 (1979).

[6] 42 UN ESCOR Supp. (No. 1) at 17, UN Doc. E/4393 (1967).

[7] See UN Doc. A/34/503, paras. 9–11 (1979). See generally Comm'n on Human Rights Res. 11 (XXXV), 35 UN ESCOR Supp. (No. 6) at 115, UN Doc. E/1979/36 (1979).

[8] See UN Doc. A/34/503, para. 12 (1979). For the consideration by the Human Rights Committee of the reports submitted by Chile under Art. 40 of the Political Covenant and the question of admissible sources of information, see Robertson, *The Implementation System: International Measures*, in The International Bill of Rights: The Covenant on Civil and Political Rights 332, 347–8 (L. Henkin ed., 1981).

[9] For a similar view, see UN Doc. CCPR/C/SR.78, at 7 (1978) (remarks by Uribe Vargas in the Human Rights Committee).

be applicable: article 8 of the Covenant on Economic, Social and Cultural Rights, article 22 of the Civil and Political Rights Covenant, a variety of ILO standards and, if it is a question of freedom of association of teachers, various UNESCO documents. All of these are procedurally and substantively different. And on top of that you have the situation occurring in Europe — you can operate under article 11 of the European Convention on Human Rights, or under article 6 of the European Social Charter.[10]

Proper 'judicial restraint' as well as knowledge of the entire *corpus juris* of international human rights are crucial for the avoidance of conflicts. In the case of *Cyprus* v. *Turkey*, the European Commission of Human Rights demonstrated its ability to avoid jurisdictional conflicts. Because the Geneva Convention Relative to the Treatment of Prisoners of War (Geneva Convention No. III)[11] was applicable and the competence of the International Committee of the Red Cross was recognized by the State concerned, the Commission refrained from examining the question of a breach of Article 5 of the European Convention on Human Rights with regard to persons accorded the status of prisoners of war.[12]

III. CLAUSES FOR AVOIDANCE OR REDUCTION OF CONFLICTS

Of particular significance are Art. 44 of the Political Covenant (interstate complaints), Art. 5(2) (a) of the Optional Protocol (individual applications), and Arts. 18 to 22 of the Economic Covenant. Art. 44 of the Political Covenant reads as follows:

[t]he provisions for the implementation of the present Covenant shall apply without prejudice to the procedures prescribed in the field of human rights by or under the constituent instruments and the conventions of the United Nations and of the specialized agencies and shall not prevent the States Parties to the present Covenant from having recourse to other procedures for settling a dispute in accordance with general or special international agreements in force between them.

---

[10] *Quoted in* Meron, *A Report on the N.Y.U. Conference on Teaching International Protection of Human Rights*, 13 N.Y.U. J. Int'l L. & Pol. 881, 930 (1981) (footnotes omitted).

[11] Geneva Convention Relative to the Treatment of Prisoners of War (Geneva Convention No. III), Aug. 12, 1949, 6 UST 3316, TIAS No. 3364, 75 UNTS 135.

[12] European Commission of Human Rights, 1 Report of the Commission on Applications Nos. 6780/74 and 6950/75, *Cyprus* v. *Turkey*, at 109 (1976, declassified in 1979).

Art. 5(2) (a) of the Optional Protocol provides that '[t]he [Human Rights] Committee shall not consider any communication from an individual unless it has ascertained that . . . [t]he same matter is not being examined under another procedure of international investigation or settlement'. The interpretation and application of this provision by the Human Rights Committee ·is discussed in Section IV below. The language of Art. 5(2) (a) inspired that of Art. 22(5) (a) of the Convention Against Torture and Other Cruel, Inhuman or Degrading Treatment or Punishment,[13] with one important difference, however, which may have been influenced by Art. 27(b) of the European Convention on Human Rights, to be discussed in Section V(b) below. Art. 22(5) (a) of the Convention Against Torture prohibits the Committee Against Torture from considering any communications from an individual not only when the communication is being examined under another procedure of international investigation or settlement (simultaneous consideration), but also when it has already been examined under such a procedure (sequential consideration).

The Political Covenant probably does not prohibit States that are parties to it and that have recognized the competence of the Human Rights Committee with regard to interstate complaints under Art. 41 from referring disputes over the interpretation or application of the Covenant to other means of settlement, including the International Court of Justice.[14] Sohn has rightly observed that the Political Covenant and the Economic Covenant show 'preference for applying UN procedures only in cases where other procedures are not available. In particular, the procedures developed by the specialized agencies . . . are given triple protection.'[15] On the other hand, the older ILO 'constitutional procedures relating to observance of ratified

---

[13]   GA Res. 39/46, opened for signature 10 Dec. 1984, 39 UN GAOR Supp. (No. 51) at 197, UN Doc. A/39/51 (1985).

[14]   See Robertson, above n. 8, at 355–6. It has been suggested that unless an international human rights agreement provides or clearly implies the contrary, special remedies under it generally supplement rather than replace the traditional remedies available between States. Draft Restatement, above n. 4, § 703, comment *a*, Reporters' Note 2.

[15]   Sohn, *Human Rights: Their Implementation and Supervision by the United Nations*, in 2 Human Rights in International Law: Legal and Policy Issues 369, 393 (T. Meron ed., 1984).

conventions [or] . . . the special procedure for complaints of violations of trade union rights . . . embody no provisions to define their relationship to other international procedures'.[16] The ILO procedures thus do not necessarily yield to UN procedures.

The procedure for the consideration of violations of human rights established in 1978 under Decision 104/EX/3.3 of the Executive Board of UNESCO presents interesting problems of jurisdictional relations. Does it constitute a procedure of international investigation or settlement for the purposes of Art. 5(2) (a) of the Optional Protocol? The UNESCO procedure allows examination both of massive and systematic violations and of individual and specific violations.[17] In presenting the new procedure to the UN Human Rights Committee, the representative of UNESCO argued that since the procedure had no 'legal character', and since UNESCO's role was not that of an international judicial body, UNESCO considered it unnecessary to specify the conditions of admissibility of communications, as is done in Art. 5(2) (a) of the Optional Protocol.[18] The insistence by UNESCO on a distinction based on the non-judicial character of the UNESCO procedure appears strange, since Art. 5(2) (a) does not require that the other procedure of investigation or settlement be judicial. UNESCO's position seems to be that it will not be precluded from examining a communication submitted to its Committee on Conventions and Recommendations under Decision 104/EX/3.3 on the ground that the same matter is being examined by the Human Rights Committee. A commentator has pointed out that 'there

---

[16] Samson, above n. 1, at 53.

[17] See UNESCO Doc. 104/EX/Dec. 3.3, para. 10 (1978). See generally Marks, *UNESCO and Human Rights: The Implementation of Rights Relating to Education, Science, Culture, and Communication*, 13 Tex. Int'l L.J. 35 (1977).

[18] See UN Doc. CCPR/C/SR. 78, at 6 (1978). The Director of the UNESCO Division of Human Rights and Peace stated:

'The problem of litispendence raised by Article 5, paragraph 2(a), of the Optional Protocol . . . concerned the procedure provided for in 104 EX/Decision 3.3 only in so far as the latter was regarded as constituting a "procedure of international investigation or settlement" within the meaning of that provision of the Optional Protocol. It was for the Human Rights Committee to decide on that point. In any event, UNESCO was not legally bound to suspend the examination of a communication in accordance with 104 EX/Decision 3.3 on the ground that it was already being examined by the Human Rights Committee.'

UNESCO Doc. 107/EX/34, para. 45 (1979).

is no specific provision in the [UNESCO] procedure to prevent simultaneous consideration as far as UNESCO is concerned, other than the organization's commitment to act in a spirit of international cooperation in human rights matters'.[19] Will this general commitment to act in a spirit of co-operation dissuade UNESCO from considering a matter which is before the Human Rights Committee?

Not surprisingly, UNESCO's position was questioned by several members of the Human Rights Committee.[20] The Committee has not yet reached a decision as to whether the UNESCO's procedure constitutes 'another procedure of international investigation or settlement', but did state that the ultimate interpretation of Art. 5(2) (a) fell within its jurisdiction.[21]

The UNESCO procedure has also aroused concern about a possible overlap with the European system for the protection of human rights. The Council of Europe's Committee of Ministers has expressed the hope that, when implementing the new system, the competent authorities of UNESCO will not lose sight of the fact that some cases may have been or are being examined by another international organ, such as the European Commission of Human Rights.[22]

In Sohn's view it would not be desirable to provide for an appeal to the United Nations from a final and binding decision rendered under the auspices of a specialized agency, but resort to appropriate UN procedures should be possible if no settlement is reached under a specialized agency procedure or if that procedure does not result in a final and binding decision.[23]

In addition to the customary stipulation that individual cases

---

[19]   Alston, *UNESCO's Procedures for Dealing with Human Rights Violations*, 20 Santa Clara L. Rev. 665, 684 (1980) (footnotes omitted).

[20]   See UN Doc. CCPR/C/SR. 78, at 6–8 (1978). Paragraph 14(a) (x) of the UNESCO Decision 104/EX/3.3 procedure provides that communications relating to matters that have been settled by the States concerned in accordance with the principles set forth in the Universal Declaration of Human Rights and the Covenants shall not be considered, but does not exclude examination of matters under consideration by another international body. But see the statement by the representative of UNESCO that paragraph 14 (a) (x) was designed to avoid conflict with other bodies. UN Doc. CCPR/C/SR.78, at 9 (1978).

[21]   33 UN GAOR Supp. (No. 40) at 105, UN Doc. A/33/40 (1978).

[22]   See Council of Europe Doc. H/Inf. (79) 4, App. IV, at 27 (1979).

[23]   Sohn, above n. 15, at 393–4.

will not be considered unless all available domestic remedies have been exhausted, some instruments provide that matters already being examined under another international procedure will not be considered. Although Art. 44 of the Political Covenant does not specifically include the procedures of regional organizations among those that are not pre-empted by the Covenant, which deprives those organizations of the 'preferred status' enjoyed by the specialized agencies under that article, Buergenthal has correctly suggested that this omission has little practical significance.[24] Art. 5(2) (a) of the Optional Protocol,[25] however, may be interpreted as embracing regional procedures.[26] The preference assigned by Art. 5(2) (a) to other procedures should be interpreted as a temporary restriction, applicable while the case is pending before another international body, rather than as an absolute prohibition on examination of a particular matter.

The International Convention on the Elimination of All Forms of Racial Discrimination, discussed in Chapter I above, contains in Art. 16 a provision aimed at avoiding jurisdictional conflicts with other procedures for settlement of disputes in the field of discrimination. Art. 16 reads as follows:

[t]he provisions of this Convention concerning the settlement of disputes or complaints shall be applied without prejudice to other procedures for settling disputes or complaints in the field of discrimination laid down in the constituent instruments of, or conventions adopted by, the United Nations and its specialized agencies, and shall not prevent the States Parties from having recourse to other procedures for settling a dispute in accordance with general or special international agreements in force between them.

Unfortunately, an avoidance of jurisdictional conflicts provision was not included in Art. 14 of the Convention, which creates a right of petition for individuals or groups of individuals within the jurisdiction of a State Party that has made a declaration recognizing the competence of the Committee to

---

[24] See Buergenthal, above n. 1, at 327-8.

[25] Art. 5(2) (a) provides that '[t]he [Human Rights] Committee shall not consider any communication from an individual unless it has ascertained that . . . [t]he same matter is not being examined under another procedure of international investigation or settlement'.

[26] See Buergenthal, above n. 1, at 328; Sohn, above n. 15, at 394.

receive and consider such communications. In accordance with Art. 14(9), upon the tenth declaration made by a State Party, the procedure outlined in Art. 14 entered into force on 3 December 1982.[27] The omission from Article 14 of a provision similar to that contained in Art. 5(2) (a) of the Optional Protocol has, however, been somewhat remedied by the adoption by the Committee on the Elimination of Racial Discrimination of a rule of procedure (83(1) (g), now (84(1) (g)), which reads as follows: '[t]he Secretary-General may request clarification from the author of a communication concerning the applicability of article 14 to his communication, in particular . . . [t]he extent to which the same matter is being examined under another procedure of international investigation or settlement.'[28] The imperfect language of Art. 14 was discussed in Chapter I, Section VII above. Since Article 14 did not specifically authorize the Committee to guard against submission of communications which had already been submitted under another procedure of investigation or settlement, the new provision was incorporated in the rule which concerns the functions of the Secretary-General, rather than in the one relating to the admissibility of communications.[29] The effectiveness of Rule 84(1) (g) remains to be seen.

IV. THE HUMAN RIGHTS COMMITTEE

While the published 'views' of the Human Rights Committee, under Art. 5(4) of the Optional Protocol, are a useful source for examining questions of interpretation and application of Art. 5(2) (a), these 'views' are not all-inclusive of the Committee's decisions under that provision. Most of the published 'views' pertain to communications that have been deemed admissible and addressed on their merits. The Committee has not always published its decisions rejecting admissibility of communications. Because consideration of communications under the Optional

[27]   38 UN GAOR Supp. (No. 18) para. 23, UN Doc. A/38/18 (1983).
[28]   UN Doc. CERD/C/35/Rev. 3, at 23 (1986). Partsch, the sponsor of the proposal to adopt such a rule, pointed out that it was identical to rule 80(1) (g) of the rules of procedure of the Human Rights Committee. UN Doc. CERD/C/SR.622, at 8 (1983).
[29]   UN Doc. CERD/C/SR.622, at 9 (1983).

Protocol takes place in closed meetings and all documents pertaining to such meetings are confidential, assessment of decisions of inadmissibility rendered by the Committee under Art. 5(2) (a) is impossible. It is, therefore, desirable that the Human Rights Committee should publish more of those decisions in which it deems communications to be inadmissible.[30]

The question of what constitutes 'another procedure of international investigation or settlement' within the meaning of Art. 5(2) (a) of the Optional Protocol has arisen in several contexts. The Human Rights Committee has determined that the procedure set up under ECOSOC Resolution 1503 (XLVIII) does not constitute such a procedure, 'since it is concerned with the examination of situations which appear to reveal a consistent pattern of gross violations of human rights and a situation is not "the same matter" as an individual complaint'.[31] The Committee has also determined that Art. 5(2) (a) relates only to procedures implemented by interstate or intergovernmental agreements or arrangements; procedures established by non-governmental organizations cannot bar consideration by the Committee of communications submitted to it under the Optional Protocol.[32]

Another question is whether an unrelated third party may deprive the Committee of its competence to examine a communication by submitting the matter to another procedure of international investigation or settlement. The Committee has determined that the submission of a complaint to another procedure by an unrelated third party subsequent to the opening of the same case before the Committee will not bar admissibility. In one case, the State Party objected to the admissibility of the communication on the grounds that the same matter had been

---

[30] The recent publication 'International Covenant on Civil and Political Rights, Human Rights Committee: Selected Decisions under the Optional Protocol (Second to Sixteenth Sessions)', UN Doc. CCPR/C/OP/1 (1985), UN Publication Sales No. E/84.XIV.2, contains, however, a number of decisions declaring a communication inadmissible.

Regarding the practice of the Human Rights Committee, see generally, Rule 90(1) (e) and 90(2) of the Rules of Procedure of the Human Rights Committee, UN Doc. CCPR/C.3/Rev.1 (1979); Robertson, above n. 8, at 364-9. For a discussion of the interpretation of draft Rule 92(2) concerning later review of a determination of inadmissibility, see 32 UN GAOR Supp. (No. 44) at 12-13, UN Doc. A/32/44 (1977).

[31] 33 UN GAOR Supp. (No. 40) at 100, UN Doc. A/33/40 (1978).

[32] Ibid.

submitted to the Inter-American Commission on Human Rights (IACHR). The author of the communication, who was acting in his capacity as legal representative of the alleged victim, claimed, however, that the Committee's competence was not excluded because the communication concerning the victim was submitted to the Human Rights Committee prior to the matter reaching the IACHR, and that the submission of the same matter to the IACHR by a third party could not prejudice the right of the victim's legal representative 'to choose the international body to protect [her] interests'.[33] The Committee agreed, stating that it was not prevented from considering the communication submitted to it 'by reason of the subsequent opening of a case by an unrelated third party under the procedure of the Inter-American Commission on Human Rights'.[34]

One should, perhaps, distinguish between a subsequent submission of a case by an unrelated third party under another procedure of international investigation or settlement and a prior submission of the same subject matter to another investigative body. In the latter instance, it appears that the Committee would not consider the communication unless the third party withdrew the prior complaint. A case in point involved a State Party contesting the admissibility of a communication submitted to the Human Rights Committee by a victim's wife where the same matter had already been submitted to the IACHR. Here the Committee ascertained from the Secretariat of the IACHR that the same matter had been submitted by a third party well in advance of the author's initial communication to the Human Rights Committee. In order to 'remove any procedural uncertainties concerning the competence of the Human Rights Committee to consider the present communication under the Optional Protocol',[35] the author of the third party communication wrote a letter to the Executive Secretary of the IACHR requesting that consideration of the case be discontinued. This information, together

[33] Communication No. R.13/56, *Celiberti de Casariego* v. *Uruguay*, 36 UN GAOR Supp. (No. 40) at 185, 186, UN Doc. A/36/40 (1981).

[34] Ibid. at 187. See also 39 UN GAOR Supp. (No. 40) at 115–16, UN Doc. A/39/40 (1984); Communication No. R.2/10, *Altesor* v. *Uruguay*, 37 UN GAOR Supp. (No. 40) at 122, 125, UN Doc. A/37/40 (1982).

[35] Communication No. R. 14/63, *Setelich* v. *Uruguay*, 37 UN GAOR Supp. (No. 40) at 114, 116, UN Doc. A/36/40 (1982).

with a copy of the third party's letter to the IACHR, was transmitted to the Human Rights Committee, which accordingly decided that Art. 5(2) (a) did not bar admissibility.[36]

In a later case, the Human Rights Committee concluded that the prior submission of a complaint by an unrelated third party to the IACHR did not constitute 'the same matter', within the meaning of Art. 5(2) (a), even though the IACHR was still considering the case.[37] Noting that Art. 5(2) (a) precludes consideration of a communication if the same matter is being examined under another procedure of international investigation or settlement, the Committee nevertheless opined that the article 'cannot be so interpreted as to imply that an unrelated third party, acting without the knowledge and consent of the alleged victim, can preclude the latter from having access to the Human Rights Committee'.[38] Following a request by the Committee to clarify the circumstances of the case pending before the IACHR, the author conducted extensive inquiries in several countries in an attempt to ascertain who had submitted the complaint to the IACHR, but was unable to obtain any information and so informed the Committee. The Committee concluded that Art. 5(2) (a) did not bar admissibility even though the third party complaint to the IACHR was not withdrawn. In another case which involved a third party communication to another international organ prior to the Human Rights Committee's being seized of the case, the State Party objected to the admissibility of the communication because the victim's name appeared in two cases pending before the IACHR. The Committee concluded, however, 'that the two-line reference . . . [to the victim] before the Inter-American Commission on Human Rights — which case lists in a similar manner the names of hundreds of other persons allegedly detained in Uruguay — did not constitute the same matter as that described in detail by the author in his communication to the Human Rights Committee. Accordingly, the communication was not inadmissible under article 5(2) (a) of the Optional Protocol.'[39]

---

[36] Ibid.
[37] Communication No. 74/1980, *Estrella* v. *Uruguay*, 38 UN GAOR Supp. (No. 40) at 150, 156, UN Doc. A/38/40 (1983).
[38] Ibid.
[39] Communication No. R.1/6, *Millán Sequeira* v. *Uruguay*, 35 UN GAOR Supp. (No. 40) at 127, 129, UN Doc. A/35/40 (1980).

The Committee's decisions concluding that the subsequent submission of a case to another international investigative body by an unrelated third party will not defeat admissibility under Art. 5(2) (a) may serve as a safeguard against the State Party encouraging such submission of a case to vitiate admissibility of a communication. These decisions protect the alleged victim from deprivation of access to the Committee by reason of an unrelated, perhaps illusory, third party complaint. In those cases where the prior submission of a complaint to another investigative body would have precluded admissibility under Art. 5(2) (a) unless the third party withdrew the complaint, the identity of the third party was ascertainable.[40] On a number of occasions where submission of a complaint by an unrelated and unknown third party would have denied the victim access to the Committee, the Committee deemed admissible communications that might be inadmissible under the plain meaning of Art. 5(2) (a).[41] While the Committee's interpretation of Art. 5(2) (a) gives some assurance that the victim's access to the Committee will not be undermined, it may permit dual examination of the same matter.

Yet another question is whether the Human Rights Committee has competence to consider a communication where the same matter has been previously submitted to another procedure of international investigation or settlement, but has either been withdrawn or is no longer being examined under the latter procedure by the time the Committee reaches a decision on the admissibility of that communication. This question has been answered in the affirmative.[42]

[40] Communication No. R.14/63, *Setelich* v. *Uruguay*, 37 UN GAOR Supp. (No. 40) at 114, 116, UN Doc. A/37/40 (1982). See also Communication No. R. 21/84, *Gilmet Dermit* v. *Uruguay*, UN Doc. CCPR/C.D (XVII)/R.21/84, Ann. at 3 (1982); Communication No. 85/1981, *Reverano de Romero* v. *Uruguay*, 39 UN GAOR Supp. (No. 40) at 159, 161, UN Doc. A/39/40 (1984).

[41] Communication No. R.18/74, (74/1980) *Estrella* v. *Uruguay*, UN Doc. CCPR/C/18/D/R.18/74, at 9 (1983), 38 UN GAOR Supp. (No. 40) at 150, 156, UN Doc. A/38/40 (1983).

[42] 34 UN GAOR Supp. (No. 40) at 123, UN Doc. A/34/40 (1979); Communication No. R.1/5, *Valentini de Bazzano* v. *Uruguay*, ibid. at 124, 126; Communication No. R.2/8, *Lanza de Netto* v. *Uruguay*, 35 UN GAOR Supp. (No. 40) at 111, 112–13; Communication No. R.1/4, *Torres Ramirez* v. *Uruguay*, ibid. at 121, 123; Communication No. R.123/1982, *Manera Johnson* v. *Uruguay*, 39 UN GAOR Supp. (No. 40) at 175, 179, UN Doc. A/39/40 (1984); Communication No. 85/1981, *Reverano de Romero* v. *Uruguay*, ibid. at 159, 161.

In one of the infrequent cases of publication of a decision on inadmissibility, the Committee had to determine whether a State Party's reservation, which will be discussed in Section V (b) below, stating that the Committee would not be competent to receive and consider individual communications relating to cases which already had been, or were being, examined under another international procedure, applied to matters that the other body had not addressed on the merits. Although the complaint had been deemed inadmissible as manifestly ill-founded by the European Commission of Human Rights, the Committee considered that because of the reservation and because the same matter had already been 'considered' by the European Commission of Human Rights, it was not competent to admit the communication.[43] In a persuasive individual opinion, Graefrath argued that the reservation did not address matters the consideration of which had been precluded by a decision of inadmissibility. He warned that

[i]f the Committee interprets the reservation in such a way that it would be excluded from considering a communication when a complaint referring to the same facts has been declared inadmissible under the procedure of the European Convention, the effect would be that any complaint that has been declared inadmissible under that procedure could later on not be considered by the Human Rights Committee, despite the fact that the conditions for admissibility of communications are set out in a separate international instrument and are different from those under the Optional Protocol.[44]

In these circumstances, a petitioner may never be able to obtain a consideration on the merits of his communication under either international procedure. In a recent decision involving this type of reservation, the Committee adopted, however, a better course of action, concurring with the respondent Government that the reservation did not apply to the case, because there was no prior examination by the European Commission of Human Rights. The Secretariat of the Commission merely pointed out to the author that the period of six months established under Art. 26 of the European Convention on

---

[43] Communication No. R.26/121, *A.M.* v. *Denmark*, 37 UN GAOR Supp. (No. 40) at 212, 213, UN Doc. A/37/40 (1982).
[44] Ibid. at 214.

Human Rights had already expired.[45] It is not clear, however, what position the Human Rights Committee would have taken had the Government argued that the reservation was applicable. The Human Rights Committee deemed the communication inadmissible on other grounds, but published the decision, nevertheless.

In another case where the State Party objected to admissibility, 'the same matter' had been brought before the European Commission of Human Rights by complainants who had submitted to the Commission their own cases, concerning claims arising from the same incident from which the communication submitted to the Human Rights Committee had also originated. The State concerned contended that the phrase 'the same matter' required a verification not only that the author of the communication himself, but also that an individual other than the author had not submitted the same matter under another international procedure. The State argued that the determinative issue was the subject matter of the communication, rather than the identity of the communication's author. The Committee disagreed, stating that the phrase 'the same matter' 'had to be understood as including the same claim concerning the same individual, submitted by him or someone else who has the standing to act on his behalf before the other international body'.[46] The Human Rights Committee has thus set forth the important rule that the words 'the same matter' should be interpreted as requiring both the same subject matter (*ratione materiae*) and the complete identity of the parties (*ratione personae*).

Yet another question addressed by the Human Rights Committee is whether a prior or ongoing investigation by another international body of events that occurred prior to the entry into force of the Political Covenant and the Optional Protocol renders inadmissible a communication concerning the same alleged victim and involving events that occurred subsequent to the entry into force of these instruments. Because the communications before the other body concerned events which

---

[45] Communication No. 158/1983, *O.F.* v. *Norway*, UN Doc. CCPR/C/23/D/ 158/1983, Ann. at 3, 8 (1984).
[46] Communication No. R.18/75, *Fanali* v. *Italy*, UN Doc. CCPR/C/18/D/R.18/ 75, at 5 (1983).

occurred prior to the entry into force of the instruments mentioned, the Committee determined that they did not constitute 'the same matter' as the alleged violations occurring after the entry into force.[47]

V. THE INTERRELATIONSHIP BETWEEN THE REGIONAL AND THE GLOBAL SUPERVISORY SYSTEMS

Problems concerning overlap and interaction arise not only between the various supervisory procedures of the United Nations and the specialized agencies, but also between global and regional instruments for the protection of human rights. The global instruments include not only the two Covenants, but also the more specialized UN conventions and instruments adopted under the auspices of the specialized agencies. The various investigatory procedures that originate in the resolutions of various organs,[48] rather than in treaties, should also be taken into account. Any one of them may conflict with parallel regional systems, such as the Organization of African Unity.[49]

A. *The American System for the Protection of Human Rights*

Ambiguous areas of possible conflict and overlap of jurisdiction can sometimes be clarified by rules of procedure or by the case law of the control organs. In the Inter-American system, the question of conflicts with procedures of other international

---

[47] Communication No. R.2/8, *Lanza de Netto* v. *Uruguay*, 35 GAOR Supp. (No. 40) at 111, 113, UN Doc. A/35/40 (1980); Communication No. R.1/6, *Millán Sequeira* v. *Uruguay*, ibid. at 127, 128; Communication No. R.2/11, *Grille Motta* v. *Uruguay*, ibid. at 132, 133; Communication No. R.7/32, *Sala de Tourón* v. *Uruguay*, 36 UN GAOR Supp. (No. 40) at 120, 122-3, UN Doc. A/36/40 (1981).

[48] Meron, *Norm Making*, above n. 1, at n. 5.

[49] The African Charter on Human and Peoples' Rights, reprinted in Human Rights Documents: Compilation of Documents Pertaining to Human Rights 155 (House Comm. on Foreign Affairs, Comm. Print 1983), which has not yet entered into force, provides that the African Commission on Human and Peoples' Rights may only deal with communications from States concerning a violation of the African Charter if local remedies are exhausted (Art. 50), but does not provide for matters being dealt with by another international procedure of investigation. However, the African Commission shall not consider communications from States Parties that 'deal with cases which have been settled by these [*sic*] States involved in accordance with the principles of the Charter of the United Nations, or the Charter of the Organization of African Unity or the provisions of the present Charter'. Art. 56(7). These provisions create the risk of overlap of procedures.

organizations for the examination of petitions or communications is governed by Art. 46(1) (c) and 47(d) of the American Convention on Human Rights[50] and Art. 36 of the Regulations of the IACHR.[51] The IACHR, an organ of the Organization of the American States, has competence to examine complaints concerning alleged violations of the American Convention on Human Rights (American Convention) and of the American Declaration of the Rights and Duties of Man

[50] OAS TS No. 36, 9 ILM 673 (1970). For the official text, see Organization of American States, Handbook of Existing Rules Pertaining to Human Rights in the Inter-American System 29, OEA/Ser.L/V/II.60, doc. 28, rev. 1 (1983) (hereinafter referred to as Handbook).

Art. 46(1) (c) reads as follows:

'Admission by the Commission [the Inter-American Commission on Human Rights] of a petition or communication lodged in accordance with Article 44 or 45 shall be subject to the following requirements:

. . .

that the subject of the petition or communication is not pending in another international proceeding for settlement . . .'

Art. 47(d) reads as follows:

'The Commission shall consider inadmissible any petition or communication submitted under Articles 44 or 45 if:

. . .

the petition or communication is substantially the same as one previously studied by the Commission or by another international organization.'

[51] Handbook, above n. 50, at 119, 134.

Art. 36 reads as follows:

'1. The Commission shall not consider a petition in cases where the subject of the petition:

a. is pending settlement in another procedure under an international governmental organization of which the state concerned is a member;

b. essentially duplicates a petition pending or already examined and settled by the Commission or by another international government [sic] organization of which the state concerned is a member.

2. The Commission shall not refrain from taking up and examining a petition in cases provided for in paragraph 1 when:

a. the procedure followed before the other organization or agency is one limited to an examination of the general situation on human rights in the state in question and there has been no decision on specific facts that are the subject of the petition submitted to the Commission, or is one that will not lead to an effective settlement of the violation denounced;

b. the petitioner before the Commission or a family member is the alleged victim of the violation denounced and the petitioner before the organizations in reference is a third party or a nongovernmental entity having no mandate from the former.'

(American Declaration).[52] Under Art. 44 of the American Convention and Art. 23(1) of the Regulations of the IACHR, 'petitions' concerning alleged violations of these instruments may be submitted to the IACHR by any person or group of persons, or any non-governmental organization legally recognized in one or more Member States of the Organization of American States. Under Art. 45 of the American Convention, 'communications' alleging violations of the Convention may also be submitted by one State Party against another, if both States have made declarations recognizing the competence of the IACHR to receive and examine such communications.

Art. 46(1) (c) of the American Convention on Human Rights provides that a petition or a communication shall not be admissible if its subject is pending in another international proceeding for settlement. Art. 47(d) provides further that to be admissible a petition or communication may not be substantially the same as one previously studied by the IACHR or by another international organization (*ne bis in idem*). Art. 36 of the Regulations (rules of procedure) of the IACHR clarified these provisions by specifying that a petition concerning a case being considered (which 'is pending settlement') under another procedure will not be admissible if the respondent State is a member of the other organization, or the petition essentially duplicates a petition pending or already examined and settled by the IACHR or by another international governmental organization of which the State concerned is a member, and if those proceedings were instituted by the victim, a member of the victim's family, or someone with a mandate to act on the victim's behalf. While Arts. 46(1) (c) and 47(d) may generally preclude admissibility of complaints already submitted to another international organization, even when the complaint was submitted to the other organization by a different party, the IACHR has carved out two exceptions in Art. 36(2) (b) of the Regulations. Art. 36(2) (b) provides that the IACHR may deem a petition admissible if the petitioner before the other organization is a third

[52] See generally, Buergenthal, *The Inter-American System for the Protection of Human Rights*, in 2 Human Rights in International Law: Legal and Policy Issues 439, 474–87 (T. Meron ed., 1984); Norris, *Bringing Human Rights Petitions Before the Inter-American Commission*, 20 Santa Clara L. Rev. 733 (1980). Regarding competing procedures, see ibid. at 743–4. See also Vargas, *Individual Access to the Inter-American Court of Human Rights*, 16 N.Y.U. J. Int'l L. & Pol. 601 (1984).

party or a non-governmental organization acting on its own behalf.

The texts discussed above present additional questions of interpretation. For example, do Arts. 46(1) (c) and 47(d) of the American Convention preclude the IACHR from considering a petition in cases where the subject of the complaint is also the subject of a communication before the Human Rights Committee, but the complaint was submitted to the Human Rights Committee after it had been submitted to the IACHR? Does the word 'pending' in Art. 46(1) (c) refer to the time the petition is submitted to the IACHR or to the time the petition is considered for admissibility by the IACHR? Given the language of Art. 5(2) (a) of the Optional Protocol, a danger exists that, if the IACHR declines to assert jurisdiction over a case that was subsequently submitted to the Human Rights Committee, then in certain circumstances the case might not be heard before either body. A result under which neither organization would have jurisdiction to examine communications submitted to both organizations must be avoided. Ideally, this problem would be resolved by establishing, through co-ordination between the two organizations, a procedure to determine which organization has more expertise and better resources to investigate and to resolve the particular case involved. In the absence of such a procedure, a possible means for the IACHR to ensure that at least one of the two organizations will have jurisdiction is to maintain a policy of admitting any otherwise admissible complaint unless the same complaint was 'pending' before the Human Rights Committee at the time the IACHR received it, rather than at the time the IACHR is considering its admissibility. This position would be consistent with the emphasis, in Art. 36(2) (a) of the Regulations, on the concept of the effectiveness of the settlement of the violation. The position of the IACHR is likely to be different if it is determined that the Human Rights Committee has already admitted the communication, despite the earlier submission of the communication to the IACHR, or if the petition is withdrawn by its author from the IACHR.

Another important question is whether Arts. 46(1) (c) and 47(d) of the American Convention preclude the IACHR from considering a petition when the subject matter of the complaint is being or has been considered by the Human Rights Committee during a study of reports by States under Art. 40 of the Political Covenant, or is being or has been considered by another UN organ in the context of a general study of human rights violations. Such general consideration by UN organs should not bar the IACHR from examination of a particular petition. The use of the term 'settlement' in Art. 46(1) (c) of the American Convention indicates that the Convention addresses examination of particular cases, which may lead to their settlement, as distinguished from studies of country-wide situations, or of reports from States, which in the case of the Political Covenant may lead only to 'general comments' by the Human Rights Committee. Similarly, when Art. 47(d) states that a petition or communication is inadmissible if it is substantially the same as one previously studied by the IACHR or by another international organization, it addresses particular cases. This conclusion is supported by Art. 36(2) (a) of the Regulations, which states that the IACHR shall not refrain from taking up and examining a petition in cases where the procedure followed before the other organization 'is one limited to an examination of the general situation on human rights in the state in question and there has been no decision on specific facts that are the subject of the petition submitted to the Commission, or is one that will not lead to an effective settlement of the violation . . .'. The conclusion that the Commission is not barred from consideration of a particular case that is being or has been addressed in a non-particularized manner by another international organization is further supported by the Commission's Resolution No. 60/81, in Case 2155.[53] In that case, the government of Uruguay argued that the IACHR should not have considered a petition concerning a case investigated by a UN body as part of a general study of the problem of disappeared persons. The IACHR, citing Art. 36(2) (a) of the Regulations, rejected the argument of Uruguay.[54]

Do Arts. 46(1) (c) and 47(d) of the American Convention preclude IACHR from considering a petition in cases in which the subject of the complaint is or was the subject of a communication before the Human Rights Committee, but where

[53] Reprinted in T. Buergenthal and R. Norris, Human Rights: The Inter-American System at 77 (Binder 3, No. 17, 1983).
[54] Ibid. at 77-8.

the definition or the scope of the rights asserted is different under the American Convention and the Political Covenant? This question is important because the Human Rights Committee in its consideration of communications will examine only whether the State charged has violated its obligations under the Political Covenant.[55] The Committee will not examine whether the State charged has violated its obligations under any other international human rights instrument, including the American Convention or the American Declaration. Obviously, the specific right violated may be defined in the Inter-American instrument differently from the way it is defined in the Political Covenant. In such a situation, a complainant who has gone first to the Human Rights Committee would not obtain consideration of a claim that the differently defined right under the Inter-American instrument has been violated, unless the Commission could admit the complaint despite the prior examination by the Human Rights Committee. A strict reading of the American Convention would probably preclude consideration by the IACHR. The Convention states no exception for complaints where the right that has allegedly been violated is defined differently in the instrument under which the subject of the complaint is being, or was, examined by another international organization. Could it nevertheless be argued that Arts. 46(1) (c) and 47(d) do not govern this situation because the complaint before the IACHR is not substantially the same as a complaint brought before another international organization when the right allegedly violated is defined differently by the other organization? Can it be maintained that even though the fact patterns involved in the two complaints are identical, the complaint is not substantially the same when the legal standard to be applied to the facts is different? Given the emphasis placed by the governing texts on the petition or communication (fact pattern) rather than on the right allegedly violated, the answers to these questions are probably in the negative.

B. *The European System for the Protection of Human Rights*

Sohn has rightly observed that the liberal attitude reflected in Art. 44 of the Political Covenant and Art. 5(2) (a) of the

---

[55] Political Covenant, Art. 41(1); Optional Protocol, Art. 1.

Optional Protocol can be contrasted with the more restrictive approach reflected in Art. 62 of the European Convention on Human Rights.[56]

As regards interstate disputes, Art. 62 of the European Convention on Human Rights provides that States Parties may submit disputes arising out of the interpretation or application of the Convention only to a means of settlement provided for in the Convention (that is the European Commission of Human Rights and possibly, after the Commission's report, the European Court of Human Rights). States Parties may not bring such disputes before other bodies such as the UN Human Rights Committee, the UN Committee on the Elimination of Racial Discrimination, the Conciliation and Good Offices Commission on Discrimination in Education of UNESCO, any of the various ILO organs, or even the International Court of Justice, except by special agreement.[57] The position of the Council of Europe and its organs has been that it is undesirable for States that have brought a case unsuccessfully under the European Convention on Human Rights later to refer the same matter to the Human Rights Committee. Even though the issue raised before the Committee would technically be a different one, because the complaint would allege a violation of a different treaty, the impression might be created that appeal from the organs of the European Convention is possible, an impression which would weaken their authority.[58] In 1970, the Committee of Ministers of the Council of Europe adopted Resolution (70) 17 dealing with States Parties to the European Convention that are also parties to the Political Covenant and have made a declaration under its Art. 41. The resolution stated that such States should normally utilize only the procedure established by the European Convention for Complaints against another party to the Convention that relate to an alleged violation of a right covered in substance by both the Convention (or its Protocols) and the

---

[56] Sohn, above n. 15, at 393.

[57] See De Meyer, *The International Control Machinery*, in Council of Europe, Directorate of Human Rights, Proceedings of the Colloquy About the European Convention on Human Rights in Relation to Other International Instruments for the Protection of Human Rights, Athens, 21–22 September 1978, at 241, 287 (1979). De Meyer suggests that reports that do not constitute a 'settlement' of the dispute do not exclude any subsequent recourse to another form of settlement. Ibid. at 292.

[58] Council of Europe Doc. CAHMP (80) 1, at 6 (1980).

Covenant. At the same time, the Committee of Ministers expressed its understanding that the procedure under the Covenant may be invoked for rights not guaranteed by the Convention or in relation to States that are not parties to it.[59]

As regards individual applications, the effect of an acceptance of the Optional Protocol by States that have accepted the right of individual petition under Art. 25 of the European Convention is that an individual alleging a violation of a right guaranteed by both the Political Covenant and the Convention would have the right to initiate proceedings under either instrument.[60] It has been suggested that such freedom of choice 'can only strengthen the protection of human rights and fundamental freedoms'.[61] On the other hand, the principle of freedom of choice might lead to difficulties as a result, *inter alia*, of divergencies in the case law of the two systems.[62] In addition, does freedom of choice include the successive use by individuals of remedies open to them?[63] Under Art. 5(2) (a) of the Optional Protocol, the Human Rights Committee is not precluded from examining a complaint previously considered by the organs of the European Convention on Human Rights. In contrast, under Art. 27(1) (b) of the Convention, the European Commission of Human Rights may not examine a complaint which is substantially the same as one previously considered by the Commission or by the Committee unless there is relevant new information (*ne bis in idem*). In order to forestall the possibility of successive applications to the Commission and the Human Rights Committee, the Committee of Ministers of the Council of Europe in its Resolution (70) 17, while recognizing the reasonableness of allowing an individual a choice of procedures under either the Convention or the Political Covenant, stated that no one should be able to bring the same case under both procedures, either simultaneously or successively. To this end, the resolution suggested that the Member States of the Council of Europe make a declaration of interpretation or a

---

[59] See Committee of Ministers Res. (70) 17, reprinted in Eissen, above n. 1, at 204–5; Council of Europe Doc. CAHMP (80) 1, at 6 (1980).
[60] Council of Europe Doc. CAHMP (80) 1, at 6 (1980); De Meyer, above n. 57, at 292.
[61] De Meyer, above n. 57, at 293.
[62] See Council of Europe Doc. CAHMP (80) 1, at 7 (1980).
[63] See De Meyer, above n. 57, at 293–5 (who asserts this is possible).

reservation to the Optional Protocol to the effect that the competence of the Human Rights Committee would not extend to receiving and considering individual complaints relating to cases that are being or have been examined under the European Convention on Human Rights. Such a declaration would apply to complaints of violations of rights protected in substance by the two instruments.[64]

VI. THE REPORTING SYSTEMS

Reporting by States on their compliance with their human rights obligations is an important component in the supervision of human rights by international organizations. The task of preparing reports focuses the attention of national administrations on weak points in internal compliance with international human rights obligations and encourages improvements. The practice, developed by the control bodies, of inviting representatives of States to be present during the discussion of their national reports has led to a dialogue, bringing about further clarification and elaboration of national reports. Nevertheless, the reporting system, to paraphrase the title of Jacques Brel's play, is alive, but is not well. As a symptom of this malaise, suffice it to cite the following paragraph from the recent report of the Committee on Elimination of Racial Discrimination (CERD):

... only five of the 63 reports received during the year were submitted on time or before the deadlines provided for under article 9, paragraph 1, of the Convention. The rest were submitted after some delay, ranging from a few days to nearly six years. In the case of 39 of the reports received during the year, 1 to 11 reminders had been sent to the States parties concerned before their reports were submitted.[65]

An earlier report indicated that despite the reporting obligations stated in Art. 9, 'no less than 89 reports ... [were] overdue from 62 States ...',[66] even after CERD's reminders.

[64] The following Council of Europe member States have made such reservations: Denmark, Iceland, Italy, Norway, Sweden, and Luxembourg. See Multilateral Treaties Deposited with the Secretary-General, Status as at 31 December 1981, UN Doc. ST/LEG/Ser.E/1, at 131 (1982); Multilateral Treaties Deposited with the Secretary-General, Supplement: Actions from 1 January to 31 December 1983, UN Doc. ST/LEG/SER.E/2/Add. 1, at Part I, page IV. 5-1 (1984).

[65] 39 UN GAOR Supp. (No. 18) para. 50, UN Doc. A/39/18 (1984).

[66] 37 UN GAOR Supp. (No. 18) at 121, UN Doc. A/37/18 (1982). See also ibid. at 131.

Similar difficulties have arisen with regard to reporting obligations under other international conventions.[67] Even some States with large national administrations have not submitted some of their reports on time. CERD's General Recommendation No. VI[68] stated that while an impressive number of States have ratified the Convention, ratification alone does not enable the control system to function effectively. In response to CERD's invitation, the General Assembly, by Resolution 37/44,[69] made an appeal to States to fulfil their obligations, while acknowledging the burden which reporting obligations placed upon States, especially those with limited resources. The Secretary-General was requested to invite the views of the Governments and to prepare a report, which was to take into account 'the overall framework of reporting obligations' under the various human rights instruments. The General Assembly could have mentioned also the burden placed on the control organs, which often cannot promptly examine the reports in the time allocated to their meetings, in addition to their personnel, administrative, and budgetary restraints.

In thoughtful comments made by Italy in response to CERD's General Recommendation No. VI, the following causes of delays in reporting were identified:

(*a*) the difficulties which may be faced by small countries, above all in preparing the first analytical report on racial discrimination in accordance with the Committee's general guidelines;

(*b*) the excessively short interval (two years) between States Parties' first reports and successive reports;

(*c*) the simultaneous preparation of four other, very complicated, reports by those States which have also ratified the International Covenants on Human Rights.[70]

One of the primary reporting difficulties stems indeed from the multiplicity of the reporting obligations under human rights treaties, declarations, and resolutions. As regards the International Convention on the Elimination of All Forms of Racial

[67] See generally UN Doc. A/39/484 (1984). See also GA Res. 39/138, 39 UN GAOR Supp. (No. 51) at 226, UN Doc. A/39/51 (1985).

[68] 37 UN GAOR Supp. (No. 18) at 121, UN Doc. A/37/18 (1982).

[69] GA Res. 37/44, 37 UN GAOR Supp. (No. 51) at 179, UN Doc. A/37/51 (1983).

[70] 37 UN GAOR Supp. (No. 18) at 144, 145, UN Doc. A/37/18 (1982).

Discrimination, Italy has proposed that States Parties which have presented their first report should merely be asked to update it periodically for the purpose of each succeeding report. Italy further proposed that the short interval between the reports could be modified by a General Assembly resolution amending Art. 9(1) of the Convention. 'This amendment should take account of the intervals laid down by the Human Rights Committee for the reports on civil and political rights (five years) and by the Economic and Social Council for the reports on economic, social and cultural rights (six years for the three reports in question); and it should be based on an overall timetable providing, for example, for two reports (or updatings) for each of the five kinds of reports in any one decade.'[71]

More far-reaching and comprehensive reforms have been proposed by Sohn. His suggestion is to consolidate all the reporting in the economic, social, and cultural fields in the sessional working group of ECOSOC.[72] This would be achieved through a resolution of ECOSOC which would authorize the sessional working group to consider reports from States non-parties to the Economic Covenant. As regards reports on civil and political rights, Sohn suggests that parties to the Political Covenant, following an invitation from ECOSOC, authorize the Human Rights Committee to consider also reports from States which are not parties to the Political Covenant regarding rights stated in that Covenant. Consideration of reports under the various human rights conventions would be transferred either to the sessional working group or to the Human Rights Committee, whenever possible by decisions, of the States Parties to those Conventions, or by a special protocol to a particular convention, or by a general protocol to the effect that whenever a convention provides for a system of reporting on human rights, the reports should be submitted to the appropriate reporting organ established by the Covenants.

While these proposals merit serious consideration, their implementation presents difficulties, especially because the control organs, while financed and serviced by the United Nations, are treaty organs. The amendment of the instruments might not

---

[71] Ibid. at 146.
[72] Sohn, above n. 15, at 377–9. See also above, Chapter IV, n. 13.

be acceptable to some States Parties. It should also be recognized that Sohn's proposals would require the two control bodies concerned to function on a full-time, or nearly full-time, basis. This would cause budgetary and administrative problems. Some eminent jurists serving on the Human Rights Committee might also be compelled to resign from it, so as to be able to continue performing their functions on other bodies, such as the European Court of Human Rights or the European Commission of Human Rights. To change the Human Rights Committee to a permanently sitting organ would transform its character. But since the Human Rights Committee (as CERD) adopts its own rules of procedure and decides on the frequency of its meetings, an amendment of the Covenant would not be required to authorize meetings on a more extended basis. Other bodies, such as the Committee on the Elimination of Discrimination Against Women established under the Convention on the Elimination of All Forms of Discrimination Against Women, could not even extend the duration of their annual meetings without an amendment of the Convention (Art. 20).

An interesting unified international reporting procedure has been proposed by Das.[73] This system would be established by a new protocol which would constitute a Human Rights Board, as a central body to which States would submit reports with regard to instruments they have accepted.

The immediate objective should be to start a process of review and amendment of the present reporting systems, aimed at their consolidation and rationalization. The difficulties in accomplishing such reform are great, and include the reluctance to amend existing instruments and adopt new ones. The United Nations should be willing, however, to emulate the example provided by States Members of the Council of Europe, which have recently started a review and examination of the implementation procedures and organs established under the European Convention on Human Rights.[74]

---

[73] Das, *Some Reflections on Implementing Human Rights*, in Human Rights: Thirty Years After the Universal Declaration 131, 146-8 (B. Ramcharan ed. 1979).

[74] See, e.g. European Ministerial Conference on Human Rights, Vienna, 19-20 March 1985, Report Submitted by the Swiss Delegation on Functioning of the Organs of the European Convention on Human Rights (Assessment, improvement

VII. CONCLUDING OBSERVATIONS

It is desirable to avoid duplication and conflict regarding organs and procedures of supervision and control, and to entrust supervision to organs with the greatest technical competence in the subject. The drafters of international human rights instruments must therefore try to prevent future overlapping or conflict of jurisdiction. Co-ordination between organizations and bodies charged with supervision of compliance should be further developed, especially in the examination of reports submitted by States. The time has come for rationalizing reporting procedures by States in the UN context. Eventually, the international community would have to consolidate supervisory systems into a more limited number of organs. Such a consolidation would resolve or reduce conflicts in supervision. It would also reduce normative conflicts through a more consistent and rational application and interpretation of human rights instruments. Even within the existing framework, however, supervisory organs should and could show due deference to other control organs and exercise a measure of 'judicial restraint'.

In some situations, simultaneous consideration of similar matters by different bodies may prove beneficial to the individuals concerned. But this cannot always be assumed to be the case. States guilty of human rights violations could take advantage of conflicting opinions of control organs by acknowledging only the milder opinion. On balance, it may therefore be preferable to encourage only sequential consideration, that is organization *b* would act only if organization *a* does not succeed in settling the matter.[75] However, the difficulty is that the principle of sequential consideration, where it is not enunciated in the governing instrument, requires a measure of interinstitutional co-ordination which is still lacking. The fact that in a

---

and reinforcement of the international control machinery set up by the Convention) (1984); European Ministerial Conference on Human Rights (Vienna, 19–20 March 1985): Texts Adopted, Resolutions Nos. 1–2, Council of Europe Doc. H (85) 7 (1985). See also Protocol No. 8 to the Convention for the Protection of Human Rights and Fundamental Freedoms, opened for signature 19 March 1985. Council of Europe Doc. H (85) 6 (1985). This Protocol aims mainly at avoiding unreasonable delays in proceedings under the European Convention. See Explanatory Memorandum, ibid. at 5.

[75] See Tardu, above n. 1, at 793–8.

number of instances the same person serves on several implementation organs may remedy somewhat this institutional deficiency and encourage cross-fertilization. Increasing awareness of co-ordination needs may lead to efforts to institutionalize the 'same person' phenomenon.[76] Another problem raised by sequential consideration is whether organization *b* should continue to desist from considering a human rights violation if the deliberations of organization *a* are unreasonably prolonged. Such a result would be clearly undesirable.[77] A distinction has been suggested [78] between the consideration of individual communications and that of more general situations of human rights. While, as regards the former, it is not desirable that 'the same matter should be examined under various procedures . . .',[79] as regards the latter, resort to inquiries or studies by various organizations is not 'in itself' open to objection. The terms of reference and the perspectives within which the different procedures are pursued are often not the same, even if there is a certain degree of overlap.'[80]

What should be the future policy on possible overlap or conflict in supervision of implementation? The availability of international forums and international remedies for individual complainants is still limited. The law of international human rights is as yet a weak instrument for the protection of individuals from sovereign States. In these circumstances, there may be advantages to double or even triple examination of individual

---

[76] It has been proposed that the Committee Against Torture should be composed, as far as possible, of persons who are members of the Human Rights Committee. UN Doc. E/CN.4/1982/L.40, Ann. II, Art. 17(2) (1982). Art. 9 of the International Convention on the Suppression and Punishment of the Crime of *Apartheid*, GA Res. 3068, 28 UN GAOR Supp. (No. 30) at 75, UN Doc. A/9030 (1973), provides that reports by States Parties be considered by a group appointed by the Chairman of the Commission on Human Rights consisting of three members of the Commission who are also representatives of States Parties to the Convention, which avoids establishing a new organ.

[77] For a view based on the *travaux préparatoires* of Art. 5(2) (a) of the Optional Protocol that the provision allowing the Human Rights Committee to consider a petition if other proceedings have been 'unreasonably prolonged' applies not only to Art. 5(2) (b) (exhaustion of domestic remedies), but also to Art. 5(2) (a) (competition with other international procedures), see 32 UN GAOR Supp. (No. 44) at 13, UN Doc. A/32/44 (1977); 2 M. Tardu, Human Rights: The International Petition System, pt. 1, § 1, at 67–9 (1980).

[78] Samson, above n. 1, at 53.

[79] Ibid.

[80] Ibid.

complaints, but such consideration should preferably be sequential rather than simultaneous. Subject to the language of the governing instruments, the interest of effective protection of human rights may justify the examination by another body of a complaint in cases where the first examination has not produced an effective remedy for a serious violation, or where it has been unreasonably prolonged. Until the procedures for the protection of human rights become comprehensive, effective, and generally accepted, there may be room for resort to complementary control mechanisms, even at the risk of a certain overlap or conflict.

The prevailing wisdom has been that it is important to improve co-ordination, to avoid conflict, and to avoid different interpretations. In addition, compelling a State to defend essentially the same case before several organs may increase apathy and cynicism about the system as a whole and give the impression of institutional chaos. Nevertheless, over-zealous efforts to rationalize the existing multiplicity of procedures might cause the most favourable procedures to be brought into line with the less far-reaching ones. As an important study by the government of the Netherlands has suggested, there may be good reason 'to allow the new procedures a certain amount of time to develop and consolidate themselves in practice. In the long run it may then prove possible to rationalize the numerous procedures, adapting the *less* effective to bring them into line with the better ones.'[81]

A similar policy should apply to complaints submitted by one State against another and to general investigations of human rights violations by States undertaken by international organizations. In the present formative stage of supervision, multiplicity of recourse procedures, which should lead to a greater observance of human rights, is more important than institutional order.

---

[81] Ministry of the Foreign Affairs of the Netherlands, Human Rights and Foreign Policy 80 (1979) (emphasis in original). For a discussion of advantages inherent in double or triple examination and in seeking out of the provision most favourable to the individual concerned, see Council of Europe Doc. CAHMP (80) 1, at 3-4 (1980). See generally Golsong, *To which Extent and for which Matters Is it Advisable to Create and Develop Special Judicial Bodies with a Jurisdiction Limited to Certain Regions or Subject Matters?*, 62 Beiträge zum ausländischen öffentlichen Recht und Völkerrecht 99, 112 (1974).

PART III

The Process of Law-Making

VI

Human Rights Law-Making Outside the United Nations and Co-ordination Between the United Nations and the Specialized Agencies

I. INTRODUCTION

ONE of the phenomena of contemporary international life is the proliferation of human rights instruments and systems of supervision. In addition to the Charter of the United Nations and comprehensive global conventions such as the International Covenant on Economic, Social and Cultural Rights[1] (Economic Covenant) and the International Covenant on Civil and Political Rights[2] (Political Covenant), instruments have been adopted within the United Nations or the specialized agencies (for instance the ILO, UNESCO) to govern particular aspects of human rights (for instance racial discrimination, rights of women) and within regional organizations (for instance the Council of Europe, the Organization of American States, the Organization of African Unity) to govern both general and particular aspects of human rights.[3] As already indicated in Chapter IV, in the United Nations, the general practice has been for each normative instrument to create its own system of

---

[1] GA Res. 2200, 21 UN GAOR Supp. (No. 16) at 49, UN Doc. A/6316 (1966).
[2] Ibid. at 52.
[3] See Human Rights; A Compilation of International Instruments, UN Doc. ST/HR/1/Rev. 2 (1983) (which lists 57 human rights instruments); Basic Documents on Human Rights (2nd edn. I. Brownlie, 1981); International Human Rights Instruments (R. Lillich ed., 1983). These compilations are necessarily selective. By the end of 1981, the ILO alone had adopted 156 international labour conventions. See generally Sohn, *The Shaping of International Law*, 8 Ga. J. Int'l & Comp. L. 1 (1978); Suy, *Innovations in International Law-Making Processes*, in The International Law and Policy of Human Welfare 187 (R. Macdonald, D. Johnston and G. Morris eds., 1978); Ramcharan, *Standard-Setting: Future Perspectives*, in Human Rights: Thirty Years After the Universal Declaration 93 (B. Ramcharan ed., 1979).

supervision whenever such systems have been established.[4] Typically, each organ of supervision applies only the norms adopted in the specific 'founding' instrument, rather than the entire *corpus juris* of international human rights or even all of the instruments comprising the International Bill of Human Rights,[5] that is, the Universal Declaration of Human Rights (Universal Declaration),[6] the Economic Covenant, the Political Covenant, and the Optional Protocol to the International Covenant on Civil and Political Rights.[7] This proliferation of normative instruments and systems of supervision has led to overlapping jurisdiction and even to conflicts between the legislative and supervisory competence, or claims of competence of various international bodies. Similar proliferation in the field of budget, programming and administration has given rise to difficult questions of co-ordination of efforts in those areas within and among international organizations.[8]

[4] E.g. the International Convention on the Elimination of All Forms of Racial Discrimination, 660 UNTS 195 (which established the Committee on the Elimination of Racial Discrimination), discussed in Buergenthal, *Implementing the UN Racial Convention*, 12 Tex. Int'l L.J. 187 (1977); the Political Covenant, above n. 2 (which established the Human Rights Committee), discussed in Robertson, *The Implementation System: International Measures*, in the International Bill of Rights: The Covenant on Civil and Political Rights 332 (L. Henkin ed., 1981). See generally van Boven, *Human Rights Fora at the United Nations. How to Select and to Approach the Most Appropriate Forum. What Procedural Rules Govern?* in International Human Rights: Law and Practice 83 (J. Tuttle ed. 1978); International Law and Fact-finding in the Field of Human Rights (B. Ramcharan ed., 1982); Guide to International Human Rights Practice (H. Hannum ed., 1984); T. Zuijdwijk, Petitioning the United Nations: A Study in Human Rights (1982). See also Franck and Fairley, *Procedural Due Process in Human Rights Fact-Finding by International Agencies*, 74 AJIL 308 (1980), for a critique of fact-finding by international agencies in the human rights area.

The trend to establish separate implementation organs for each UN human rights instrument is continuing. For example, the Convention on the Elimination of All Forms of Discrimination against Women provides for the establishment of a Committee on the Elimination of Discrimination against Women. GA Res. 34/180, 34 UN GAOR Supp. (No. 46) at 193, UN Doc. A/34/46 (1979) (Art. 17); the Convention against Torture and Other Cruel, Inhuman or Degrading Treatment or Punishment provides for the establishment of a Committee against Torture (Art. 17). GA Res. 39/46, opened for signature 10 Dec. 1984, 39 UN GAOR Supp. (No. 51) at 197, UN Doc. A/39/51 (1985). But see Chapter IV n. 73 above.

[5] See Chapter IV nn. 70–1, above.

[6] GA Res. 217A, UN Doc. A/810, at 71 (1948).

[7] GA Res. 2200, 21 UN GAOR Supp. (No. 16) at 59, UN Doc. A/6316 (1966).

[8] See e.g. Sharp, *Program Coordination and the Economic and Social Council*, in UN Administration of Economic and Social Programs 102 (G. Mangone ed., 1966); Meron, *Administrative and Budgetary Coordination by the General Assembly*, in ibid. at 37; Meron, *Budget Approval by the General Assembly of the United Nations: Duty or Discretion?*, 42 Brit. Y.B. Int'l L. 91 (1967).

The extent of human rights law-making[9] in the international organizations is impressive, in terms of both the quantity of output and of the number of organs which are involved in the law-making activities. Law-making is carried out in the United Nations General Assembly and ECOSOC and in the many subsidiary organs of the General Assembly and ECOSOC, including the functional commissions of the latter organ. States are involved in the human rights law-making activity of the various specialized agencies of the United Nations, particularly in the ILO and UNESCO, and in the activities of various regional organizations such as the Council of Europe, the Organization of American States, and the Organization of African Unity, and in conferences convened outside the framework of either universal or regional organizations (for example, conferences on humanitarian law convened by Switzerland and initiated and prepared largely by the International Committee of the Red Cross). While the chaotic pace of legislative activity places a heavy burden on States and on international organizations, the main difficulty lies in the often unsatisfactory quality of the law-making instruments produced. As observed by Szasz in the context of the multilateral treaty-making process by international organizations, treaties 'frequently deal inadequately with the problems to which they are addressed'.[10] This inadequacy of the instruments adopted has been discussed in Chapters I–III above.

This chapter will discuss human rights law-making by major

---

[9] The 1973 Report of the *Ad Hoc* Inter-Agency Meeting of Legal Experts on Co-ordination of Legislative Work of Organizations within the UN system suggested that the concept of 'legislative work' should be interpreted: 'in the widest sense as including all international and regional norms and standards designed to be applied by the member States of the various organizations, whether they were in the form of Conventions, Declarations, Recommendations, Resolutions and Regulations such as the International Health Regulations or Codex Alimentarius Standards, or model codes and other guides to national legislative activity.' Report of the *Ad Hoc* Inter-Agency Meeting of Legal Experts on Co-ordination of Legislative Work of Organizations, UN Doc. Co-ordination/R.1003, at 1 (1973) (hereinafter cited as Co-ordination Report).

Law-making as a process whereby international organizations adopt human rights instruments should not be confused with the jurisprudential process which explains how provisions contained in such instruments become 'law'. On the jurisprudential aspects of law-making, see generally Law Making in the Global Community (N. Onuf ed., 1982).

[10] Szasz, *Improving the International Legislative Process*, 9 Ga. J. Int'l & Comp. L. 519, 521 (1979).

international organizations outside the United Nations and review the institutional co-ordination in that field.[11]

The complexity of law-making is reflected by the following questions posed by Australia and other delegations and listed in a report of the Secretary-General of the United Nations, prepared in the context of reviewing the UN multilateral treaty-making process:

[W]hat is the best first approach to a new topic for treaty-making — an inquiry by a single expert, by the Secretariat or by a committee? If by a committee, then should it be a committee comprising all Members or only some? Should it consist of government representatives or of experts? Is it right to assume that these are the only alternatives? Should there perhaps be supplementary machinery whose responsibility it would be to co-ordinate the activities of all elements interested in a particular subject and ensure that an appropriate report is prepared which seeks to reflect all points of view? What should be the form of reports — whether of such a body or of any other person or entity? . . . Should there be a requirement that an attempt be made to assess the extent and nature of the impact of proposals upon the domestic law of the Member States? Is there a need or scope for an indication of uniform methods of State implementation of treaty commitments? What is the best stage at which to inject the views of States into the treaty-making process? How may such views best be conveyed — by answers to questionnaires, by comments on drafts or by discussion in committees? And when should a proposal be deemed ripe for consideration by a diplomatic conference? Is the present general practice of diplomatic conferences satisfactory? . . . Is it sufficient that when the conference concludes its work it should do so only with a convention? Or should the conference prepare a report containing an explanation or a commentary upon the convention — in a manner comparable to the explanatory memoranda which in some States accompany legislation?[12]

[11] See generally International Complaint System, Council of Europe Doc. CAHMP (80) 2 (1980) (this Secretariat Information Memorandum prepared by the Directorate of Human Rights for the *Ad Hoc* Committee on the Multiplication of Complaint Procedures at the International Level of the Council of Europe, is a particularly useful compilation); Meron, *Norm Making and Supervision in International Human Rights: Reflections on Institutional Order*, 76 AJIL 754 (1982) (hereinafter cited as Meron, *Norm Making*); Jenks, *The Conflict of Law-Making Treaties*, 30 Brit. Y.B. Int'l L. 401 (1953); Jenks, *Co-ordination: A New Problem of International Organization*, 77 Recueil des cours 157 (1950–II); Jenks, *Co-ordination in International Organization: an Introductory Survey*, 28 Brit. Y.B. Int'l L. 29 (1951).

[12] 1 Review of the Multilateral Treaty-Making Process, UN Doc. ST/LEG/SER. B/21, at 4–5 (Provisional Version, 1982) (quoting UN Doc. A/32/143, and corrigendum dated 18 July 1977 entitled 'Request for the Inclusion of an Item in the Provisional Agenda of the Thirty-second Session, Review of the Multilateral Treaty-Making Process, Letter dated 19 July 1977 from the representatives of Australia, Egypt, Indonesia, Kenya, Mexico, the Netherlands and Sri Lanka to the United Nations, addressed to the Secretary General') [hereinafter cited as 1 Review].

Certainly, the structural and procedural weaknesses of the treaty-making process often reflect political considerations. The fact that States are unlikely to agree in the near future upon far-reaching reforms does not, however, obviate the need for critical analysis, which can identify the necessary elements for constructive changes.

II. MODELS OF LAW-MAKING OUTSIDE THE UNITED NATIONS

A. *In the Specialized Agencies*

1. *The International Labour Organisation*   The ILO has an efficient, structured treaty-making procedure consisting of a number of steps carried out according to a predetermined timetable. The relevant rules are contained in Arts. 19–23 of the Constitution of the International Labour Organisation and in Part II, Section E (Convention and Recommendation Procedure) of the Standing Orders of the International Labour Conference (Conference).[13] This procedure provides for an orderly consideration of conventions and recommendations and clearly states the respective roles of the Conference, the International Labour Office (Office), and the Members. While, in certain cases, a single-discussion procedure is used,[14] the usual practice is to follow the double-discussion procedure,[15] which takes up to thirty months altogether.[16] As a preliminary observation to explanation of the double-discussion procedure, it should be noted that the International Labour Conference is the only body within the ILO which has the authority to adopt international labour conventions. The consideration of instruments is initiated by the inclusion of the subject matter on the agenda of the Conference. The agenda of the Conference is

[13] See Constitution of the International Labour Organisation and Standing Orders of the International Labour Conference 13–17 (International Labour Office, 1982). For Section E of the Standing Orders, see ibid. at 48.

[14] Art. 38 of the Standing Orders, ibid. at 50; 2 Review of the Multilateral Treaty-Making Process 239–40, UN Doc. ST/LEG/SER.B/21 (Provisional Version, 1982) (hereinafter cited as 2 Review). Regarding ILO law-making in general, see International Labour Standards (International Labour Office, 1984); ILO Doc. GB.228/4/2 (1984).

[15] Art. 39 of the Standing Orders, above n. 13, at 51; 2 Review, above n. 14, at 237–9.

[16] 1 Review, above n. 12, at 15.

settled by the Governing Body generally eighteen months prior to the opening of the session. The Conference itself may include an item on the agenda of its following session.

The double-discussion procedure consists of the following: after the inclusion of the item on the agenda, the Office prepares a preliminary report, which sets out the law and practice in the different countries and other useful information, together with a questionnaire. The preliminary report and the questionnaire must reach the governments no later than twelve months prior to the opening of the Conference at which the question is to be discussed initially. The report highlights problems and indicates which of them could be resolved through the adoption of an instrument. The purpose of the questionnaire is to ascertain what standards States would be prepared to accept and thus, if possible, to identify the obstacles to a generally acceptable instrument. On the basis of the replies from States, the preparation of the first draft of an instrument begins. In preparing replies to the questionnaire, governments are required to consult with employers' and workers' organizations.[17] The replies are to reach the Office no later than eight months before the opening of the session of the Conference. On the basis of the replies, the Office prepares a second report which identifies the primary questions requiring consideration by the Conference. This report should reach governments not less than four months before the Conference. This report contains a summary of the replies to the questionnaire, and conclusions proposed in the light of the replies as to the form of the instrument (convention, recommendation, or convention accompanied by a recommendation) and as to the content of the substantive provisions of the new instrument. Both reports are discussed at the Conference, and constant practice is to refer them to a specially constituted tripartite committee. After a general discussion, the committee analyses each provision individually and votes on the draft provisions and on the amendments. A simple majority of the votes cast by the members of the committee who are present is required under a system of weighted voting. To be

[17] See Convention (No. 144) concerning Tripartite Consultations to promote the Implementation of International Labour Standards, International Labour Conventions and Recommendations, 1919–1981, at 198 (International Labour Office, 1982).

valid, the votes cast for and against may not be less than two-fifths of the total.[18]

Each committee must set up a drafting committee which reviews the text for internal consistency, verifies the conformity of the authentic versions of the instrument in English and in French, and attempts to ensure conformity with the style and presentation of other ILO instruments. After approval by the committee, the text established by the drafting committee is presented for adoption to the plenary session of the Conference. The plenary adopts the text together with a resolution formally including the subject matter in the agenda of its next session for second and final discussion.

Immediately following the first session of the Conference, the Office prepares the text of a draft convention, which must reach governments no later than two months after the closing of the Conference. The governments then have three months in which to state whether they wish to propose amendments. On the basis of the replies, the Office prepares a final report containing a revised draft text of the instrument. This report must reach the governments not less than three months before the opening of the session of the Conference in which the question is to be discussed for the second time. The procedure followed during the second session of the Conference is similar to that followed during the first session, until the draft instrument is submitted by the technical committee to the plenary. The plenary then votes on each clause and on such amendments as are presented. After the adoption of all the provisions, the text is referred to the Conference Drafting Committee which reviews the technical provisions for the last time and adds the final clauses in accordance with the pattern followed for ILO instruments. The text as approved by the Conference Drafting Committee is circulated to the delegations. No further amendments may be presented without the permission of the President of the Conference after consultation with the Vice-Presidents. The text is put to the Conference for a final vote and must be approved by two-thirds of the votes cast by delegates present and voting.

[18] 2 Review, above n. 14, at 238.

2. *United Nations Educational, Scientific and Cultural Organization*[19]   A rather structured law-making procedure is followed by UNESCO. According to current practice, proposals which call for the preparation of a preliminary study leading to the formulation of a normative instrument take the form of draft resolutions submitted to the General Conference of UNESCO. The preliminary study is carried out by the Secretariat and submitted to the Executive Board. The Board then decides whether to include a suitable item on the provisional agenda of the General Conference. On the basis of the proposal to draft a new normative instrument and of the preliminary study, the Executive Board decides whether to instruct the Secretariat or one or more experts, or a committee of experts, to prepare a thorough study in addition to a report on the subject for communication to the General Conference. The Board communicates to the General Conference any comments it may deem necessary. When a proposal for the regulation of a particular subject matter on an international basis is included in the provisional agenda of the General Conference, the Director-General transmits to States, at least seventy days before the opening of the conference, a copy of the preliminary study, the Executive Board's comments, and other information. The General Conference must decide whether the question should be regulated on an international basis and, if so, whether the international regulation should be in the form of a convention or a recommendation. Conventions require, for their submission to States, a two-thirds majority in the General Conference; recommendations require a simple majority only. When the General Conference has decided that the question should be regulated on an international basis and has chosen the form such regulation should take, it must decide whether the Director-General's final report comprising a draft text should be submitted directly to the General Conference or to a special committee consisting of technical or legal experts appointed by States. If it is decided to convene such a special committee, that committee must meet at least four months before the opening of the General Conference. The preparation of drafts of conventions and recommendations is a function of the

[19] Ibid. at 255–60.

Director-General, who takes into account comments by governments. Draft texts and any amendments are submitted to the General Conference for adoption.

The General Conference is thus involved in the law-making process in three stages: first, when it approves the programme and the budget providing for the preparation of the preliminary study; second, if the question has been included in its provisional agenda by the Executive Board, when it decides on the advisability of regulating the subject on an international basis and the form of regulation appropriate; and finally, when it adopts the instrument. The entire process requires a minimum of four years.

On a number of occasions the General Conference of UNESCO has concluded that a treaty should be adopted by an international conference.[20] The procedure leading to the establishment of instruments by such conferences is less structured than that leading to the preparation of instruments which are adopted by the General Conference. The convening of a conference is usually preceded by resolutions of the General Conference calling for meetings of governmental experts to study the desirability of regulating the subject concerned on an international basis and, later, to draft the instruments for submission to an international conference.

B. *In the Regional Organizations: The Council of Europe*[21]

The initiative for the conclusion of an international instrument may originate in one of several sources: the Parliamentary Assembly; committees of experts; committees established under various treaties of the Council of Europe (treaty organs), which may propose improvements in the operation of the treaties concerned by means of an amending protocol or of an additional treaty on the subject; committees charged with the elaboration of the programme of work of the Council of Europe; meetings of ministers charged with special questions, such as environment or education; governments; the Committee of Ministers; or the Secretariat. Most proposals for new instruments originate in the Parliamentary Assembly or in committees of experts, but at

---

[20] Ibid. at 258-9.
[21] Ibid. at 319-22. See also Chapter VII nn. 54-7 and accompanying text, below.

times the source of their proposals can be traced to a government or to a non-governmental organization. Members of expert committees are appointed by their governments.

The decision to elaborate an international instrument is always taken by the Committee of Ministers, normally after it receives a report from a committee of experts suggesting that the proposal is desirable and feasible. Before deciding on the formulation of an instrument, the Committee of Ministers insists on a determination that the proposed instrument is of interest to States. Although the report of the committee of experts provides the Committee of Ministers with important legal and factual data, in many cases the decision concerning the form of the instrument (convention, agreement, recommendation, and so on) is made at a later stage, after the work has begun.

The usual practice is for an expert committee to formulate draft texts, with the assistance of the Secretariat. Only in exceptional cases are preliminary texts submitted to the expert committee by the Secretariat or by the Parliamentary Assembly.[22] Expert committees usually meet twice a year and after each meeting transmit a report to the Committee of Ministers. They may seek guidance from the Committee of Ministers concerning special difficulties. When a draft instrument has been completed, it is transmitted to the Committee of Ministers for the Committee's decision whether to adopt the instrument and open it for signature. The drafts are accompanied by explanatory memoranda, which are prepared by the committee of experts or by the Secretariat. In formulating that decision, the Committee may request the opinion of the Parliamentary Assembly.

The experience of the Council of Europe suggests that the procedure of entrusting the drafting of a treaty to a small committee of governmental experts has some advantages. While experts ensure the necessary quality, the small membership facilitates consensus. The experts take into account the situation prevailing in their countries.[23]

Most treaties have been concluded within three to four years from the beginning of the process, but in some cases the

----

[22] 1 Review, above n. 12, at 84.
[23] Ibid.

law-making process lasted for shorter or longer periods.[24] The practice of the Council of Europe as regards the extension of rights is considered in Chapter IV above and in Chapter VII below.

III. CO-ORDINATION BETWEEN THE UNITED NATIONS AND THE SPECIALIZED AGENCIES

A. *The Legal Setting*

The principal provisions of the Charter regarding co-ordination

[24] In 1975, the Committee of Ministers approved paragraph 26 of a report prepared at its request by the Permanent Representative of Sweden in co-operation with the Secretariat on the 'advisability of replacing in certain cases the elaboration of conventions by more efficient machinery and of the desirability of a selective policy regarding the detailed follow-up of resolutions'. 2 Review, above n. 14, at 326–38. The report by Sweden suggests the possibility of making more frequent use in relation to technical subjects 'of the framework or outline treaty approach'. Ibid. at 332. The content of a proposed convention would be limited to general undertakings or principles. The authority to draft more detailed provisions would be delegated to treaty organs. 'Such a system could be accompanied by "contracting-out" procedures on the lines of those followed within the International Civil Aviation Organization.' Ibid. Detailed provisions could be appended to the convention by a particular treaty organ which would have responsibility for amending or developing those provisions whenever necessary.

Paragraph 26 of the report, which was approved by the Committee of Ministers for its own future guidance and for the guidance of committees of experts set up under Article 17 of the Statute of the Council of Europe, read, in part, as follows: '(1) [a] topic should be considered as being suitable for the drafting of a *convention* if there is a need for compulsory State undertakings, taking into account the need to assure the security of international relations. In this respect, it should be noted that a convention may be drafted not only so as to contain itself compulsory provisions but also to act as a framework for further enactments or the elaboration of compulsory regulations.

(ii) A *recommendation* should be regarded as the appropriate instrument if its purpose is mainly to establish principles of conduct for member States in the particular area under examination and to organize an exchange of information on how those principles are to be implemented in member States, possibly with a view to further examination within the council of Europe as to the follow-up which might be required as a result of the experience gained in implementing these principles.'
Ibid. at 336.

It should be observed that while recommendations take effect automatically with regard to all member States of the Council of Europe, they are not usually binding and, moreover, require for their adoption the unanimous vote of the representatives casting a vote *and* of a majority of the representatives entitled to sit on the Committee of Ministers. Ibid. at 333. A recommendation thus may tend to reflect the lowest common denominator or a minimum solution. On the other hand, to adopt a treaty, *only* a majority of the representatives casting a vote and a majority of the representatives entitled to sit on the Committee of Ministers is required. Ibid.

of activities with the Specialized Agencies are Articles 57,[25] 58,[26] and 63.[27] Pursuant to Art. 63 of the Charter, the United Nations has entered into a series of relationship agreements with the specialized agencies regarding a number of matters of mutual concern. Of particular importance is the provision concerning the recommendations of the United Nations to the specialized agency concerned. A typical provision of this kind is that contained in Article IV of the Agreement between the United Nations and the International Labour Organisation.[28]

[25] Art. 57(1) reads as follows:
'[T]he various specialized agencies, established by intergovernmental agreement and having wide international responsibilities, as defined in their basic instruments, in economic, social, cultural, educational, health, and related fields, shall be brought into relationship with the United Nations in accordance with the provisions of Article 63.'
[26] Art. 58 reads as follows:
'[t]he Organization shall make recommendations for the co-ordination of the policies and activities of the specialized agencies.'
[27] Art. 63 reads as follows:
'1. [t]he Economic and Social Council may enter into agreements with any of the agencies referred to in Article 57, defining the terms on which the agency concerned shall be brought into relationship with the United Nations. Such agreements shall be subject to approval by the General Assembly.

2. It may co-ordinate the activities of the specialized agencies through consultation with and recommendations to the General Assembly and to the Members of the United Nations.'
[28] This provision reads as follows:
'[r]ecommendations of the General Assembly and of the Council:

1. [t]he International Labour Organisation, having regard to the obligation of the United Nations to promote the objectives set forth in Article 55 of the Charter and the function and power of the Council under Article 62 of the Charter, to make or initiate studies and reports with respect to international economic, social, cultural, educational, health and related matters and to make recommendations concerning these matters to the specialized agencies concerned, and having regard, also to the responsibility of the United Nations, under Articles 58 and 63 of the Charter, to make recommendations for the co-ordination of the policies and activities of such specialized agencies, agrees to arrange for the submission, as soon as possible, to the Governing Body, the Conference or such other organ of the International Labour Organisation, as may be appropriate, of all formal recommendations which the General Assembly or the Council may make to it.

2. The International Labour Organisation agrees to enter into consultation with the United Nations upon request, with respect to such recommendations, and in due course to report to the United Nations on the action taken, by the Organisation or by its members, to give effect to such recommendations, or on the other results of their consideration.

3. The International Labour Organisation affirms its intention of co-operating in whatever further measures may be necessary to make co-ordination of the activities of specialized agencies and those of the United Nations fully effective.

It follows from Articles 58, 62(1), and 63(1) (Chapter IX of the Charter) and from the relationship agreements that ECOSOC may make formal recommendations to the specialized agencies which the latter are required to take into account. Under Art. 60, responsibility for the discharge of the functions of the Organization set forth in Chapter IX is vested in the General Assembly and, under the authority of the General Assembly, in ECOSOC. The General Assembly, too, has thus authority to make formal recommendations to the specialized agencies. This 'power of recommendation' has not been used by the General Assembly or ECOSOC to obtain any systematic legislative co-ordination with the agencies.[29] If difficulties with regard to legislative co-ordination are not resolved by drafting, that failure often must be explained by substantive or political, rather than technical, considerations. Such factors include the lack of co-ordination with national governments, the special interests of international organizations, and the 'empire building' tendencies of international secretariats.

Conflicts between the legislative activities of the United Nations and those of the specialized agencies reflect the overlap between certain provisions of the Charter and some of the broad constitutional provisions of the specialized agencies particularly concerned with human rights, for instance the ILO,[30] UNESCO,[31] and the World Health Organization (WHO).[32] This overlap is discernable in the goals of the organizations, the

In particular, it agrees to participate in, and to co-operate with, any body or bodies which the Council may establish for the purpose of facilitating such co-ordination, and to furnish such information as may be required for the carrying out of this purpose.'

Agreements between the United Nations and the Specialized Agencies and the International Atomic Energy Agency. UN Doc. ST/SG/14, at 1, 3–4 (1961).

[29] 1 Review, above n. 12, at 17.

[30] 62 Stat. 3485, TIAS No. 1868, 15 UNTS 35; amended by 7 UST 245, TIAS No. 3500, 191 UNTS 143; 14 UST 1039, TIAS No. 5401, 466 UNTS 323; 25 UST 3253, TIAS No. 7987 (ILO Constitution). The constitutions of the specialized agencies are collected in A. Peaslee, International Governmental Organizations: Constitutional Documents (3rd rev. edn., 1974).

[31] 61 Stat. 2495, TIAS No. 1580, 4 UNTS 275; amended by 6 UST 6157, TIAS No. 3469, 575 UNTS 270; 10 UST 959, TIAS No. 4230, 575 UNTS 252; 22 UST 1699, TIAS No. 7197; 29 UST 3379, TIAS No. 9016; 29 UST 3384, TIAS No. 9017 (UNESCO Constitution).

[32] 62 Stat. 2679, TIAS No. 1808, 14 UNTS 185; amended by 26 UST 990, TIAS No. 8086; 28 UST 2088, TIAS No. 8534 (WHO Constitution).

vagueness of the relationship agreements concluded between the United Nations and the specialized agencies,[33] and the autonomy and independent legal personality of each of the specialized agencies.[34] During the last few years the specialized agencies have increasingly complained that the General Assembly 'is legislating more and more, and in ever greater detail' in fields that 'are clearly the responsibility' of one of the specialized agencies,[35] which may lead to 'confusion, overlapping of activities and even conflicting decisions'.[36] With regard to UNESCO, for example, such conflicts have resulted from UN activities involving the right to education,[37] the right to information,[38] and the rights to science and technology.[39] UNESCO has asserted that these activities encroach on its Constitution and tend to modify the functionally decentralized system established by the UN Charter, the constitutive instruments of the specialized agencies, and the relationship agreements. Similar conflicts have also arisen between the United Nations and the ILO, for example, concerning the rights of migrant workers. Following the adoption of General Assembly Resolution 32/197, on Restructuring of the Economic and Social Sectors of the United Nations System,[40] the International Organisations Committee of the Governing Body of the ILO found it necessary to emphasize that the relationship agreement between the ILO and the United Nations recognizes the competence of the ILO, as defined in its Constitution, as an autonomous organization, with its own international personality.[41]

Measures taken by the General Assembly, such as General

---

[33] See generally Agreements between the United Nations and the Specialized Agencies and the International Atomic Energy Agency, above n. 28. On the activities of the specialized agencies in the field of human rights, see UN Doc. E/CN.4/1193 (1976); UN Doc. E/CN.4/1433 (1980).

[34] For a proposal to review the various relationship agreements, see UN Doc. E/1981/3, para. 73 (1980).

[35] UNESCO Doc. 110/EX/19, para. 67 (1980).

[36] Director-General of UNESCO, quoted in UN Doc. A/AC.198/13, para. 20 (1980).

[37] See UN Doc. A/35/148, at 8 (Decision 7.1.1, para. 4 of the Executive Board of UNESCO) (1980); UNESCO Doc. 110/EX/19, para. 68 (1980).

[38] See UN Doc. A/35/362 (1980); UN Doc. A/AC.198/13, paras. 21-2 (1980).

[39] See UNESCO Doc. 109/EX/22 (1980); UNESCO Doc. 109/EX/Dec.5.3.2 (1980).

[40] 32 UN GAOR Supp. (No. 45) at 121, UN Doc A/32/45 (1977).

[41] ILO Doc. GB.212/IO/1/9, para. 2(a) (1980).

Assembly Resolution 34/172, towards formulating a new UN convention on the protection of rights of all migrant workers, exemplify the conflicts in the 'legislative' standard-setting context.[42] In response to that resolution, the ILO emphasized that its constitutional mandate had always included the protection of migrant workers and that 'it would be preferable for standard-setting for the protection of migrant workers to continue to be entrusted to the ILO, as the agency with specific constitutional responsibility for this question'.[43] Many delegations at the General Assembly, however, were of the view that existing instruments had a 'sectoral' approach, such as those of the ILO in labour and those of UNESCO in education. These delegations wished to establish a new instrument covering the whole range of political, civil, cultural, economic and social aspects of the rights of migrant workers.[44] It should be pointed out that while the ILO's work on the question of migrant workers has been carried out through bodies possessing considerable expertise, the work of the United Nations in preparing a convention on the rights of migrant workers is carried out by an open-ended working group of delegates to the General Assembly.[45] This process illustrates the drafting of human rights instruments by generalists, some of them experienced and knowledgeable, rather than experts.

B. *The Institutional Setting*

Although most universal organizations have more or less the same membership, there arise serious difficulties of co-ordination

[42] GA Res. 34/172, 34 UN GAOR Supp. (No. 46) at 188, UN Doc. A/34/46 (1979). See also Chapter VII n. 34, below.

[43] ILO Doc. GB.212/IO/1/8, para. 17 (1980). See generally ILO Doc. GB.212/15/28 (1980); UN Doc. E/1980/16 (1980).

[44] See ILO Doc. GB.212/IO/1/8, para. 19 (1980).
On the work of the ILO for the protection of migrant workers, see UN Doc. A/C.3/35/1 (1980); International Labour Conference, Survey of the Reports Relating to Conventions Nos. 97 and 143 and Recommendations Nos. 86 and 151 concerning Migrant Workers (Report III, Part 4B, 66th Sess. 1980); International Labour Office, International Labour Standards 36 (1978). See generally Valticos, *The Role of the ILO. Present Action and Future Perspectives*, in Human Rights: Thirty Years After the Universal Declaration 212 (B. Ramcharan ed., 1979).

[45] GA Res. 34/172, 34 UN GAOR Supp. (No. 46) at 188, UN Doc. A/34/46 (1979); GA Res. 35/198, 35 UN GAOR Supp. (No. 48) at 209, UN Doc. A/35/48 (1980); GA Res. 36/160, 36 UN GAOR Supp. (No. 51) at 190, UN Doc. A/36/51 (1981); GA Res. 37/170, 37 UN GAOR Supp. (No. 51) at 196, UN Doc. A/37/51 (1982).

with delegations of the same State sometimes taking inconsistent positions in various organizations. It is often assumed that such problems are caused exclusively by lack of co-ordination on the national level. However, if a government adopts inconsistent positions in various organizations, this may in fact be a reflection of national policy and national interests of a political, economic, or other nature.

The present system is not only inefficient and wasteful, with too many bodies involved, often not in sufficient depth, in the law-making process; it is a system in which priorities are difficult to establish and to follow. The system stretches the material and personnel resources of organizations and governments. The uneven quality of the instruments and the gaps, overlap, and conflicts between instruments which result damage the credibility of the law-making process.

What then are the objects of co-ordination in human rights law-making? Regarding normative provisions, as indicated in Chapter IV, the development of an integrated system of international treaty law governing human rights has a number of goals. Such a system would prevent unnecessary duplication, conflicts, and variations in the interpretation and implementation of instruments adopted by different organizations, and it would ensure that statutory provisions on complex technical subjects are established and supervised by the most competent organizations. Szasz has observed rightly that the object of co-ordination is to create a coherent body of international law, avoiding both gaps and overlap.[46]

The purposes of rationalizing and co-ordinating the systems of supervision of human rights, which are similar to the goals of integrating the substantive treaty law on human rights have already been discussed. Problems of co-ordination arise not only between the United Nations and the specialized agencies, or between the organizations belonging to the UN system and regional organizations. They arise also within the United Nations. Co-ordination in international human rights is particularly needed in the United Nations family of organizations because of its decentralized structure. With regard to regional organizations, which have different memberships, it is possible

---

[46] Szasz, above n. 10, at 524.

to envisage a continued divergence in the character and scope of human rights undertakings.

When there is a structured method for law-making, including detailed research and study at early stages of the process, it should not be difficult to identify the already existing instruments which are relevant to the subject matter of new law-making. Such research should lead to the clarification of areas of potential gaps, overlap, or conflict. The ILO Secretariat has developed a salutary system for identifying existing instruments of relevance, whether concluded in the ILO or in other organizations,[47] and of ensuring that gaps, overlap, or conflicts will be avoided as far as possible. At an early stage (by the use of preliminary questionnaires) the ILO Secretariat draws the attention of members of the ILO to existing conventions and recommendations which are relevant to the subject being considered for new law-making. Also at a very early stage, and no later than the first draft of the new instrument, the Secretariat prepares a text for inclusion in the preamble of the new instrument which recalls the existing instruments and, if necessary, clarifies the gap which the new standards should fill.[48] The Secretariat draws the attention of the competent bodies of the International Labour Conference to provisions paralleling existing provisions, so that variations in language are used only to reflect intended differences in meaning.[49]

Despite the lip-service paid to the importance of co-ordination and the thousands of pages consecrated to this subject in the records of international organizations, there exists at present only limited co-ordination on the inter-secretariat level.[50]

---

[47] 1 Review, above n. 12, at 25. The International Labour Office has stated that: 'given the very substantial body of international labour Conventions already in existence, new Conventions which are not designed to replace existing ones may overlap, parallel or otherwise impinge on instruments already binding on some Members. Methods have had to be evolved, in the elaboration of new Conventions, to take account of this, and to avoid duplication, conflict and doubt as to legislative intent.' 2 Review, above n. 14, at 241. See also N. Valticos, International Labour Law 70–4 (1979). Concerning ILO Law-making techniques, see International Labour Office, International Labour Standards 6–23 (1984).

[48] 2 Review, above n. 14, at 242.

[49] Ibid.

[50] On the Administrative Committee on Co-ordination (ACC) and the machinery for inter-organizational co-ordination, see Meron, *Status and Independence of the International Civil Servant*, 167 Recueil des cours 289, 295, and n. 6 (1980-II). Of particular importance are the inter-secretariat meetings on human rights organized by the UN Centre for Human Rights.

No representative or expert organ or body has been charged with the continuous oversight of 'legislative' activities with a view to avoiding gaps, overlap, or conflicts.

A proposal to create an inter-organizational committee for co-ordination of human rights 'legislation', composed of the legal advisers of the various international organizations and other experts was discussed in Chapter IV, Section IX. Another possibility would be for the General Assembly or ECOSOC to establish a small body of experts and charge it with a continuous review of human rights instruments proposed in the entire UN system, including specialized agencies. Such a review would lead to an early identification and warning of gaps, overlap, or conflicts. The success of this body would depend on the quality of the research that it would carry out and on the support that it would obtain from the General Assembly and ECOSOC. The results of research conducted by such a group should be circulated rapidly and widely through a special bulletin of 'legislative' activities. The General Assembly and ECOSOC should be ready, whenever necessary, to follow up on the warnings of the group by resolutions directed to the bodies involved in the preparation of the relevant instruments. This would help to eliminate or at least reduce conflicts between new instruments and old ones.

Given the 'growing incoherence in the UN legislative system . . . [and] lack of co-ordination among the proliferating *ad hoc* law-making bodies',[51] it is important that responsibility for co-ordination be given to a body enjoying the necessary prestige, credibility, and authority. Responsibility for co-ordination, envisaged by Art. 63 of the Charter with regard to specialized agencies, should have been exercised by ECOSOC far more vigorously and consistently. This role should have been exercised also with regard to law-making activities in the United Nations. The Commission to Study the Organization of Peace has observed that ECOSOC could give more attention and perform co-ordinating functions more effectively than the General Assembly,[52] which

[51] M. El Baradei, T. Franck, and R. Trachtenberg; The International Law Commission: The Need for a New Direction 17 (UNITAR Policy and Efficacy Studies No. 1, 1981), summarized in 76 AJIL 630 (1982).

[52] Restructuring the United Nations System for Economic and Social Co-operation for Development 10 (Commission to Study the Organization of Peace, 1980).

already has a very heavy workload. The question is, however, whether ECOSOC, whose functions are not infrequently pre-empted by the General Assembly, particularly in issuing instructions directly to the Commission on Human Rights,[53] has at present the necessary status to carry out effectively the function of co-ordinating human rights law-making. In a different context, it rightly has been observed that the interest of the General Assembly in the work of the Commission on Human Rights and of the Sub-Commission on Prevention of Discrimination and Protection of Minorities 'has reached the point where it can be said that the real parent body of the Commission, and hence of the Sub-Commission, is no longer their constitutional parent, the Economic and Social Council, but the General Assembly'.[54] The active involvement of the General Assembly in guiding and instructing these bodies and in giving them urgent mandates to draft various instruments has 'interfered to some extent with [their] regular work . . .'.[55]

Given the present reality, it may be necessary perhaps to confer the function of co-ordination within the United Nations on the General Assembly. As regards co-ordination with the specialized agencies, ECOSOC must remain the organ of first instance, so as to avoid a breach of Art. 63 of the Charter. It would be best if the final recommendation on co-ordination with the specialized agencies were made by the General Assembly under the authority conferred upon it by Art. 60. But the General Assembly has neither the necessary expertise nor the time required to engage in a systematic co-ordination of law-making. Despite the reluctance to establish new subsidiary organs, the General Assembly should establish a small expert body to assist and advise it and to act as a focus for inter-organizational consultations.

The co-ordinating functions of the General Assembly should consist of the gathering, dissemination, and exchange of data about law-making activities. This would encompass distribution of studies prepared by the expert body or the secretariats about

[53] Among the resolutions adopted on the recommendations of the Third Committee, several include such direct instructions to the Commission, See, e.g. GA Res. 37/180, 37 UN GAOR Supp. (No. 51) at 202, UN Doc. A/37/51 (1982).

[54] Humphrey, *The United Nations Sub-Commission on the Prevention of Discrimination and the Protection of Minorities*, 62 AJIL 869, 883 (1968).

[55] Ibid.

specific areas of concern, such as potential overlap or gaps between particular instruments. But the co-ordinating role of the General Assembly should not be restricted to these activities, important and essential as they may be. The General Assembly should also attempt to influence the law-making process by proposing subjects to be considered and by identifying the most appropriate and competent organs to which the subjects may be referred. At the same time, ECOSOC and the General Assembly should make sure that the United Nations respects the prerogatives and the special expertise and competence of the specialized agencies. ECOSOC and the General Assembly should refrain from law-making in fields where the specialized agencies have higher competence and greater expertise, for example the ILO with regard to the question of migrant workers. Whenever necessary, the General Assembly should make decisions addressed to the organs of the United Nations over which it has the necessary authority under the Charter, and make appropriate recommendations to other intergovernmental organizations. Recommendations to such other organizations might be to consider for law-making subjects within their competence, or to refrain from considering for law-making subjects which would best be left to other organizations. While discouraging undesirable law-making, the General Assembly should stimulate necessary law-making. The General Assembly may not *determine* which subjects should or should not be appropriate for law-making by other intergovernmental organizations, as this would encroach on their competence. With regard to the ILO such an encroachment would give rise to special difficulties, since the decision-making organs of the ILO are not exclusively governmental.

The practical and conceptual difficulties involved in co-ordination should not be underestimated, especially in light of the broad spectrum of the subjects and of the organs involved. While attempting to co-ordinate and to rationalize, care must be taken to avoid excessive centralization and not to slow down unduly the law-making process.

It must be remembered that the powers of the United Nations with regard to specialized agencies are powers of recommendation (which must be given due consideration by the agencies), not of decision. Each specialized agency has an independent legal personality and an area of competence for which it has been given primary responsibility, although, as already observed, there is considerable overlap between the purposes of the United Nations and of some of the agencies and between those of a number of the agencies themselves.

The General Assembly should be particularly careful in making recommendations to regional organizations,[56] which are not part of the United Nations system and have their own peculiar geographical, ideological, cultural, economic, or other characteristics.

The broad goals of co-ordination have already been defined. These goals can often be attained by means of close and constant consultations between those responsible for the drafting of instruments dealing with related subjects within different organs or organizations. The Administrative Committee on Co-ordination (ACC) has made an interesting proposal in this regard: each organization should include in its rules of procedure a provision requiring mutual consultation before the adoption of international conventions by intergovernmental bodies and the submission to the organ by which an instrument is to be adopted of any comments on the draft made by another organization.[57] It was hoped that such a practice would eliminate unintentional conflicts and bring potential conflicts into the open before the proposed instruments become final. Jenks has proposed that such consultations include not only the United Nations and the specialized agencies, but all international and regional organizations.[58] In some cases there is a formal provision for such consultations in agreements between global and regional organizations.[59] The Standing Orders of the Conference[60] and of the Governing Body of the

---

[56] It may be noted that one of the questions listed by the UN Secretariat for discussion by the Sixth Committee of the General Assembly was whether the General Assembly should assume a co-ordinating role in respect of multilateral treaty-making activities of all intergovernmental organizations, as distinguished from those within the UN system. UN Doc. A/35/312, at 30 (1980). The Council of Europe and the Organization for Economic Co-operation and Development expressed reservations to such a role for the General Assembly. 1 Review, above n. 12, at 66–8.

[57] Jenks, *The Conflict of Law-Making Treaties*, above n. 11, at 429–30. See also above n. 50.

[58] Jenks, *The Conflict of Law-Making Treaties*, above n. 11, at 430.

[59] Ibid.

[60] Article 17 *bis* of the Standing Orders, above n. 13 at 39.

ILO[61] provide for prior consultation in respect of proposals for new activities relating to matters of direct concern to the United Nations or other specialized agencies.[62] It does not appear, however, that the ACC recommendation with regard to rules of procedure has been fully implemented in all the organizations which participate in the ACC.[63]

Jenks emphasized that, for consultations to be fruitful, there should develop on the part of all who are involved in the law-making process 'a habit of regarding the international statute book as a whole and attempting to judge of the value, proper scope, and detailed content of any proposed instrument not in isolation but in relation to the complex of law-making treaties on a wide range of intricately interrelated subjects of which it will form a part'.[64] This salutary wish, which is characteristic of the uniquely high standards practised and advocated by Jenks, should become the goal of all the individuals involved in law-making in governments or in international organizations.

---

[61] Article 16 of the Standing Orders of the Governing Body (International Labour Office, 1977).
[62] UN Doc. A/36/553, at 49 (1981).
[63] See generally Meron, above n. 50.
[64] Jenks, *The Conflict of Law-Making Treaties*, above n. 11, at 430.

VII

Human Rights Law-Making in the United Nations: A Case for Reforms

I. INTRODUCTION

THE extent of human rights law-making in the United Nations has been impressive, in terms of the quantity of both its output and the number of organs involved. Law-making, as a process by which organs of the United Nations adopt international human rights instruments, has naturally attracted the critical attention of governments and scholars, for whom such processes have always held a special fascination. Recent studies have drawn attention to this process in the United Nations in general, and in the human rights area in particular.[1] They point to deficiencies in both the process and the quality of the instruments which have been adopted. These deficiencies are not always rooted in political factors, but often in incompetence, hasty consideration and approval, lack of adequate research and editing, and so on and therefore must not be viewed as inevitable and beyond reasonable prospects for reform. The

---

[1] Schachter, *The Nature and Process of Legal Development in International Society*, in The Structure and Process of International Law 745 (R. Macdonald and D. Johnston eds., 1983); Sohn, *The Shaping of International Law*, 8 Ga. J. Int'l & Comp. L. 1 (1978); Suy, *Innovations in International Law-Making Processes*, in The International Law and Policy of Human Welfare 187 (R. Macdonald, D. Johnston, and G. Morris eds., 1978); Szasz, *Improving the International Legislative Process*, 9 Ga. J. Int'l & Comp. L. 519 (1979); M. El Baradei, T. Franck, and R. Trachtenberg, The International Law Commission: The Need for a New Direction (UNITAR Policy and Efficacy Studies No. 1, 1981), summarized in 76 AJIL 630 (1982); Review of the Multilateral Treaty-Making Process, UN Doc. ST/LEG/SER.B/ 21 (Provisional Version, 1982); Alston, *Conjuring up New Human Rights: A Proposal for Quality Control*, 78 AJIL 607 (1984); Ramcharan, *Standard-Setting: Future Perspectives*, in Human Rights: Thirty Years After the Universal Declaration 93 (B. Ramcharan ed., 1979); Meron, *Norm Making and Supervision in International Human Rights: Reflections on Institutional Order*, 76 AJIL 754 (1982). On codification of international law in general, see Rosenne, *Codification of International Law*, in [Instalment 7] Encyclopedia of Public International Law 34 (R. Bernhardt ed., 1984) and bibliography ibid. at 41.

important volume of essays on the International Covenant on Civil and Political Rights edited by Henkin contains many examples of poorly drafted provisions and, worse, of provisions which conflict with each other.[2] It is not unusual to find that provisions drafted during a later session of the law-making organ conflict with those drafted earlier, and that no attempt is made subsequently to revise the conflicting texts.

Some of the unfortunate language involved in one of the major human rights instruments, the Convention on the Elimination of All Forms of Racial Discrimination, was discussed in Chapter I.[3] Other instruments, for example the Convention on the Elimination of All Forms of Discrimination Against Women (Chapter II), pose equal or even greater problems, as demonstrated in an unusually candid memorandum of law by the Department of State.[4] Inconsistencies and the potential for conflict between norms contained in different instruments have been observed.[5] UN Secretariat studies have noted the lack of structure in human rights law-making processes[6] and unhappiness with the present situation has been voiced openly by governments. The government of the United States thus observed in the Third (Social, Humanitarian and Cultural Questions) Committee of the General Assembly that

[2] See, e.g. Cassese, *The Self-Determination of Peoples* in The International Bill of Rights: The Covenant on Civil and Political Rights 92, 103-5 (L. Henkin ed., 1981); Ramcharan, *Equality and Nondiscrimination*, in ibid. at 246, 251, 256-7.

[3] See also Meron, *The Meaning and Reach of the International Convention on the Elimination of All Forms of Racial Discrimination*, 79 AJIL 283 (1985).

[4] *Convention on the Elimination of All Forms of Discrimination Against Women, Message from the President of the United States Transmitting the Convention on the Elimination of All Forms of Discrimination Against Women, Adopted by the United Nations General Assembly on December 18, 1979, and Signed on Behalf of the United States of America on July 17, 1980*, S. Ex. R, 96th Cong. 2d Sess. (1980).
In addition to many substantive difficulties, there is a serious inconsistency between the duty of the Committee on the Elimination of Discrimination Against Women, under Art. 21, to examine the reports submitted by States Parties under Art. 18, and the language of Art. 20, which states that '[t]he Committee shall normally meet for a period of not more than two weeks annually in order to consider the reports submitted in accordance with article 18 of the present Convention'. Since by 21 January 1985, 65 States were parties to the Convention and the Committee has been considering six reports in every one of its sessions, one member of the Committee has observed that, at this pace, 'the discussion of all reports would be completed by the year 2000'. UN Doc. CEDAW/C/1985/L.1, para. 29 (1985); 40 UN GAOR Supp. (No. 45) at 1, UN Doc. A/40/45 (1985).

[5] See Meron, above n. 1, at 756-64.

[6] 1 Review, above n. 1, at 12.

much of the work in this area proceeds without planning, in a kind of haphazard manner, at a desultory pace and with overlapping jurisdictions. We have working groups in the Third Committee, in the Commission on Human Rights, and in the Subcommission. It is difficult to keep track of the different drafts. There is a lack of continuity and expertise among the persons working on the drafts. It makes no sense, for example, for a body of this size to attempt to draft a convention from its inception. As it is, one often has to reinvent the wheel each time a working group reconvenes. The result is neither fast nor fruitful.[7]

The problem, however, cannot be attributed merely to a lack of co-ordination or of cost-efficiency in the system; it also derives from the quality of the instruments themselves and has a far-reaching impact on prospects for acceptance of instruments by States, respect for the norms stated, and the interpretation of those norms. As the government of Spain observed in the general context of UN treaty-making, politicization of the negotiating process and inadequate preparation of the relevant texts help to explain 'the legal inadequacies of many of the treaties adopted recently, a situation which in turn creates major problems in terms of the interpretation and application of such treaties'.[8]

A fresh look at the law-making structure of the United Nations is therefore needed. Such an inquiry is particularly timely in light of the examination recently begun by the Sub-Commission on Prevention of Discrimination and Protection of Minorities (the Sub-Commission) of its role in the human rights law-making process and of its relationship with the Commission on Human Rights (the Commission).

---

[7] Verbatim text of remarks by Jerome J. Shestack (13 Nov. 1980), summarized in UN Doc. A/C.3/35/SR. 56, at 12–14 (1980).

[8] 1 Review, above n. 1, at 43.

Scholars have complained about the high degree of abstraction and generality in which international human rights instruments have been drafted and which makes their application in specific cases difficult. Lillich, *Civil Rights*, in 1 Human Rights in International Law: Legal and Policy Issues 115, at 121 (T. Meron ed., 1984); Greenberg, *Race, Sex and Religious Discrimination in International Law*, in 2 ibid. 307, at 318, 330.

Abstraction helps, however, in many cases to attain the necessary consensus. In national laws and constitutions, highly abstract provisions are clarified through practice and jurisprudence. In international human rights the process of creating interpretative jurisprudence is slow in time and incomprehensive in scope. This makes good drafting essential.

II. THE PRESENT STRUCTURE OF UN HUMAN RIGHTS LAW-MAKING

In the United Nations, law-making in the human rights area is carried out by the General Assembly, ECOSOC, and the many subsidiary organs of these two principal organs, including the functional commissions of ECOSOC. The key provisions on human rights law-making are found in Arts. 13 and 62 of the Charter of the United Nations, which suggest that the law-making powers of the General Assembly and ECOSOC are largely concurrent or shared and, as regards the relationship between the General Assembly and ECOSOC, in Art. 60. Although both the General Assembly and ECOSOC are mentioned in Art. 7 among the principal organs of the United Nations, ECOSOC's position is subordinate to that of the General Assembly.[9] The Charter empowers the General Assembly to exercise an overall authority over the law-making activities of the United Nations, but this power either has not been exercised or has not been exercised effectively. Rather than creating an effective infrastructure to carry out their law-making responsibilities, both the General Assembly, under Art. 22 of the Charter, and ECOSOC, under Art. 68, have established a plethora of standing and *ad hoc* bodies and entrusted them with the performance of human rights functions, including 'legislative' activities.

Among those bodies, the Commission and the Sub-Commission are of particular importance in human rights law-making. The terms of reference of the Commission,[10] as approved by ECOSOC in Res. 5(I) and amended by Res. 9(II), encompass the preparation of law-making human rights instruments. By Res. 9(II), ECOSOC authorized the Commission to call in *ad hoc* working groups of non-governmental experts in specialized fields or individual experts without further reference to ECOSOC but with the approval of the Council's President and the UN Secretary-General.[11] While the Commission generally

[9] See generally J. Renninger, ECOSOC: Options for Reform (UNITAR Policy and Efficacy Studies No. 4, at 4 (1981)).

[10] L. Sohn and T. Buergenthal, International Protection of Human Rights 739–40 (1973).

[11] United Nations Action in the Field of Human Rights, UN Doc. ST/HR/2/Rev. 2, at 282 (1983).

executes the directives of ECOSOC,[12] on many occasions the General Assembly has addressed requests directly to the Commission, rather than through ECOSOC.[13] The Commission has been involved in the drafting of many human rights instruments. It is composed of forty-three representatives of States Members of the United Nations elected by ECOSOC on the basis of equitable geographical distribution. ECOSOC resolutions provide that the Secretary-General shall consult with governments selected to serve on the Commission before the representatives are finally nominated by their governments and confirmed by the Council.[14] Consultation with the Secretary-General, however, is routine.

The original terms of reference of the Sub-Commission, as clarified and extended by the Commission in 1949,[15] do not explicitly mention law-making. Law-making functions may, however, be entrusted to the Sub-Commission by specific resolutions of the Commission or of ECOSOC. On many occasions the Commission has called on the Sub-Commission to prepare drafts of human rights instruments. The Sub-Commission is composed of twenty-six members (and their alternates), who are elected by the Commission as individuals and not as representatives of States. Their selection is made in consultation with the Secretary-General and was originally subject to the consent of the governments of the States of which they were nationals.[16] The latter requirement is now obsolete, however, since ECOSOC Res. 1334 (XLIV) of 31 May 1968 provides for the nomination of experts by their governments.[17]

The Commission and the Sub-Commission perform other functions as well as law-making, such as the preparation of

---

[12] L. Sohn &.T. Buergenthal, above n. 10, at 740.

[13] United Nations Action, in the Field of Human Rights, UN Doc. ST/HR/2/ Rev. 1 at 274 n. 14 (1980). For an example of such a resolution, see GA Res. 37/ 180, 37 UN GAOR Supp. (No. 51) at 202, UN Doc. A/37/51 (1982).

[14] L. Sohn and T. Buergenthal, above n. 10, at 740.

[15] Ibid. at 744.

[16] United Nations Action, above n. 13, at 276. On the Sub-Commission, see generally Haver, *The United Nations Sub-Commission on the Prevention of Discrimination and the Protection of Minorities*, 21 Colum. J. Transnat'l L. 103 (1982); Humphrey, *The United Nations Sub-Commission on the Prevention of Discrimination and the Protection of Minorities*, 62 AJIL 869 (1968).

[17] See, e.g. UN Doc. E/CN.4/1984/47 and Addenda 1–7 (1984); UN Doc. E/ CN.4/1985/SR.37, at para. 3 (1985).

studies and programmes and the consideration of violations. Thus, only part of their time, and usually a small part, is devoted to law-making.[18] Both bodies devote the major portion of their time to studying particular violations of human rights and situations prevailing in countries accused of infringement of human rights. The preponderance of studies of human rights violations over law-making does not appear to reflect a deliberate decision that, at the present stage of development of the law, the former are more important than the latter;[19] rather, it is explained by the greater urgency of investigations as well as by the time constraints on the Commission. Although the international community may have passed the zenith of its law-making activity, at least in so far as broadly orientated global instruments focusing on civil and political rights are concerned,[20] work on such subjects as, *inter alia*, rights of the child, is continuing[21] and new subjects, such as the right to development, are coming up, especially in the economic and social fields. The need for disciplined and informed law-making is thus as great as ever.

In addition to 'standard-setting', the Sub-Commission deals with various studies, considers gross violations of human rights in accordance with Res. 8 (XXIII) of the Commission and ECOSOC Res. 1235 (XLII), and handles communications under the procedure established by ECOSOC Res. 1503 (XLVIII). The Sub-Commission sends missions to various areas in which human rights are threatened. It adopts 'rather hurriedly a large number of resolutions',[22] particularly on the situation in

[18] Tolley, *Decision-Making at the United Nations Commission on Human Rights, 1979–82*, 5 Human Rights Q. 27, 43 (1983).

[19] For a discussion of the several historical stages in the work of the Commission, see Schwelb and Alston, *The Principal Institutions and Other Bodies Founded under the Charter*, in 1 The International Dimensions of Human Rights 231, 250–1 (K. Vasak ed., P. Alston Eng. ed., 1982).

[20] Meron, above n. 1, at 771–2.

[21] UN Doc. E/CN.4/1984/71 (1984); UN Doc. E/CN.4/1985/64 (1985).
A recent report of the UN Secretary-General lists the following human rights instruments which are under preparation: a convention on the rights of the migrant workers, a convention on the rights of the child, a declaration on the rights of minorities, a declaration on the rights of non-citizens, a declaration on the rights of detained or imprisoned persons, an instrument on the protection of persons detained in mental health institutions, and an instrument on the rights and responsibilities of those who seek to defend human rights. UN Doc. A/40/348, at 40 (1985).

[22] UN Doc. E/CN.4/Sub.2/1984/2, at 4 (1984).

countries where gross violations of human rights are occurring. Because so much of the Sub-Commission's work is related neither to discrimination nor to protection of minorities, it has been suggested that its name be changed to 'Committee of Experts on Human Rights'.[23]

A perusal of the documents of the Sub-Commission, including the annotated agenda for its 1984 session,[24] and my own observation of the Sub-Commission's work during that session reveal that little time and little priority are given to its law-making role. With the encouragement of the Commission, the Sub-Commission is now reviewing its role, decision-making processes, agenda, rationalization of work, and relationship with the Commission.[25] In acknowledgement of the low priority now accorded to law-making, suggestions 'that the drafting of norms should be one of its priorities'[26] have been advanced. In a candid and thoughtful statement before the Working Group on the Review of the Work of the Sub-Commission, Kurt Herndl, the Assistant Secretary-General for Human Rights, argued the need to consider the Sub-Commission's methods of preparing standards:

In the earlier years of the Sub-Commission standards were prepared with much deliberation. They usually were a direct follow-up to a study and were often based on the study's conclusions. Nowadays, draft standards may be proposed by one or more individual members of the Sub-Commission, appended to a resolution, sometimes discussed by a working group, and then sent by the Sub-Commission to the Commission. Would there not seem to be some need for better procedures and organization in this area . . .?[27]

Herndl also called for rationalization of the Sub-Commission's procedure for selecting and preparing studies, which is a matter

[23] Ibid. at 3.
[24] UN Doc. E/CN.4/Sub.2/1984/1/Add.1 (1984). See also Report of the Sub-Commission on Prevention of Discrimination and Protection of Minorities on its Thirty-Seventh Session, UN Doc. E/CN.4/1985/3, E/CN.4/Sub.2/1984/43 (1984).
[25] UN Doc. E/CN.4/1985/3, E/CN.4/Sub.2/1984/43 at 23–5 (1984). See also UN Doc. E/CN.4/Sub.2/1984/2 (1984); UN Doc. E/CN.4/Sub.2/1984/3 (1984).
[26] UN Doc. E/CN.4/Sub.2/1984/2, at 3–4 (1984). See also Garber and O'Connor, *The 1984 UN Sub-Commission on Prevention of Discrimination and Protection of Minorities*, 79 AJIL 168, 178 (1985).
[27] Verbatim text (8 Aug. 1984), summarized in UN Doc. E/CN.4/Sub.2/1984/SR.5, at 7 (1984).

of importance in the present context since studies frequently lead to law-making projects.

The quality of the members of the Commission and the Sub-Commission is a significant factor in the success or lack of success of their work. Alluding to the practice of many governments of designating as their representatives on the Commission persons possessing special competence in human rights, the United States government observed, correctly, that 'such representatives have been able to make the most significant contributions to the Commission's work'.[28] Clearly, the fact that the Commission initially had as members persons of the calibre of René Cassin and Eleanor Roosevelt is an important reason for the speedy adoption of a truly remarkable instrument: the Universal Declaration of Human Rights. But the overall experience with regard to the quality of representatives on the Commission is not reassuring, since some States appoint representatives who lack the necessary expertise and standing.[29] The Commission is not only a political organ, composed of representatives of States, but also a politicized one. The Sub-Commission is, of course, composed of experts, but their quality is uneven.[30] There is some evidence of its growing politicization as well.[31]

---

[28] 1978 Digest of United States Practice in International Law 439 (M. Nash ed. 1980).

[29] Biographical data of representatives to the Commission are available in the Office of Secretariat Services for Economic and Social Matters of the UN Secretariat but are not circulated as UN documents. UN Doc. E/1983/5 (1983).

Referring to some distinguished members of the Commission in its early years, Tolley has observed that '[t]he calibre and effectiveness of Commission members vary not only among delegations but also over time'. Above n. 18, at 34.

[30] For biographical data of candidates to the Sub-Commission nominated by governments and submitted by them, see UN Doc. E/CN.4/1984/47 and Addenda 1-7 (1984).

[31] See e.g. UN Doc. E/CN.4/Sub.2/1984/2, at 3 (1984); UN Doc. E/CN.4/Sub.2/1984/3, at 3 (1984). The Chairman of the Sub-Commission acknowledged the relevance of the issue of the independence of the members of the Sub-Commission: '[o]ne must be careful to stress that independence, since there was no escaping the fact that members were nominated by Governments and were exposed, as were the members of the Commission to many different pressures, not only from their own Governments but from others and from non-governmental and other organizations.' UN Doc. E/CN.4/1905/SR.37 at para. 3 (1985). Austria called for the strengthening of the expert character of the Sub-Commission and 'the depoliticization of its work'. UN Doc. E/CN.4/1985/SR.35 (1985). In Res. 1985/28, on the 'Report of the Sub-Commission on Prevention of Discrimination and Protection of Minorities on its thirty-seventh session', the Commission stressed that States should 'nominate as

One should not lose sight of the fact that human rights law-making is also carried out outside the Commission and the Sub-Commission. Thus, the important Convention on the Elimination of All Forms of Discrimination Against Women[32] was elaborated largely by the Commission on the Status of Women, another functional commission of ECOSOC, composed of thirty-two representatives of Member States.[33]

Some law-making projects are undertaken by the General Assembly itself without any serious preparatory work by more expert organs. For example, the new UN Convention on the Protection of the Rights of All Migrant Workers and Their Families[34] is being drafted by the General Assembly despite the greater expertise and considerable achievements of the ILO in this area.[35] Such work is carried out at the United Nations by an open-ended working group of delegates to the General Assembly, in a process which exemplifies the drafting of human rights instruments by generalists, rather than by experts. The General Assembly is also considering, through another open-ended working group, the elaboration of a declaration on the human rights of individuals who are not citizens of the country in which they live.[36]

It should not be assumed, however, that a generalist governmental representative is necessarily incompetent. Talented academics, parliamentarians, lawyers, and members of women's organizations, among others, have served on the Third Committee and other organs composed of representatives of governments; but this is not enough to guarantee the necessary 'legislative'

members and alternates persons meeting the criteria of independent experts, not subject to Government instructions in the performance of their functions as members of the Sub-Commission . . .'. UN Doc. E/CN.4/1985/L.11/Add.2, at 20, para. 4 (1985). See also Garber and O'Connor, above n. 26, at 178–9; UN Doc. E/CN.4/1985/SR.36/Add.1 at 3, 7 (1985).

[32] GA Res. 34/180, 34 UN GAOR Supp. (No. 46) at 193, UN Doc. A/34/46 (1979).

[33] United Nations Action, above n. 11, at 83–5, 290; L. Sohn and T. Buergenthal, above n. 10, at 526.

[34] See UN Doc. A/C.3/38/WG.1/CRP.2/Rev.1 (1983); UN Doc. A/C.3/38/1 (1983); UN Doc. A/C.3/38/5 (1983); UN Doc. A/C.3/39/1 (1984); UN Doc. A/C.3/39/4 (1984).

[35] See Meron, above n. 1, at 760 and n. 39.

[36] GA Res. 37/169, 37 UN GAOR Supp. (No. 51) at 196, UN Doc. A/37/51 (1982); GA Res. 38/87, UN Doc. A/RES/38/87 (1983); UN Doc. A/C.3/39/9 and Corr. 1 (1984).

skill when the initial draft is not prepared by experts. While national law-makers may not always be well qualified, they are usually assisted by governmental and legislative experts and function in a more structured setting. Although the General Assembly often performs elaborate and complex drafting functions, such an organ is not well equipped to prepare a good text on the basis of many, sometimes conflicting proposals. The General Assembly can effectively deal with the adoption of multilateral instruments mostly in cases where the draft does not require much additional revision or negotiation before its adoption. Some topics, however, because of their highly political content, may require a greater degree of involvement by governments throughout the law-making process. In such cases it might be necessary to entrust a subject to law-making by the General Assembly since it is an appropriate body for negotiation and for the formation of consensus. While conferences of plenipotentiaries may also be hampered by the difficulty inherent in a broad membership, their rules of procedure, working methods, and available time are better-suited to the requirements of law-making than those of a main committee of the General Assembly.[37]

Of course, the contents of the instruments reflect the parameters of political consensus. But the technical quality of the instruments often falls short even of the reach of political consensus (where there has been deficient drafting, inconsistencies as between different provisions of the same instrument, gaps, overlap, or conflicts between instruments).[38] Problems of particular concern are the frequent lack of adequate research prior to the decision to initiate the law-making process, and inadequate supporting research throughout that process. However, these problems are not limited to human rights. The Legal Counsel of the United Nations has complained that the time left to the Secretariat for study and research in the codification and progressive development of international law 'has dwindled almost to a vanishing point'.[39]

Whether there is a need for an instrument and what form this instrument should take, for instance a treaty or a declaration,

[37] See 1 Review, above n. 1, at 112 (remarks by Austria).
[38] See generally Meron, above n. 1.
[39] Suy, above n. 1, at 196.

are often insufficiently considered. Texts are frequently drawn up by representative organs with a large membership, without the benefit of a carefully formulated initial draft prepared by experts. There is inadequate resort to special rapporteurs, drafting committees, and expert working groups. The process suffers from lack of direction and structure. Authority is displaced among many bodies. While several organs are involved in the drafting of human rights instruments, not a single organ is engaged exclusively in law-making. Organs that specialize in human rights devote the bulk of their time to 'non-legislative' work. The centre of gravity of the Sub-Commission as well as that of the Commission has shifted from law-making to other activities, especially to the consideration of gross violations of human rights.

III. ALTERNATIVE LAW-MAKING MODELS

In considering possible reforms of law-making in the human rights field, it may be worthwhile to take a brief look at some other models of law-making. In the United Nations, three areas are particularly instructive: outer space treaties, international trade law, and the general law-making activities of the International Law Commission.

For the preparation of treaties regulating activities in outer space,[40] a structured procedure has been developed by the Committee on the Peaceful Uses of Outer Space[41] and its Legal Sub-Committee. This process is characterized by successive consideration of texts by a working group of the Legal Sub-Committee, the Legal Sub-Committee itself, and the Committee, all of which are composed of members from the same fifty-three States, and finally by a main committee of the General Assembly (at present, the Special Political Committee). The report of each organ to the next senior one records problems and progress.[42] The treaty is eventually adopted and opened for signature by the General Assembly. In the drafting process, the

---

[40] 2 Review, above n. 1, at 137.
[41] For the Committee's initial mandate, see GA Res. 1348, 13 UN GAOR Supp. (No. 18) at 5, UN Doc. A/4090 (1958). Regarding the role of the Scientific and Technical Sub-Committee, see 2 Review, above n. 1, at 141.
[42] 1 Review, above n. 1, at 12.

working group is sometimes assisted by a drafting committee, as is the Committee itself when completing the preparation of a particular text.

The procedures of the United Nations Commission on International Trade Law (UNCITRAL) are regular and relatively structured.[43] The usual practice is to request the Secretariat to prepare studies on the issues pertaining to the adoption of a proposed convention. UNCITRAL has adopted the salutary policy of referring a subject matter to a working group only 'after preparatory studies . . .[have] been made by the Secretariat and the consideration of these studies by the Commission . . . [has] indicated not only that the subject-matter . . . [is] a suitable one in the context of the unification and harmonization of a law, but that the preparatory work . . . [is] sufficiently advanced . . .'.[44]

When UNCITRAL decides that a particular subject merits further study, possibly with a view to the preparation of a treaty, it assigns the subject to a working group. While UNCITRAL is composed of representatives of thirty-six governments, not of experts elected in their individual capacities, States are encouraged to send to each working group representatives who are experts in the field. Working groups are central to UNCITRAL's functioning. They benefit from the constant input of research by the Secretariat and comments by governments. Background studies by the Secretariat analyse various questions, as requested by the working group, examine the existing law, highlight problems, and suggest ways of harmonizing or unifying the law. They often contain draft provisions intended to facilitate the efforts of the working group. At various stages of the working group's endeavours, the Secretariat circulates questionnaires to all States and interested organizations soliciting comments and suggestions for consideration by the working group. Working groups establish drafting committees to recommend the text of the draft provisions and their place in the draft treaty.

When the draft treaty reaches an advanced stage, the working group often requests the Secretariat to prepare an explanatory memorandum on the draft treaty, which is intended to aid the

---

[43] For UNCITRAL's initial mandate, see GA Res. 2205, 21 UN GAOR Supp. (No. 16) at 99, UN Doc. A/6316 (1966).

[44] 2 *Review*, above n. 1, at 227.

working group but not to constitute an official commentary. A careful editorial review is undertaken and a final text is prepared for submission to UNCITRAL. The draft text as approved by the working group is circulated to governments and interested organizations, together with a commentary. At the final stages, it is considered by UNCITRAL, with the assistance of a drafting committee. The revised text is submitted by UNCITRAL to the General Assembly with the recommendation that a diplomatic conference be convened to adopt the draft convention.[45]

The Law-making by the International Law Commission (ILC), a body of thirty-four experts elected by the General Assembly upon nomination by governments,[46] is characterized by the recourse to one expert for the basic preparatory work through the use of a special rapporteur, the subsequent careful scrutiny of the successive drafts, the progressive and gradual elaboration of texts with constant input from governments and organizations until the texts are ready for adoption, and a careful recording of the preparatory work, which is crucial to the proper study of the legislative histories and interpretation of the text.

Normally, the principal stages in the ILC's work are: the appointment of a special rapporteur; the preparation of a special report or series of reports (which contain analyses, draft articles, and commentaries); the consideration of these reports by the ILC at several readings; the use of drafting committees, which play a central role; the assignment of various tasks to the Secretariat; the input of governmental comments on the evolving texts through written observations and debate in the Sixth Committee of the General Assembly; and the convening by the General Assembly of a diplomatic conference which would use the articles adopted by the ILC as the basis for discussion,[47] or the adoption of the articles by the Assembly itself.

When final articles on a given subject are submitted by the ILC to the General Assembly, they are accompanied by a

[45] Ibid. at 224–32; 1 ibid. at 11.

[46] 2 ibid., at 173–223. For the Statute of the ILC, see UN Doc. A/CN.4/4/Rev.2 (1982). The initial terms of reference of the ILC are contained in GA Res. 174(II), UN Doc. A/519, at 105 (1947). They have been amended on several occasions by other resolutions. The amended terms of reference are contained in The Work of the International Law Commission 103 (United Nations, 3rd edn., 1980).

[47] 1 Review, above n. 1, at 3.

commentary and by a recommendation on whether they should form the basis of a convention. The General Assembly is thus called upon to decide whether or not such a convention should be concluded and, if so, what organ should be entrusted with the task.[48] The General Assembly, through the Sixth (Legal) Committee, has adopted several conventions on the basis of the articles adopted by the ILC, but far more have been adopted by conferences convened by the Assembly.[49]

The primary reasons for the success of the ILC drafts lie in the procedure followed and, as one commentary has suggested, in the high quality of the scholarship of its members and in their independent expert character.[50] The fact that the ILC has included some of the leading international lawyers and benefited from the services of a number of outstanding special rapporteurs has helped to build up support for the drafts it has prepared. 'Negotiations between states which were based on a draft prepared by the Commission have been . . . more successful than those which began without a first draft, or where the first draft was negotiated by state representatives.'[51]

Outside the United Nations, the ILO procedure for the adoption of conventions and recommendations by the International Labour Conference is of particular interest, because of its proven effectiveness, continuity, and highly structured character.[52]

---

[48]   2 ibid. at 202.

[49]   Ibid. at 205–10.

[50]   This is not to suggest that the work of the ILC has been above criticism. For a recent critical appraisal of its work and role, see El Baradei, Franck, and Trachtenberg, above n. 1.

[51]   Ibid. at 22.

[52]   See generally 2 Review, above n. 1, at 237–40; 1 ibid. at 14–15. On law-making in the ILO see also ILO Doc. GB.228/4/2 (1984); International Labour Standards 6–23 (International Labour Office, 1984).

Outside the United Nations, the specialized agencies, and regional organizations, the law-making techniques employed by the International Committee of the Red Cross (ICRC) in the preparation of draft Geneva conventions and protocols for the protection of victims of war are of interest. They are characterized by the consultation of private experts followed, when the results warrant, by the consultation of governmental experts. Drafts prepared by the ICRC are revised in meetings with governmental experts and eventually submitted for approval to a diplomatic conference convened by the Swiss Government, as the depository of the four Geneva Conventions of 12 August 1949 for the Protection of Victims of War. 2 Review, above n. 1, at 364–83. The ICRC has published comprehensive commentaries on each of these four Conventions, but not, so far, on the two Protocols Additional to the Geneva Conventions of 12 August 1949, which were opened for signature on 12 Dec. 1977.

Although this procedure is rooted in the statutory provisions of the ILO[53] and in its tripartite character, there is no reason why some of its features could not inspire appropriate reforms in UN human rights law-making.

The law-making experience of the Council of Europe, which is characterized by the formulation of draft texts by small committees of governmental experts with the assistance of the Secretariat, also merits attention.[54] The Council of Europe has taken a methodical approach towards carefully expanding the political and civil rights stated in the European Convention for the Protection of Human Rights and Fundamental Freedoms by a series of protocols, of which Protocols Nos. 6,[55] 7,[56] and 8[57] are the most recent. Through this process, some important protections, including those inspired by a number of the substantive provisions of the International Covenant on Civil and Political Rights, have been incorporated in the additional protocols.

[53] Constitution of the International Labour Organisation, Arts. 19–23; Pt. II, Sec. E (Convention and Recommendation Procedure) of the Standing Orders of the International Labour Conference, International Labour Office, Constitution of the International Labour Organisation and Standing Orders of the International Labour Conference at 13–17, 48 (1982); see also Convention (No. 144) concerning Tripartite Consultations to Promote the Implementation of International Labour Standards, in International Labour Conventions and Recommendations 1919–1981, at 198 (International Labour Office, 1982).

[54] 1 Review, above n. 1, at 84. An important example of such a committee is the Committee of Experts for the Extension of the Rights Embodied in the European Convention on Human Rights.

[55] Council of Europe Doc. H (83) 3 (1983). On extension of rights in the Council of Europe in general, see also Council of Europe Doc. H/ONG (82) 3; Parliamentary Assembly of the Council of Europe, Recommendation 838 (1978) on widening the scope of the European Convention on Human Rights; Parliamentary Assembly of the Council of Europe, Recommendation 839 (1978) on the revision of the European Social Charter; Reply from the Committee of Ministers to Recommendation No. 838 (1978), Council of Europe Doc. H/Inf. (79)4, App. III, at 21 (1979); Report of the Committee of Experts on Human Rights to the Committee of Ministers on Problems Arising from the Co-existence of the United Nations Covenants on Human Rights and the European Convention on Human Rights, Council of Europe Doc. H(70)7 (1970); Council of Europe, Directorate of Human Rights, Proceedings of the Colloquy About the European Convention on Human Rights in Relation to Other International Instruments for the Protection of Human Rights, Athens, 21–22 September 1978 (1979).

[56] Council of Europe Doc. H (84) 5 (1984).

[57] Protocol No. 8 to the Convention for the Protection of Human Rights and Fundamental Freedoms, opened for signature 19 March 1985, (Council of Europe Doc. H (85) 6 (1985)) is aimed mainly at avoiding delays in proceedings under the European Convention. See explanatory memorandum, ibid. at 5.

The Council of Europe has encountered greater difficulties, however, in trying to identify economic, social, and cultural rights which might be included in an additional protocol to the European Convention. The United Nations should emulate the example given by the Council of Europe and regard the task of human rights law-making not as an operation designed to produce a particular instrument, but as a continuing process, which includes extension, elaboration, consolidation, and revision. The work begun on the possible elaboration of a Second Optional Protocol to the International Covenant on Civil and Political Rights, Aiming at the Abolition of the Death Penalty[58] points in the right direction.

IV. PROPOSED REFORMS

To rationalize the adoption of so-called 'new rights', Philip Alston has recently proposed a set of procedures involving the UN Secretariat, the General Assembly, and the Commission.[59] Such procedures would indeed be useful and could also be applied to rights not regarded as 'new'. It is far from certain, however, that the General Assembly would have the necessary incentive to adopt such procedures. It is even more doubtful whether the General Assembly and other organs would have the self-discipline to follow such a procedure as long as the existing framework for human rights law-making is not modified. Procedures operate best when they are tied to institutional arrangements, as in the area of outer space law or international trade law, where law-making organs have been established.

What is needed is an organ that would devote its entire time to, and specialize exclusively in, human rights law-making. Future law-making activity should be concentrated in such an organ, a UN Human Rights Law Commission (UNHRLC), which would function according to well-defined, structured processes particularly suitable for human rights, which is a broad, but nevertheless specialized field.[60] The law-making processes would gain in efficiency and the instruments in quality.

---

[58]   See UN Doc. A/39/535 (1984); Meron, *Towards a Humanitarian Declaration on Internal Strife*, 78 AJIL 859, 865 n. 37 (1984).

[59]   Alston, above n. 1, at 617–21.

[60]   UN Doc. A/37/444, at 6 (1982) (comments by Australia).

The creation of a single expert body would not mean that that body would necessarily monopolize the entire law-making activity in the field of human rights, any more than the ILC monopolizes law-making in other areas of international law. But the UNHRLC should be entrusted, at least, with the drafting of major instruments of general interest. It may be possible and even desirable from time to time to refer a particular subject to a different, perhaps an *ad hoc*, organ, especially where the subject requires particular expertise, or to a broadly representative political organ, if the subject is politically very sensitive. To paraphrase Schachter's discussion of the ILC, when the objectives are not well agreed and when the technical issues do not fall within the purview of the general international lawyer, there may be good reason to have recourse to a more specialized body, in which the particular subject can be handled by technical experts, governmental officials, and lawyers knowledgeable in the field.[61] In the present state of human rights law, much of the work of the UNHRLC would be devoted to progressive development rather than to codification. However, the UNHRLC could also be charged with the preparation of drafts consolidating, improving, and revising some of the instruments which have already been adopted. This would include filling lacunae and improving implementation clauses. When one considers how many instruments have already been adopted, the tasks of revision and consolidation and, in some cases, of extending rights by drafting additional protocols to the major human rights treaties, as in the Council of Europe, takes on special importance.

It might be possible to restructure the present Commission and the Sub-Commission and carve out from them the new law-making organ. But except for the law-making activities of these organs, their present form and mandates might better be left unaltered. Their agenda is demanding enough without law-making, especially if it is recalled that their mandate under resolutions adopted by the General Assembly and ECOSOC extends to all the Member States of the United Nations and not only, as is the case with organs established by various human rights treaties, to States Parties to particular instruments. Of

---

[61] Schachter, above n. 1, at 786.

course, the Commission and the Sub-Commission could also benefit from reforms. The Sub-Commission has begun to review its role on an excessively timid note. Let us hope that this examination develops into a significant critique and, eventually, reform.

Leaving aside for a moment the question of the UNHRLC composition, let us focus first on the process to be followed. There should be prior discussion at the political level, normally by the General Assembly, but possibly at times by ECOSOC, of the need to initiate the law-making process. Some general guidelines might be adopted at this time. To be well informed, the participants in the preliminary discussion should have at their disposal prior studies carried out by the Secretariat or outside experts. The preparatory work would include canvassing the membership and interested governmental and non-governmental organizations (NGOs), whose role in the law-making process is often important, by means of detailed questionnaires. Before deciding to start working on an instrument, States should have a clear perception of the need for it and its feasibility. Another question which merits consideration at an early stage of the law-making process is the form appropriate to an instrument, that is whether it should be a binding agreement- or a recommendation. In some circumstances it might be desirable to start work on two parallel instruments, one binding, the other recommendatory, as in the ILO.[62] The decision as to the type

---

[62] See 1 Review above n. 1, at 19.

Regarding the legal value of declarations, see Schachter, above n. 1, at 787–95, and bibliography, ibid. at 804 n. 97; Schachter, *The Crisis of Legitimation in the United Nations*, 50 Nordisk Tidsskrift for International Ret 3 (1981).

In the ILO and in UNESCO, a decision as to the form of an instrument is required at early stages of the law-making process. In the United Nations human rights law-making there is no structured rational process for making an informed choice between a declaration' and a convention. In a number of cases, a declaration has preceded the adoption of a convention on the subject. The advantages involved in beginning with a declaration are several. A declaration enables the provision of a faster remedy for, or amelioration of, the underlying problems. Certain principles, as well as the reach of the political consensus, can be tested in practice before a commitment is made to elaborate a convention. At the same time, guidelines are established which are useful for the elaboration of a future convention. Where an instrument contains a developed system of supervision, the form of a binding instrument (a convention) may be especially desirable. See generally 1 Review, above n. 1, at 19; N. Valticos, International Labour Law 55–7 (1979). See also Ch. VI n. 24 above. In the United Nations it is often assumed that declarations should, almost as a matter of course, be sooner or later followed by conventions. This subject should,

of instrument might have to be reconsidered as more is learned about the problems and the limits of state support for, and interest in, the new instrument.

In the elaboration of the instruments, the UNHRLC would be given constant research support by the Secretariat. The work of the UNHRLC would be modeled *mutatis mutandis* on the working procedures of the ILC and, perhaps, when useful, on some elements of the procedures of UNCITRAL or of other bodies. The UNHRLC should not, however, slavishly follow the ILC model. It should guard against such undesirable features as undue fragmentation of the discussion of the draft articles over the course of many sessions, and the slow pace characteristic of the ILC. There should be constant resort to special rapporteurs, drafting committees, researchers, and governments for comments. A single person, however, would have primary responsibility for preparing the first draft. The evolving texts would go through a fixed number of readings by the UNHRLC according to a predetermined timetable. When the drafting and editing are completed, the instrument should be submitted to a representative organ for adoption; it must be clear that the UNHRLC role would be limited to formulating the text of the instrument.

As a general but not inflexible rule, major instruments should be submitted to conferences of plenipotentiaries for adoption, after a decision by the General Assembly. Such conferences would have more time, more expertise, and more appropriate working methods than the General Assembly for the negotiation and adoption of human rights instruments. The General Assembly should be given the task of adopting a human rights instrument only if the draft approved by the UNHRLC is, in view of both its content and the political context, likely to be adopted without prolonged negotiations and major revisions. When a text is submitted to the General Assembly for adoption, the Sixth Committee could be involved usefully in the process by the referral of some matters to it by the Third Committee,

---

however, be approached with caution. A declaration accepted by consensus or quasi-unanimity may have a greater influence on the behaviour of States than a sparsely ratified convention. Moreover there is a danger that in the course of the drafting of a convention, norms already accepted in a declaration would be called into question and perhaps revised and narrowed.

or by the creation of a joint committee constituted of these two main committees, or by the formation of a working group drawn from members of these committees. The General Assembly ought to consider reviewing Annex II to its Rules of Procedure, entitled 'Methods and Procedures of the General Assembly for Dealing with Legal and Drafting Questions',[63] which inadequately addresses human rights law-making, and drawing up more effective rules for its adoption of human rights instruments.

To ensure that the new scheme of things meets with success, adequate and efficient resources must be provided for the Centre for Human Rights of the UN Secretariat. Such resources might make it possible to institute 'pre-initiation' studies, along the lines of the ILO practice, where they are statutorily required.[64] The UNHRLC will also need strong support from the Secretariat when the preparatory studies are carried out by independent experts or special rapporteurs (unless such persons can call upon their national governments for help, a practice which is not always in the best interest of the international community). At present, it is unrealistic to expect the Centre for Human Rights to be able to respond to the proliferating requests for in-depth background research and studies.

One facet of the process that cries for improvement is the recording of the preparatory work for the human rights instruments. A strengthened Secretariat could prepare analytical collections of records, as was done, *inter alia*, for the Vienna Convention on Diplomatic Relations,[65] the Vienna Convention on Consular Relations,[66] and the Vienna Convention on the Law of Treaties,[67] but not for even the most important instruments

---

[63]   UN Doc. A/520/Rev. 14, at 41 (1982).

[64]   UN Doc. A/36/553, at 48 (1981).

[65]   See 2 Official Records, United Nations Conference on Diplomatic Intercourse and Immunities, UN Doc. A/CONF.20/14/Add.1 (1962).

[66]   See 2 Official Records, United Nations Conference on Consular Relations, UN Doc. A/Conf.25/16/Add.1 (1963).

[67]   Official Records, Documents of the Conference, United Nations Conference on the Law of Treaties, UN Doc. A/CONF.39/11/Add.2 (1971).

See also 2 Official Records, Documents of the Conference, United Nations Conference on the Representation of States in their Relations with International Organizations, UN Doc. A/CONF.67/18/Add.1 (1976); 3 Official Records, Documents of the Conference, United Nations Conference on Succession of States in Respect of Treaties, UN Doc. A/CONF.80/16/Add.2 (1979).

For a list of commentaries on conventions pertaining to narcotic drugs and similar substances, see UN Doc. A/35/312/Add.1, at 30 n. 6.

in the human rights field. This is not to suggest that official explanatory memoranda on the various instruments should be prepared for adoption by the conferences that are to adopt the texts of the instruments, as this course of action would pose serious problems.[68] Rather, means for improving access to the records of preparatory work[69] should be created. The UNHRLC should prepare commentaries on the draft articles which it adopts, following the pattern established by the ILC. Such commentaries would aid the plenipotentiary conferences or the General Assembly in considering the text for adoption and would constitute an important resource for the interpretation of the instruments. However, they would not be approved formally by these bodies and would not acquire the status of an authoritative commentary.

Let us now turn to the composition and character of the UNHRLC. This body should be relatively small, preferably with a smaller number of members than the ILC. Like the Commission on Human Rights, it should be elected by ECOSOC and constitute another functional commission of that organ, or by the Commission on Human Rights as its second Sub-Commission. The basic choice appears to be between an organ of representatives of States, such as the Legal Sub-Committee of the Committee on the Peaceful Uses of Outer Space or UNCITRAL, and a committee of experts elected in their individual capacity, such as the ILC, the Human Rights Committee established under Art. 28 of the Political Covenant, the Committee on the Elimination of Racial Discrimination established under Art. 8 of the International Convention on the Elimination of All Forms of Racial Discrimination, the Committee on the Elimination of Discrimination Against Women established under Art. 17 of the Convention on the Elimination of All Forms of Discrimination Against Women, and the Committee Against Torture established under Art. 17 of the recently adopted Convention Against Torture and Other Cruel, Inhuman or Degrading Treatment or Punishment.[70] While the latter pattern is clearly preferable because it creates better prospects for a high degree of expertise

---

[68] UN Doc. A/35/312/Add.1, at 5, 9 (1980) (comments by Austria).
[69] Ibid. at 30 (comments by the United Kingdom).
[70] GA Res. 39/46, opened for signature 10 Dec. 1984, 39 UN GAOR Supp. (No. 51) at 197, UN Doc. A/39/51 (1985).

and continuity, and a lesser involvement in politics, the establishment of an organ composed of governmental experts is not necessarily calamitous. The experience with UNCITRAL and the Council of Europe has shown that when governments are interested enough in influencing the formulation of an instrument of importance to them, they can and do appoint competent experts. Careful selection of experts is therefore essential. Moreover, any independent observer of the work of the United Nations cannot avoid becoming increasingly cynical about the independence from their governments of individually elected experts from many Member States, especially serving officials of government ministries and state institutions. Nor is the procedure of electing individual experts a guarantee of their professional competence.. The crucial point, therefore, is not that members be elected in their individual capacity, but that they should be genuine experts.

Those advocating that even the preliminary formulation of UN treaties should be entrusted to government representatives argue that this would ensure greater sensitivity to political considerations[71] and a more reliable assessment of the support by States for a new instrument. Obviously, draft texts have to stand the test of acceptance by States.[72] I am not suggesting that human rights law-making could or should be apolitical, for law-making is a political process. The Secretary-General of the United Nations himself has emphasized that the ILC does not stand aloof from political realities.[73] While excessive politicization of human rights law-making should be avoided, the prospects for depoliticizing United Nations human rights activities in general are unrealistic, as recently demonstrated by Franck.[74] What is needed urgently is a better balance between the participation of experts and that of generalist diplomats. In any event, the political perspective would be provided by constant input from governmental comments, guidelines and instructions from the political organs, and by the knowledge of the UNHRLC members that their drafts would be submitted for

[71] See generally UN Doc. A/36/553, at 62 (1981).
[72] See UN Doc. A/35/312/Add.1, at 3 (1980) (comments by Austria).
[73] UN Press Release SG/SM/494, at 3–4 (4 July 1983).
[74] Franck, *Of Gnats and Camels: Is There a Double Standard at the United Nations?* 78 AJIL 811, 819–30 (1984).

adoption to the political organs. The fact that human rights law-making occurs largely in the domain of progressive development should not make the preparation of drafts any less appropriate for a group of individual experts to undertake.

The Secretary-General's recent Report on the Work of the Organization calls upon Member States to 'give serious thought to the best way of doing business',[75] and to examine 'existing United Nations practices and consider ways and means to make them more effective in dealing with gross violations of human rights wherever they occur'.[76] This challenge merits being taken up also in the field of law-making.

The proposal to establish the UNHRLC is likely to be greeted with scepticism, well justified no doubt, about the prospects for reform. It will be said that the United Nations already suffers from a proliferation of organs and that there is no guarantee that the UNHRLC would measure up to our hopes and expectations if it were established. Yet the subject of human rights law-making is crucial, the present system inadequate, and reform needed. The academic community therefore has both the moral and professional obligation to lead the way, to suggest reforms, and to work for their adoption. Are human rights less important than the fields in which the United Nations has established better structures and procedures for law-making?

---

[75] 39 UN GAOR Supp. (No. 1) at 2, UN Doc. A/39/1 (1984).
[76] Ibid. at 5.

ANNEXES

Annex I

INTERNATIONAL COVENANT ON CIVIL AND POLITICAL RIGHTS

Adopted and opened for signature, ratification and accession by General Assembly resolution 2200 A (XXI) of 16 December 1966

ENTRY INTO FORCE: 23 March 1976, in accordance with article 49.

Preamble

The States Parties to the present Covenant,

Considering that, in accordance with the principles proclaimed in the Charter of the United Nations, recognition of the inherent dignity and of the equal and inalienable rights of all members of the human family is the foundation of freedom, justice and peace in the world,

Recognizing that these rights derive from the inherent dignity of the human person,

Recognizing that, in accordance with the Universal Declaration of Human Rights, the ideal of free human beings enjoying civil and political freedom and freedom from fear and want can only be achieved if conditions are created whereby everyone may enjoy his civil and political rights, as well as his economic, social and cultural rights,

Considering the obligation of States under the Charter of the United Nations to promote universal respect for, and observance of, human rights and freedoms,

Realizing that the individual, having duties to other individuals and to the community to which he belongs, is under a responsibility to strive for the promotion and observance of the rights recognized in the present Covenant,

Agree upon the following articles:

Part I

Article 1

1. All peoples have the right of self-determination. By virtue of that right they freely determine their political status and freely pursue their economic, social and cultural development.

2. All peoples may, for their own ends, freely dispose of their natural wealth and resources without prejudice to any obligations arising out of international economic co-operation, based upon the principle of mutual benefit, and international law. In no case may a people be deprived of its own means of subsistence.

3. The States Parties to the present Covenant, including those having responsibility for the administration of Non-Self-Governing and Trust Territories, shall promote the realization of the right of self-determination,

and shall respect that right, in conformity with the provisions of the Charter of the United Nations.

Part II

Article 2

1. Each State Party to the present Covenant undertakes to respect and to ensure to all individuals within its territory and subject to its jurisdiction the rights recognized in the present Covenant, without distinction of any kind, such as race, colour, sex, language, religion, political or other opinion, national or social origin, property, birth or other status.

2. Where not already provided for by existing legislative or other measures, each State Party to the present Covenant undertakes to take the necessary steps, in accordance with its constitutional processes and with the provisions of the present Covenant, to adopt such legislative or other measures as may be necessary to give effect to the rights recognized in the present Covenant.

3. Each State Party to the present Covenant undertakes:

(*a*) To ensure that any person whose rights or freedoms as herein recognized are violated shall have an effective remedy, notwithstanding that the violation has been committed by persons acting in an official capacity;

(*b*) To ensure that any person claiming such a remedy shall have his right thereto determined by competent judicial, administrative or legislative authorities, or by any other competent authority provided for by the legal system of the State, and to develop the possibilities of judicial remedy;

(*c*) To ensure that the competent authorities shall enforce such remedies when granted.

Article 3   The States Parties to the present Covenant undertake to ensure the equal right of men and women to the enjoyment of all civil and political rights set forth in the present Covenant.

Article 4

1. In time of public emergency which threatens the life of the nation and the existence of which is officially proclaimed, the States Parties to the present Covenant may take measures derogating from their obligations under the present Covenant to the extent strictly required by the exigencies of the situation, provided that such measures are not inconsistent with their other obligations under international law and do not involve discrimination solely on the ground of race, colour, sex, language, religion or social origin.

2. No derogation from articles 6, 7, 8 (paragraphs 1 and 2), 11, 15, 16 and 18 may be made under this provision.

3. Any State party to the present Covenant availing itself of the right of derogation shall immediately inform the other States Parties to the present Covenant, through the intermediary of the Secretary-General of the United Nations, of the provisions from which it has derogated and of the reasons by which it was actuated. A further communication shall be made,

through the same intermediary, on the date on which it terminates such derogation.

Article 5

1. Nothing in the present Covenant may be interpreted as implying for any State, group or person any right to engage in any activity or perform any act aimed at the destruction of any of the rights and freedoms recognized herein or at their limitation to a greater extent than is provided for in the present Covenant.

2. There shall be no restriction upon or derogation from any of the fundamental human rights recognized or existing in any State Party to the present Covenant pursuant to law, conventions, regulations or custom on the pretext that the present Covenant does not recognize such rights or that it recognizes them to a lesser extent.

Part III

Article 6

1. Every human being has the inherent right to life. This right shall be protected by law. No one shall be arbitrarily deprived of his life.

2. In countries which have not abolished the death penalty, sentence of death may be imposed only for the most serious crimes in accordance with the law in force at the time of the commission of the crime and not contrary to the provisions of the present Covenant and to the Convention on the Prevention and Punishment of the Crime of Genocide. This penalty can only be carried out pursuant to a final judgement rendered by a competent court.

3. When deprivation of life constitutes the crime of genocide, it is understood that nothing in this article shall authorize any State Party to the present Covenant to derogate in any way from any obligation assumed under the provisions of the Convention on the Prevention and Punishment of the Crime of Genocide.

4. Anyone sentenced to death shall have the right to seek pardon or commutation of the sentence. Amnesty, pardon or commutation of the sentence of death may be granted in all cases.

5. Sentence of death shall not be imposed for crimes committed by persons below eighteen years of age and shall not be carried out on pregnant women.

6. Nothing in this article shall be invoked to delay or to prevent the abolition of capital punishment by any State Party to the present Covenant.

Article 7
No one shall be subjected to torture or to cruel, inhuman or degrading treatment or punishment. In particular, no one shall be subjected without his free consent to medical or scientific experimentation.

Article 8

1. No one shall be held in slavery; slavery and the slave-trade in all their forms shall be prohibited.

2. No one shall be held in servitude.

3. (*a*) No one shall be requried to perform forced or compulsory labour;

(*b*) Paragraph 3 (*a*) shall not be held to preclude, in countries where imprisonment with hard labour may be imposed as a punishment for a crime, the performance of hard labour in pursuance of a sentence to such punishment by a competent court;

(*c*) For the purpose of this paragraph the term 'forced or compulsory labour' shall not include:

(i) Any work or service, not referred to in sub-paragraph (*b*), normally required of a person who is under detention in consequence of a lawful order of a court, or of a person during conditional release from such detention;

(ii) Any service of a military character and, in countries where conscientious objection is recognized, any national service required by law of conscientious objectors;

(iii) Any service exacted in cases of emergency or calamity threatening the life of well-being of the community;

(iv) Any work or service which forms part of normal civil obligations.

Article 9

1. Everyone has the right to liberty and security of person. No one shall be subjected to arbitrary arrest or detention. No one shall be deprived of his liberty except on such grounds and in accordance with such procedure as are established by law.

2. Anyone who is arrested shall be informed, at the time of arrest, of the reasons for his arrest and shall be promptly informed of any charges against him.

3. Anyone arrested or detained on a criminal charge shall be brought promptly before a judge or other officer authorized by law to exercise judicial power and shall be entitled to trial within a reasonable time or to release. It shall not be the general rule that persons awaiting trial shall be detained in custody, but release may be subject to guarantees to appear for trial, at any other stage of the judicial proceedings, and, should occasion arise, for execution of the judgement.

4. Anyone who is deprived of his liberty by arrest or detention shall be entitled to take proceedings before a court, in order that that court may decide without delay on the lawfulness of his detention and order his release if the detention is not lawful.

5. Anyone who has been victim of unlawful arrest or detention shall have an enforceable right to compensation.

Article 10

1. All persons deprived of their liberty shall be treated with humanity and with respect for the inherent dignity of the human person.

2. (*a*) Accused persons shall, save in exceptional circumstances, be segregated from convicted persons and shall be subject to separate treatment appropriate to their status as unconvicted persons;

(*b*) Accused juvenile persons shall be separated from adults and brought as speedily as possible for ajudication.

3. The penitentiary system shall comprise treatment of prisoners the essential aim of which shall be their reformation and social rehabilitation. Juvenile offenders shall be segregated from adults and be accorded treatment appropriate to their age and legal status.

Article 11 No one shall be imprisoned merely on the ground of inability to fulfil a contractual obligation.

Article 12

1. Everyone lawfully within the territory of a State shall, within that territory, have the right to liberty of movement and freedom to choose his residence.

2. Everyone shall be free to leave any country, including his own.

3. The above-mentioned rights shall not be subject to any restrictions except those which are provided by law, are necessary to protect national security, public order (*ordre public*), public health or morals or the rights and freedoms of others, and are consistent with the other rights recognized in the present Covenant.

4. No one shall be arbitrarily deprived of the right to enter his own country.

Article 13 An alien lawfully in the territory of a State Party to the present Covenant may be expelled therefrom only in pursuance of a decision reached in accordance with law and shall, except where compelling reasons of national security otherwise require, be allowed to submit the reasons against his expulsion and to have his case reviewed by, and be represented for the purpose before, the competent authority or a person or persons especially designated by the competent authority.

Article 14

1. All persons shall be equal before the courts and tribunals. In the determination of any criminal charge against him, or of his rights and obligations in a suit at law, everyone shall be entitled to a fair and public hearing by a competent, independant and impartial tribunal established by law. The Press and the public may be excluded from all or part of a trial for reasons of morals, public order (*ordre public*) or national security in a democratic society, or when the interest of the private lives of the parties so requires, or to the extent strictly necessary in the opinion of the court in special circumstances where publicity would prejudice the interests of justice; but any judgement rendered in a criminal case or in a suit at law shall be made public except where the interest of juvenile persons otherwise requires or the proceedings concern matrimonial disputes of the guardianship of children.

2. Everyone charged with a criminal offence shall have the right to be presumed innocent until proved guilty according to law.

3. In the determination of any criminal charge against him, everyone shall be entitled to the following minimum guarantees, in full equality:

(*a*) To be informed promptly and in detail in a language which he understands of the nature and cause of the charge against him;

(*b*) To have adequate time and facilities for the preparation of his defence and to communicate with counsel of his own choosing;

(*c*) To be tried without undue delay;

(*d*) To be tried in his presence, and to defend himself in person or through legal assistance of his own choosing; to be informed, if he does not have legal assistance, of this right; and to have legal assistance assigned to him, in any case where the interests of justice so require, and without payment by him in any such case if he does not have sufficient means to pay for it;

(*e*) To examine, or have examined, the witnesses against him and to obtain the attendance and examination of witnesses on his behalf under the same conditions as witnesses against him;

(*f*) To have the free assistance of an interpreter if he cannot understand or speak the language used in court;

(*g*) Not to be compelled to testify against himself or to confess guilt.

4. In the case of juvenile persons, the procedure shall be such as will take account of their age and the desirability of promoting their rehabilitation.

5. Everyone convicted of a crime shall have the right to his conviction and sentence being reviewed by a higher tribunal according to law.

6. When a person has by a final decision been convicted of a criminal offence and when subsequently his conviction has been reversed or he has been pardoned on the ground that a new or newly discovered fact shows conclusively that there has been a miscarriage of justice, the person who has suffered punishment as a result of such conviction shall be compensated according to law, unless it is proved that the non-disclosure of the unknown fact in time is wholly or partly attributable to him.

7. No one shall be liable to be tried or punished again for an offence for which he has already been finally convicted or acquitted in accordance with the law and penal procedure of each country.

Article 15

1. No one shall be held guilty of any criminal offence on account of any act or omission which did not constitute a criminal offence, under national or international law, at the time when it was committed. Nor shall a heavier penalty be imposed than the one that was applicable at the time when the criminal offence was committed. If, subsequent to the commission of the offence, provision is made by law for the imposition of the lighter penalty, the offender shall benefit thereby.

2. Nothing in this article shall prejudice the trial and punishment of any person for any act or omission which, at the time when it was committed, was criminal according to the general principles of law recognized by the community of nations.

Article 16 Everyone shall have the right to recognition everywhere as a person before the law.

Article 17
1. No one shall be subjected to arbitrary or unlawful interference with his privacy, family, home or correspondence, nor to unlawful attacks on his honour and reputation.
2. Everyone has the right to the protection of the law against such interference or attacks.

Article 18
1. Everyone shall have the right to freedom of thought, conscience and religion. This right shall include freedom to have or to adopt a religion or belief of his choice, and freedom, either individually or in community with others and in public or private, to manifest his religion or belief in worship, observance, practice and teaching.
2. No one shall be subject to coercion which would impair his freedom to have or to adopt a religion or belief of his choice.
3. Freedom to manifest one's religion or beliefs may be subject only to such limitations as are prescribed by law and are necessary to protect public safety, order, health, or morals or the fundamental rights and freedoms of others.
4. The States Parties to the present Covenant undertake to have respect for the liberty of parents and, when applicable, legal guardians to ensure the religious and moral education of their children in conformity with their own convictions.

Article 19
1. Everyone shall have the right to hold opinions without interference.
2. Everyone shall have the right to freedom of expression; this right shall include freedom to seek, receive and impart information and ideas of all kinds, regardless of frontiers, either orally, in writing or in print, in the form of art, or through any other media of his choice.
3. The exercise of the rights provided for in paragraph 2 of this article carries with it special duties and responsibilities. It may therefore be subject to certain restrictions, but these shall only be such as are provided by law and are necessary:
(*a*) For respect of the rights or reputations of others;
(*b*) For the protection of national security or of public order (*ordre public*), or of public health or morals.

Article 20
1. Any propaganda for war shall be prohibited by law.
2. Any advocacy of national, racial or religious hatred that constitutes incitement to discrimination, hostility or violence shall be prohibited by law.

Article 21 The right of peaceful assembly shall be recognized. No restrictions may be placed on the exercise of this right other than those imposed in conformity with the law and which are necessary in a democratic society in the interests of national security or public safety, public order (*order public*), the protection of public health or morals or the protection of the rights and freedoms of others.

Article 22

1. Everyone shall have the right to freedom of association with others, including the right to form and join trade unions for the protection of his interests.

2. No restrictions may be placed on the exercise of this right other than those which are prescribed by law and which are necessary in a democratic society in the interests of national security or public safety, public order (*ordre public*), the protection of public health or morals or the protection of the rights and freedoms of others. This article shall not prevent the imposition of lawful restrictions on members of the armed forces and of the police in their exercise of this right.

3. Nothing in this article shall authorize States Parties to the International Labour Organisation Convention of 1948 concerning Freedom of Association and Protection of the Right to Organize to take legislative measures which would prejudice, or to apply the law in such a manner as to prejudice the guarantees provided for in that Convention.

Article 23

1. The family is the natural and fundamental group unit of society and is entitled to protection by society and the State.

2. The right of men and women of marriageable age to marry and to found a family shall be recognized.

3. No marriage shall be entered into without the free and full consent of the intending spouses.

4. States Parties to the present Covenant shall take appropriate steps to ensure equality of rights and responsibilities of spouses as to marriage, during marriage and at its dissolution. In the case of dissolution, provision shall be made for the necessary protection of any children.

Article 24

1. Every child shall have, without any discrimination as to race, colour, sex, language, religion, national or social origin, property or birth, the right to such measures of protection as are required by his status as a minor, on the part of his family, society and the State.

2. Every child shall be registered immediately after birth and shall have a name.

3. Every child has the right to acquire a nationality.

Article 25 Every citizen shall have the right and the opportunity, without any of the distinctions mentioned in article 2 and without unreasonable restrictions:

(*a*) To take part in the conduct of public affairs, directly or through freely chosen representatives;

(*b*) To vote and to be elected at genuine periodic elections which shall be by universal and equal suffrage and shall be held by secret ballot, guaranteeing the free expression of the will of the electors;

(*c*) To have access, on general terms of equality, to public service in his country.

Article 26   All persons are equal before the law and are entitled without any discimination to the equal protection of the law. In this respect, the law shall prohibit any discrimination and guarantee to all persons equal and effective protection against discrimination on any ground such as race, colour, sex, language, religion, political or other opinion, national or social origin, property, birth or other status.

Article 27   In those States in which ethnic, religious or linguistic minorities exist, persons belonging to such minorities shall not be denied the right, in community with the other members of their group, to enjoy their own culture, to profess and practise their own religion, or to use their own language.

Part IV

Article 28

1. There shall be established a Human Rights Committee (hereafter referred to in the present Covenant as the Committee). It shall consist of eighteen members and shall carry out the functions hereinafter provided.

2. The Committee shall be composed of nationals of the States Parties to the present Covenant who shall be persons of high moral character and recognized competence in the field of human rights, consideration being given to the usefulness of the participation of some persons having legal experience.

3. The members of the Committee shall be elected and shall serve in their personal capacity.

Article 29

1. The members of the Committee shall be elected by secret ballot from a list of persons possessing the qualifications prescribed in article 28 and nominated for the purpose by the States Parties to the present Covenant.

2. Each State Party to the present Covenant may nominate not more than two persons. These persons shall be nationals of the nominating State.

3. A person shall be eligible for renomination.

Article 30

1. The initial election shall be held no later than six months after the date of the entry into force of the present Covenant.

2. At least four months before the date of each election to the Committee, other than an election to fill a vacancy declared in accordance with

article 34, the Secretary-General of the United Nations shall address a written invitation to the States Parties to the present Covenant to submit their nominations for membership of the Committee within three months.

3. The Secretary-General of the United Nations shall prepare a list in alphabetical order of all the persons thus nominated, with an indication of the States Parties which have nominated them, and shall submit it to the States Parties to the present Covenant no later than one month before the date of each election.

4. Elections of the members of the Committee shall be held at a meeting of the States Parties to the present Covenant convened by the Secretary-General of the United Nations at the Headquarters of the United Nations. At the meeting, for which two thirds of the States Parties to the present Covenant shall constitute a quorum, the persons elected to the Committee shall be those nominees who obtain the largest number of votes and an absolute majority of the votes of the representatives of States Parties present and voting.

Article 31

1. The Committee may not include more than one national of the same State.

2. In the election of the Committee, consideration shall be given to equitable geographical distribution of membership and to the representation of the different forms of civilization and of the principal legal systems.

Article 32

1. The members of the Committee shall be elected for a term of four years. They shall be eligible for re-election if renominated. However, the terms of nine of the members elected at the first election shall expire at the end of two years; immediately after the first election, the names of these nine members shall be chosen by lot by the Chairman of the meeting referred to in article 30, paragraph 4.

2. Elections at the expiry of office shall be held in accordance with the preceding articles of this part of the present Covenant.

Article 33

1. If, in the unanimous opinion of the other members, a member of the Committee has ceased to carry out his functions for any cause other than absence of a temporary character, the Chairman of the Committee shall notify the Secretary-General of the United Nations, who shall then declare the seat of that member to be vacant.

2. In the event of the death or the resignation of a member of the Committee, the Chairman shall immediately notify the Secretary-General of the United Nations, who shall declare the seat vacant from the date of death or the date on which the resignation takes effect.

Article 34

1. When a vacancy is declared in accordance with article 33 and if the term of office of the member to be replaced does not expire within six

months of the declaration of the vacancy, the Secretary-General of the United Nations shall notify each of the States Parties to the present Covenant, which may within two months submit nominations in accordance with article 29 for the purpose of filling the vacancy.

2. The Secretary-General of the United Nations shall prepare a list in alphabetical order of the persons thus nominated and shall submit it to the States Parties to the present Covenant. The election to fill the vacancy shall then take place in accordance with the relevant provisions of this part of the present Covenant.

3. A member of the Committee elected to fill a vacancy declared in accordance with article 33 shall hold office for the remainder of the term of the member who vacated the seat on the Committee under the provisions of that article.

Article 35   The members of the Committee shall, with the approval of the General Assembly of the United Nations, receive emoluments from United Nations resources on such terms and conditions as the General Assembly may decide, having regard to the importance of the Committee's responsibilities.

Article 36   The Secretary-General of the United Nations shall provide the necessary staff and facilities for the effective performance of the functions of the Committee under the present Covenant.

Article 37

1. The Secretary-General of the United Nations shall convene the initial meeting of the Committee at the Headquarters of the United Nations.

2. After its initial meeting, the Committee shall meet at such times as shall be provided in its rules of procedure.

3. The Committee shall normally meet at the Headquarters of the United Nations or at the United Nations Office at Geneva.

Article 38   Every member of the Committee shall, before taking up his duties, make a solemn declaration in open committee that he will perform his functions impartially and conscientiously.

Article 39

1. The Committee shall elect its officers for a term of two years. They may be re-elected.

2. The Committee shall establish its own rules of procedure, but these rules shall provide, *inter alia*, that:

(*a*) Twelve members shall constitue a quorum;

(*b*) Decisions of the Committee shall be made by a majority vote of the members present.

Article 40

1. The States Parties to the present Covenant undertake to submit reports on the measures they have adopted which give effect to the rights

recognized herein and on the progress made in the enjoyment of those rights:

(a) Within one year of the entry into force of the present Covenant for the States Parties concerned;

(b) Thereafter whenever the Committee so requests.

2. All reports shall be submitted to the Secretary-General of the United Nations, who shall transmit them to the Committee for consideration. Reports shall indicate the factors and difficulties, if any, affecting the implementation of the present Covenant.

3. The Secretary-General of the United Nations may, after consultation with the Committee, transmit to the specialized agencies concerned copies of such parts of the reports as may fill within their field of competence.

4. The Committee shall study the reports submitted by the States Parties to the present Covenant. It shall transmit its reports, and such general comments as it may consider appropriate, to the States Parties. The Committee may also transmit to the Economic and Social Council these comments along with the copies of the reports it has received from States Parties to the present Covenant.

5. The States Parties to the present Covenant may submit to the Committee observations on any comments that may be made in accordance with paragraph 4 of this article.

Article 41

1. A State Party to the present Covenant may at any time declare under this article that it recognizes the competence of the Committee to receive and consider communications to the effect that a State Party claims that another State Party is not fulfilling its obligations under the present Covenant. Communications under this article may be received and considered only if submitted by a State Party which has made a declaration recognizing in regard to itself the competence of the Committee. No communication shall be received by the Committee if it concerns a State Party which has not made such a declaration. Communications received under this article shall be dealt with in accordance with the following procedure:

(a) If a State Party to the present Covenant considers that another State Party is not giving effect to the provisions of the present Covenant, it may, by written communication, bring the matter to the attention of that State Party. Within three months after the receipt of the communication the receiving State shall afford the State which sent the communication an explanation, or any other statement in writing clarifying the matter which should include, to the extent possible and pertinent, reference to domestic procedures and remedies taken, pending, or available in the matter.

(b) If the matter is not adjusted to the satisfaction of both States Parties concerned within six months after the receipt by the receiving State of the initial communication, either State shall have the right to refer the matter to the Committee, by notice given to the Committee and to the other State.

(*c*) The Committee shall deal with a matter referred to it only after it has ascertained that all available domestic remedies have been invoked and exhausted in the matter, in conformity with the generally recognized principles of international law. This shall not be the rule where the application of the remedies is unreasonably prolonged.

(*d*) The Committee shall hold closed meetings when examining communications under this article.

(*e*) Subject to the provisions of sub-paragraph (*c*), the Committee shall make available its goods offices to the States Parties concerned with a view to a friendly solution of the matter on the basis of respect for human rights and fundamental freedoms as recognized in the present Covenant.

(*f*) In any matter referred to it, the Committee may call upon the States Parties concerned, referred to in sub-paragraph (*b*), to supply any relevant information.

(*g*) The States Parties concerned, referred to in sub-paragraph (*b*), shall have the right to be represented when the matter is being considered in the Committee and to make submissions orally and/or in writing.

(*h*) The Committee shall, within twelve months after the date of receipt of notice under sub-paragraph (*b*), submit a report:

(i) If a solution within the terms of sub-paragraph (*e*) is reached, the Committee shall confine its report to a brief statement of the facts and of the solution reached;

(ii) If a solution within the terms of sub-paragraph (*e*) is not reached, the Committee shall confine its report to a brief statement of the facts; the written submissions and record of the oral submissions made by the States Parties concerned shall be attached to the report.

In every matter, the report shall be communicated to the States Parties concerned.

2. The provisions of this article shall come into force when ten States Parties to the present Covenant have made declarations under paragraph 1 of this article. Such declarations shall be deposited by the States Parties with the Secretary-General of the United Nations, who shall transmit copies thereof to the other States Parties. A declaration may be withdrawn at any time by notification to the Secretary-General. Such a withdrawal shall not prejudice the consideration of any matter which is the subject of a communication already transmitted under this article; no further communication by any State Party shall be received after the notification of withdrawal of the declaration has been received by the Secretary-General, unless the State Party concerned has made a new declaration.

Article 42

1. (*a*) If a matter referred to the Committee in accordance with article 41 is not resolved to the satisfaction of the States Parties concerned, the Committee may, with the prior consent of the States Parties concerned, appoint an *ad hoc* Conciliation Commission (hereinafter referred to as the Commission). The good offices of the Commission shall be made available

to the States Parties concerned with a view to an amicable solution of the matter on the basis of respect for the present Covenant;

(*b*) The Commission shall consist of five persons acceptable to the States Parties concerned. If the States Parties concerned fail to reach agreement within three months on all or part of the composition of the Commission, the members of the Commission concerning whom no agreement has been reached shall be elected by secret ballot by a two-thirds majority vote of the Committee from among its members.

2. The members of the Commission shall serve in their personal capacity. They shall not be nationals of the States Parties concerned, or of a State not party to the present Covenant, or of a State Party which has not made a declaration under article 41.

3. The Commission shall elect its own Chairman and adopt its own rules of procedure.

4. The meetings of the Commission shall normally be held at the Headquarters of the United Nations or at the United Nations Office at Geneva. However, they may be held at such other convenient places as the Commission may determine in consultation with the Secretary-General of the United Nations and the States Parties concerned.

5. The secretariat provided in accordance with article 36 shall also service the commissions appointed under this article.

6. The information received and collated by the Committee shall be made available to the Commission and the Commission may call upon the States Parties concerned to supply any other relevant information.

7. When the Commission has fully considered the matter, but in any event not later than twelve months after having been seized of the matter, it shall submit to the Chairman of the Committee a report for communication to the States Parties concerned:

(*a*) If the Commission is unable to complete its consideration of the matter within twelve months, it shall confine its report to a brief statement of the status of its consideration of the matter;

(*b*) If an amicable solution to the matter on the basis of respect for human rights as recognized in the present Covenant is reached, the Commission shall confine its report to a brief statement of the facts and of the solution reached;

(*c*) If a solution within the terms of sub-paragraph (*b*) is not reached, the Commission's report shall embody its findings on all questions of fact relevant to the issues between the States Parties concerned, and its views on the possibilities of an amicable solution of the matter. This report shall also contain the written submissions and a record of the oral submissions made by the States Parties concerned;

(*d*) If the Commission's report is submitted under sub-paragraph (*c*), the States Parties concerned shall, within three months of the receipt of the report, notify the Chairman of the Committee whether or not they accept the contents of the report of the Commission.

8. The provisions of this article are without prejudice to the responsibilities of the Committee under article 41.

9. The States Parties concerned shall share equally all the expenses of the members of the Commission in accordance with estimates to be provided by the Secretary-General of the United Nations.

10. The Secretary-General of the United Nations shall be empowered to pay the expenses of the members of the Commission, if necessary, before reimbursement by the States Parties concerned, in accordance with paragraph 9 of this article.

Article 43   The members of the Committee, and of the *ad hoc* conciliation commissions which may be appointed under article 42, shall be entitled to the facilities, privileges and immunities of experts on mission for the United Nations as laid down in the relevant sections of the Convention on the Privileges and Immunities of the United Nations.

Article 44   The provisions for the implementation of the present Covenant shall apply without prejudice to the procedures prescribed in the field of human rights by or under the constituent instruments and the conventions of the United Nations and of the specialized agencies and shall not prevent the States Parties to the present Covenant from having recourse to other procedures for settling a dispute in accordance with general or special international agreements in force between them.

Article 45   The Committee shall submit to the General Assembly of the United Nations, through the Economic and Social Council, an annual report on its activities.

Part V

Article 46   Nothing in the present Covenant shall be interpreted as impairing the provisions of the Charter of the United Nations and of the constitutions of the specialized agencies which define the respective responsibilities of the various organs of the United Nations and of the specialized agencies in regard to the matters dealt with in the present Covenant.

Article 47   Nothing in the present Covenant shall be interpreted as impairing the inherent right of all peoples to enjoy and utilize fully and freely their natural wealth and resources.

Part VI

Article 48

1. The present Covenant is open for signature by any State Member of the United Nations or member of any of its specialized agencies, by any State Party to the Statute of the International Court of Justice, and by any other State which has been invited by the General Assembly of the United Nations to become a party to the present Covenant.

2. The present Covenant is subject to ratification. Instruments of ratification shall be deposited with the Secretary-General of the United Nations.

3. The present Covenant shall be open to accession by any State referred to in paragraph 1 of this article.

4. Accession shall be effected by the deposit of an instrument of accession with the Secretary-General of the United Nations.

5. The Secretary-General of the United Nations shall inform all States which have signed this Covenant or acceded to it of the deposit of each instrument of ratification or accession.

Article 49

1. The present Covenant shall enter into force three months after the date of the deposit with the Secretary-General of the United Nations of the thirty-fifth instrument of ratification or instrument of accession.

2. For each State ratifying the present Covenant or acceding to it after the deposit of the thirty-fifth instrument of ratification or instrument of accession, the present Covenant shall enter into force three months after the date of the deposit of its own instrument of ratification or instrument of accession.

Article 50

The provisions of the present Covenant shall extend to all parts of federal States without any limitations or exceptions.

Article 51

1. Any State Party to the present Covenant may propose an amendment and file it with the Secretary-General of the United Nations. The Secretary-General of the United Nations shall thereupon communicate any proposed amendments to the States Parties to the present Covenant with a request that they notify him whether they favour a conference of States Parties for the purpose of considering and voting upon the proposals. In the event that at least one third of the States Parties favours such a conference, the Secretary-General shall convene the conference under the auspices of the United Nations. Any amendment adopted by a majority of the States Parties present and voting at the conference shall be submitted to the General Assembly of the United Nations for approval.

2. Amendments shall come into force when they have been approved by the General Assembly of the United Nations and accepted by a two-thirds majority of the States Parties to the present Covenant in accordance with their respective constitutional processes.

3. When amendments come into force, they shall be binding on those States Parties which have accepted them, other States Parties still being bound by the provisions of the present Covenant and any earlier amendment which they have accepted.

Article 52

Irrespective of the notifications made under article 48, paragraph 5, the Secretary-General of the United Nations shall inform all

States referred to in paragraph 1 of the same article of the following particulars:

(a) Signatures, ratifications and accessions under article 48;

(b) The date of the entry into force of the present Covenant under article 49 and the date of the entry into force of any amendments under article 51.

Article 53

1. The present Covenant, of which the Chinese, English, French, Russian and Spanish texts are equally authentic, shall be deposited in the archives of the United Nations.

2. The Secretary-General of the United Nations shall transmit certified copies of the present Covenant to all States referred to in article 48.

Annex II

OPTIONAL PROTOCOL TO THE INTERNATIONAL COVENANT
ON CIVIL AND POLITICAL RIGHTS

Adopted and opened for signature, ratification and accession by General
Assembly resolution 2200 A (XXI) of 16 December 1966

ENTRY INTO FORCE: 23 March 1976, in accordance with article 9.

The States Parties to the present Protocol,
Considering that in order further to achieve the purposes of the Covenant on Civil and Political Rights (hereinafter referred to as the Covenant)
and the implementation of its provisions it would be appropriate to enable
the Human Rights Committee set up in part IV of the Covenant (hereinafter referred to as the Committee) to receive and consider, as provided in
the present Protocol, communications from individuals claiming to be
victims of violations of any of the rights set forth in the Covenant.
Have agreed as follows:

Article 1 A State Party to the Covenant that becomes a party to the
present Protocol recognizes the competence of the Committee to receive
and consider communications from individuals subject to its jurisdiction
who claim to be victims of a violation by that State Party of any of the
rights set forth in the Covenant. No communication shall be received by
the Committee if it concerns a State Party to the Covenant which is not a
party to the present Protocol.

Article 2 Subject to the provisions of article 1, individuals who claim
that any of their rights enumerated in the Covenant have been violated and
who have exhausted all available domestic remedies may submit a written
communication to the Committee for consideration.

Article 3 The Committee shall consider inadmissible any communication
under the present Protocol which is anonymous, or which it considers to
be an abuse of the right of submission of such communications or to be
incompatible with the provisions of the Covenant.

Article 4
1. Subject to the provisions of article 3, the Committee shall bring any
communications submitted to it under the present Protocol to the attention of the State Party to the present Protocol alleged to be violating any
provision of the Covenant.
2. Within six months, the receiving State shall submit to the Committee
written explanations or statements clarifying the matter and the remedy, if
any, that may have been taken by that State.

Article 5

1. The Committee shall consider communications received under the present Protocol in the light of all written information made available to it by the individual and by the State Party concerned.

2. The Committee shall not consider any communication from an individual unless it has ascertained that:

(*a*) The same matter is not being examined under another procedure of international investigation or settlement;

(*b*) The individual has exhausted all available domestic remedies. This shall not be the rule where the application of the remedies is unreasonably prolonged.

3. The Committee shall hold closed meetings when examining communications under the present Protocol.

4. The Committee shall forward its views to the State Party concerned and to the individual.

Article 6 The Committee shall include in its annual report under article 45 of the Covenant a summary of its activities under the present Protocol.

Article 7 Pending the achievement of the objectives of resolution 1514 (XV) adopted by the General Assembly of the United Nations on 14 December 1960 concerning the Declaration on the Granting of Independence to Colonial Countries and Peoples, the provisions of the present Protocol shall in no way limit the right of petition granted to these peoples by the Charter of the United Nations and other international conventions and instruments under the United Nations and its specialized agencies.

Article 8

1. The present Protocol is open for signature by any State which has signed the Covenant.

2. The present Protocol is subject to ratification by any State which has ratified or acceded to the Covenant. Instruments of ratification shall be deposited with the Secretary-General of the United Nations.

3. The present Protocol shall be open to accession by any State which has ratified or acceded to the Covenant.

4. Accession shall be effected by the deposit of an instrument of accession with the Secretary-General of the United Nations.

5. The Secretary-General of the United Nations shall inform all States which have signed the present Protocol or acceded to it of the deposit of each instrument of ratification or accession.

Article 9

1. Subject to the entry into force of the Covenant, the present Protocol shall enter into force three months after the date of the deposit with the Secretary-General of the United Nations of the tenth instrument of ratification or instrument of accession.

2. For each State ratifying the present Protocol or acceding to it after the deposit of the tenth instrument of ratification or instrument of accession,

the present Protocol shall enter into force three months after the date of the deposit of its own instrument of ratification or instrument of accession.

Article 10 The provisions of the present Protocol shall extend to all parts of federal States without any limitations or exceptions.

Article 11
1. Any State Party to the present Protocol may propose an amendment and file it with the Secretary-General of the United Nations. The Secretary-General shall thereupon communicate any proposed amendments to the States Parties to the present Protocol with a request that they notify him whether they favour a conference of States Parties for the purpose of considering and voting upon the proposal. In the event that at least one third of the States Parties favours such a conference, the Secretary-General shall convene the conference under the auspices of the United Nations. Any amendment adopted by a majority of the States Parties present and voting at the conference shall be submitted to the General Assembly of the United Nations for approval.
2. Amendments shall come into force when they have been approved by the General Assembly of the United Nations and accepted by a two-thirds majority of the States Parties to the present Protocol in accordance with their respective constitutional processes.
3. When amendments come into force, they shall be binding on those States Parties which have accepted them, other States Parties still being bound by the provisions of the present Protocol and any earlier amendment which they have accepted.

Article 12
1. Any State Party may denounce the present Protocol at any time by written notification addressed to the Secretary-General of the United Nations. Denunciation shall take effect three months after the date of receipt of the notification by the Secretary-General.
2. Denunciation shall be without prejudice to the continued application of the provisions of the present Protocol to any communication submitted under article 2 before the effective date of denunciation.

Article 13 Irrespective of the notifications made under article 8, paragraph 5, of the present Protocol, the Secretary-General of the United Nations shall inform all States referred to in article 48, paragraph 1, of the Covenant of the following particulars:
(*a*) Signatures, ratifications and accessions under article 8;
(*b*) The date of the entry into force of the present Protocol under article 9 and the date of the entry into force of any amendments under article 11;
(*c*) Denunciations under article 12.

Article 14

1. The present Protocol, of which the Chinese, English, French, Russian and Spanish texts are equally authentic, shall be deposited in the archives of the United Nations.

2. The Secretary-General of the United Nations shall transmit certified copies of the present Protocol to all States referred to in article 48 of the Covenant.

Annex III

INTERNATIONAL CONVENTION ON THE ELIMINATION OF ALL FORMS OF RACIAL DISCRIMINATION

Adopted and opened for signature and ratification by General Assembly resolution 2106 A (XX) of 21 December 1965

ENTRY INTO FORCE: 4 January 1969, in accordance with article 19.

The States Parties to this Convention,

Considering that the Charter of the United Nations is based on the principles of the dignity and equality inherent in all human beings, and that all Member States have pledged themselves to take joint and separate action, in co-operation with the Organization, for the achievement of one of the purposes of the United Nations which is to promote and encourage universal respect for and observance of human rights and fundamental freedoms for all, without distinction as to race, sex, language or religion,

Considering that the Universal Declaration of Human Rights proclaims that all human beings are born free and equal in dignity and rights and that everyone is entitled to all the rights and freedoms set out therein, without distinction of any kind, in particular as to race, colour or national origin,

Considering that all human beings are equal before the law and are entitled to equal protection of the law against any discrimination and against any incitement to discrimination,

Considering that the United Nations has condemned colonialism and all practices of segregation and discrimination associated therewith, in whatever form and wherever they exist, and that the Declaration on the Granting of Independence to Colonial Countries and Peoples of 14 December 1960 (General Assembly resolution 1514 (XV)) has affirmed and solemnly proclaimed the necessity of bringing them to a speedy and unconditional end,

Considering that the United Nations Declaration on the Elimination of All Forms of Racial Discrimination of 20 November 1963 (General Assembly resolution 1904 (XVIII)) solemnly affirms the necessity of speedily eliminating racial discrimination throughout the world in all its forms and manifestations and of securing understanding of and respect for the dignity of the human person,

Convinced that any doctrine of superiority based on racial differentiation is scientifically false, morally condemnable, socially unjust and dangerous, and that there is no justification for racial discrimination, in theory or in practice, anywhere,

Reaffirming that discrimination between human beings on the grounds of race, colour or ethnic origin is an obstacle to friendly and peaceful relations among nations and is capable of disturbing peace and security among peoples and the harmony of persons living side by side even within one and the same State,

Convinced that the existence of racial barriers is repugnant to the ideals of any human society,

Alarmed by manifestations of racial discrimination still in evidence in some areas of the world and by governmental policies based on racial superiority or hatred, such as policies of *apartheid*, segregation or separation,

Resolved to adopt all necessary measures for speedily eliminating racial discrimination in all its forms and manifestations, and to prevent and combat racist doctrines and practices in order to promote understanding between races and to build an international community free from all forms of racial segregation and racial discrimination,

Bearing in mind the Convention concerning Discrimination in respect of Employment and Occupation adopted by the International Labour Organisation in 1958, and the Convention against Discrimination in Education adopted by the United Nations Educational, Scientific and Cultural Organization in 1960,

Desiring to implement the principles embodied in the United Nations Declaration on the Elimination of All Forms of Racial Discrimination and to secure the earliest adoption of practical measures to that end,

Have agreed as follows:

Part I

Article 1

1. In this Convention, the term 'racial discrimination' shall mean any distinction, exclusion, restriction or preference based on race, colour, descent, or national or ethnic origin which has the purpose or effect of nullifying or impairing the recognition, enjoyment or exercise, on an equal footing, of human rights and fundamental freedoms in the political, economic, social, cultural or any other field of public life.

2. This Convention shall not apply to distinctions, exclusions, restrictions or preferences made by a State Party to this Convention between citizens and non-citizens.

3. Nothing in this Convention may be interpreted as affecting in any way the legal provisions of States Parties concerning nationality, citizenship or naturalization, provided that such provisions do not discriminate against any particular nationality.

4. Special measures taken for the sole purpose of securing adequate advancement of certain racial or ethnic groups or individuals requiring such protection as may be necessary in order to ensure such groups or individuals equal enjoyment or exercise of human rights and fundamental freedoms shall not be deemed racial discrimination, provided, however, that such measures do not, as a consequence, lead to the maintenance of separate rights for different racial groups and that they shall not be continued after the objectives for which they were taken have been achieved.

Article 2

1. States Parties condemn racial discrimination and undertake to pursue by all appropriate means and without delay a policy of eliminating racial discrimination in all its forms and promoting understanding among all races, and, to this end:

(*a*) Each State Party undertakes to engage in no act or practice of racial discrimination against persons, groups of persons or institutions and to ensure that all public authorities and public institutions, national and local, shall act in conformity with this obligation;

(*b*) Each State Party undertakes not to sponsor, defend or support racial discrimination by any persons or organizations;

(*c*) Each State Party shall take effective measures to review governmental, national and local policies, and to amend, rescind or nullify any laws and regulations which have the effect of creating or perpetuating racial discrimination wherever it exists;

(*d*) Each State Party shall prohibit and bring to an end, by all appropriate means, including legislation as required by circumstances, racial discrimination by any persons, group or organization;

(*e*) Each State Party undertakes to encourage, where appropriate, integrationist multiracial organizations and movements and other means of eliminating barriers between races, and to discourage anything which tends to strengthen racial division.

2. States Parties shall, when the circumstances so warrant, take, in the social, economic, cultural and other fields, special and concrete measures to ensure the adequate development and protection of certain racial groups or individuals belonging to them, for the purpose of guaranteeing them the full and equal enjoyment of human rights and fundamental freedoms. These measures shall in no case entail as a consequence the maintenance of unequal or separate rights for different racial groups after the objectives for which they were taken have been achieved.

Article 3 States Parties particularly condemn racial segregation and *apartheid* and undertake to prevent, prohibit and eradicate all practices of this nature in territories under their jurisdiction.

Article 4 States Parties condemn all propaganda and all organizations which are based on ideas or theories of superiority of one race or group of persons of one colour or ethnic origin, or which attempt to justify or promote racial hatred and discrimination in any form, and undertake to adopt immediate and positive measures designed to eradicate all incitement to, or acts of, such discrimination and, to this end, with due regard to the principles embodied in the Universal Declaration of Human Rights and the rights expressly set forth in article 5 of this Convention, *inter alia*:

(*a*) Shall declare an offence punishable by law all dissemination of ideas based on racial superiority or hatred, incitement to racial discrimination, as well as all acts of violence or incitement to such acts against any race or group of persons of another colour or ethnic origin, and also the provision of any assistance to racist activities, including the financing thereof;

(*b*) Shall declare illegal and prohibit organizations, and also organized and all other propaganda activities, which promote and incite racial discrimination, and shall recognize participation in such organizations or activities as an offence punishable by law;

(*c*) Shall not permit public authorities or public institutions, national or local, to promote or incite racial discrimination.

Article 5 In compliance with the fundamental obligations laid down in article 2 of this Convention, States Parties undertake to prohibit and to eliminate racial discrimination in all its forms and to guarantee the right of everyone, without distinction as to race, colour, or national or ethnic origin, to equality before the law, notably in the enjoyment of the following rights:

(*a*) The right to equal treatment before the tribunals and all other organs administering justice;

(*b*) The right to security of person and protection by the State against violence or bodily harm, whether inflicted by government officials or by any individual group or institution;

(*c*) Political rights, in particular the rights to participate in elections — to vote and to stand for election — on the basis of universal and equal suffrage, to take part in the Government as well as in the conduct of public affairs at any level and to have equal access to public service;

(*d*) Other civil rights, in particular:

  (i) The right to freedom of movement and residence within the border of the State;

  (ii) The right to leave any country, including one's own, and to return to one's country;

  (iii) The right to nationality;

  (iv) The right to marriage and choice of spouse;

  (v) The right to own property alone as well as in association with others;

  (vi) The right to inherit;

  (vii) The right to freedom of thought, conscience and religion;

  (viii) The right to freedom of opinion and expression;

  (ix) The right to freedom of peaceful assembly and association;

(*e*) Economic, social and cultural rights, in particular:

  (i) The rights to work, to free choice of employment, to just and favourable conditions of work, to protection against unemployment, to equal pay for equal work, to just and favourable remuneration;

  (ii) The right to form and join trade unions;

  (iii) The right to housing;

  (iv) The right to public health, medical care, social security and social services;

  (v) The right to education and training;

  (vi) The right to equal participation in cultural activities;

(*f*) The right of access to any place or service intended for use by the general public, such as transport, hotels, restaurants, cafés, theatres and parks.

Article 6 States Parties shall assure to everyone within their jurisdiction effective protection and remedies, through the competent national tri-bunals and other State institutions, against any acts of racial discrimi-nation which violate his human rights and fundamental freedoms contrary to this Convention, as well as the right to seek from such tribunals just and adequate reparation or satisfaction for any damange suffered as a result of such discrimination.

Article 7 States Parties undertake to adopt immediate and effective measures, particularly in the fields of teaching, education, culture and information, with a view to combating prejudices which lead to racial dis-crimination and to promoting understanding, tolerance and friendship among nations and racial or ethical groups, as well as to propagating the purposes and principles of the Charter of the United Nations, the Universal Declaration of Human Rights, the United Nations Declaration on the Elimination of All Forms of Racial Discrimination, and this Convention.

Part II

Article 8

1. There shall be established a Committee on the Elimination of Racial Discrimination (hereinafter referred to as the Committee) consisting of eighteen experts of high moral standing and acknowledged impartiality elected by States Parties from among their nationals, who shall serve in their personal capacity, consideration being given to equitable geographical distribution and to the representation of the different forms of civilization as well as of the principal legal systems.

2. The members of the Committee shall be elected by secret ballot from a list of persons nominated by the States Parties. Each State Party may nominate one person from among its own nationals.

3. The initial election shall be held six months after the date of the entry into force of this Convention. At least three months before the date of each election the Secretary-General of the United Nations shall address a letter to the States Parties inviting them to submit their nominations within two months. The Secretary-General shall prepare a list in alpha-betical order of all persons thus nominated, indicating the States Parties which have nominated them, and shall submit it to the States Parties.

4. Elections of the members of the Committee shall be held at a meet-ing of States Parties convened by the Secretary-General at United Nations Headquarters. At that meeting, for which two thirds of the States Parties shall constitute a quorum, the persons elected to the Committee shall be nominees who obtain the largest number of votes and an absolute majority of the votes of the representatives of States Parties present and voting.

5. (*a*) The members of the Committee shall be elected for a term of four years. However, the terms of nine of the members elected at the first election shall expire at the end of two years; immediately after the first election the names of these nine members shall be chosen by lot by the Chairman of the Committee.

(*b*) For the filling of casual vacancies, the State Party whose expert has ceased to function as a member of the Committee shall appoint another expert from among its nationals, subject to the approval of the Committee.

6. States Parties shall be responsible for the expenses of the members of the Committee while they are in performance of Committee duties.

Article 9

1. States Parties undertake to submit to the Secretary-General of the United Nations, for consideration by the Committee, a report on the legislative, judicial, administrative or other measures which they have adopted and which give effect to the provisions of this Convention: (*a*) within one year after the entry into force of the Convention for the State concerned; and (*b*) thereafter every two years and whenever the Committee so requests. The Committee may request further information from the States Parties.

2. The Committee shall report annually, through the Secretary-General, to the General Assembly of the United Nations on its activities and may make suggestions and general recommendations based on the examination of the reports and information received from the States Parties. Such suggestions and general recommendations shall be reported to the General Assembly together with comments, if any, from States Parties.

Article 10

1. The Committee shall adopt its own rules of procedure.

2. The Committee shall elect its officers for a term of two years.

3. The secretariat of the Committee shall be provided by the Secretary-General of the United Nations.

4. The meetings of the Committee shall normally be held at United Nations Headquarters.

Article 11

1. If a State Party considers that another State Party is not giving effect to the provisions of this Convention, it may bring the matter to the attention of the Committee. The Committee shall then transmit the communication to the State Party concerned. Within three months, the receiving State shall submit to the Committee written explanations or statements clarifying the matter and the remedy, if any, that may have been taken by that State.

2. If the matter is not adjusted to the satisfaction of both parties, either by bilateral negotiations or by any other procedure open to them, within six months after the receipt by the receiving State of the initial communication, either State shall have the right to refer the matter again to the Committee by notifying the Committee and also the other State.

3. The Committee shall deal with a matter referred to it in accordance with paragraph 2 of this article after it has ascertained that all available domestic remedies have been invoked and exhausted in the case, in conformity with the generally recognized principles of international law. This

shall not be the rule where the application of the remedies is unreasonably prolonged.

4. In any matter referred to it, the Committee may call upon the States Parties concerned to supply any other relevant information.

5. When any matter arising out of this article is being considered by the Committee, the States Parties concerned shall be entitled to send a representative to take part in the proceedings of the Committee, without voting rights, while the matter is under consideration.

Article 12

1. (*a*) After the Committee has obtained and collated all the information it deems necessary, the Chairman shall appoint an *ad hoc* Conciliation Commission (hereinafter referred to as the Commission) comprising five persons who may or may not be members of the Committee. The members of the Commission shall be appointed with the unanimous consent of the parties to the dispute, and its good offices shall be made available to the States concerned with a view to an amicable solution of the matter on the basis of respect for this Convention.

(*b*) If the States parties to the dispute fail to reach agreement within three months on all or part of the composition of the Commission, the members of the Commission not agreed upon by the States parties to the dispute shall be elected by secret ballot by a two-thirds majority vote of the Committee from among its own members.

2. The members of the Commission shall serve in their personal capacity. They shall not be nationals of the States parties to the dispute or of a State not Party to this Convention.

3. The Commission shall elect its own Chairman and adopt its own rules of procedure.

4. The meetings of the Commission shall normally be held at United Nations Headquarters or at any other convenient place as determined by the Commission.

5. The secretariat provided in accordance with article 10, paragraph 3, of this Convention shall also service the Commission whenever a dispute among States Parties brings the Commission into being.

6. The States parties to the dispute shall share equally all the expenses of the members of the Commission in accordance with estimates to be provided by the Secretary-General of the United Nations.

7. The Secretary-General shall be empowered to pay the expenses of the members of the Commission, if necessary, before reimbursement by the States parties to the dispute in accordance with paragraph 6 of this article.

8. The information obtained and collated by the Committee shall be made available to the Commission, and the Commission may call upon the States concerned to supply any other relevant information.

Article 13

1. When the Commission has fully considered the matter, it shall prepare and submit to the Chairman of the Committee a report embodying

its findings on all questions of fact relevant to the issue between the parties and containing such recommendations as it may think proper for the amicable solution of the dispute.

2. The Chairman of the Committee shall communicate the report of the Commission to each of the States parties to the dispute. These States shall, within three months, inform the Chairman of the Committee whether or not they accept the recommendations contained in the report of the Commission.

3. After the period provided for in paragraph 2 of this article, the Chairman of the Committee shall communicate the report of the Commission and the declarations of the States Parties concerned to the other States Parties to this Convention.

Article 14

1. A State Party may at any time declare that it recognizes the competence of the Committee to receive and consider communications from individuals or groups of individuals within its jurisdiction claiming to be victims of a violation by that State Party of any of the rights set forth in this Convention. No communication shall be received by the Committee if it concerns a State Party which has not made such a declaration.

2. Any State Party which makes a declaration as provided for in paragraph 1 of this article may establish or indicate a body within its national legal order which shall be competent to receive and consider petitions from individuals and groups of individuals within its jurisdiction who claim to be victims of a violation of any of the rights set forth in this Convention and who have exhausted other available local remedies.

3. A declaration made in accordance with paragraph 1 of this article and the name of any body established or indicated in accordance with paragraph 2 of this article shall be deposited by the State Party concerned with the Secretary-General of the United Nations, who shall transmit copies thereof to the other States Parties. A declaration may be withdrawn at any time by notification to the Secretary-General, but such a withdrawal shall not affect communications pending before the Committee.

4. A register of petitions shall be kept by the body established or indicated in accordance with paragraph 2 of this article, and certified copies of the register shall be filed annually through appropriate channels with the Secretary-General on the understanding that the contents shall not be publicly disclosed.

5. In the event of failure to obtain satisfaction from the body established or indicated in accordance with paragraph 2 of this article, the petitioner shall have the right to communicate the matter to the Committee within six months.

6. (*a*) The Committee shall confidentially bring any communication referred to it to the attention of the State Party alleged to be violating any provision of this Convention, but the identity of the individual or groups of individuals concerned shall not be revealed without his or their express consent. The Committee shall not receive anonymous communications.

(*b*) Within three months, the receiving State shall submit to the Committee written explanations or statements clarifying the matter and the remedy, if any, that may have been taken by that State.

7. (*a*) The Committee shall consider communications in the light of all information made available to it by the State Party concerned and by the petitioner. The Committee shall not consider any communication from a petitioner unless it has ascertained .that the petitioner has exhausted all available domestic remedies. However, this shall not be the rule where the application of the remedies is unreasonably prolonged.

(*b*) The Committee shall forward its suggestions and recommendations, if any, to the State Party concerned and to the petitioner.

8. The Committee shall include in its annual report a summary of such communications and, where appropriate, a summary of the explanations and statements of the States Parties concerned and of its own suggestions and recommendations.

9. The Committee shall be competent to exercise the functions provided for in this article only when at least ten States Parties to this Convention are bound by declarations in accordance with paragraph 1 of this article.

Article 15

1. Pending the achievement of the objectives of the Declaration on the Granting of Independence to Colonial Countries and Peoples, contained in General Assembly resolution 1514 (XV) of 14 December 1960, the provisions of this Convention shall in no way limit the right of petition granted to these peoples by other international instruments or by the United Nations and its specialized agencies.

2. (*a*) The Committee established under article 8, paragraph 1, of this Convention shall receive copies of the petitions from, and submit expressions of opinion and recommendations on these petitions to, the bodies of the United Nations which deal with matters directly related to the principles and objectives of this Convention in their consideration of petitions from the inhabitants of Trust and Non-Self-Governing Territories and all other territories to which General Assembly resolution 1514 (XV) applies, relating to matters covered by this Convention which are before these bodies.

(*b*) The Committee shall receive from the competent bodies of the United Nations copies of the reports concerning the legislative, judicial, administrative or other measures directly related to the principles and objectives of this Convention applied by the administering Powers within the Territories mentioned in subparagraph (*a*) of this paragraph, and shall express opinions and make recommendations to these bodies.

3. The Committee shall include in its report to the General Assembly a summary of the petitions and reports it has received from United Nations bodies, and the expressions of opinion and recommendations of the Committee relating to the said petitions and reports.

4. The Committee shall request from the Secretary-General of the United Nations all information relevant to the objectives of this Convention and

available to him regarding the Territories mentioned in paragraph 2 (*a*) of this article.

Article 16   The provisions of this Convention concerning the settlement of disputes or complaints shall be applied without prejudice to other procedures for settling disputes or complaints in the field of discrimination laid down in the constituent instruments of, or conventions adopted by, the United Nations and its specialized agencies, and shall not prevent the States Parties from having recourse to other procedures for settling a dispute in accordance with general or special international agreements in force between them.

Part III

Article 17

1. This Convention is open for signature by any State Member of the United Nations or member of any of its specialized agencies, by any State Party to the Statute of the International Court of Justice, and by any other State which has been invited by the General Assembly of the United Nations to become a Party to this Convention.

2. This Convention is subject to ratification. Instruments of ratification shall be deposited with the Secretary-General of the United Nations.

Article 18

1. This Convention shall be open to accession by any State referred to in article 17, paragraph 1, of the Convention.

2. Accession shall be effected by the deposit of an instrument of accession with the Secretary-General of the United Nations.

Article 19

1. This Convention shall enter into force on the thirtieth day after the date of the deposit with the Secretary-General of the United Nations of the twenty-seventh instrument of ratification or instrument of accession.

2. For each state ratifying this Convention or acceding to it after the deposit of the twenty-seventh instrument of ratification or instrument of accession, the Convention shall enter into force on the thirtieth day after the date of the deposit of its own instrument of ratification or instrument of accession.

Article 20

1. The Secretary-General of the United Nations shall receive and circulate to all States which are or may become Parties to this Convention reservations made by States at the time of ratification or accession. Any State which objects to the reservation shall, within a period of ninety days from the date of the said communication, notify the Secretary-General that it does not accept it.

2. A reservation incompatible with the object and purpose of this Convention shall not be permitted, nor shall a reservation the effect of which

would inhibit the operation of any of the bodies established by this Convention be allowed. A reservation shall be considered incompatible or inhibitive if at least two thirds of the States Parties to this Convention object to it.

3. Reservations may be withdrawn at any time by notification to this effect addressed to the Secretary-General. Such notification shall take effect on the date on which it is received.

Article 21   A State Party may denounce this Convention by written notification to the Secretary-General of the United Nations. Denunciation shall take effect one year after the date of receipt of the notification by the Secretary-General.

Article 22   Any dispute between two or more States Parties with respect to the interpretation or application of this Convention, which is not settled by negotiation or by the procedures expressly provided for in this Convention, shall, at the request of any of the parties to the dispute, be referred to the International Court of Justice for decision, unless the disputants agree to another mode of settlement.

Article 23
1. A request for the revision of this Convention may be made at any time by any State Party by means of a notification in writing addressed to the Secretary-General of the United Nations.
2. The General Assembly of the United Nations shall decide upon the steps, if any, to be taken in respect of such a request.

Article 24   The Secretary-General of the United Nations shall inform all States referred to in article 17, paragraph 1, of this Convention of the following particulars:
   (*a*) Signatures, ratifications and accessions under articles 17 and 18;
   (*b*) The date of entry into force of this Convention under article 19;
   (*c*) Communications and declarations received under articles 14, 20 and 23;
   (*d*) Denunciations under article 21.

Article 25
1. This Convention, of which the Chinese, English, French, Russian and Spanish texts are equally authentic, shall be deposited in the archives of the United Nations.
2. The Secretary-General of the United Nations shall transmit certified copies of this Convention to all States belonging to any of the categories mentioned in article 17, paragraph 1, of the Convention.

Annex IV

CONVENTION ON THE ELIMINATION OF ALL FORMS OF DISCRIMINATION AGAINST WOMEN

Adopted and opened for signature, ratification and accession
by General Assembly resolution 34/180 of 18 December 1979

ENTRY INTO FORCE: 3 September 1981, in accordance with article 27 (i).

The States Parties to the present Convention,

Noting that the Charter of the United Nations reaffirms faith in fundamental human rights, in the dignity and worth of the human person and in the equal rights of men and women,

Noting that the Universal Declaration of Human Rights affirms the principle of the inadmissibility of discrimination and proclaims that all human beings are born free and equal in dignity and rights and that everyone is entitled to all the rights and freedoms set forth therein, without distinction of any kind, including distinction based on sex,

Noting that the States parties to the International Covenants on Human Rights have the obligation to ensure the equal right of men and women to enjoy all economic, social, cultural, civil and political rights,

Considering the international conventions concluded under the auspices of the United Nations and the specialized agencies promoting equality of rights of men and women,

Noting also the resolutions, declarations and recommendations adopted by the United Nations and the specialized agencies promoting equality of rights of men and women,

Concerned, however, that despite these various instruments extensive discrimination against women continues to exist,

Recalling that discrimination against women violates the principles of equality of rights and respect for human dignity, is an obstacle to the participation of women, on equal terms with men, in the political, social, economic and cultural life of their countries, hampers the growth of the prosperity of society and the family and makes more difficult the full development of the potentialities of women in the service of their countries and of humanity,

Concerned that in situations of poverty women have the least access to food, health, education, training and opportunities for employment and other needs,

Convinced that the establishment of the new international economic order based on equity and justice will contribute significantly towards the promotion of equality between men and women,

Emphasizing that the eradication of *apartheid*, all forms of racism, racial discrimination, colonialism, neo-colonialism, aggression, foreign occupation and domination and interference in the internal affairs of States is essential to the full enjoyment of the rights of men and women,

Affirming that the strengthening of international peace and security, the relaxation of international tension, mutual co-operation among all States irrespective of their social and economic systems, general and complete disarmament, in particular nuclear disarmament under strict and effective international control, the affirmation of the principles of justice, equality and mutual benefit in relations among countries and the realization of the right of peoples under alien and colonial domination and foreign occupation to self-determination and independence, as well as respect for national sovereignty and territorial integrity, will promote social progress and development and as a consequence will contribute to the attainment of full equality between men and women,

Convinced that the full and complete development of a country, the welfare of the world and the cause of peace require the maximum participation of women on equal terms with men in all fields,

Bearing in mind the great contribution of women to the welfare of the family and to the development of society, so far not fully recognized, the social significance of maternity and the role of both parents in the family and in the upbringing of children, and aware that the role of women in procreation should not be a basis for discrimination but that the upbringing of children requires a sharing of responsibility between men and women and society as a whole,

Aware that a change in the traditional role of men as well as the role of women in society and in the family is needed to achieve full equality between men and women,

Determined to implement the principles set forth in the Declaration on the Elimination of Discrimination against Women and, for that purpose, to adopt the measures required for the elimination of such discrimination in all its forms and manifestations,

Have agreed on the following:

Part I

Article 1   For the purposes of the present Convention, the term 'discrimination against women' shall mean any distinction, exclusion or restriction made on the basis of sex which has the effect or purpose of impairing or nullifying the recognition, enjoyment or exercise by women, irrespective of their marital status, on a basis of equality of men and women, of human rights and fundamental freedoms in the political, economic, social, cultural civil or any other field.

Article 2   States Parties condemn discrimination against women in all its forms, agree to pursue by all appropriate means and without delay a policy of eliminating discrimination against women and, to this end, undertake:

(*a*) To embody the principle of the equality of men and women in their national constitutions or other appropriate legislation if not yet incorporated therein and to ensure, through law and other appropriate means, the practical realization of this principle;

(*b*) To adopt appropriate legislative and other measures, including sanctions where appropriate, prohibiting all discrimination against women;

(*c*) To establish legal protection of the rights of women on an equal basis with men and to ensure through competent national tribunals and other public institutions the effective protection of women against any act of discrimination;

(*d*) To refrain from engaging in any act or practice of discrimination against women and to ensure that public authorities and institutions shall act in conformity with this obligation;

(*e*) To take all appropriate measures to eliminate discrimination against women by any person, organization or enterprise;

(*f*) To take all appropriate measures, including legislation, to modify or abolish existing laws, regulations, customs and practices which constitute discrimination against women;

(*g*) To repeal all national penal provisions which constitute discrimination against women.

Article 3 States Parties shall take in all fields, in particular in the political, social, economic and cultural fields, all appropriate measures, including legislation, to ensure the full development and advancement of women, for the purpose of guaranteeing them the exercise and enjoyment of human rights and fundamental freedoms on a basis of equality with men.

Article 4

1. Adoption by States Parties of temporary special measures aimed at accelerating *de facto* equality between men and women shall not be considered discrimination as defined in the present Convention, but shall in no way entail as a consequence the maintenance of unequal or separate standards; these measures shall be discontinued when the objectives of equality of opportunity and treatment have been achieved.

2. Adoption by States Parties of special measures, including those measures contained in the present Convention, aimed at protecting maternity shall not be considered discriminatory.

Article 5 States Parties shall take all appropriate measures:

(*a*) To modify the social and cultural patterns of conduct of men and women, with a view to achieving the elimination of prejudices and customary and all other practices which are based on the idea of the inferiority or the superiority of either of the sexes or on stereotyped roles for men and women;

(*b*) To ensure that family education includes a proper understanding of maternity as a social function and the recognition of the common responsibility of men and women in the upbringing and development of their children, it being understood that the interest of the children is the primoridal consideration in all cases.

Article 6 States Parties shall take all appropriate measures, including legislation, to suppress all forms of traffic in women and exploitation of prostitution of women.

Part II

Article 7 States Parties shall take all appropriate measures to eliminate discrimination against women in the political and public life of the country and, in particular, shall ensure to women, on equal terms with men, the right:

(*a*) To vote in all elections and public referenda and to be eligible for election to all publicly elected bodies;

(*b*) To participate in the formulation of government policy and the implementation thereof and to hold public office and perform all public functions at all levels of government;

(*c*) To participate in non-governmental organizations and associations concerned with the public and political life of the country.

Article 8 States Parties shall take all appropriate measures to ensure to women, on equal terms with men and without any discrimination, the opportunity to represent their Governments at the international level and to participate in the work of international organizations.

Article 9

1. States Parties shall grant women equal rights with men to acquire, change or retain their nationality. They shall ensure in particular that neither marriage to an alien nor change of nationality by the husband during marriage shall automatically change the nationality of the wife, render her stateless or force upon her the nationality of the husband.

2. States Parties shall grant women equal rights with men with respect to the nationality of their children.

Part III

Article 10 States Parties shall take all appropriate measures to eliminate discrimination against women in order to ensure to them equal rights with men in the field of education and in particular to ensure, on a basis of equality of men and women:

(*a*) The same conditions for career and vocational guidance, for access to studies and for the achievement of diplomas in educational establishments of all categories in rural as well as in urban areas; this equality shall be ensured in pre-school, general, technical, professional and higher technical education, as well as in all types of vocational training;

(*b*) Access to the same curricula, the same examinations, teaching staff with qualifications of the same standard and school premises and equipment of the same quality;

(*c*) The elimination of any stereotyped concept of the roles of men and women at all levels and in all forms of education by encouraging co-education and other types of education which will help to achieve this aim and, in particular, by the revision of textbooks and school programmes and the adaptation of teaching methods;

(*d*) The same opportunities to benefit from scholarships and other study grants;

(*e*) The same opportunities for access to programmes of continuing education, including adult and functional literacy programmes, particularly those aimed at reducing, at the earliest possible time, any gap in education existing between men and women;

(*f*) The reduction of female student drop-out rates and the organization of programmes for girls and women who have left school prematurely;

(*g*) The same opportunities to participate actively in sports and physical education;

(*h*) Access to specific educational information to help to ensure the health and well-being of families, including information and advice on family planning.

Article 11

1. States Parties shall take all appropriate measures to eliminate discrimination against women in the field of employment in order to ensure, on a basis of equality of men and women, the same rights, in particular:

(*a*) The right to work as an inalienable right of all human beings;

(*b*) The right to the same employment opportunities, including the application of the same criteria for selection in matters of employment;

(*c*) The right to free choice of profession and employment, the right to promotion, job security and all benefits and conditions of service and the right to receive vocational training and retraining including apprenticeships, advanced vocational training and recurrent training;

(*d*) The right to equal remuneration, including benefits, and to equal treatment in respect of work of equal value, as well as equality of treatment in the evaluation of the quality of work;

(*e*) The right to social security, particularly in cases of retirement, unemployment, sickness, invalidity and old age and other incapacity to work, as well as the right to paid leave;

(*f*) The right to protection of health and to safety in working conditions, including the safeguarding of the function of reproduction.

2. In order to prevent discrimination against women on the grounds of marriage or maternity and to ensure their effective right to work, States Parties shall take appropriate measures:

(*a*) To prohibit, subject to the imposition of sanctions, dismissal on the grounds of pregnancy or of maternity leave and discrimination in dismissals on the basis of marital status;

(*b*) To introduce maternity leave with pay or with comparable social benefits without loss of former employment, seniority or social allowances;

(*c*) To encourage the provision of the necessary supporting social services to enable parents to combine family obligations with work responsibilities and participation in public life, in particular through promoting the establishment and development of a network of child-care facilities;

(*d*) To provide special protection to women during pregnancy in types of work proved to be harmful to them.

3. Protective legislation relating to matters covered in this article shall be reviewed periodically in the light of scientific and technological knowledge and shall be revised, repealed or extended as necessary.

Article 12

1. States Parties shall take all appropriate measures to eliminate discrimination against women in the field of health care in order to ensure, on a basis of equality of men and women, access to health care services, including those related to family planning.

2. Notwithstanding the provisions of paragraph 1 of this article, States Parties shall ensure to women appropriate services in connexion with pregnancy, confinement and the post-natal period, granting free services where necessary, as well as adequate nutrition during pregnancy and lactation.

Article 13 States Parties shall take all appropriate measures to eliminate discrimination against women in other areas of economic and social life in order to ensure, on a basis of equality of men and women, the same rights, in particular:

(*a*) The right to family benefits;

(*b*) The right to bank loans, mortgages and other forms of financial credit;

(*c*) The right to participate in recreational activities, sports and all aspects of cultural life.

Article 14

1. States Parties shall take into account the particular problems faced by rural women and the significant roles which rural women play in the economic survival of their families, including their work in the non-monetized sectors of the economy, and shall take all appropriate measures to ensure the application of the provisions of the present Convention to women in rural areas.

2. States Parties shall take all appropriate measures to eliminate discrimination against women in rural areas in order to ensure, on a basis of equality of men and women, that they participate in and benefit from rural development and, in particular, shall ensure to such women the right:

(*a*) To participate in the elaboration and implementation of development planning at all levels;

(*b*) To have access to adequate health care facilities, including information, counselling and services in family planning;

(*c*) To benefit directly from social security programmes;

(*d*) To obtain all types of training and education, formal and non-formal, including that relating to functional literacy, as well as, *inter alia*, the benefit of all community and extension services, in order to increase their technical proficiency;

(*e*) To organize self-help groups and co-operatives in order to obtain equal access to economic opportunities through employment or self-employment;

(*f*) To participate in all community activities;

(*g*) To have access to agricultural credit and loans, marketing facilities, appropriate technology and equal treatment in land and agrarian reform as well as in land resettlement schemes;

(*h*) To enjoy adequate living conditions, particularly in relation to housing, sanitation, electricity and water supply, transport and communications.

Part IV

Article 15

1. States Parties shall accord to women equality with men before the law.

2. States Parties shall accord to women, in civil matters, a legal capacity identical to that of men and the same opportunities to exercise that capacity. In particular, they shall give women equal rights to conclude contracts and to administer property and shall treat them equally in all stages of procedure in courts and tribunals.

3. States Parties agree that all contracts and all other private instruments of any kind with a legal effect which is directed at restricting the legal capacity of women shall be deemed null and void.

4. States Parties shall accord to men and women the same rights with regard to the law relating to the movement of persons and the freedom to choose their residence and domicile.

Article 16

1. States Parties shall take all appropriate measures to eliminate discrimination against women in all matters relating to marriage and family relations and in particular shall ensure, on a basis of equality of men and women:

(*a*) The same right to enter into marriage;

(*b*) The same right freely to choose a spouse and to enter into marriage only with their free and full consent;

(*c*) The same rights and responsibilities during marriage and at its dissolution;

(*d*) The same rights and responsibilities as parents, irrespective of their marital status, in matters relating to their children; in all cases the interests of the children shall be paramount;

(*e*) The same rights to decide freely and responsibly on the number and spacing of their children and to have access to the information, education and means to enable them to exercise these rights;

(*f*) The same rights and responsibilities with regard to guardianship, wardship, trusteeship and adoption of children, or similar institutions where these concepts exist in national legislation; in all cases the interests of the children shall be paramount;

(g) The same personal rights as husband and wife, including the right to choose a family name, a profession and an occupation;

(h) The same rights for both spouses in respect of the ownership, acquisition, management, administration, enjoyment and disposition of property, whether free of charge or for a valuable consideration.

2. The betrothal and the marriage of a child shall have no legal effect, and all necessary action, including legislation, shall be taken to specify a minimum age for marriage and to make the registration of marriages in an official registry compulsory.

Part V

Article 17

1. For the purpose of considering the progress made in the implementation of the present Convention, there shall be established a Committee on the Elimination of Discrimination against Women (hereinafter referred to as the Committee) consisting, at the time of entry into force of the Convention, of eighteen and, after ratification of or accession to the Convention by the thirty-fifth State Party, of twenty-three experts of high moral standing and competence in the field covered by the Convention. The experts shall be elected by States Parties from among their nationals and shall serve in their personal capacity, consideration being given to equitable geographical distribution and to the representation of the different forms of civilization as well as the principal legal systems.

2. The members of the Committee shall be elected by secret ballot from a list of persons nominated by States Parties. Each State Party may nominate one person from among its own nationals.

3. The initial election shall be held six months after the date of the entry into force of the present Convention. At least three months before the date of each election the Secretary-General of the United Nations shall address a letter to the States Parties inviting them to submit their nominations within two months. The Secretary-General shall prepare a list in alphabetical order of all persons thus nominated, indicating the States Parties which have nominated them, and shall submit it to the States Parties.

4. Elections of the members of the Committee shall be held at a meeting of States Parties convened by the Secretary-General at United Nations Headquarters. At that meeting, for which two thirds of the States Parties shall constitute a quorum, the persons elected to the Committee shall be those nominees who obtain the largest number of votes and an absolute majority of the votes of the representatives of States Parties present and voting.

5. The members of the Committee shall be elected for a term of four years. However, the terms of nine of the members elected at the first election shall expire at the end of two years; immediately after the first election the names of these nine members shall be chosen by lot by the Chairman of the Committee.

6. The election of the five additional members of the Committee shall

be held in accordance with the provisions of paragraphs 2, 3 and 4 of this article, following the thirty-fifth ratification or accession. The terms of two of the additional members elected on this occasion shall expire at the end of two years, the names of these two members having been chosen by lot by the Chairman of the Committee.

7. For the filling of casual vacancies, the State Party whose expert has ceased to function as a member of the Committee shall appoint another expert from among its nationals, subject to the approval of the Committee.

8. The members of the Committee shall, with the approval of the General Assembly, receive emoluments from United Nations resources on such terms and conditions as the Assembly may decide, having regard to the importance of the Committee's responsibilities.

9. The Secretary-General of the United Nations shall provide the necessary staff and facilities for the effective performance of the functions of the Committee under the present Convention.

Article 18

1. States Parties undertake to submit to the Secretary-General of the United Nations, for consideration by the Committee, a report on the legislative, judicial, administrative or other measures which they have adopted to give effect to the provisions of the present Convention and on the progress made in this respect:

(*a*) Within one year after the entry into force for the State concerned;

(*b*) Thereafter at least every four years and further whenever the Committee so requests.

2. Reports may indicate factors and difficulties affecting the degree of fulfilment of obligations under the present Convention.

Article 19

1. The Committee shall adopt its own rules of procedure.

2. The Committee shall elect its officers for a term of two years.

Article 20

1. The Committee shall normally meet for a period of not more than two weeks annually in order to consider the reports submitted in accordance with article 18 of the present Convention.

2. The meetings of the Committee shall normally be held at United Nations Headquarters or at any other convenient place as determined by the Committee.

Article 21

1. The Committee shall, through the Economic and Social Council, report annually to the General Assembly of the United Nations on its activities and may make suggestions and general recommendations based on the examination of reports and information received from the States Parties. Such suggestions and general recommendations shall be included in

the report of the Committee together with comments, if any, from States Parties.

2. The Secretary-General of the United Nations shall transmit the reports of the Committee to the Commission on the Status of Women for its information.

Article 22   The specialized agencies shall be entitled to be represented at the consideration of the implementation of such provisions of the present Convention as fall within the scope of their activities. The Committee may invite the specialized agencies to submit reports on the implementation of the Convention in areas falling within the scope of their activities.

Part VI

Article 23   Nothing in the present Convention shall affect any provisions that are more conducive to the achievement of equality between men and women which may be contained:

(*a*) In the legislation of a State Party; or

(*b*) In any other international convention, treaty or agreement in force for that State.

Article 24   States Parties undertake to adopt all necessary measures at the national level aimed at achieving the full realization of the rights recognized in the present Convention.

Article 25

1. The present Convention shall be open for signature by all States.

2. The Secretary-General of the United Nations is designated as the depositary of the present Convention.

3. The present Convention is subject to ratification. Instruments of ratification shall be deposited with the Secretary-General of the United Nations.

4. The present Convention shall be open to accession by all States. Accession shall be effected by the deposit of an instrument of accession with the Secretary-General of the United Nations.

Article 26

1. A request for the revision of the present Convention may be made at any time by any State Party by means of a notification in writing addressed to the Secretary-General of the United Nations.

2. The General Assembly of the United Nations shall decide upon the steps, if any, to be taken in respect of such a request.

Article 27

1. The present Convention shall enter into force on the thirtieth day after the date of deposit with the Secretary-General of the United Nations of the twentieth instrument of ratification or accession.

2. For each State ratifying the present Convention or acceding to it after the deposit of the twentieth instrument of ratification or accession, the Convention shall enter into force on the thirtieth day after the date of the deposit of its own instrument of ratification or accession.

Article 28

1. The Secretary-General of the United Nations shall receive and circulate to all States the text of reservations made by States at the time of ratification or accession.

2. A reservation incompatible with the object and purpose of the present Convention shall not be permitted.

3. Reservations may be withdrawn at any time by notification to this effect addressed to the Secretary-General of the United Nations, who shall then inform all States thereof. Such notification shall take effect on the date on which it is received.

Article 29

1. Any dispute between two or more States Parties concerning the interpretation or application of the present Convention which is not settled by negotiation shall, at the request of one of them, be submitted to arbitration. If within six months from the date of the request for arbitration the parties are unable to agree on the organization of the arbitration, any one of those parties may refer the dispute to the International Court of Justice by request in conformity with the Statute of the Court.

2. Each State Party may at the time of signature or ratification of the present Convention or accession thereto declare that it does not consider itself bound by paragraph 1 of this article. The other States Parties shall not be bound by that paragraph with respect to any State Party which has made such a reservation.

3. Any State Party which has made a reservation in accordance with paragraph 2 of this article may at any time withdraw that reservation by notification to the Secretary-General of the United Nations.

Article 30

The present Convention, the Arabic, Chinese, English, French, Russian and Spanish texts of which are equally authentic, shall be deposited with the Secretary-General of the United Nations.

IN WITNESS WHEREOF the undersigned, duly authorized, have signed the present Convention.

Annex V

DECLARATION ON THE ELIMINATION OF ALL FORMS OF
INTOLERANCE AND OF DISCRIMINATION BASED ON
RELIGION OR BELIEF

Proclaimed by the General Assembly of the United Nations
on 25 November 1981 (resolution 36/55)

The General Assembly,

Considering that one of the basic principles of the Charter of the United Nations is that of the dignity and equality inherent in all human beings, and that all Member States have pledged themselves to take joint and separate action in co-operation with the Organization to promote and encourage universal respect for and observance of human rights and fundamental freedoms for all, without distinction as to race, sex, language or religion,

Considering that the Universal Declaration of Human Rights and the International Covenants on Human Rights proclaim the principles of non-discrimination and equality before the law and the right to freedom of thought, conscience, religion and belief,

Considering that the disregard and infringement of human rights and fundamental freedoms, in particular of the right to freedom of thought, conscience, religion or whatever belief, have brought, directly or indirectly, wars and great suffering to mankind, especially where they serve as a means of foreign interference in the internal affairs of other States and amount to kindling hatred between peoples and nations,

Considering that religion or belief, for anyone who professes either, is one of the fundamental elements in his conception of life and that freedom of religion or belief should be fully respected and guaranteed,

Considering that it is essential to promote understanding, tolerance and respect in matters relating to freedom of religion and belief, and to ensure that the use of religion or belief for ends inconsistent with the Charter of the United Nations, other relevant instruments of the United Nations and the purposes and principles of the present Declaration is inadmissible,

Convinced that freedom of religion and belief should also contribute to the attainment of the goals of world peace, social justice and friendship among peoples and to the elimination of ideologies or practices of colonialism and racial discrimination,

Noting with satisfaction the adoption of several, and the coming into force of some, conventions, under the aegis of the United Nations and of the specialized agencies, for the elimination of various forms of discrimination,

Concerned by manifestations of intolerance and by the existence of discrimination in matters of religion or belief still in evidence in some areas of the world,

Resolved to adopt all necessary measures for the speedy elimination of such intolerance in all its forms and manifestations and to prevent and combat discrimination on the ground of religion or belief,

Proclaims this Declaration on the Elimination of All Forms of Intolerance and of Discrimination Based on Religion or Belief:

Article 1

1. Everyone shall have the right to freedom of thought, conscience and religion. This right shall include freedom to have a religion or whatever belief of his choice, and freedom, either individually or in community with others and in public or private, to manifest his religion or belief in worship, observance, practice and teaching.

2. No one shall be subject to coercion which would impair his freedom to have a religion or belief of his choice.

3. Freedom to manifest one's religion or beliefs may be subject only to such limitations as are prescribed by law and are necessary to protect public safety, order, health or morals or the fundamental rights and freedoms of others.

Article 2

1. No one shall be subject to discrimination by any State, institution, group of persons, or person on grounds of religion or other beliefs.

2. For the purposes of the present Declaration, the expression 'intolerance and discrimination based on religion or belief' means any distinction, exclusion, restriction or preference based on religion or belief and having as its purpose or as its effect nullification or impairment of the recognition, enjoyment or exercise of human rights and fundamental freedoms on an equal basis.

Article 3

Discrimination between human beings on grounds of religion or belief constitutes an affront to human dignity and a disavowal of the principles of the Charter of the United Nations, and shall be condemned as a violation of the human rights and fundamental freedoms proclaimed in the Universal Declaration of Human Rights and enunciated in detail in the International Covenants on Human Rights, and as an obstacle to friendly and peaceful relations between nations.

Article 4

1. All States shall take effective measures to prevent and eliminate discrimination on the grounds of religion or belief in the recognition, exercise and enjoyment of human rights and fundamental freedoms in all fields of civil, economic, political, social and cultural life.

2. All States shall make all efforts to enact or rescind legislation where necessary to prohibit any such discrimination, and to take all appropriate measures to combat intolerance on the grounds of religion or other beliefs in this matter.

Article 5

1. The parents or, as the case may be, the legal guardians of the child have the right to organize the life within the family in accordance with their religion or belief and bearing in mind the moral education in which they believe the child should be brought up.

2. Every child shall enjoy the right to have access to education in the matter of religion or belief in accordance with the wishes of his parents or, as the case may be, legal guardians, and shall not be compelled to receive teaching on religion or belief against the wishes of his parents or legal guardians, the best interests of the child being the guiding principle.

3. The child shall be protected from any form of discrimination on the ground of religion or belief. He shall be brought up in a spirit of understanding, tolerance, friendship among peoples, peace and universal brotherhood, respect for freedom of religion or belief of others, and in full consciousness that his energy and talents should be devoted to the service of his fellow men.

4. In the case of a child who is not under the care either of his parents or of legal guardians, due account shall be taken of their expressed wishes or of any other proof of their wishes in the matter of religion or belief, the best interests of the child being the guiding principle.

5. Practices of a religion or beliefs in which a child is brought up must not be injurious to his physical or mental health or to his full development, taking into account article 1, paragraph 3, of the present Declaration.

Article 6   In accordance with article 1 of the present Declaration, and subject to the provisions of article 1, paragraph 3, the right to freedom of thought, conscience, religion or belief shall include, *inter alia*, the following freedoms:

(*a*) To worship or assemble in connection with a religion or belief, and to establish and maintain places for these purposes;

(*b*) To establish and maintain appropriate charitable or humanitarian institutions;

(*c*) To make, acquire and use to an adequate extent the necessary articles and materials related to the rites or customs of a religion or belief;

(*d*) To write, issue and disseminate relevant publications in these areas;

(*e*) To teach a religion or belief in places suitable for these purposes;

(*f*) To solicit and receive voluntary financial and other contributions from individuals and institutions;

(*g*) To train, appoint, elect or designate by succession appropriate leaders called for by the requirements and standards of any religion or belief;

(*h*) To observe days of rest and to celebrate holidays and ceremonies in accordance with the precepts of one's religion or belief;

(*i*) To establish and maintain communications with individuals and communities in matters of religion and belief at the national and international levels.

Article 7 The rights and freedoms set forth in the present Declaration shall be accorded in national legislation in such a manner that everyone shall be able to avail himself of such rights and freedoms in practice.

Article 8 Nothing in the present Declaration shall be construed as restricting or derogating from any right defined in the Universal Declaration of Human Rights and the International Covenants on Human Rights.

Index